THE HISTORY OF THE
U.S. AIR FORCE

THE HISTORY OF THE
U.S. AIR FORCE

David A. Anderton

Hamlyn – Aerospace
London · New York · Sydney · Toronto

A Hamlyn/Aerospace Book

Published by
The Hamlyn Publishing Group Limited
London • New York • Sydney • Toronto
Astronaut House, Hounslow Road,
Feltham, Middlesex,
England

Created and produced by Stan Morse
Aerospace Publishing Ltd
10 Barley Mow Passage
London W4 4PH

© Copyright Aerospace Publishing Ltd 1981

Colour profiles © Pilot Press Ltd

First published 1981

ISBN 0 600 34985 3

Credits

Additional editorial material: Bill Gunston
Chris Chant

Design Rod Teasdale

Artwork Keith Fretwell (large three-views)

Typesetting Modern Text Typesetting

Monochrome Tenreck Ltd

Colour reproduction Process Colour Scanning Ltd

Film work Precise Litho Ltd

Acknowledgments
We are most grateful to the U.S. Air Force for
the photographs, information and help they have
provided for this book.

Foreword

This book is a history of the United States Air Force tracing, in broad narrative form, the major events that have, through the years, shaped today's USAF.

While writing my books on the Strategic and Tactical Air Commands I was constantly puzzled as to why things were being done the way they were, how USAF policies had evolved, or what the traditions were that had caused things to happen the way they had. So, believing in the old maxim "If you would learn, teach", I decided that someday I should try to write a broad-based history of the USAF. That my growing desire to do so coincided with a suggestion made by publisher Stan Morse was a fortunate happenstance.

Mine is a very personal approach to history, as if you and I were sometimes in the cockpit, or watching air battles from an ethereal vantage point. I have tried in that way to take this exciting portion of America's history out of yesterday's archives and into today's age of visual experience.

I hope that you will find in my words some of the excitement, the danger, the heroism and the politics that have made the USAF what it is today.

David A. Anderton
Ridgewood, NJ
February, 1981

Contents

Pioneering years: few who saw the Signal Corps' original Wright Model A fly in 1908 could have appreciated the tremendous future in store for U.S. air power. But the Army had already been in the air business for 45 years with their balloons. O, ye of little faith!

The Army's Balloons and Dirigibles

"Ballooning can be made a very useful implement in warfare. All depends on the encouragement it receives."

John La Mountain's words were in a letter to Maj. Gen. Benjamin F. Butler, Commander of the Department of Virginia for the Union in the summer of 1861.

"I am well convinced in my mind," La Mountain had written, "that at an expense not to exceed eight or nine thousand dollars, I can build a balloon in a month's time, and with it shell, burn or destroy Norfolk or any city near our camps."

He was optimistic about the specific details, but accurate about the concept. Ballooning was to become a very useful implement in warfare, and John La Mountain was one of four men who introduced the new weapon in the field with the Union armies.

Observation balloons were not new to war when the Civil War broke out April 12, 1861. The French had used them successfully in campaigns against the Austrians at the end of the 18th century. During the intervening years, balloons had been considered for military use by U.S. forces at least twice, first in the Seminole War of 1840.

The Seminole Indians were to be deported from their homeland in Florida to a remote Western reservation. Masters of movement through Florida's swamps, they evaded troops under Col. John H. Sherburne for several years. But Sherburne conceived the idea of equipping his infantry with hot-air balloons for night observations when enemy campfires would be visible for long distances. By plotting and triangulation, the positions of the Seminoles could be determined. Sherburne unofficially wrote to balloonist Charles Durant, who offered to sell a new balloon for $900 and a used one for $600. That is as far as Sherburne got, because his official request for balloon support was rejected.

Within five years, the U.S. was at war with Mexico. Balloonist John Wise, of Lancaster, Pennsylvania, wrote the War Department, suggesting that he be hired to make balloon observations of Mexico City and to bomb it, if that would help. He never received a reply.

When the first shot was fired at Fort Sumter by the forces of rebellion, starting the Civil War, the technology of balloon construction and operation was well established. Wise had set a world distance record July 1, 1859, flying from St. Louis to Jefferson County, New York, a distance of 809 miles, in 19 hours and 40 minutes. Wise made other contributions to the art. He invented the rip panel, for almost instantaneous deflation of the balloon after landing. He discovered that a ripped balloon envelope would billow to the top of its covering network of ropes, to serve as a rudimentary, but effective, parachute.

James Allen was the first balloonist to volunteer for service in the Civil War. One week after the capture of Ft. Sumter, he headed for Washington, D.C., with two balloons, offering his four years of experience to the Union. His first balloon was inflated June 9 from a gas main at Massachusetts Avenue and Third Street, hauled by a ground crew to Caton's Farm about one mile north of the Capitol building, and launched on a trial flight. The first attempt to use the balloon tactically was made July 9; Allen expected to observe rebel positions just outside Washington. The attempt failed; the balloon could not be fully inflated because of an inefficient gas generator.

But Lt. Henry L. Abbot, Topographical Engineers, was impressed. In his report, he wrote that balloons would be very useful in coming campaigns. He also singled out, at that early stage, the major factor that was to frustrate the balloon corps and its people: command and control. For all the time that balloons

Men of Lowe's detachment inflate the observation balloon "Intrepid" during the Battle of Fair Oaks. Bedevilled by personal animosity and political bickering, the balloon corps of the Union armies nevertheless managed to play a prophetic if indecisive part in the Civil War.

were in service with the Union armies, dedicated troops never were assigned. Instead, individual soldiers were temporarily detached from regular troops in the area. Their commanders objected, and kept the pressure on to get their men back as soon as possible. Further, there was no continuity of service under such an arrangement; ground crews never developed proficiency in operating and maintaining the balloons.

Allen got another chance when Brig. Gen. Irvin McDowell's troops moved out in the first Manassas campaign in July 1861. Both balloons were inflated with coal gas at a plant in Alexandria, Virginia, the morning of July 14. One burst; it was old and in poor condition. The second was man-handled along the road toward Falls Church, but a gusty and strengthening wind drove balloon and handling crew off the road and toward a canal. A telegraph pole impaled the balloon; it collapsed in a final sigh of gas, and ended Allen's early hopes of service to the Union cause.

The Topographic Engineers' office had enough faith to keep trying. On June 26 they telegraphed the experienced balloonist John Wise for an estimate of the cost and delivery date of a new balloon of 20,000 cubic feet capacity, made of the best Indian silk and with linen cordage. Wise replied that it would take two weeks and cost $850.

Wise was appointed a balloonist in the Federal service July 1, 1861. He was 53 years old, with more than a quarter-century of ballooning experience behind him. The balloon was finished July 16 and moved to Washington. Ordered to Centreville, Virginia, and duty with Gen. McDowell's headquarters, Wise and the inflated balloon started out in the early light of July 21. He met Maj. Albert J. Myer, Signal Officer of the Army, and commander of the unit that would take the

balloon to battle. Myer was impatient; he could hear the guns of battle ahead and, seeking faster transport, ordered that the balloon be moored to a wagon and towed by a team of horses. The hitch was made, and the horses were urged into a trot. Near Fairfax Courthouse, the inevitable happened. The balloon was snared by the thick foliage of the trees lining the road. Over Wise's objections, Myer ordered the wagon ahead. The balloon tore and collapsed, and the first Battle of Bull Run was fought without aerial reconnaissance.

Wise managed a first successful ascent July 24, at Arlington, Virginia, just across the Potomac from Washington. He saw some Confederate artillery about five miles distant, and spotted rebel reconnaissance parties out in front of the Union positions.

The following morning, while moving the inflated balloon from Arlington toward Ball's Cross Roads, the wind again ruined Wise's day. The handling lines were worn through by constant chafing against the telegraph wires along the route, and the balloon broke loose, headed south. It was brought down by gunfire from soldiers at Arlington, and landed in a pathetic pile of tangled cordage and torn cloth near Gen. Robert E. Lee's former home.

Wise urged the Army to buy transportable hydrogen generators, because moving an inflated balloon around the countryside was not practical. The suggestion was referred to a major with whom Wise had exchanged bitter words. The major killed the recommendation, and Wise resigned in frustration.

Enter John La Mountain, once an associate of Wise and partner with him in an attempted crossing of the Atlantic by balloon. He volunteered, twice; but no response came from the War Department. Instead,

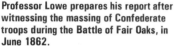

Professor Lowe prepares his report after witnessing the massing of Confederate troops during the Battle of Fair Oaks, in June 1862.

Gen. Butler, from his headquarters at Fortress Monroe, wrote and offered a job as an aerial observer. Butler's position on the coast of southern Virginia by Hampton Roads made him vulnerable to both land and sea assaults. He was receiving intelligence reports of enemy movements, but was unable to confirm any of them. Butler believed that balloon observations would help his situation.

La Mountain arrived at the site, unloaded his balloon, and made his first ascent July 25, 1861. Between then and August 10, he was aloft six times and filed detailed reports of each trip. He made a few errors and omissions, but the bulk of his reporting was accurate. More important, it was timely. He estimated troop numbers by counting tents and huts, and discovered some units not known to be in the area.

He was innovative: he attached one of his balloons to a windlass at the stern of an armed transport named *Fanny*, and on August 3 ascended to 2,000 feet to discover some previously undetected Confederate artillery. It was in a position to shell the Fortress, and the Union ships that lay in, or moved through, the roads.

August 10 was one of his most productive days. La Mountain went aloft five times, once as high as 3,500 feet, and including one night ascent. He made his first sketch in the air, instead of just taking notes. He discovered a rebel force of about 5,000 men to the northwest, another strong force to the northeast of the Fortress, and spotted two large men-of-war anchored off Norfolk. His sketch was copied, and Butler forwarded it and La Mountain's reconnaissance report, to Gen. Winfield Scott, commander of the Union armies.

La Mountain left temporarily on August 16 to get a larger balloon and his own gas generator. He left the letter quoted in part above with Gen. Butler, who passed it along with a strong endorsement to the War Department. Butler moved to another command, his successor was not told of La Mountain's service, and so when the aeronaut did return with his larger balloon, nobody was expecting him. Finally he was ordered to report to the Army of the Potomac, under Maj. Gen. George B. McClellan. There his path crossed that of Thaddeus S. C. Lowe, and fireworks followed.

Lowe was 29 years old, and experienced as a balloonist. He also had planned to fly the Atlantic. On a test ascent he had lifted off from Cincinnati, Ohio, a Union stronghold, and had landed well to the south in secessionist territory. Suspected of being a spy, he was jailed; the abolitionist newspapers he was carrying with him didn't help his case. But his fame had preceded him; he was recognized, released and returned to Cincinnati. He abandoned the trans-Atlantic venture and volunteered to join the Union, with his balloons.

In Washington, on June 18, 1861, he demonstrated the use of captive balloons for observation and telegraphed a message from his *Enterprise* to the White House, relayed by the Alexandria office of the telegraph company. The next day, Lowe made ascensions from the White House lawn, watched by President Abraham Lincoln and Cabinet members.

Lincoln was fascinated, and wrote letters of introduction to Gen. Scott on Lowe's behalf. But he finally had to escort Lowe personally into the office of the crusty old general to persuade him to hire Lowe and his new-fangled contraption. Lowe began work on a 25,000 cubic foot balloon August 2, and started drawing a daily pay of $5, to be increased to $10 when the balloon was complete and operating.

The *Union* first flew August 29 outside Washington. On September 24, Lowe first directed artillery fire by Union batteries, advising them of the position of their shots around targets in the Falls Church area. The following day, the Army Quartermaster General ordered four more new balloons from Lowe, together

with the gas generating plants necessary to inflate them.

By then both Lowe and La Mountain were aeronauts in the Army of the Potomac, and each was doing his best to minimize the skills and accomplishments of the other. The two rivals were called into a meeting with Brig. Gen. Fitz John Porter, one of McClellan's staff officers and himself a balloon enthusiast. Porter suggested a truce in the best interests of the Union cause, and the two agreed to cooperate. La Mountain went on the payroll at the same $10 daily rate that Lowe was receiving.

In addition to his captive flights, La Mountain began a series of free-balloon missions. He would ascend to a level above the reach of enemy ground fire, drift over their lines and positions behind the lines, and then ascend to a higher altitude to catch the prevailing winds blowing back toward the Union positions. He did this four times between October 4 and December 10, 1861, soaring once as high as 18,000 feet to find the wind that would return him to safety.

La Mountain's daring flights forced the development and use of camouflage techniques by the Confederates. Their commanders grasped the deep meaning of the

The cumbersome paraphernalia associated with balloon operations is clear in this photograph taken at Ft. Myer. The hydrogen gas used for lift was expensive and vulnerable, and the balloon's military value was also eroded by the type's size and complexity. All in all, the airplane offered far greater scope.

sinister sphere overhead, and began to take pains to hide troop movements and campsites from airborne eyes.

By November, Lowe's four new balloons were ready, and waiting with *Union* in Washington for orders. These arrived and Lowe, with his troop of aeronauts, joined McClellan's forces along the Potomac.

Late in 1861, contemporary history recorded the first use of an aircraft carrier, specifically built for the mission. One of Lowe's aeronauts, William Paullin, was in charge of the balloon *Constitution*, and attached to Brig. Gen. Joseph Hooker's corps near Washington. Paullin operated occasionally from the flat deck of the remodeled coal barge, *George Washington Parke Custis*. She had been modified for balloon operations, and carried the balloon, its windlass and restraining lines, the gas generator, spare parts and materials. The 112-foot long vessel usually was towed by a steam tug, but for operations in shallow water she was supplied with long poles and oars.

The new year saw two smaller balloons added to the force, now totaling seven: *Union, Intrepid, Constitution, Washington, United States, Eagle* and *Excelsior.* Lowe's corps now included Paullin; James Allen, the first balloonist with the Union forces and his brother, Ezra; John B. Starkweather; John H. Steiner (who was to write from his remote station with the Army of the Mississippi: ". . . the officers here are as dum as a set of asses . . no one seems to know any thing abought this thing . . . "); Ebenezer Seaver; John R. Dickinson; and Jacob C. Freno, who turned out to be a throughly unsavory character, a gambler on the side, and—when dismissed—a saboteur.

Lowe had all the balloons and La Mountain was fuming. His own *Atlantic* was aging and too small; his larger *Saratoga* had broken loose and disappeared on a southern heading. Two of Lowe's balloons were stored in Washington, and La Mountain decided to ask for one to be released to him. Unfortunately, he accompanied his request with a denunciation of Lowe. It took three months of angry exchanges before Lowe was able to counter La Mountain's charges successfully. On February 19, 1862, orders came from Gen. McClellan, discharging La Mountain.

"Yesterday There Was a Balloon in the Air All Day"

A Richmond, Virginia, newspaper for May 26, 1862, carried the latest battle report on its front page:

The enemy are fast making their appearance on the banks of the Chickahominy. Yesterday there was a balloon in the air all day. They evidently discovered something of importance for at 4 a.m. this morning brisk cannonading was heard at Mechanicsville and the Yankees now occupy that place.

A major engagement was in the making between the Union Army of the Potomac and the Confederate Army of Northern Virginia, and Thaddeus Lowe and the balloonists were ready. McClellan's army was split by the Chickahominy river, normally mild-mannered, but now approaching flood stages because of the recent heavy rains. A few units under Brig. Gen. Samuel P. Heintzelman had crossed, but the main body of the force was waiting at Mechanicsville for reinforcements to arrive from Washington, where they had been posted to defend the capital.

Lowe had three balloons on station: *Washington, Intrepid* and *Constitution.* Observations made routinely from them convinced him that Confederate forces were massing for an attack on Heintzelman's force across the river. In later years, Lowe included this description of the events of the battle in his unpublished memoirs:

From eleven o'clock until dark, on the 29th of May, the enemy commenced to concentrate their forces in front of Fair Oaks, moving on roads entirely out of sight of our pickets, and concealing themselves as much as possible in and behind woods where none of their movements could be seen except from the balloon . . .

On the 31st of May, at noon, I ascended at Mechanicsville and discovered bodies of the enemy and trains of wagons moving from Richmond toward Fair Oaks. I remained in the air watching their movements until nearly two o'clock when I saw the enemy form in line of battle, and cannonading immediately commenced.

I made an observation that showed that the Confederates were marching to attack our troops on the right bank of Chickahominy before the completion of the bridge would permit those on the left bank to join them. This would mean the destruction of our army. I descended immediately and sent off the most important dispatch of any during my whole experience in the military service.

Lowe advised McClellan's staff of the situation: Confederate troops were in position, and wagon trains and artillery were moving up rapidly to engage Hentzelman's force.

The armies clashed; within minutes, heavy smoke from the volleys of rifle and cannon fire drifted above the battleground, making observations difficult. But it seemed that the Union line was holding.

Time dragged; across the river, two divisions of Union troops were waiting in reserve. Finally, late in the afternoon, their orders arrived, and they began to cross on a floating log bridge. The noise of battle urged them on. The Union line retreated under the fierce pressure of the rebel assault, and was holding tenaciously to its second line of defense.

The fresh Union troops hit the field at a run, shouting and firing; they pressed the attack, forcing the grey-clad troops into retreat. And the Union command staff, inexperienced and lacking any real brilliance in tactics, thought that was the end of it. Tomorrow the Union forces could continue their march southward, and in a few weeks the rag-tag armies of secession would be crushed decisively. The Rebs were retreating; they'd keep going until they were in Richmond.

Lowe made one more ascent on that busy day, the huge balloon lifting him into the night sky, giving him a vantage point to observe lights across the river where the Confederates had held the field. There were far too many, he thought, for stretcher bearers and doctors. There were enough for a whole army.

His first ascent the following morning confirmed his suspicions. The Confederates had held their positions after falling back, and were readying a second attack. Worse, Lowe could see reinforcements on the road up from Richmond, infantry and cavalry columns kicking up the dust against the pale morning light. It was a major Confederate effort that almost emptied Richmond of its defenders, and without Lowe's reports it would have caught the Union armies unprepared. The war between the states might well have ended right there on the banks of the flooded Chickahominy river.

The two armies met again in a charnelhouse that turned field and forest into plains of the dead. Close combat and point-blank range dropped Johnny Reb and Billy Yank within arm's reach of each other.

Through it all, Lowe kept *Washington* and *Intrepid* in the air, observing and reporting four times each hour to ground headquarters, enabling them to update their battle intelligence and redeploy troops.

A contemporary photograph shows Lowe in his balloon, ready to rise above the tree line. The basket is painted with red and white vertical stripes, topped by a blue field with two large white stars on each of the four sides. About two dozen men handle four lines from the ground to the balloon, and another six or so observe. In the background are four tents, pitched along the edge of a small grove of trees.

Lowe is standing, one hand on his hip and the other resting on the basket suspension cordage just above the spreader hoop. The lines under the picture tell us that " . . . for the next few moments shells and bullets from the shrapnels will be bursting and whistling about his ears."

The observation balloon proved its value on that frightful day on the Chickahominy, but the lessons learned did not remain long in the hidebound minds of the war's leaders in the field. In spite of continuing successes, the Union observation force never was allowed to operate as planned or promised. After a new commander had arbitrarily cancelled Lowe's contract and reduced his daily pay to $6, Lowe resigned. His assistants asked for other duties. By June 1863, with many major battles of the war yet to come, the balloon corps was disbanded.

As a measure of its accomplishments, note that Lowe himself made more than 3,000 ascents, spending several hundred hours aloft observing enemy operations. He and his aeronauts made a major and unrecognized contribution to the eventual Union victory.

A Hill in Cuba

Adolphus W. Greely, a veteran of the Civil War, rose from private in that conflict to become a brigadier general, and Chief Signal Officer of the reconstituted Signal Corps on July 1, 1891. Greely was progressive; one of the first actions of his new command was to create a balloon section, the first true military aeronautical activity in U. S. history. (Civil War balloonists all were hired as civilians, and never were commissioned in the Union Army.)

When the United States and Spain went to war in April 1898, the Signal Corps' sole balloon was in dead storage in Denver, and there were no trained personnel to rehabilitate it and get it operational. Under the urgency of war, the Corps personnel did manage to get the balloon repaired by mid-May, and to Daiquiri, Cuba, by June 28. The following day the detachment reached their headquarters and prepared for the first ascent.

The balloon was a mess; its varnished envelope was stuck together in places from the humidity. But it was inflated, and three ascents were made, one of them confirming the presence and position of the main Spanish battle fleet in Santiago harbor.

On July 1, the balloon was moved toward El Poso Hill, and made its first ascent. The two observers, Lt. Cols. Joseph E. Maxfield and George McC. Derby, saw American units on the advance, but could not make out the Spanish forces because thick woods blocked their view from that position. The balloon was hauled down partway and moved nearer to San Juan Hill. On the way, its maneuvering lines were fouled by trees and shrubs, and the balloon could not get enough altitude either for safety or for observation. Even so, the first ascent from the new location revealed the position and strength of the entrenched Spanish forces. American artillery was swung to bear on them and to support the American advance up the hill.

Spanish infantry fired on the balloon, which took so many hits that it was hauled down for repair. Enemy fire increased, and the balloon detachment was forced out of action for the rest of the battle. The men went to other duties.

The official report of the Battle of San Juan Hill, filed by Maj. Gen. William Shafter, stated that the service rendered by the balloon observers was satisfactory. Enthusiasts have credited the observers with making the victory possible. At the time, the unofficial view was that the balloon drew enemy fire. Worse, long rounds landed among troops in reserve and even rewounded casualties waiting for treatment at aid stations well behind the main line of battle.

It had been an almost impossible task from the start. The balloon was aged and in bad condition. personnel were hastily gathered, and lacked experience as a team. There was no time for a test ascent before deployment to battle. But in spite of all that, the balloon was made airworthy, was operated in three different locations, and did furnish useful and timely intelligence to Shafter's staff.

The balloon corps languished again after that war, its equipment concentrated in storage at Ft. Myer, Virginia, for economy reasons. In 1902 the Signal Corps tried again, establishing a Balloon Detachment at Ft. Myer. Some funds were found to order and construct a few new balloons. More aeronauts were trained to fly them, and Army officers observed and entered the great balloon races of the early 20th century.

Ballooning was a field that the Signal Corps saw as a useful adjunct to the primary mission of communications for the Army, and one to which the Corps had staked an early claim. So it was logical for them to take one more step forward, and to create the first of the predecessor organizations of the United States Air Force.

A scene typical of the halcyon days before the advent into U.S. Army service of those noisy aircraft: groundcrew walk an inflated balloon from its shed at Fort Myer during the summer of 1908.

The order was issued August 1, 1907, by the Office of the Chief Signal Officer, War Department. It stated:

An Aeronautical Division of this office is hereby established to take effect this date.
This Division will have charge of all matters pertaining to military ballooning, air machines, and all kindred subjects. All data on hand will be carefully classified and perfected for future experiments. The operations of this Division are strictly confidential . . .

A major undertaking for the Corps was the acquisition of a newer kind of air machine, the dirigible. Several had been flown in the United States and Europe, and their performance offered the prospect of freeing the military balloonist from dependence on the wind. The dirigibles combined the lifting power of the balloon with a powerplant for propulsion, and control surfaces for steering.

The Corps Buys a Dirigible

Brig. Gen. James Allen, then Chief Signal Officer, was an official observer at the 1907 James Gordon Bennett International Balloon Race in St. Louis. An air meet was scheduled to follow the races, and Gen. Allen stayed on to watch the flying.

A dirigible competition was a feature of the air meet, and one of them was well demonstrated by Thomas Scott Baldwin, a former wire-walker, parachute jumper, and general daredevil. Allen talked with Baldwin about acquiring a dirigible for the Corps, and Baldwin was interested.

Soon after, the Corps issued a specification and a request for bids for a dirigible to carry two persons plus 100 pounds of ballast at a maximum speed of 20 mph. The material for the envelope, a lamination of silk and rubber, would be furnished by the government.

Most prospective bidders were furious; they knew nothing about the proposed material which, in fact, was one of Baldwin's ideas turned to reality by a fabric manufacturer. It was an unfair restriction, they argued, and they won. The Corps issued revised Specification S. C. 483 on January 21, 1908. It made the contractor responsible for choosing the envelope material, but it specified a breaking strength for the fabric, and the restriction that varnished material could not be used.

Hydrogen was to be the lifting gas; developed lift had to be sufficient to carry two persons weighing a total of 350 pounds, plus ballast weighing 100 pounds. Dimensions were left to the contractor with the single restriction that overall length could not exceed 120 feet. Required speed was still 20 mph., with penalties for every mile per hour below that speed, and rejection if the craft did not exceed 16 mph. Endurance was to be two hours. Three speed and three endurance trials were allowed, to be conducted by the contractor within 30 days after delivery of the craft to Ft. Myer, and the costs of the trials were to be borne by the contractor.

Baldwin was low bidder, at $6,750 and 150 days until delivery, and received a contract February 24, 1908. Other bids varied to a high of $33,000 and a delivery time of 250 days. Glenn Curtiss, whose lightweight engines had powered Baldwin's earlier dirigibles, began work on a new, water-cooled, four-cylinder engine to deliver 20 hp.

Baldwin's design was typical. An openwork nacelle was slung below a cylindrical gas bag with pointed ends. At the forward end of the nacelle was a propeller, driven by a 22-ft. long shaft that extended from the Curtiss engine, mounted in the nacelle about one-third of the way back. Just behind the engine sat the forward pilot, who controlled the engine and the movements of the dirigible in a vertical plane. He operated a set of control surfaces like short-span wings extending from the sides of the nacelle. Toward the rear sat the second pilot, whose function was to man the rudder and provide directional control of the airship.

Final lift figure was approximately 1,350 pounds; 500 pounds of that was charged to two pilots, ballast, fuel, and useful load items.

Signal Corps Dirigible No. 1 was delivered to Ft. Myer during the week of July 20, and was ready for flight tests by August 4. The first flight lasted seven minutes and reached an altitude of 250 feet, but proved the ability of the machine to fly. Over the next week, Baldwin and Curtiss, his co-pilot, made several tests, including two over the course that had been selected for the official speed trials.

On August 12 the official test flights began, and the engine promptly failed on the way. Repaired on the site by Curtiss, the engine was restarted and returned the dirigible to Ft. Myer, but the test was a failure. On August 14, the two aeronauts completed the course, at an average speed of 19.61 mph., and the trials board concluded that figure was close enough.

The next day, the dirigible passed its endurance tests and on August 18 Baldwin was notified officially of its acceptance by the Corps. All that remained was to instruct two officers to fly it. Baldwin started with three pupils: Lts. Frank P. Lahm, Benjamin D. Foulois, and Thomas E. Selfridge.

Dirigible No. 1 led a short life, first at Ft. Myer and later at Ft. Omaha, Nebraska, the Signal Corps' designated site for lighter-than-air development.

Hydrogen gas was made then by treating iron filings with sulphuric acid, collecting and separating the gas that resulted. A small quantity of moisture-laden gas, still holding some particles of acid, always got through the gas processors and into the envelope. It ate pinholes in the fabric, reducing the lift by allowing gas to escape. Within two years after its purchase, No. 1's lift had been reduced to the point where only small, light men were able to fly her from the forward position.

Finally, even that weight was too much, and the dirigible was jury-rigged to permit flights by a single pilot from the rear position. He also had to move fore and aft along the framework of the nacelle to change the trim of the ship, and it was soon apparent that this was no way to fly. Besides, the airplane was now coming into its own, and offered more promise than an ungainly bag of gas. Signal Corps Dirigible No. 1 was condemned and publicly auctioned in 1912.

A Goodyear kite balloon floats steadily in the hot breeze over the border area during the American-Mexican conflict of 1917. In the absence of hostile aircraft and anti-aircraft guns, kite balloons were a considerable aid in the accurate registering of artillery fire.

The Signal Corps buys the Airplane

The Wright brothers made the first controlled, powered flights in history on December 17, 1903. As late as three years after the fact, scientific journals still pointed out the total impossibility of many-carrying, powered flight. By then, the Wrights had been flying in public view from Huffman's pasture outside Dayton, Ohio.

The British government approached the Wrights at the end of 1904 with an offer to buy their airplane, but were politely refused. The patriotic brothers wanted their own government to benefit, and tried three times in 1905 to interest the War Department. The last of the three replies they received, from the Recorder of the Board of Ordnance and Fortification, the responsible agency for funding new weapons of war, was a classic:

... the Board does not care to formulate any requirements for the performance of a flying machine or to take any further action until a machine is produced which by actual operation is shown to be able to produce horizontal flight and to carry an operator.

By then, the Wrights had made more than 150 flights, many of them in full view of reporters and spectators.

They continued to experiment, undaunted, and during 1906 designed and built a much better engine than their original powerplant of 1903. In 1907, the Aero Club of America took action, going directly to President Theodore Roosevelt and politely demanding some action to acquire the Wright invention for development as a weapon. Official channels led the Wrights back to the Board of Ordnance and Fortification with outline specifications for their latest airplane proposal. They emphasized that they did not want advance payments, and that they were not asking for financial support until a successful article was delivered. The Board responded that funds were not available,

and that any action would require an act of Congress.

Wilbur Wright went to Washington to tell the Chief of Ordnance and the Board's Secretary what he and his brother had done. He was invited to appear before the Board on December 5, 1907, and was at last able to convince the Board that he was a serious, believable co-inventor of an operational flying machine.

The Aeronautical Division drafted Specification No. 486, basing it on Wilbur's estimates of the performance of his proposed aircraft, and issued it for competitive bidding on December 23, 1907. The specification outlined an airplane that would carry two persons with combined weight of 350 pounds, and enough fuel for a 125-mile flight. Required speed was a minimum of 40 mph. A 10% bonus was offered for each mile per hour speed gain to a top of 44 mph., and a 10% penalty would be assessed for each mile per hour below 40 mph., with total rejection if the craft did not meet or exceed 36 mph. It was desirable that the machine could be easily assembled and taken apart for transportation in army wagons. It should take about one hour to assemble and put into operational condition.

The machine had to be able to takeoff "... in any country which might be encountered in field service." The starting system had to be simple and transportable, and the plane had to be able to land on an unprepared field without damage. Further, it had to have some device to permit safe descent in case the propulsion system broke down.

And finally, "It should be sufficiently simple in its construction and operation to permit an intelligent man to become proficient in its use within a reasonable length of time."

When the specification became public knowledge, the Army became the target for an outcry of disbelief. Newspaper editorials pointed out that nothing even approaching such a machine had been built, let alone flown. Even the *American Magazine of Aeronautics,*

This Wright Model B was the second military flying machine in the world (the first was also a Wright bought by the U.S. War Department in 1907). The photograph was probably taken in 1911 at Simms Station, in the centre of what is today the mighty Wright-Patterson AFB, the Air Force's technical headquarters.

A stark view of a stark event as the camera catches the moment just after the crash on September 17, 1908 at Ford Myer in which Lieutenant Thomas E. Selfridge was killed and Orville Wright seriously injured.

supposedly a learned journal, criticized the Army for asking the impossible; such performance requests could lead only to failure to achieve them. There would be no bidders, the magazine predicted.

There were 41 bidders, and 22 were considered as worth detailed investigation. Prices varied from a low of $500 to a high of $10,000,000. The choice finally narrowed to three who met all the terms of the specification: J. F. Scott, who asked for $1,000 and 185 days; A. M. Herring, who wanted $20,000 and 180 days; and the Wrights, who asked for $25,000 and 200 days.

All three looked promising, but there was only enough money for the two lowest bids. The Army desperately wanted to get the Wright airplane as well, and found a special fund, available only to the President, for purchases or services. There was money left in the fund from an appropriation made for the Spanish-American War some ten years earlier, and—with Roosevelt's approval—that fund was to be tapped for the purchase of the Wright machine.

Neither Scott nor Herring completed his contract. Scott withdrew his bid, and Herring, after being granted two extensions of time, finally failed to produce.

The Wright *Flyer* reached Ft. Myer on August 20, 1908, within the time specified by contract, and was readied for flight trials. By early September, the plane had set a new world endurance record and had carried its first military observer, Lt. Lahm. On September 17, Orville was flying the aircraft with Lt. Selfridge as passenger. On the fourth circuit of the field at Ft. Myer, one propeller deflected enough to slice a bracing wire attached to the rudder frame. The severed wire and the splintered propeller threw the airplane out of control; it crashed to the ground, fatally injuring Selfridge and injuring Wright. The trials were postponed by the War Department until the summer of 1909.

Orville had done all the flying in the 1908 trials, and he continued as the only pilot when the tests were resumed the following year. Wilbur was there, with encouragement and his special knowledge.

The first endurance test flight was scheduled for the evening of July 27, 1909. Orville was pilot as usual, and Lt. Lahm the passenger. It was Orville's first passenger-carrying flight since the fatal accident. The plane stayed in the air for one hour, 12 min. and 40 sec., establishing a new endurance record and easily passing the military requirement.

President William Howard Taft was among the crowd that came to Ft. Myer that summer evening. It was relatively calm; the earlier gusty winds had abated before the flight.

The Associated Press night report, dated July 27, gave this description of the endurance run:

Round and round the aëroplane went, seventy-four times about the great drill ground—4,000 feet in circumference, some times in shorter circles. The machine kept sixty feet high, save where some stray currents of air rocked her up or down.

After the seventieth turn, a great shout went up, automobile horns were tooted in a deafening chorus and handclapping and cheers and waving of hats and handkerchiefs told the men in the flying craft that their task was accomplished.

Orville again flew for the ten-mile cross-country speed trial required by the contract. On July 30, he and passenger Lt. Foulois flew the measured course in 14 min., 42 sec., for an average speed greater than 42 mph. The course ran between Ft. Myer and Shooter's Hill in Alexandria, the present site of the Masonic Memorial to George Washington. More than 7,000 people crowded the perimeter of the drill ground to watch the takeoff and cheer the return.

The Associated Press story that night said this about the drama of the takeoff:

As if drawn by invisible power, it rose higher and higher, reached the end of the field, turned at a slight angle and came about, facing the madly-cheering multitude.

Hats and handkerchiefs were waving, automobile horns were tooting, some overwrought spectators even wept as the great white creature turned again southward at the starting tower.

President Taft was there again to greet Orville and Foulois on their return, and " . . . to participate in the wild demonstration which welcomed the triumphant aviator."

The final report of the trials recorded that the airplane had met its requirement for endurance, and that the official speed according to the terms of the contract was 42.583 mph. The Wrights received $30,000 instead of $25,000 for their aircraft as a result.

Lahm and Foulois had been selected as pilot trainees under the terms of the Wright contract, but Foulois was sent abroad as a delegate to the International Congress of Aeronautics, and his place was taken by 2nd Lt. Frederic E. Humphreys. The training site was a field near the Maryland Agricultural College at College Park, Maryland. It was leased, cleared and readied for flight training which began October 8, 1909.

Both students soloed October 26, Humphreys with a total logged dual time of three hours, three minutes and 36 sec., Lahm with three hours, seven minutes, and 24 sec. On November 5, the airplane was damaged in a minor crash. While the pilots waited for parts from the factory, the weather turned cold and windy. Clearly, College Park was not suited for year-round flying training; those earliest airplanes were defeated by a light wind, and winter flying clothing had yet to be developed.

The government owned land near San Antonio, Texas, and had established Ft. Sam Houston there years earlier. It seemed a logical choice for a training site, and its selection was approved. The airplane and the mechanics were shipped to the Texas site, but there was a problem with the officers.

Humphreys, detached from the Corps of Engineers temporarily for flight training, was reassigned to the

Engineer School. Lahm, detached from the cavalry for the legal limit of four years, was ordered back to the horses. So the Army had an airplane, but no pilots. Only Lt. Foulois, with about three hours of flying time in training, was left to be considered. He became the Army's pilot, and went to Ft. Sam Houston, where he made the first flight, which was also his first solo flight, March 2, 1910.

The Army lacked funds to buy more aircraft, in spite of repeated requests to Congress for appropriations. But it got one anyway, in February 1911. A new Type B Wright plane, purchased by Robert F. Collier and loaned by him to the Army, arrived at Ft. Sam Houston, along with Wright pilot P. O. Parmelee, who checked Lt. Foulois out in the different control system of the new plane.

The first appropriation for military aeronautics as such followed when Congress approved the War Department appropriations for fiscal year 1912. In those funds was $125,000 specifically for aeronautics, and $25,000 of that was made immediately available. Three Wright airplanes and two Curtiss types were ordered.

Lt. G. E. M. Kelly's death in the crash of one of the Curtiss airplanes was followed by an order ending flying from the drill ground at Ft. Sam Houston. By then the War Department was committed to training in the College Park area again. It was established, and training began there, moving to winter quarters in Augusta, Georgia, when the weather turned cooler, moving back in the spring.

Pioneering continued at College Park. A rudimentary bomb sight had been developed by a Coast Artillery Corps officer and tested during 1911 at the school. In 1912, Col. Isaac N. Lewis brought one of his first sample machine guns to the school and requested that it be tested from the air. It was reasonably successful, even though the gun had no sight and was hand-held, its muzzle braced against a footrest. Night flying was tried, after one pilot was delayed on the way home and made a successful emergency landing by the light of ignited gasoline and oil puddles. Acetylene lamps were placed along the runway as guides.

Up to this time, the Army had not established its own qualifications for pilots, relying instead on the Fédération Aéronautique Internationale to set standards and issue licenses. But in the summer of 1912, the Army announced the new rating of Military Aviator. The candidate had to show his ability to climb his aircraft to at least 2,500 ft., operate in a wind of at least 15 mph., carry a passenger to 500 ft. and then dead-stick the airplane to a landing within 150 ft. of a designated point. He also had to make a cross-country flight of at least 20 miles at an average altitude of 1,500 ft.

The aviators flew their first missions in support of Army troop maneuvers in the area of New York City from August 10 to 17, 1912. They made reconnaissance flights, reporting the position of Red forces by radio, and including an hour-long mission over the triangle formed by Stratford, Derby and New Haven, Connecticut, spotting both Red and Blue forces in the field.

In November, 1912, Lts. H. H. Arnold and Thomas DeW. Milling were detached to Ft. Riley, Kansas, with two Type C Wright aircraft, to experiment with artillery regulation from the air. Several types of signalling were tried, but radio messages in code worked best.

The same year, the Army opened an aviation school at Ft. William McKinley, near Manila in the Philippine Islands. Summer rains flooded the flying area, and the unit moved to the shore of Manila Bay, installing floats on their three airplanes. One by one, the three planes were destroyed in accidents, and the school closed.

Both College Park and the winter site in Augusta continued in the training mission until February 25,

1913, when equipment and personnel were ordered to Texas City, Texas, in case the Mexican revolution required a U. S. presence.

The second Congressional appropriation of aeronautical funds again allocated $125,000, but $1 million had been requested. But Congress authorized 35% extra pay for officers regularly assigned to flying duty, limiting the number who could receive this largesse to 30.

In mid-1913, the lease at College Park expired, and was not renewed. All the equipment stored there after the move to Texas City was shipped to the Army's new flying school at North Island, near San Diego, California. The site had first been exploited by Glenn Curtiss as an alternate to Hammondsport, New York, for pilot training. The Army rented space and began flight training, continuing with its experiments with new ideas and equipment. There were further tests on a bomb sight, and Lt. Milling developed the first practical safety belt.

The Signal Corps had begun keeping flight records in 1911, with one stated reason being the need to keep track of accidents. They were occurring often enough to cause concern; each fatal crash was followed by a sudden loss of interest by the War Department and an expressed desire to shut the program down. From September 17, 1908, until February 28, 1914, 11 fatalities occurred in the Army's aviation program, killing eight pilots.

Records showed that conditions had improved in the three years. In 1911, there was a fatal accident for every 65 hours flown; by 1914, the rate was one every 125 hours. In 1911, Corps aviators made 372 flights per fatal accident; in 1914, the number was 515. The mortality rate had been reduced substantially, but it was still too high.

In a memorandum dated February 28, 1914, the Signal Corps noted that the greatest number of fatal accidents had occurred with the Wright Type C aircraft, and accordingly had grounded the airplane by telegraph messages February 16. An investigative board would be convened to evaluate the problem.

The board recommended that future flying be done only on the Burgess and Curtiss aircraft, both tractor types rather than the pusher type pioneered by the Wrights. It is speculative to suggest that the officers of the board believed that an engine to the rear was a sure route to fatal injuries in any crash.

The military still had not faced the problems first outlined in 1861 in Abbot's criticism of the balloon

After its single Wright Model A, the Signal Corps then bought two Model B and seven Model C aircraft from the Wrights. These last two models were almost identical: the forward stabilizer of the Model A was abandoned in favour of a rear-mounted unit, wheels were incorporated in the landing gear, and other detail improvements were incorporated. Both models were intended for training, but whereas on the Model B the pupil and instructor had to share some of the controls, on the Model C they were each provided with their own set.

Seen on the Curtiss airfield in 1916 are the experimental S-1 scout triplane and an R-3 biplane workhorse. Some 18 R-3s were ordered by the Air Service, and these were delivered in 1917 as R-6s. Some were later fitted with twin-float landing gears.

operations. Aviation personnel were detailed on temporary duty, officer pilots coming from other branches of the Army generally, and enlisted men from the Signal Corps. There was no guarantee that either officers or men would have any future in the aeronautical service.

But the Sixty-Third Congress, in its second session, passed a landmark bill, H.R. 5304, "An Act to Increase the Efficiency of the Aviation Service of the Army, and for Other Purposes." The wording of the bill stated that:

. . . there shall hereafter be, and there is hereby created, an aviation section, which shall be a part of the Signal Corps of the Army, and which shall be, and hereby is, charged with the duty of operating or supervising the operation of all military aircraft, including balloons and aeroplanes, all appliances pertaining to said craft, and signalling apparatus of any kind when installed on said craft; also with the duty of training officers and enlisted men in matters pertaining to military aviation.

The bill went on to increase the authorized strength of the Signal Corps by 60 aviation officers and 260 enlisted men, and directed that the strength increase be maintained by a flow of a sufficient number of aviation students. Further, there would be two classes of officers, junior military aviators and military aviators, and pay increments would be made available for this type of duty. The bill was signed into law by President Woodrow Wilson July 18, 1914.

The Influence of the Mexican Revolution

The many machinations of the Mexican revolution that began late in 1910 had a major effect on the development of airpower in the United States. It was not that the use of airpower was particularly successful; it wasn't. But the attempted use of airpower was very educational.

The first incident followed the seizure of power by

Gen. Victoriano Huerta on February 22, 1913. His government was not recognized by the United States and, in a period of tense relations, officers and men in training at Augusta were ordered to Texas City. The unit arrived in a special train March 2, and unloaded their five airplanes and began flying.

Texas City had been chosen as the site of a training school earlier, and the concentration of aeronautical materiel there prompted the Chief Signal Officer to suggest that the operation be organized properly. The 1st Provisional Aero Squadron was established officially on March 5, 1913, formed with personnel and equipment from Augusta and Texas City. It included a headquarters staff of three officers, and two aero companies of three officers and 24 and 27 enlisted men, respectively.

The situation in Mexico quieted down, and the 1st was split. Headquarters stayed at Texas City with three officers, 26 men and two airplanes; the rest moved to the North Island training center.

The revolution aroused the U. S. again when American sailors were arrested ashore in Tampico early in 1914. They were released, following an exchange of notes. The U.S.A. resented Huerta's attitude and ordered Marines to land at Vera Cruz, almost due east of Mexico City, in an obvious threat to the capital city. The invasion was met by demonstrations and strong reactions, and the 1st Aero Squadron was sent to Ft. Crockett, Galveston, Texas. Five aviators, 30 men, and three Burgess tractor biplanes went as a detachment: 1st Company, 1st Aero Squadron. The remainder of personnel and equipment at North Island became the 2nd Company. The 1st Company arrived April 30, but the pressure was off. The planes stayed in their crates, and the unit returned to North Island July 13.

On August 5, 1914, the 1st Aero Squadron dropped the word "Provisional" from its title, and officially reorganized to comply with War Department General Order No. 75, of December 4, 1913, setting out the table of organization for aero squadrons.

For more than a year the revolution moved in a number of directions, eventually splitting into three major forces under three leaders; Carranza, Zapata, and Francisco "Pancho" Villa. In the fighting among the factions, Villa was defeated in March 1915 and retreated north.

On April 13, two officers of the 1st were detached and sent to Brownsville, Texas, with a single Martin T airplane, for service with the border patrol. Lts. Milling and B. Q. Jones planned to use the aircraft for spotting Villa's gun positions across the river from Brownsville, near Matamoros. But the Martin T had no radio, and Villa had abandoned the positions and the town two days before the aviators arrived on April 17.

Villa believed in airpower, and had his own force of at least three American airplanes flown by at least five American pilots. In April, while a U. S. Martin plane was scouting Villa's abandoned positions, a new Wright Model HS was being delivered from the Dayton factory to Villa's men in El Paso, Texas.

Late in October 1915, the U. S. recognized Carranza's government, and that act cut off Villa's supply of arms and other weapons from the U.S.A. In January, 1916, Villa ordered the execution of some U. S. citizens he had captured, and on March 9 his forces crossed the border to attack the town of Columbus, New Mexico, killing 19 Americans.

President Wilson immediately sent a punitive force of 15,000 men under the command of Brig. Gen. John J. Pershing to the border near Columbus, with orders to get Villa and bring him back, dead or alive. The 1st Aero Squadron was ordered to join the expedition.

By then, the squadron was at Ft. Sam Houston, and it was about 620 miles, airline distance, to Columbus. The planes were aging; there were few landing fields and fuel depots between the two towns. The 1st crated its aircraft and set out by rail March 13, 1916. They arrived two days later, and set up shop. Their eight Curtiss JN-3s were assembled and covered with tarpaulins until a hanger could be built. Their motor transport was requisitioned by the Quartermaster Corps and used for troop supply.

Their mission was reconnaissance. Villa's cavalry moved fast over country that they knew well. The American force, new to the region, and operating in a wilderness state that had only recently joined the United States, was in strange territory indeed.

The JN-3s had been flying for more than a year as trainers, receiving harsh treatment. Their 90-hp. engines were operating in the heat and sand of the southwest. There were high mountains in the area with attendant turbulence and altitude problems, and it was a long distance from one point to another.

Capts. Townsend F. Dodd and Foulois made one reconnaissance flight from Columbus, and then the 1st moved with Pershing to Casas Grandes, Mexico, about 100 miles south of Columbus. All eight aircraft headed south to Casas Grandes. None made it the first try; all landed somewhere else. Six did get to the base area the next day, but one was abandoned after a crash, and the second missing plane had yet to be recovered after being downed by a leak in its fuel tank.

Flying conditions were abysmal. Planes of the 1st encountered hail, extreme turbulence that forced the planes down to treetop height in the rugged mountains, severe rain, and snowstorms. Propellers delaminated in the hot, dry climate and squadron mechanics removed the prop as soon as an airplane returned from its mission, placing it in a humidor to keep the glue holding. When an airplane was scheduled for flight, a different propeller was taken out of storage and mounted. But all this effort was almost wasted; the basic performance of the JN-3 was simply insufficient to have any real value in the campaign.

Relegated to carrying dispatches between elements of Pershing's forces, the planes performed better. They still ran into rain, hail and snow, but they didn't have to operate in the Sierra Madre mountains, and that made the difference.

On March 31, Congress enacted legislation to correct some urgent deficiencies in military materiel, and part of the $500,000 alloted to the Aviation Section was used to buy some new equipment for the 1st. On April 20 the squadron was ordered back to Columbus to take charge of their new aircraft. By then, they were down to two JN-3s in commission, and those were flown to Columbus and junked. To replace them, the 1st received four Curtiss N-8 machines, which turned out to be equally unsuited to the Mexican theater of operations. Hardly a year later, the four Curtiss aircraft were condemned as unfit. Seven pilots had evaluated them officially, and reported that they would not fly them except in an extreme military emergency.

The 1st stayed on duty with Pershing until August 15, 1916, and then moved back to Columbus, where they were stationed when the unit was called to France in August 1917.

The squadron's experiences had been as wild and turbulent as the weather conditions they flew in. But the lessons that were learned paid off in an appreciation that aircraft had to be designed to meet the requirements of military forces in the field.

The campaign is often viewed as a comic-opera war, with daredevil fliers, hair-raising flights, and splintering crashes that killed nobody. But Villa was never captured, and it was in reality a guerrilla war that the

Of considerable historical importance was the first use of a machine gun in the air-to-ground role. The tests, made in June 1912 in a Wright Model B, used a Lewis gun operated by Captain Charles de F. Chandler. His pilot was Lieutenant De Witt Milling.

Major H.A. Dargue poses by his Curtiss JN-2 on the outskirts of Chihuahua City in 1917. Forced down while on a reconnaissance flight, the major was stoned by the hostile Mexicans.

U. S. lost, a history that was destined to be repeated a half-century later.

Gen. Pershing, the cavalryman with some disdain for airplanes, praised the men by saying that they had " . . . too often risked their lives in old and often useless machines which they have patched up and worked over in an effort to do their share of the duty this expedition has been called upon to perform." He called the officers devoted and fearless, and when Christmas 1916 rolled around, "Black Jack" Pershing sent a message to Capt. Dodd, then commanding the 1st:

. . . kindly extend my warmest thanks to your command for the faithful and efficient service it has performed as a part of this expedition.

It must have been a source of some official embarrassment that the Mexican air effort was so pathetic.

One of the superannuated types fobbed off on the Americans in France was the Voisin Type 8, and elderly pusher design of only limited use even for training.

In Europe, World War 1 was raging, and airplanes were in daily use. The bombing and fighting aircraft designs were far in advance of anything the U. S. had to offer.

By December, 1916, German Zeppelins had bombed London; air-to-air combat was a reality, as were the synchronized machine guns, firing through the propeller disc, that made it practical; airmen had developed the arts of artillery regulation and of tactical support, and were planning strategic bombing with an independent force whose heavy four-engined bomber was already well advanced in development and construction.

In August, 1916, Congress had authorized $13,281,666 for aeronautical development, a quantum leap over the paltry sums of earlier years. But war was coming to the U.S.A., it was felt, and the country had to be ready. Seven aero squadrons were authorized that year, but only the 1st was equipped and ready for action, even though its antique aircraft would have been useless in the skies of France.

Perhaps 125 U. S. airplanes were in commission at the end of 1916. All of them were trainers, or communications and reconnaissance types, and not one was suited for combat. The majority—less than 80—were Curtiss JN-4s and JN-4Bs. Another 17 or so were also Curtiss, the Models R-2, and R-4, best described as a larger and more powerful JN. The rest were five different trainers built by five different companies: L-W-F, Martin, Sloane, Standard and Sturtevant.

They were based at three training fields and three "operational" bases. Signal Corps Aviation Schools had been established at North Island; at Mineola, on Long Island, New York; and at Memphis, Tennessee. The 1st Aero Squadron was stationed at Columbus, New Mexico, and equipped with 11 Curtiss R-2 and three R-4 machines. The 2nd Aero Squadron had been formed at San Antonio, Texas, and was operating five Curtiss JN-4s and three R-4s.

And that was the total strength of American airpower just before the country entered World War 1. But within less than two years, it was to become a major force in the air, and had begun to develop the concepts and doctrines that became the foundation stones of the United States Air Force in later years.

The Air Service in World War I

Steely-eyed aces, squinting through the sights of their Vickers machine guns, shooting down Fokkers and Gothas by the score, destroying the Flying Circuses, raiding the German aerodromes . . .

These are the images that a generation acquired of the United States Air Service in World War 1. They are, like their sources—the pulp fiction of the '30s—also fiction.

The hard facts are disillusioning. No American-trained airmen fought in the skies of France until more than one year after the entry of the United States into the war. The most experienced squadrons served only a total of seven months in the war zone. Most American air strength was not committed—or available—to battle until two months before the end of the war. The airmen flew castoffs from the French and British air arms, outmoded airplanes whose performance ranged from indifferent to dangerous. Spare parts were lacking; they were improvised, in some extreme cases, from discarded French farm machinery. Aircraft in-

struments, primitive anyway, were in poor shape, and malfunctioned so much that pilots trusted only their clocks and their wristwatches. Their claims of victories were, in all likelihood, exaggerated by two or three times. Their losses were great enough to put whole squadrons out of action for a time. The industry back home failed them; its products were inferior, and only a few American-built aircraft ever reached the front and combat. And yet . . .

And yet there were heroes that the war gave to a generation, real heroes who did, in fact, shoot down brightly painted Fokkers, and who flamed observation balloons and bombed German targets. From that terrible crucible of war came the principles, concepts and, unfortunately, some dogmas, that governed the development of air power in the years afterward.

The United States declared war April 6, 1917. The only experienced U. S. air unit was the 1st Aero Squadron, tested in fruitless pursuit of a remarkable Mexican guerrilla leader. Their antique airplanes

MacDonald and Krout, bundled against the late autumn chill and the cutting cold of the slipstream, pose in Number 7, "Peaches", of the 135th Aero Squadron. She was an American-built DH-4, powered by the Liberty engine, and painted in the overall olive drab finish characteristic of the last few months of the war. MacDonald's twin guns are the standard Lewis model used by observers in the Allied air forces; Krout's battery consists of twin Marlin machine guns, located on the upper fuselage decking just ahead of his face.

The Pioneering Years

On the ground and in the mud of France, 1st Lieutenant Ray W. Krout, USAS, poses in front of his Liberty-powered DH-4 with his ground crew of four specialists. From the left these are: Sgt. Nandick, Sgt. Parker, Krout, Sgt. Halseth, and Armorer Anderson. Krout's original caption for this photo revealed his British training with the Royal Air Force. He spelled Anderson's title "Armourer" and did not identify him by rank. The ground crewmen are wearing thigh-length rubber boots, and you need only one glance at the picture to know why. You read, in the old stories, about the ever-present mud of the Western Front; but you can't appreciate it without seeing pictures like this one, that make the point better than any description.

should have been condemned as scrap. At the war's beginning, the U. S. ranked 14th among air powers of the world. In 14 years since the invention of the airplane by two Americans, the United States had let its potential in the skies fall into other hands.

The Army saw no real importance for aviation, and expected that it would play a relatively insignificant part in the conflict. There were no approved plans for its use, no approved programs to build its strength. The in-service force was pathetic: about 100 pilots, perhaps 125 planes in commission, and not one of them fit for rough service, let alone combat. There were fewer balloons than the Union armies had in the Peninsular Campaign of 1862. The aviation industry was a handful of companies who had delivered about 15% of their orders in the year before the war, and were hopelessly behind the very modest production schedules established for trainer aircraft.

But by April 6, 1917, a few American airmen had

been fighting in France for a year. The pilots were volunteers, members of the French Escadrille N.124 *Lafayette*, perhaps the most famous squadron in military history. For a year after their country entered the war, these airmen were the only Americans to see aerial combat and to profit from the terrible experience. Formed in April, 1916, the Lafayette Escadrille was a major influence on the development of U. S. pursuit aviation. It taught a nucleus of American airmen who later led other squadrons or contributed their expertise to the air fighting. By its publicized example, it probably was a recruiting aid. But in spite of all these positive contributions to the American air arm, it was long after the declaration of war before any formal action was taken to welcome the Lafayette pilots into their own country's air service and to use their expertise. They were commissioned in the U. S. Signal Corps on February 18, 1918, and the Lafayette Escadrille became the 103rd Aero Squadron that day.

The pace of that transfer was typical of the measured march that moved American airmen to the war. When the first American-trained air crews arrived in Europe in early 1918, ready to fly and fight, they found that many of their castoff aircraft had arrived from training bases and were not only unarmed but also in bad repair; that machine guns were not available to install on the pursuit planes; that their pilot training had been sadly lacking in any of the aspects of air combat, including gunnery.

It was standard practice to send fresh American units to the area around Toul, France, on the southern flank of the forward zone. There was enough enemy action to gain some experience of combat, but not enough to overwhelm new pilots. There were two "tame" German Jagdstaffels covering the sector, and occasionally they offered battle.

The 94th Aero Squadron, later to become famed as the *Hat-in-the-Ring* unit under Capt. Eddie Rickenbacker, arrived at Toul April 9, 1918, two days more than a year after the U. S. entered the war. They were equipped with Nieuport 28s, a clean-looking aircraft briefly used by the French and pulled out of front-line service because it often shed its upper-wing fabric during a highspeed dive. No guns were available; when they did arrive, there were not enough to arm all the

Looking remarkably clean in muddy surroundings, this American-built DH-4 of the 85th Aero Squadron stands in the open near the end of the war. The last weeks are already passing, and the 85th is late on the scene. No post-war reports available indicate that the squadron saw combat, so this picture must have been taken a few days before or after the Armistice. The squadron insigne is a winged cherub, wearing a U. S. campaign hat, and sitting on a globe. The airplane is named "Marie", and its crew is pilot Robert T. Palmer and observer H. M. Rice. Serial number is 23114.

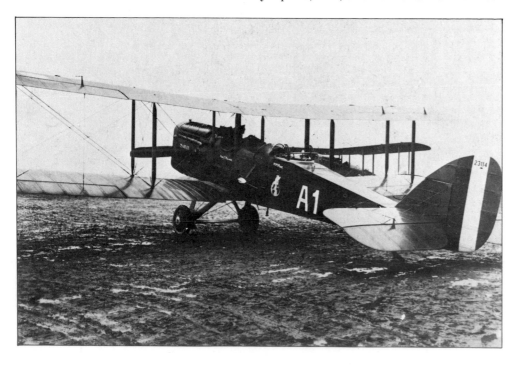

airplanes with the twin weapons for which the cowling mounts had been designed. So each of the 94th's Nieuports sallied forth to battle with a single .30-cal. machine gun mounted to the left of the cowling.

One can only imagine the frustrations of the pilots and ground crews. After such a string of experiences, they needed something—anything—to boost their morale. It came, in the unexpected arrival of two German fighters on a rainy April 14th.

Lts. Douglas Campbell and Alan Winslow were killing time, playing cards on a table that held the squadron's field telephone. It was a foul day, with a 500-foot ceiling and little air activity. The telephone jangled; two German planes are on the way, said the tinny voice of a forward observer, and you'd better send up a patrol. The two officers were off the ground in little more than a minute, a tribute to one good characteristic of the Nieuports.

They climbed fast, intercepted the Germans, and shot them down, Winslow scoring first and Campbell moments later. The wreckage landed almost on their aerodrome at Gengault, and the Americans had their first aerial victories.

The two landed to be greeted by an enthusiastic group of mechanics. One sergeant in Campbell's ground crew, oblivious to the military niceties, slapped Campbell on the back and said, "That's the stuff, Lieutenant, old kid!"

It had been a very long road to those two victories. The country had started from such an inferior postiion that any progress toward forging a combat arm would have been remarkable. Major, massive problems had stood between plans and accomplishments, and they would not be solved in the short time America spent in the war.

There were fundamental differences in the proposed use of American forces. The British and French, exhausted by the years of war, wanted them as a manpower pool, to replace their own losses and reinforce their divisions. The U. S. would have none of that; American troops would be commanded by American officers and serve in American armies.

There was also a basic difference of belief in the proper role of airpower between Gen. John J. Pershing, who commanded the American Expeditionary Force in Europe, and Col. (later Brig. Gen.) William Mitchell, the AEF's top air commander.

Pershing was wedded to the concept of air in support of ground armies, who would naturally do the fighting, defeat the enemy, and seize the objectives. Mitchell saw the air force as a strategic one, hammering the enemy sources of production and supplies, and eliminating his ability to win battles and the war.

Pershing wanted to see friendly planes above his lines, keeping enemy aircraft away and furnishing top cover for his advancing armies. Mitchell wanted to destroy enemy air on the ground, or keep it there by cutting off its supply lines.

It was a difference that extended throughout the military, and which found proponents of both concepts in both the ground and the air services. It is a difference that still exists, half a century and several wars later, between a mechanized, mobile Army and an independent strategically minded Air Force.

The fact is that during its entire employment in the conflict, American air power was subordinated to ground armies and their immediate tactical needs. The Air Service tried, but was never officially permitted, to develop a strategic bombardment force to strike deep into Germany's industry.

1st Lieutenant Ray W. Krout, U. S. Air Service, posed for this formal portrait in France, in 1918, dressed in his best uniform. Krout survived his war, stayed in the service and was killed in a crash during war games a decade or so later.

Number 11 is an S.E.5a, serial F.8040, built by Austin Motor Co. (1914) Ltd., of Northfield, Birmingham. One of only 38 bought from Britain in October 1918. She's on the roster of the 25th Aero Squadron, whose executioner insigne adorns her sides. The stripe on the upper left wing is white, indicating that the plane is part of the 2nd Flight of the 25th Squadron.

The Pioneering Years

French Premier Alexandre Ribot cabled President Wilson May 24, 1917, proposing that the U. S. send an air arm of 4,500 planes, 5,000 pilots and 15,000 mechanics overseas by June, 1918. It was the first of many overly ambitious plans and programs, none realized, that characterized America's first war air effort.

The National Advisory Committee for Aeronautics, established in 1915 "...to supervise and direct the scientific study of the problems of flight..." had proposed a more modest, even realistic, program six days after the U. S. entered the fray: build 3,700 planes in 1918, 6,000 in 1919, and 10,000 in 1920.

The War Department developed its own goal, based on Ribot's stated needs: 12,000 airplanes and 24,000 engines, to be produced between January 1 and June 30, 1918.

But what to build? Only Britain and France were producing contemporary fighter, bomber and reconnaisance aircraft. The answer was obvious: make arrangements to build those airplanes in the United States. So a group of aviation officers under Maj. Raynal C. Bolling were sent to Europe in June 1917 to investigate and negotiate with the British, French and Italians for American production of their aircraft.

Six types were recommended by two of Bolling's staff, Capts. Virginius E. Clark and Edgar S. Gorrell, in their report of August 17, 1917: the Bristol Scout for advanced training; the Bristol F.2B fighter for army cooperation; the de Havilland D.H.4 for long-range reconnaissance and bombing by day; the 200-hp. S.P.A.D. as one fighter, and a new S.P.A.D. design with a Gnome rotary engine as the other; and the Caproni triplane for night bombing.

Aircraft design, never static, was a very dynamic art in those years. Before the final report could be acted upon, the list began to change as superior models became available. The D.H.9 replaced the D.H.4; the Caproni triplane gave way to a smaller biplane design; the Handley Page O/400 was also considered as a night bomber; the new S.P.A.D. was a failure.

Contracts were placed in September and October, 1917. The Curtiss Aeroplane Co. was signed to build 3,000 S.P.A.D. fighters, 500 Caproni bombers, and 1,000 Bristol F.2Bs. The Dayton-Wright Airplane Co. was to produce 2,000 de Havilland D.H.9 day bombers, and the Fisher Body Co. was to build 3,000 more.

The industry had nine months to meet those goals. It would have been impossible under the best of conditions, but the production program produced some of the worst. The Italians wanted to redesign their bomber in the U.S. The British wouldn't send a sample Handley Page until long after it was in full production. The French claimed they could produce all the fighters needed, so American plans for fighter production were cancelled.

There were conflicting reports from Europe, command changes, and organization of the Air Service with two branches, one responsible for training and operations, and the other for production. They were independent agencies, and without a single commander initially.

The final result was nothing to brag about. Only one type of airplane—the U.S.-built DH-4 day bomber and reconnaissance aircraft—was delivered to Europe in any quantity. Although 1,100 per month were being built by the Armistice, only 1,213 were shipped to France and the combat zone. Of those, 499 were sent to front-line squadrons, and 417 of those were actually used in combat operations.

It was, incidentally, loved by the observation squadron and hated by the day bomber units. Loaded with bombs, its performance was mediocre; with 500 pounds of bombs it took one hour to climb to 10,000 feet and its top speed was under 100 mph. But without those bombs, it was not a bad performer. Even so, the

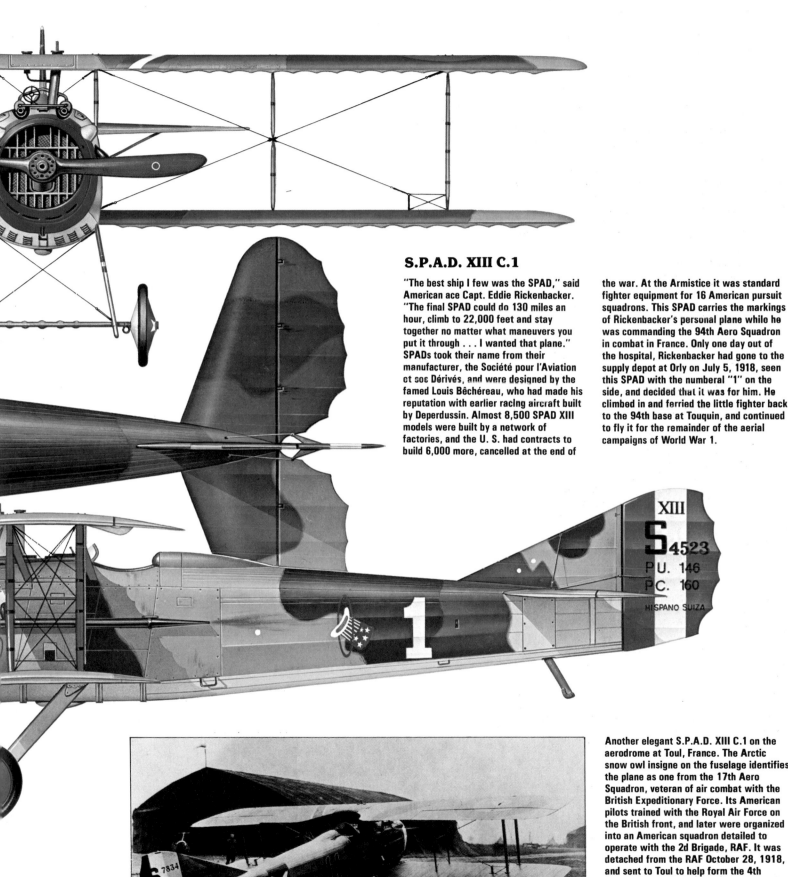

S.P.A.D. XIII C.1

"The best ship I few was the SPAD," said American ace Capt. Eddie Rickenbacker. "The final SPAD could do 130 miles an hour, climb to 22,000 feet and stay together no matter what maneuvers you put it through . . . I wanted that plane." SPADs took their name from their manufacturer, the Société pour l'Aviation et ses Dérivés, and were designed by the famed Louis Bêchéreau, who had made his reputation with earlier racing aircraft built by Deperdussin. Almost 8,500 SPAD XIII models were built by a network of factories, and the U. S. had contracts to build 6,000 more, cancelled at the end of

the war. At the Armistice it was standard fighter equipment for 16 American pursuit squadrons. This SPAD carries the markings of Rickenbacker's personal plane while he was commanding the 94th Aero Squadron in combat in France. Only one day out of the hospital, Rickenbacker had gone to the supply depot at Orly on July 5, 1918, seen this SPAD with the numeral "1" on the side, and decided that it was for him. He climbed in and ferried the little fighter back to the 94th base at Touquin, and continued to fly it for the remainder of the aerial campaigns of World War 1.

Another elegant S.P.A.D. XIII C.1 on the aerodrome at Toul, France. The Arctic snow owl insigne on the fuselage identifies the plane as one from the 17th Aero Squadron, veteran of air combat with the British Expeditionary Force. Its American pilots trained with the Royal Air Force on the British front, and later were organized into an American squadron detailed to operate with the 2d Brigade, RAF. It was detached from the RAF October 28, 1918, and sent to Toul to help form the 4th Pursuit Group. Operational there November 1, it was hampered by lack of replacement aircraft, and never did see action again. The unit used a white dumbbell insigne during its stay with the British; the snow owl was used later.

This S.P.A.D. XIII C.1, to these eyes the epitome of the Allied fighter, has been trundled out onto the snow-covered field late in 1918 for an engine run. She belongs to the 141st Aero Squadron, a unit headquartered at Toul as part of the 4th Pursuit Group. The 141st became operational October 23, and was scheduled to be joined by three other squadrons: 17th, 25th and 148th. But airplanes were hard to come by, and only the 141st ever engaged in its combat mission of pursuit. Before the Armistice, the squadron was in only 13 engagements, and shot down two enemy aircraft at no loss to itself. The squadron insigne is a tiger, mauling a spiked German helmet.

observation units preferred the French Salmson 2A.2.

America did build a total of 11,760 airplanes during its war years, and the bulk of them were Curtiss JN-4 trainers. At the Armistice, the annual production rate was 23,000 aircraft of all types. For comparison, the British rate in July 1918 was 41,000 per year and the French, 31,000.

The Air Campaigns of 1918

April, May and most of June 1918 were spent in quiet activity on the Toul sector: patrols, occasional combat, and training. Other types of aircraft joined the pursuit units. Observation and bombing squadrons practised their arts. And on June 28, all four squadrons of the newly organized First Pursuit Group—27th, 94th, 95th and 147th—were ordered north to Touquin, in the Champagne country, to help establish control of the air over the looming battle at Château-Thierry. There they were joined by the First Corps Observation Group, with its veteran 1st Aero Squadron plus the 12th and 88th. The 1st and 2nd Balloon Companies also were deployed to the new sector. The pursuit and observation units together constituted the First Air Brigade, commanded by Col. Mitchell.

Opposing them, and the other Allied air units in the area, the Germans had concentrated 46 of their available 78 fighter squadrons, including the three crack units known as "Flying Circuses" because of their brightly painted aircraft.

Château-Thierry was the first of the three major battles in which American airmen were to play any significant part. The war had less than five months to run; the Germans were beginning to feel the pinch, but were still capable of mounting a major offensive.

One of these had been kicked off in March and had advanced inexorably on Paris. It was temporarily held at the Marne river, but the Germans were obviously massing forces for an attempted breakthrough near Château-Thierry, a small town about 50 miles from Paris. The French were reinforced by the American First Army Corps, and with it went the First Air Brigade.

One of the reconnaissance pilots flying on the morning of July 15 when the German attack moved forward was Mitchell. He found five pontoon bridges that the Germans had thrown across the Marne the previous night, and which they were using to move troops to the battle. It's interesting to note that the bridges were not bombed; instead, ground forces were shifted to meet the oncoming German troops.

Mitchell had devised an overall plan for his force. He wanted to attack the German supply base at Fère-en-Tardenois with a strong day bombardment force and draw in the German pursuits to defend the area. His pursuits would then engage the German fighters and, with some luck and skill, kill enough of the enemy to reduce their quantitative superiority.

For most of the Americans, it was their first real air operation of any consequence. For all, it was dangerous, because the Germans controlled the air from the start of the battle. Into this cauldron flew 54 Nieuport 28s, flown by 40 or more inexperienced Americans and a handful with some time over the lines in combat. The results were predictable. The First Pursuit Group lost 36 pilots—killed, wounded, missing, or prisoners—during the six-week offensive. They were outnumbered and outfought.

The 27th Pursuit suffered especially; six of its pilots were lost on August 1st. The unit had to drop out of the action, and was sent to the rear to recover and to re-equip with the more rugged S.P.A.D. XIII.

The corps observation squadrons did somewhat better, losing only one plane and crew per week on the average. The balloon companies lost all their balloons to enemy air action, but none of the observers, because

This angular, slab-sided airplane is a Breguet 14A.2 day bomber, assigned to the 96th Aero Squadron. These planes had first served with an instruction center, and were received by the 96th in wretched condition. The inventive mechanics of the unit improvised spare parts from farm machinery, and readied the planes for combat long before the ordered spares could be delivered. The 96th was the first American bomber unit to enter combat, beginning operations on May 18, 1918 from Amanty, near Toul. The unlovely lines of the Breguet concealed its excellent performance; the Americans operated it routinely at 10,000 feet with a 600-lb. bomb load which is clearly marked on the rudder placarding. The French stencils read "P.U.310K" (Useful load, 310 kilograms). Note the Browning machine gun mounted on the left side of the forward fuselage, the many cooling vents on the cowling, and the hand-painted camouflage finish with brush stokes showing on the side-view photograph.

they wore parachutes.

The German offensive was blunted, and the Germans retreated to positions along the Vesle River in August.

The U. S. campaign at St.-Mihiel, which followed, was planned as a drive to pinch off the German salient on the Meuse River south of Verdun. The support air force was placed again under Mitchell's command. He assembled 101 squadrons totalling 1,476 aircraft assigned. More than 700 of them were from the French Division Aérienne, a highly mobile and flexible tactical air force. About 600 were drawn from U. S. squadrons, perhaps 130 from the British, and the rest from Italian units.

When the offensive began September 12, 1918, Mitchell's force actually numbered about 959 planes available to fly. But the weather was bad, so that most missions on the opening day were limited to single-plane reconnaissance flights. One was by Mitchell himself, who flew daily reconnaissance flights during the campaign.

There was moderate fighting after the weather cleared, with the major losses suffered by the newer and inexperienced units as usual. There was not that much pursuit action, and both their losses and victories were low.

One army and four corps observations squadrons flew the bulk of the St.-Mihiel missions on reconnaissance and artillery regulation flights. The 91st Army Obs. Sq., the only experienced and well-equipped unit in its group, flew penetration missions as deep as 50 miles behind the German front, and at altitudes below 3,000 feet, in carrying out its mission.

The 91st operated French Salmson 2A.2 aircraft, and had gradually evolved their observation missions to meet the conditions of the Western Front. Before St.-Mihiel, most of their missions had been flown at dawn, and at an altitude of 16,000 feet. At St.-Mihiel they shifted to low-altitude flights, and were most sucessful.

The 91st was part of the First Army Observation Group, along with the 24th and 9th Squadrons, which had been formed on September 6 during the buildup for the St.-Mihiel campaign.

The 9th was a unique outfit: the only night observation unit in the A.E.F. It was equipped with the ubiquitous Breguet 14, but it was the Corps d'Armée model, or 14A, for short. The planes were painted black, and some had rather elaborate decorations, the forerunners of shark's mouths and other wild animal and fish adaptations to aircraft noses.

The Château-Thierry campaign had brought out the need for some kind of night observation, and Mitchell authorized establishment of an experimental flight to test airplanes and techniques for the mission. The 9th drew the assignment and began a series of test flights to learn about the problem. Landings and takeoffs were guided by small arc lights, placed on the field to outline the runway. Beacon towers were placed on the home aerodrome and in the battle zone, flashing a light signal in the International Code. Map coordination with the tower positions marked gave them approximate check point data, and observations of the ground were made by the light from parachute flares.

The 9th scored first on a night mission September 14, at the end of the St.-Mihiel offensive, with a flight from 8:06 PM to 9:50 PM. Two days later, a night-flying Breguet encountered German night fighters for the first time, at no loss to either side.

There also were 21 balloon companies in the campaign, 15 of them American and six French. They lost ten balloons.

In the exuberance of flight, Ray Krout hauls his DH-4 up into the beginning of a chandelle, starting the steep climbing, banking turn to the right above the clouds that covered France near Toul on a day late in Oct 1918. Hunter MacDonald, Krout's observer, is silhouetted against the clouds as Charles Fleet, known as "Fleety" to all the pilots and observers of the 135th Aero Squadron, United States Air Service, snaps the picture. MacDonald seems to be almost casually leaning against the side of the fuselage; but he's securely strapped in with the canvas and leather harness used in the rear seats of these craft. There was occasional time to do things like this between combat missions when their serious work was artillery observation and regulation of battery fire.

The First Day Bombardment Group was the hardest hit during the St.-Mihiel campaign. It had been organized just a few days before the offensive began, and was composed of the 96th Day Bombardment Squadron, equipped with the Breguet 14B.2, and the 11th and 20th Squadrons, both flying the Liberty-engined de Havilland DH-4.

On the very first day, four officers and eight aircraft were lost from the strength of the First. Four days later, the 96th was withdrawn from action; it had lost 14 aircraft and 16 pilots and observers in the four days of the St.-Mihiel battle. Two days later it was the turn of the 11th to leave. It had flown against Mars-la-Tour to bomb the German troops and supplies there, and only one DH-4 returned from the six dispatched.

The 96th was dogged by bad luck almost from the start. It began operations May 18 in the relative peace and quiet of the Toul sector. Its Breguets had come from a previous assignment at a French training field, and were somewhat the worse for wear. Spares were impossible to procure, and the planes were finally made airworthy by clever mechanics who improvised parts from discarded French farm machinery, a good source of high-strength wood and some useful steel fittings.

With the Breguets in good repair, their performance was excellent. The 14B.2 could carry three times the bomb load of a DH-4 to a higher altitude, and operated smoothly at 10,000 feet with a 600-pound bomb load. It had been flown to, and operated at, altitudes above 18,000 feet, with a load of 12 Michelin 90-mm. bombs. It protected the pilot with an armored seat, and gave the gunner a brace of Lewis guns with six drums of .30-cal. ammunition. The tank held fuel for five hours of flight.

The 96th flew its first mission in France June 12, with the Breguets loaded with 500 pounds of bombs each, and dropping from 12,000 feet. Their primary targets on that, and later missions, were railway yards. The observer acted as bombardier, and steered the pilot on the bomb run by pulling on the left or right rein attached to the pilot's arms to indicate the course correction. The crews had no electrically heated flying suits, and no oxygen systems, yet they bombed routinely from altitudes of 10,000 to 15,000 feet in the latter months of 1918.

When the attack at St.-Mihiel began September 15, the Germans already had begun to move back. The salient was reduced and all objectives met in a single day of fighting, with a few days after that left for mopping up and consolidating positions. The Germans were at the start of their last long retreat, and the war was nearing an end.

Over the Western Front

As is almost too well known, the U.S. Army Air Service was woefully ill equipped when the United States entered World War 1 in April 1917. Despite this, the air arm was eventually able to play a significant part in air operations as a result of the production efforts of France and the United Kingdom combined with the forceful tactical precepts of 'Billy' Mitchell. Flying French aircraft for the most part, plus a number of British types built in the U.S.A. and powered with the magnificent Liberty engine, the American air service soon began to exert tremendous pressure on the German air units facing them, and the American use of their squadrons in massed support of the ground formations set the pattern on which American tactical air developments were built up so successfully in the inter-war years.

1. The 135th Aero Squadron base at Ourches on July 30, 1918.

2. The aircraft operated by the 135th Squadron were American-built DH-4 day bombers of British design.

3. Typical of the terrain over which the Air Service operated was the Remenauvillé sector near St.-Mihiel, seen here on May 7, 1918.

4. The 135th Squadron, like its sister squadron the 100th Squadron of the 2d Day Bombardment Group, operated Liberty-engined DH-4s.

5. Krout and MacDonald in their DH-4 over France.

6. A captured example of World War 1's most formidable fighter, the Fokker D.VII.

7. Sleek and at times deadly, the Albatros D.Va suffered from a distressing willingness to shed its lower wings.

8. The handsome lines of the Pfalz D.IIIa fighter were not reflected by the type's generally disappointing performance.

2

1

3

There was one more big push for the Americans, the Meuse-Argonne Offensive, moving northward between the river on their right and the heavily wooded Argonne forest on their left. Mitchell's air forces had released most of the French units, the Division Aérienne having been deployed elsewhere. Only the French night bombardment and corps observation squadrons remained on the scene. The total aircraft strength was 594 in commission out of 836 assigned.

The mission of the three pursuit groups had been clearly defined. The First was to clear the front area of balloons and low-flying German aircraft; the Second and Third Pursuit Groups were to provide high cover for the First, and to escort the day bombers. The S.P.A.D. aircraft of the Second and Third also carried two 25-pound bombs each to bomb infantry at will.

The offensive began September 25. The weather closed in the next day and stayed bad into November and the Armistice. There were 10 days considered fit for flying in that time, and only three of them were clear enough to permit useful photo missions. On the last three days of October, Army observation squadrons were finally able to photograph all of the long-range artillery objectives for the Army.

The corps observation squadrons told much the same story, but they had additional problems. The signalling system of pre-positioned panels that linked ground and air units depended on some experience on the ground among the troops who would receive the supplies or messages dropped. The soldiers in the Meuse-Argonne offensive were largely new and fresh, and not used to working with observation aircraft.

The Germans had stationed eight of their best fighter squadrons opposite the corps observation squadrons, but they concentrated their attacks on the day bombers and the observation planes were able to work relatively safely.

The sixteen balloon companies lost 21 balloons, 15 to aircraft and six to enemy shelling.

It was the fighters that saw most of the action, flying their low-level intercepts under clouds, through rain and fog. On their first day of action—September 26—they shot down five German balloons and six airplanes.

On the evening of September 29, the irrepressible Frank Luke, the Arizona balloon-buster, was killed, following an epic battle he waged alone against German aircraft, balloons and ground troops. He is credited with bringing down three balloons and two airplanes, and with dropping bombs that killed 11 Germans before being forced to land. In the tradition of the gunslinger of the wild West, Luke faced the

Above: A new DH-4, in its factory finish of khaki and cream at Toul in November, 1918. Note the wind-driven generator mounted externally forward and above the fuselage insigne. It was used to power the on-board radio equipment that the observers used for direct contact with the artillery batteries they were assisting.

Above right The insigne of the 135th Aero Squadron was a painting of the famed Statue of Liberty. This particular example was on one of the planes of the 135th, and was photographed for Krout's scrapbook.

Imagine yourself to be 2nd Lt. Howard B. ("Shorty") Maguire, of the 135th Aero Squadron, and you're coming home after a mission, back to the aerodrome at Toul. In a few seconds he's going to cut the power way down and the big Liberty is going to cough and chug and the prop is going to swing slowly and this DH-4 is going to drop like a brick because it has a lot of drag when the power is off.

Germans with his .45-cal. pistol until rifle fire dropped him.

During October and November, until the Armistice, the First Pursuit Group alone claimed 101 German aircraft destroyed at a cost of 15 American casualties. The Second and Third Groups, being newer, were less successful.

And that was the end of it. The Meuse-Argonne offensive sped ahead, the Germans retreated, and finally the years of blood-letting came to an end in the fields of France and Belgium, just where the war had started.

Airpower had played an important part in the three campaigns, but not nearly as important a part as its proponents have contended since then.

When the Armistice was declared November 11, 1918, American air units had 740 planes assigned to 45 squadrons. That was less than ten percent of the Allied air strength, still less if one considers that the planes in commission were considerably fewer, perhaps as few as 450.

American fliers claimed a total of 781 enemy aircraft and 73 balloons shot down or destroyed. There were 71 officially recognized American aces, each credited with five or more enemy aircraft or balloons. But less than 100 of these victories were confirmed by either capture or inspection of the wreckage. The AEF lost a verifiable 289 aircraft and 48 balloons; the Germans probably lost a similar number to the Americans.

U. S. pilots and observers killed or missing in action totalled 237. Many might have been saved, had they worn available parachutes. The Germans used them, as did balloon observers on both sides. But Allied airmen rejected the chute, in retrospect on the flimsiest of grounds: It would have been, they believed, an insult to their bravery, their skill, and their faith in their own abilities, to rely on a means of escape from a burning or bullet-ridden aircraft. It almost smacked of cowardice, or fleeing in the face of the enemy. So they died instead.

American bomber forces made 150 attacks on targets, penetrating into German territory routinely about 50 miles, and on one occasion as deep as 160 miles. They dropped 138 tons of bombs. Most of the bombing was done by one squadron during the day, normally equipped with 12 aircraft and probably with nine or ten in commission. At a probably high bomb-load weight of 500 pounds per sortie, that computes to a total of 552 sorties into German territory.

Because of the short time the U. S. forces were in combat, these figures only hint at the developing potential. Growth curves for almost any activity were swooping upward after the summer of 1918, and historians are fond of impressing the reader with what might have been, had the war lasted well into 1919.

From a starting point of essentially zero in April 1917, the United States had sent to France 6,861 officers and 51,229 enlisted men in aviation service only. Another 1,000 officers and nearly 20,000 men were still in training.

American pilots at the front numbered 1,402 and there were 769 observers. Some were waiting specific assignments; the squadron totals were 767 pilots, 481 observers, and 23 gunners assigned.

The impressive growth rate of the U. S. Air Service is reflected in total personnel strengths, all ranks. In 1916, the Aviation Section, Signal Corps, comprised 311 officers and men. By 1917, that figure had risen four-fold to 1,218. But during 1918, it jumped to 195,023 officers and men, a 627-fold increase. There has not been an expansion like that since, at least not in the United States air forces.

No wonder there were problems.

The Golden Age of Biplane Bombers

The bombers streamed down the Hudson River Valley, past Storm King Mountain, their roaring Hornet engines echoing across the wide water below. Their shadows raced under them, a mirror formation of the long column of three-plane Vees. Bright overhead sun reflected from their yellow wings and highlighted the insignia at each wingtip.

The mood was captured by a photographer in one of the planes, from the forward gunner's position, and spread across the New York *Herald Tribune*'s Sunday rotogravure section on May 31, 1932. The bombers were part of an "... Army air armada .." that had been on maneuvers in New England, and they staged the aerial parade down the Hudson and over Manhattan as a show of air power.

They were Keystone B-3As, strutted and wire-braced biplanes, and the show of force over Manhattan that day was, in all probability, the entire serviceable bomber strength of the United States Army Air Corps.

There were other pictures of the times that reflected the sport of open-cockpit flying: a formation of delicate Boeing P-12Es suspended against a backdrop of fluffy cumulus; a right echelon of blunt-nosed Curtiss P-6Es, their noses and landing gears painted with the Arctic snow owl markings of the 17th Pursuit Squadron based at Selfridge Field, Michigan.

It was the glorious era of the biplane, a golden age of fragile airplanes with yellow wings and olive drab bodies, another epoch in the development of American air power. But behind the pleasant-looking facade of aerial maneuvers with brightly painted pursuits and bulky biplane bombers lay a murky arena of Byzantine maneuvering for recognition of air power. Implicit in that recognition would be the creation of an independent air force, the evolution of a strategic doctrine, and the development of a long-range, heavy bomber to execute that doctrine.

For the two decades between the wars, proponents of air power fought their battles, sometimes in silence, sometimes loudly and publicly. During those 20 years, they endured the decimation of demobilization, statements of missions that placed air power in a very subordinate position to infantry, innumerable arguments with the establishment of the Army, Navy and War Department, and internal dissension between the protagonists of a separate air force and those who were

Fourteen Boeing P-12Es from the 27th Pursuit Squadron of the 1st Pursuit Group roar out of the sky in a stepped-up formation of five Vees. These aircraft have the modified headrests containing liferafts, giving them the horizontal line aft of the cockpit. Markings enthusiasts should note that these planes carry chevrons on both the upper and lower surfaces of the upper wing, and tail fins of different hues, probably to identify flights within the squadron. The characteristic "broken-axle" look of the P-12 landing gear is caused by the hinged truss design. With the airplane on the ground, the axle straightens.

The Pioneering Years

Curtiss P-6E Hawk

One of two classic Army biplane pursuit aircraft designs of the 1920s and 1930s, the long-lived Hawk series was epitomized by the last of the production versions, the P-6E. Its basic shape had evolved through a long line of Hawk biplanes, originating with Army and Navy racers that Curtiss built between 1921 and 1925. The developed B-P-6E form was elegant, with tapered wings and a fuselage that faired into the 600-hp Curtiss Conqueror liquid-cooled engine. The initial order was for 46 of these E models, and most were delivered to the 17th and 94th Pursuit Squadrons during 1932. The single-leg landing gear and the belly radiator position were the major differences between the P-6E and earlier Hawks, with their more-conventional landing gear and nose radiators. This particular aircraft is painted in the characteristic black and white markings and Army Air Corps insignia of the 17th Pursuit Squadron of the 1st Pursuit Group, while based at Selfridge Field, Michigan. This scheme, named after the Arctic snow owl painted on the fuselage band, was a short-lived one; but it is the best-remembered, as well as the most elaborate, of all Hawk markings.

convinced that it was wise to stay as a combat arm of the Army.

They suffered very tight budgetary restraints, a worldwide depression and a national revulsion against total war and the mass bombing of cities. They survived more than 15 public investigations and hearings, helped sponsor—and saw fail—a dozen pieces of legislation proposing a Department of Aeronautics and 17 bills proposing a single and unified Department of Defense, and rearranged their structure in accordance with two major reorganization acts affecting the Army and its air service.

Their training and operational experience was poor, and it showed in the limited tactical exercises conducted in the field, and especially and publicly in what has been interpreted falsely as the fiasco of the 1934 air mail affair. Their leading spokesman, the charismatic

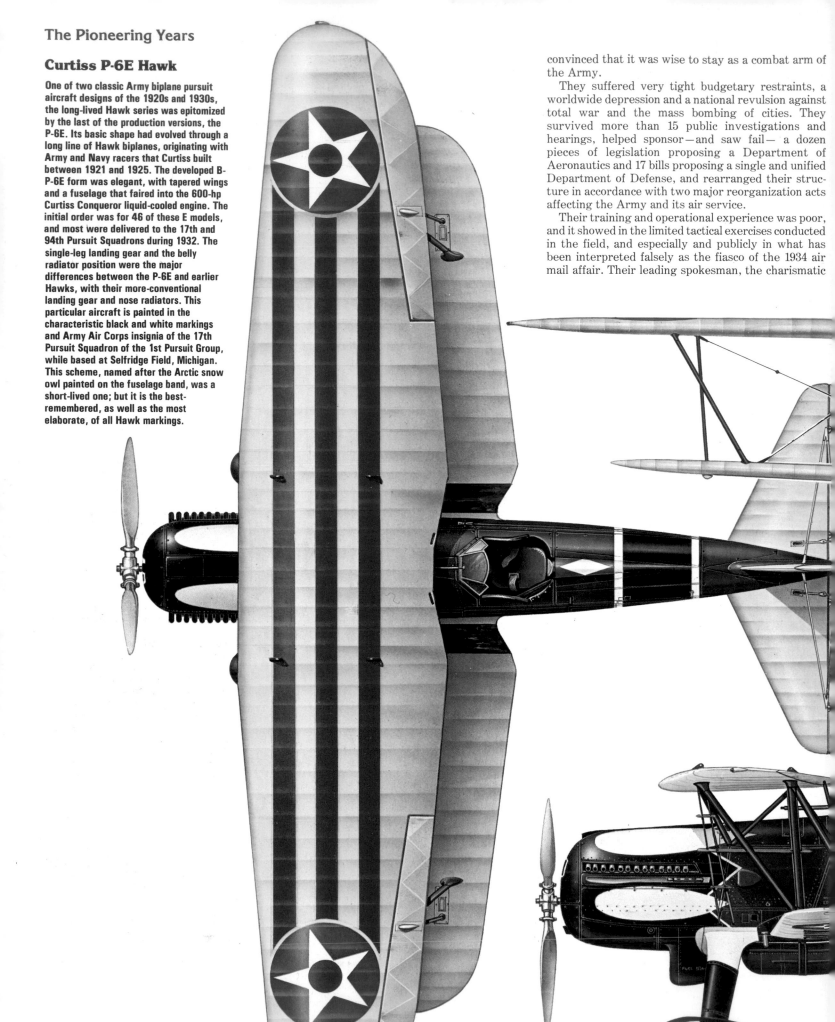

Billy Mitchell, was exiled, disgraced by court martial, and eventually vindicated.

Strangely, public support of aviation was never higher than during those years. Starting with Capt. Charles A. Lindbergh's solo crossing of the Atlantic in May 1927, public enthusiasm built with each successive record flight. Radio broadcasts and movie newsreels chronicled the adventures of brave and daring airmen, both civilian and military.

When the decades ended in the roar of artillery fire and the clangor of tank engines across the Polish border in September 1939, the air arm had accomplished much. It had achieved a degree of independence with an Air Corps-controlled tactical offensive strike force, then called the General Headquarters Air Force. It had evolved a basic strategic doctrine that was the cornerstone for its future building. And it had com-

pleted the acquisition process that gave the Air Corps its first strategic bomber design.

Demobilization and Decimation

World War 1 had not changed anything, in spite of the best efforts of the airmen. The Army General Staff could not, or would not, see any advantage in a separate air arm commanded by air generals. The proper role of the airplane, the Staff held, was to serve as the eyes of the Army, and to support the ground forces in the ways the ground forces thought best.

At the Armistice, demobilization took precedence over defense. The air service was hard hit. Its personnel and aircraft strengths were decimated. Its supporting industry was almost bankrupted by the abrupt cancellations of contracts for thousands of aircraft and

One of the most famous airplane photographs of all time, this familiar shot shows nine Curtiss P-6Es of the 17th Pursuit Squadron, 1st Pursuit Group, operating out of Selfridge Field, Michigan. The planes are marked with the characteristic white splashes and black backgrounds that were adopted to show off the squadron insigne of the Arctic snow owl, painted on the fuselages on a black band with white edges. That insigne dates back to the end of World War 1, and was worn proudly by the Hawks of the 17th. These planes are fitted with a 50-gallon jettisonable belly tank to augment the internal fuel capacity of 50 gal.

The Pioneering Years

Designed in the transition period between advanced biplanes and monoplanes with retractable undercarriages, the Seversky P-35 was not wholly successful. However, the type is of considerable importance as a linear precursor of the mighty Republic P-47 Thunderbolt. Seen here is the P-35 flown by the commander of the 94th Pursuit Squadron in 1938 and 1939.

The nine planes of the 17th Pursuit reformed in three elements of three planes each, stepped-up from the lead element and in a right echelon. The formation leader is flying the Hawk at the extreme lower left; element leaders are stepped up from him in echelon, holding on him as their wingmen in turn hold on each element leader. It's a pretty tight formation, and not a lot of distance separates the wingtips. Number two man in the top element does seem a little misaligned, though, and you can bet he heard about it after this picture appeared in print.

engines. Airplanes became a drug on the market, and could be bought, still in their original wartime shipping crates, for a few hundred dollars. Many were burned in huge bonfires in French fields, rather than cost the money to ship them back to the U. S.

Congress cut budgets for new weapons, aircraft included. Typical was their treatment of a 1918 plan, developed by the Air Service and the Army General Staff, which envisioned a total force of 24,000 personnel, with appropriate numbers of aircraft. Congress slashed the request to less than one-third of the amount. The postwar strength of the Air Service fell to 12,000 personnel in 1920, and there literally was no money to fund the procurement of new aircraft. The squadrons flew aircraft left over from the war.

To draw attention to the capabilities of air power and to win public support, the Air Service embarked on a series of record-breaking and pioneering flights right after the war. Altitude and speed records were set and broken. Technical developments, less conspicuous, paralleled these historic flights.

The Air Service sought recognition, begged the

public to pay attention to this weapon that could fly long distances, break speed and altitude records, and carry a useful load.

In later years, writers have given Brig. Gen. Billy Mitchell heroic stature for what they perceived as his single-handed fight for recognition of an independent air force. In truth, Mitchell was one of many who held those views and who spoke out for them. But he was the top-ranking airman with those views, he was a flamboyant publicity seeker, and he knew how to make headlines. He was doomed to fail; he and his associates had the courage and the enthusiasm, but his opponents had the rank. And in that kind of battle, there is only one outcome.

Mitchell was a fanatic about air power. It obsessed him. Fanatics get things done, however; they are movers and shakers, even though it often costs them their careers and their lives. Then they are called martyrs, and that term also has been applied to Mitchell.

He had a popular argument: air power was economical, cheaper than battleships and ground armies. It

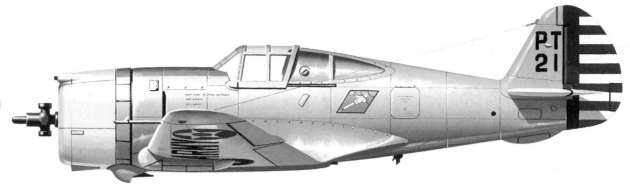

The Curtiss P-36 was another interim type that served in limited numbers in the late 1930s. Designed under the Curtiss Model 75 designation, the airplane did better in the export market, and was of historical importance as the starting point of the design trail that led to the widely produced P-40 series of inline-engined fighters and fighter-bombers.

could sink any enemy fleet that was bringing troops in an invasion attempt, and it could destroy the industrial might, and therefore the will to resist, of any enemy country. Why spend money on sinkable battleships, he argued, when you can buy far more strength for less, and sink enemy ships?

Mitchell ached to back his concepts with positive public proof. He wrote about it, spoke about it, and finally got to do something about it, because his views were shared by some high-placed Navy admirals.

So the Navy, willing to put the principle to the test, carried out its own bombing attacks on the USS *Indiana*, an obsolete battleship, during the week of October 28 to November 3, 1920. The result was predictable; it also was suppressed. Not one word of the test report became public knowledge until the *Illustrated London News* published a picture in its issue of December 11, 1921, of the damaged *Indiana*.

In January 1921, Mitchell appeared before the House of Representatives' Appropriations Committee and said, among other comments, ".. we can either destroy or sink any ship in existence today ... all we want is a

chance to demonstrate these things ... " In rebuttal, Secretary of the Navy Josephus Daniels made a foot-in-the-mouth statement about his willingness to stand, bare-headed, on the deck or at the wheel of any battleship under attack from the air by bombers.

Opportunity for Air Power

Mitchell got his chance when some German warships were turned over to the Navy for experimental purposes, with a stipulation that they had to be destroyed before early August 1921. The Navy decided to run its own bombing tests—with the unstated purpose of proving Mitchell wrong—and on February 7, 1921, so notified the Army. The tests were to be under the complete control of the Commander in Chief, Atlantic Fleet. Mitchell agreed to commit the Air Service under those conditions, as a partner in the bombing experiments.

Navy rules of engagement limited the number of hits allowed, the size and weight of bombs, and retained the right to call off the bombing at any time so that

This photo has been used everywhere, but it is so redolent of the times, so absolutely nostalgic in its appearance, that we make no apologies for using it again. Look and listen, and above the whine of the engines you can hear the sounds of the 1930s: A victrola playing "Buddy, Can You Spare a Dime?" from the porch of a summer cottage; the horn of the neighbor's "Tin Lizzie"; the early morning horse-drawn wagon that brought the milk.

The forward fuselage of this Keystone B-4A, serial number 32-135, is simply a prop for the studied pose of Miss Whatever and Daring Air Corps Pilot. She's resting her arm on what would normally be a red-hot exhaust pipe and sitting on a wingwalk trod by dirty-booted grease monkeys. Keystone built 25 of these behemoths, powering them with Pratt & Whitney R-1860-7 radials that developed 575 bhp each. They weighed about 13,000 pounds, ready to go, and had a top speed of 121 mph on a good day. The five-man crew included a forward gunner whose open-air perch, within inches of the whirling propeller blades, must have been a precarious one. Who are those people, anyway?

If you were a kid who built model airplanes in the 1930s, you hung around airports, hoping to catch a glimpse of some rare and new military ship. Holy Cow, there's one! Hey, that's a Douglas O-38B! Wow, look at the insignia! And yes, kid, it is an O-38B, and it's from the 119th Observation Squadron of the New Jersey National Guard, and it's attached to the 44th Infantry Division. It's hard to see that insigne, but it's a pair of numeral fours, back to back, in black on a yellow field, with a black ring around it. And hey, kid, get the Hell off the field, will ya? Ya could get hurt!

boarding parties could inspect the damage. The target ships were to be anchored in deep water, 75 miles at sea off the mouth of Chesapeake Bay and about 100 miles airline distance from the Army's bomber base at Langley Field, Virginia.

Mitchell prodded the Army Ordnance Corps to develop a 2,000-pound bomb for the tests. The biggest weapon then in the arsenal was an 1,000-pounder, and Mitchell wanted the larger weapon to take full advantage of the devastating effect of an underwater burst near the hull of a target. The big bombs were to be carried by the relatively new Martin MB-2, standard heavy bomber of the 1921 Air Service.

Mitchell organized the First Provisional Air Brigade at Langley Field. From Langley's tenant units he drew the 50th and 88th Squadrons, operating DH-4 day bombers and SE-5 pursuits. Up from Kelly Field, Texas, came the 49th and 96th Squadrons, flying their MB-2s, and also bringing along their DH-4s and one Handley Page O/400, assigned to the 96th. The 1st and 5th Squadrons deployed from Mitchel Field, NY, with DH-4 day bombers.

They began streaming in May 6, 1921, and started a combined training and practice program. They bombed stationary targets, made dummy runs on moving automobiles, dropped live ordnance on the wrecks of the *Indiana* and her sister ship, the *Texas*, lying in the waters off Langley.

The official test program began June 21, with an attack by three Naval Air Service flying boats that sank a German submarine, the U-117. The Navy bombed again June 29, dropping 80 dummy bombs of various sizes on the moving, remotely controlled battleship USS *Iowa*. The Navy airmen scored two hits; the *Iowa* stayed afloat.

The Air Service had its first turn July 13 against a German destroyer adrift 100 miles offshore. Bomb size was limited by Navy rules to a maximum of 300 pounds. A dozen SE-5 pursuits strafed the ship and dropped 25-pound bombs in simulation of an anti-personnel attack to clear the decks and the defensive gun positions. The second wave was scheduled to be 14 DH-4s with 100-pounders, but Mitchell signalled them away and sent in his heavies, 16 MB-2s each carrying six of the 300-pound bombs. One by one they dropped; by the 44th explosion, the destroyer was sinking, 20 minutes after the start of the attack.

Ten strikes were scheduled against the next target, the German light cruiser *Frankfurt*, alternating Navy and Army aircraft. The first six strikes dropped the

stipulated bombs of either 250-lb. or 300-lb. size, and did no damage to the hull, although they did smash some of the superstructure. The seventh wave was the Navy's, three planes with 520-lb. bombs. They dropped seven and scored three hits before being waved off for an inspection by the umpires. The eighth strike was made by the MB-2s, and six of them, armed with 600-lb. bombs, began their attack at 4:15 PM. At 4:50 the *Frankfurt* sank.

The toughest target was next: the German heavy battleship *Ostfriesland*, whose true tonnage had been concealed and never reported accurately, a stratagem used later in the case of the German "pocket battleships" of World War 2. On July 20, both Navy and Army aircraft dropped 52 bombs with very little effect, even though the largest weighed 1,000 lb.

On July 21, six Martin MB-2s and one Handley Page O/400, each carrying the special 2,000-lb. bombs that Ordnance had rushed through the development and production cycle, took to the air accompanied by other MB-2s carrying 1,000-lb. bombs. These latter planes formed the first wave of the attack, dropped five bombs and were waved off. An argument followed over the rules while the MB-2s circled, waiting with the 2,000-pounders. The issue was resolved, and the olive drab biplanes swung into a column at 2,500 feet. The first bomb was dropped at 12:18 PM; the sixth, at 12:31. At 12:40 the *Ostfriesland* vanished below the surface, leaving a widening ring of bubbles and debris as she plunged toward the bottom. The Handley Page, denied a drop before the sinking, made its pass and dropped its single one-tonner in the center of the roiled water.

After that, anything was anti-climax. "We don't sink battleships; we loop them!" scrawled one enthusiastic flier on a hangar wall back at Langley. The tests continued, and the Army pilots sank the obsolete battleship USS *Alabama*. The major thesis of Mitchell's crusade had been demonstrated, finally, in those tests off the Virginia shore.

The tests, conclusive as they might have appeared to be, didn't change anything. The advocates of bombardment had made their point; the Army and Navy remained unconvinced and continued to regard air power as just another way to help surface forces win their battles.

More tests were conducted in 1923, and they proved the same points once again. Mitchell spoke, wrote and crusaded, growing more impatient, more abrasive, and more reckless. He was exiled, in effect, sent to San Antonio to keep him out of the public eye.

Then, on September 5, 1925, the USS *Shenandoah*, a giant dirigible operated by the Navy, crashed in a line squall over Ohio. Fourteen of the 43 crewmen were killed, and Mitchell used their deaths as the reason for releasing a statement to the press blasting both the Army and the Navy. He blamed the accident, and others before it, on the ". . . incompetency, criminal negligence and almost treasonable administration of the national defense by the war and navy departments."

It was the last straw. Orders for the court martial of Brig. Gen William Mitchell, USAS, were cut that weekend and announced September 7. He was tried, found guilty, and suspended from the Army, forfeiting half his pay and allowances. He died February 19, 1936, never to see the ultimate proof of his concepts in the great strategic bomber raids of World War 2.

Gestation of the Strategic Bomber

For long years, the preponderant Army aircraft were observation types. In 1921, the fleet included about 1,100 de Havilland DH-4B observation aircraft, capable of carrying a small bomb load over a short range; 179 British-designed SE-5E pursuits; and an even dozen Martin MB-2 heavy bombers. A majority of those

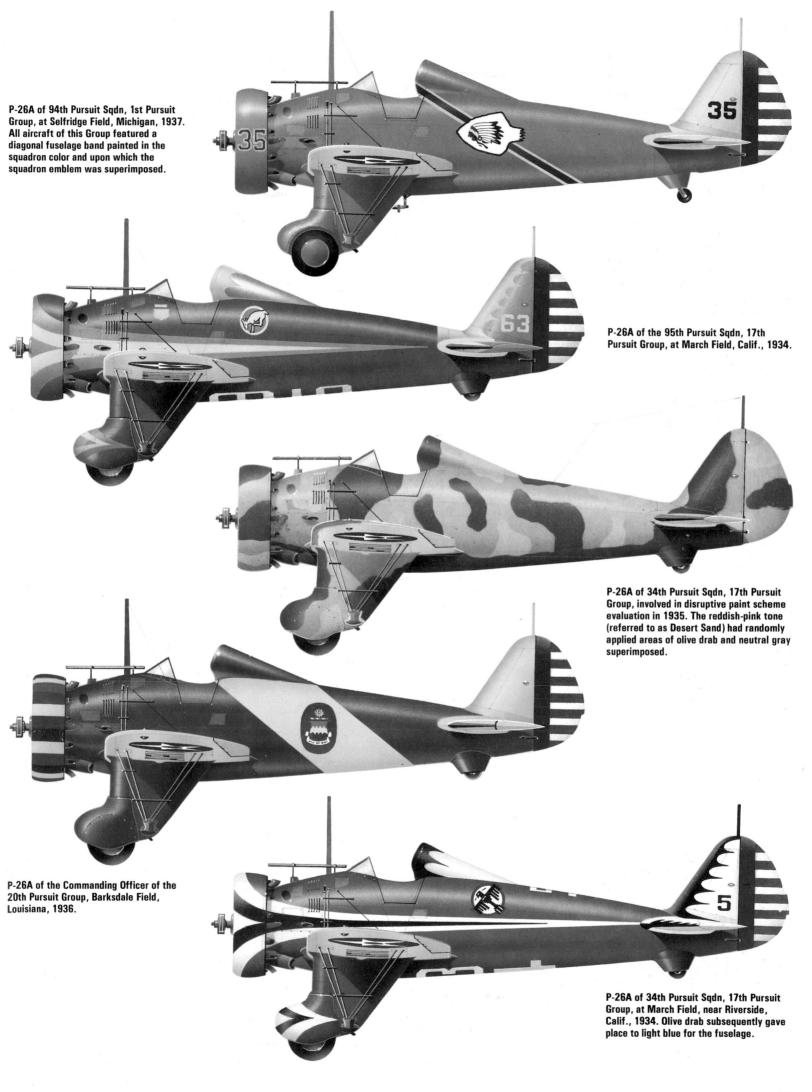

P-26A of 94th Pursuit Sqdn, 1st Pursuit Group, at Selfridge Field, Michigan, 1937. All aircraft of this Group featured a diagonal fuselage band painted in the squadron color and upon which the squadron emblem was superimposed.

P-26A of the 95th Pursuit Sqdn, 17th Pursuit Group, at March Field, Calif., 1934.

P-26A of 34th Pursuit Sqdn, 17th Pursuit Group, involved in disruptive paint scheme evaluation in 1935. The reddish-pink tone (referred to as Desert Sand) had randomly applied areas of olive drab and neutral gray superimposed.

P-26A of the Commanding Officer of the 20th Pursuit Group, Barksdale Field, Louisiana, 1936.

P-26A of 34th Pursuit Sqdn, 17th Pursuit Group, at March Field, near Riverside, Calif., 1934. Olive drab subsequently gave place to light blue for the fuselage.

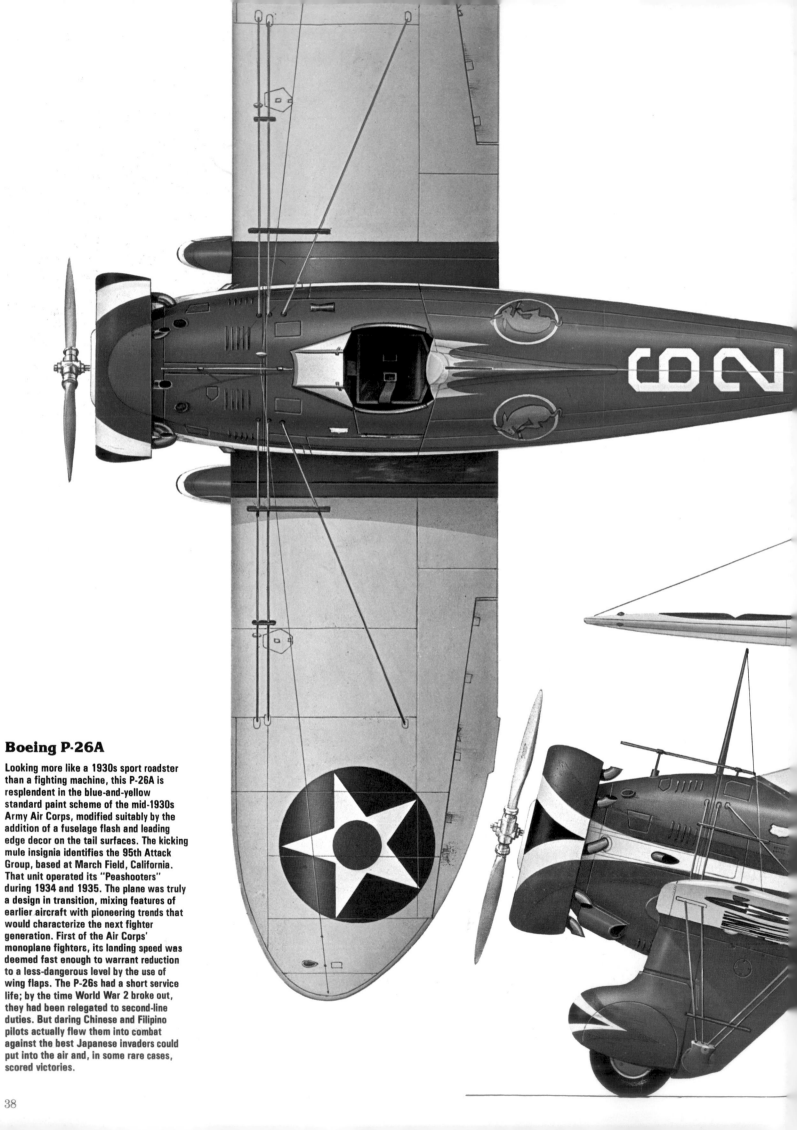

Boeing P-26A

Looking more like a 1930s sport roadster than a fighting machine, this P-26A is resplendent in the blue-and-yellow standard paint scheme of the mid-1930s Army Air Corps, modified suitably by the addition of a fuselage flash and leading edge decor on the tail surfaces. The kicking mule insignia identifies the 95th Attack Group, based at March Field, California. That unit operated its "Peashooters" during 1934 and 1935. The plane was truly a design in transition, mixing features of earlier aircraft with pioneering trends that would characterize the next fighter generation. First of the Air Corps' monoplane fighters, its landing speed was deemed fast enough to warrant reduction to a less-dangerous level by the use of wing flaps. The P-26s had a short service life; by the time World War 2 broke out, they had been relegated to second-line duties. But daring Chinese and Filipino pilots actually flew them into combat against the best Japanese invaders could put into the air and, in some rare cases, scored victories.

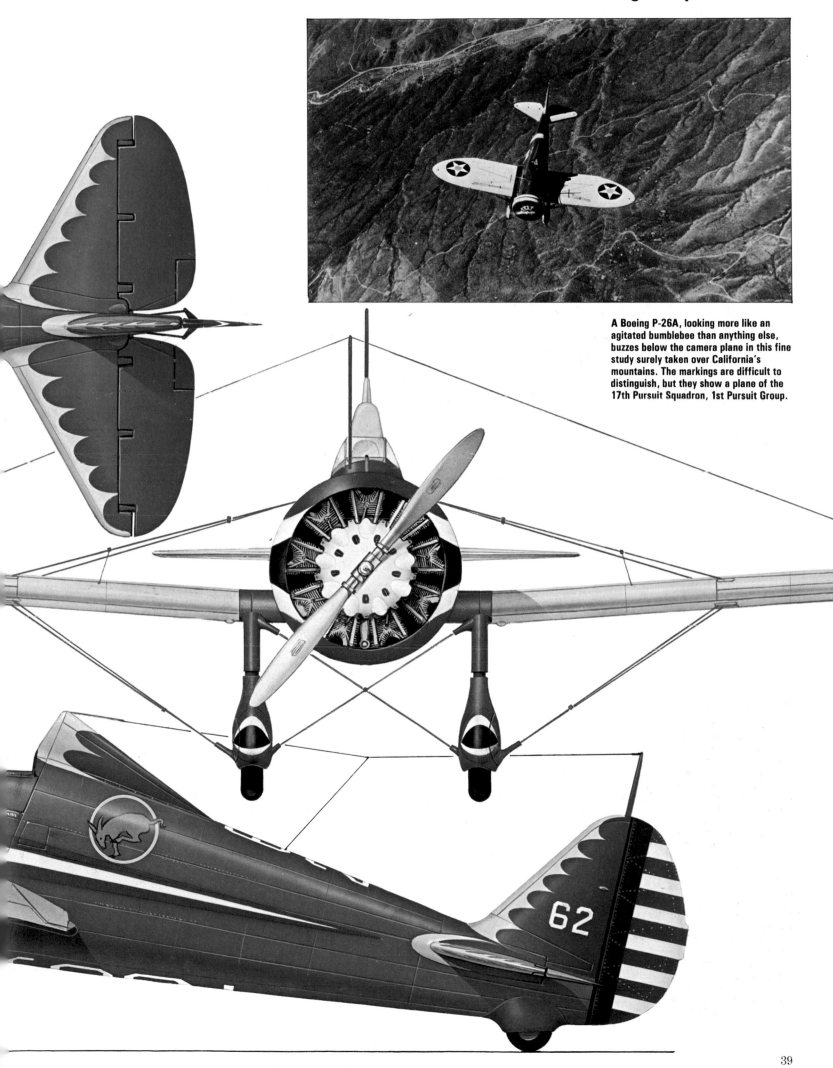

A Boeing P-26A, looking more like an agitated bumblebee than anything else, buzzes below the camera plane in this fine study surely taken over California's mountains. The markings are difficult to distinguish, but they show a plane of the 17th Pursuit Squadron, 1st Pursuit Group.

The Pioneering Years

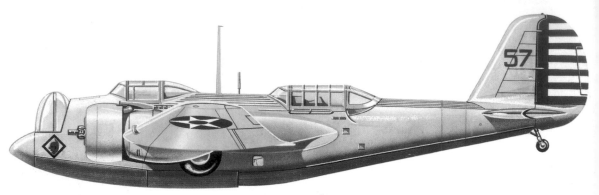

One of the Martin B-10Bs of the 28th Bombardment Squadron, USAAC, which operated from Camp Nichols, Luzon, Philippines from 1937 to 1941.

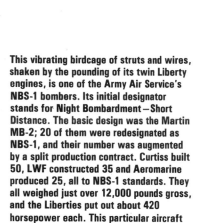

This vibrating birdcage of struts and wires, shaken by the pounding of its twin Liberty engines, is one of the Army Air Service's NBS-1 bombers. Its initial designator stands for Night Bombardment—Short Distance. The basic design was the Martin MB-2; 20 of them were redesignated as NBS-1, and their number was augmented by a split production contract. Curtiss built 50, LWF constructed 35 and Aeromarine produced 25, all to NBS-1 standards. They all weighed just over 12,000 pounds gross, and the Liberties put out about 420 horsepower each. This particular aircraft carries the insigne of the 11th Bombardment Squadron in an unusual rear-fuselage location.

aircraft was in storage, not available to fly on operations.

By the middle of 1924, the Air Service only had 754 planes in commission; 457 of them were for observation. The bomber fleet had increased to 59 by then, and there were eight attack planes capable of light tactical bombing. A total of 78 pursuits rounded out the airpower roster.

During the 1920s, the total offensive strength of the United States in the air never exceeded one pursuit, one attack, and one bombardment group.

The efficiencies of these planes had not improved very much over the capabilities exhibited over the Western Front in 1917/1918. The best biplane bomber of the late 1920s—the Curtiss B-2 Condor—had a bomb load of 2,500 pounds. Fully loaded, the plane had a combat radius of less than 300 miles, and a cruise speed of about 100 mph. It was regarded as much too costly a weapon; only twelve were bought, and they were delivered during 1928 and 1929.

The technology of that time produced inferior bombers. They would have been hammered out of the skies by any of the swifter, maneuverable biplanes operated by the world's air forces.

The tactical exercises of the times showed the obvious; the lumbering bombers were sitting ducks in daylight. Their only chance of survival would be night operations. Bombing accuracy, never very good, would be even worse at night. The advantage of tight formation flying to mass the bombs would be lost in the looser formations demanded by the increased risk of collision in night flying.

After a number of abortive starts, bomber technology reached a turning point in 1930. The Air Corps issued a circular request for a new bomber, and its results revolutionized bomber design and tactics.

In response, Boeing developed its Models 214 and 215 (later the Y1B-9 and YB-9, respectively) with corporate funds. They both flew in 1931, were tested by the Air Corps, and the biplane bomber was instantly obsolete. The sleek, low-winged Boeing design was a revolution in technology.

Unfortunately for Boeing, the Glenn L. Martin Co. was developing a similar aircraft with even better performance. The XB-907 was built, flown February 18, 1932, and was chosen by the Army for production as the B-10.

For the first time, the Air Corps had a modern

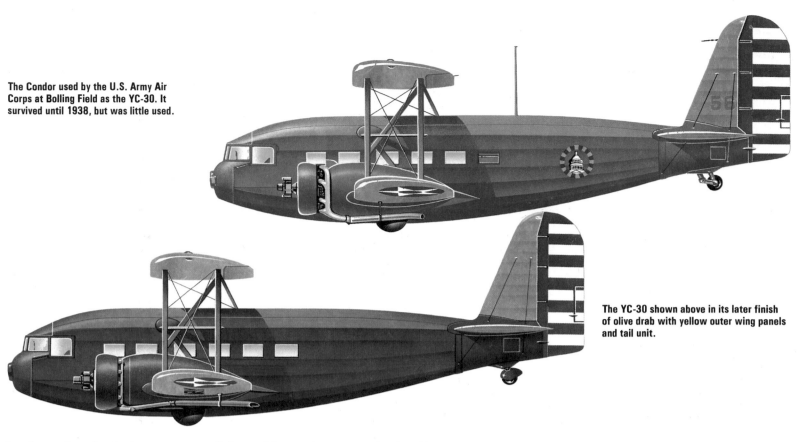

The Condor used by the U.S. Army Air Corps at Bolling Field as the YC-30. It survived until 1938, but was little used.

The YC-30 shown above in its later finish of olive drab with yellow outer wing panels and tail unit.

bomber, miles ahead of contemporary fighters. Flat out, it could outrun them.

Air Corps fortunes received another boost in January 1931, in an agreement between Gen. Douglas Mac-Arthur, Army Chief of Staff, and Admiral William V. Pratt, Chief of Naval Operations. The Air Corps assumed the responsibility for the land-based air defense of the coastlines of the United States and of its possessions. That agreement finally gave the Air Corps a mission that was independent of ground forces and their control, and Air Corps leadership immediately tried to turn the agreement into a reason to create an independent air arm. In 1933, the Corps recommended the creation of a General Headquarters Air Force (GHQAF), with pursuit, attack and bombardment squadrons organized for coastal defense under Air Corps control. The concept was tested experimentally with the establishment of a Provisional GHQAF, organized specifically to concentrate the Air Corps on the west coast for exercises in the late spring. It was the first opportunity to try out the idea, and it was also the first opportunity for the new Martin B-10 to show its capabilities. Both were the harbingers of greater things to come.

Project A, the Materiel Division's July 1933 study for a long-range bomber, showed that in theory a bomber could be designed to carry a ton of bombs for a distance of 5,000 miles at a speed of 200 mph. The giant Boeing XB-15 was the direct result of the Project A concept. But it was ahead of its powerplants; aerodynamically and structurally, it taught the Air Corps a lot about big bombers.

In May 1934, the Air Corps circulated requests for design proposals for a multi-engined bomber. Everybody except Boeing assumed that multi-engined meant two engines; Boeing interpreted it to mean multi-engined, and developed its Model 299. It was a four-engined heavyweight that gave Boeing the unique distinction of having revolutionized bomber design twice in five years. Model 299 first flew July 28, 1935, and was ferried to Wright Field for official tests August 20. It made the flight non-stop, 2,000 miles at an average speed of 252 mph. Model 299 crashed October 30, when the Army pilot neglected to unlock the controls before takeoff.

No matter; the new bomber was such a major improvement over any other bomber in the air or on

the drawing boards that its success was assured. It went into production as the B-17 Flying Fortress, the progenitor of the long-range, heavy strategic bomber that the Air Corps had been seeking for so long.

The Corps Carries the Mail

For 102 days in 1934, the Army Air Corps flew domestic air mail routes, assigned to the job by an Executive Order from the White House. It followed a year-long investigation that alleged fraud and collusion among the dozen or so airlines who hauled the mail for a subsidy of 54¢ per mile flown.

It was not a new experience for the military fliers. Air mail service in the U. S. had been started by the Army on May 15, 1918. By August that year, the flights were transferred to the supervision of the Post Office Department, and civilian pilots were hired to fly the planes.

Private carriers started flying some mail and making connections between Post Office routes in 1920. But it

In later years, you kick yourself for not recording the times and places of snapshot like this one of a Curtiss A-3B Falcon. Curtiss built 78 of them, delivering them beginning in 1930, and they were pretty tame for attackers. Top speed was about 140 mph, and the Curtiss V-1150-5 engine in that blunt nose with its bulky radiator probably caused more drag than the rest of the airplane. Ready to fly, the A-3B weighed 4,400 lb, including the two-man crew of pilot and rear gunner. The upper wing, its outer panels swept back slightly, spanned 38 ft, and the overall length was 27 ft 2 in.

This mighty armada of Keystone B-3As is on its way down the Hudson River to parade above New York City in a display of America's aerial strength. These hulking bombers could speed through the air slightly slower than a World War 1 fighter, which would have made them easy prey for a determined attacker in any contemporary pursuit plane. But there they go, brave lads all, pounding downriver past the Storm King mountain on the right, in stepped-up formation of Vees of three each, twin Pratt & Whitneys roaring and the wind whistling in the wires that braced the 75-foot wingspan. They're probably doing about 100 mph.

Can you believe this shot? One of the Army's 12 Curtiss B-2 Condor bombers hauls into a left bank under the attack of a tight formation of Boeing P-12D pursuits, and all above the beach and boardwalk at Atlantic City, New Jersey? The Condor is from the 11th Bombardment Squadron, and carries a special nose flash, probably red and white, on fuselage and nacelles.

took government action to transfer all the business to private hands. In June 1927, the airlines started to phase in their air mail work, and by December 31, 1927, the government was out of the business, and private enterprise was flying the mail.

Maj. Gen. Foulois was asked on February 9, 1934, if the Air Corps could carry the mail in the event that domestic air mail contracts were cancelled. Foulois answered yes, but it would take four to six weeks to get ready. When he reported to Gen. Douglas MacArthur later that day, he was handed the Executive Order, dated February 9, directing the airlines to stop carrying the mail just ten days later.

Foulois faced a formidable task. The airlines were moving about three million pounds of mail each year with a fleet of about 500 airplanes, operating over a route network of more than 25,000 miles. The Army Air Corps had about 250 airplanes that could fly the routes, but they were obsolescent at best. The Corps' pilots were inexperienced in night and bad-weather flying. Facilities were limited, and the chosen aircraft had some serious deficiencies in instrumentation.

February 19 brought a long period of foul weather over most of the country. Inevitably, there were crashes, and some of them were fatal. There was a press outcry, and public reaction, followed by Congressional investigations. The popular perception then — a wrong one — remains even today in a belief that the Air Corps' carriage of the mail was a tremendous fiasco during which planes rained out of the skies and crashed in flames.

The facts are different. During the days between February 19 and June 1, when the Army handed over to the airlines again, the pilots moved 777,389 pounds of mail. They flew almost 1.6 million route miles, and logged 14,109 hours of flying time. Those numbers, extrapolated to a full year's effort, about match the performance of the commercial carriers. And the Air Corps did it with about half the number of airplanes.

That fleet was diminished severely by the 57 crashes that did occur, more than one every other day. Only four fatalities resulted on mail routes, and the total cost in lives was either 11 or 12, depending on whose data one believes at this time.

In retrospect, then, it was not a fiasco, even though

it wiped out a substantial portion of the Air Corps' strength in aircraft. It was more than an adequate job, given the state of the planes and of the Air Corps' readiness to perform such a mission. It spurred development of instrument flight in the Corps, and led to the introduction of new equipment and techniques for that kind of flying. It was, in a way, a forerunner of the surge operations begun by Tactical Air Command in the 1970s, an exercise that strained the capabilities of aircraft, pilots, ground crews and facilities. And it proved that the Air Corps had a long way to go before it could think of operations around the clock, in all kinds of weather, over any kind of terrain.

In March 1935, the GHQAF became a permanent, instead of a provisional, organization. All tactical aircraft from the nine Army corps areas were assigned to the GHQAF, which made its headquarters at Langley Field, Va. Its three operational wings were based at Langley, Barksdale Field, La., and March Field, Cal.

It was more form than substance. The GHQAF had no heavy bombers, and didn't get any for more than two years after its formation. The first batch of 13 service-test Y1B-17s, ordered in January 1936, and delivered between March and August 1937, was earmarked for the GHQAF. Planned procurement of heavy bombers for 1938 was a further 29 B-17s, production models this time, with 11 more scheduled for 1938. But by September 1939, when war broke out in Europe, only 13 B-17s and the sole XB-15 actually formed the long-range, heavy bomber striking force of the GHQAF.

But that didn't seem to worry the Joint Board of the Army and Navy. It remained unconvinced that there was any need at all for advanced bombers with longer range and larger capacity than the B-17 offered. In June 1938, with another world war about 15 months off, the Board opined that the B-17 was as far as the United States needed to go in bomber design. There was no requirement the Board could see for greater ferry range, increased combat radius, or larger bomb load.

On the eve of battle, the Air Corps still had to win its primary fight. It was soon to do so, but only with the help of the Germans and the Japanese.

Rearming for War

They stood in the hallway of the dormitory, listening to the slightly nasal, Harvard-accented voice coming from the loudspeakers of several radios tuned to the same station. Franklin Delano Roosevelt, just starting his unprecedented third term as President, was asking industry to build 50,000 airplanes a year for war.

The three, finishing their third year as aeronautical engineering students, dismissed the request with ridicule. They knew what industry could do; it was producing a few thousand planes a year. Now Roosevelt was asking industry to increase its production tenfold. It was clearly impossible, and they said so, loudly and jeeringly.

On May 16, 1940, Roosevelt's message did seem farfetched, if not impossible. The U. S. aviation industry had built a total of 921 military aircraft during 1939. But spurred by foreign sales, it would turn out a noteworthy 6,019 during 1940. By the time of the attack on Pearl Harbor, the industry was crowding the 20,000 mark — it actually delivered 19,433 military planes during 1941 — and within weeks would be outproducing any of the Axis countries and Great Britain.

Roosevelt was thoroughly aware of the reality of the world situation then. He had first addressed the subject in his annual message to the Congress early in 1938. The growing menace of military build-up in Europe was obvious to all except those who wouldn't see it. FDR asked Congress for a major increase in defense appropriations, mostly to be spent on Naval strength. He got it.

Hardly a year later, he was back. On January 12, 1939, FDR told Congress that U. S. air strength, then at an official figure of 1,700 planes, 1,600 officers, and 18,000 enlisted men, was "utterly inadequate". But it was even worse than Roosevelt said. Those 1,700 planes were obsolescent. The Army Air Corps owned a total of about 800 first-line planes. For comparison, the Royal Air Force fielded about 2,000 first-line airplanes

then, and the Luftwaffe numbered about 4,000. Total RAF personnel exceeded 100,000, and the Luftwaffe counted a half-million men and women.

It would require a massive investment to strengthen the U. S. air arm, and FDR asked Congress for $300 million in appropriations earmarked solely to buy new military planes for the Army Air Corps. By April, Congress had written, reported out, and passed legislation to build the air arm to 5,500 aircraft. The bill doubled the authorized officer strength, and increased enlisted strength by 150 percent.

It marked a shift in American policy away from isolationism, away from the concept of disarmament, and toward rearmament. Later in 1939, after the invasion of Poland, the United States declared that its policy would be one of neutrality, but that — in accordance with the Monroe Doctrine — it would fight to keep the Axis powers out of the Western Hemisphere.

As the fortunes of war buffeted France and Britain, it became apparent to U. S. leaders that the country might have to fight to defend the Western Hemisphere. Consequently, a new defense policy began to evolve, one that was based on dynamic concepts, using mobile forces, rather than on a static concept, waiting for the enemy to arrive on your shores.

It also was apparent that the United States would tilt its neutrality toward France and Britain; on no account could it be seen as supporting the black deeds of the Nazis. Gradually the tilt increased: in 1940, with open aid to the Allies, and in 1941, with Lend-Lease.

Because of the effective use of air power by the Germans in the early phases of the war, and the superb defensive use of limited fighter strength by the British during 1940, the military leadership of the United States began to think more favorably about air power. By the eve of the country's entry into war, air power had become a major factor in the advanced plans and strategy of the U. S.

Bottom left: While the European combatants in World War 2 were driving ahead relentlessly with the development of more advanced combat airplanes, in 1940 and 1941 the U.S. forces could devote greater effort to the development of trainer craft such as these Beech AT-11 bombing and gunnery trainers. In a way this proved a long-term advantage, for training went ahead more smoothly once the U.S.A. had entered the war.

In September 1939, on the day World War 2 began, the Curtiss P-36C pursuits of the 27th PS, 1st PG, were all painted in different camouflage schemes to display at the National Air Races at Cleveland. In the background are the 1st PG's Seversky P-35s and a Lockheed C-40.

In 1937 Vultee Aircraft, at Downey, launched a family of trainers and fighters sharing as many common parts as possible. Most never left the drawing board, but a few Model 48 Vanguards saw service with China, and the BT-13 Valiant basic trainer became a standard USAAF type, with 11,537 delivered. This was one of the first batch, in use at Randolph Field in 1939.

Greatest trainer in all history, the North American AT-6 is known by a score of designations and names. This AT-6A (NA-77) was used by the Army Air Corps in early 1941 as a gunnery trainer, with a "·30-caliber" in the rear cockpit, at Harlingen, Texas—now home of the Confederate AF.

The pace of the buildup before World War 2 was unique; it outran the frantic requirements of World War 1. Within a very few years, the United States went from a fifth-rate air power to a first-rate one. But it started from a very low point.

At the end of 1938, the first-line strength of the Army Air Corps stood at less than 500 airplanes. By late 1939, it was about 800. In September that year, the AAC had a total bomber force of 23 B-17 models of two types. About 700 of the first-line planes were one of three types: The Douglas B-18A, of which 350 were produced; the Northrop A-17A, with 239 built; and the Curtiss P-36A, with 243 produced. All were outdated.

In spite of major efforts by the AAC and by industry, the strength of the air arm did not significantly increase but, in fact, decreased as the war drew nearer. In the summer of 1941, with war less than six months away, the striking arm of the GHQAF included two groups of heavy bombers with a total of 70 planes; two groups with 114 medium bombers total; two groups of light bombers with the same strength; and three pursuit groups with a total of 225 aircraft. The numbers added to 523, the entire usable, operational fighting strength of the U. S. Army Air Corps. No wonder that Maj. Gen. Henry H. Arnold, Chief of the Air Corps, said that the Corps was at "zero strength."

There was one contributing factor that subtracted strength from the U. S. forces: the delivery of large numbers of warplanes to France and Great Britain. The involvement of those countries in the American aircraft production buildup, and the subsequent influence of their purchases on production, is a major part of Air Corps history.

Importance of Foreign Sales

Foreign sales always had taken a large portion of American output, not only in the aircraft industry. China was the most important customer from 1925 through 1938, buying approximately 13 percent of the total U. S. export volume. During those years, the Chinese bought 19,392 military planes from the United States.

Aircraft exports in the late 1930s accounted for about one-third of total sales, but they brought in about one-half of the profits. It was good business, and Congress, ever alert to the needs of free enterprise, passed a 1937 law allowing arms sales to non-belligerent customers. The items had to be paid for in cash, and the customer had to take delivery in the United States. Remember that the country was isolationist then, and there was still strong public sentiment against arms sellers as "merchants of death". Hence the specification for non-belligerent customers by Congress.

Early in 1938, a French military mission asked for, and received, permission to fly the Curtiss P-36A, then the latest service pursuit. In January, 1939, another French mission visited the Douglas plant, and one officer flew in the experimental Douglas Model 7B. The plane crashed, and the officer was taken to hospital and admitted under an assumed name. The secret leaked out; there was a Congressional outcry from a few of the die-hard isolationists. They thought it was illegal, or immoral, or something to allow a foreign military officer to fly in a U. S. military craft. But no law had been broken, and the incident opened the door wide to foreign sales.

A month after the accident, the British purchasing mission increased its U. S. orders to 650 aircraft. Their investment in planes and facilities at Lockheed and North American alone totalled $25 million. A few days later, the French ordered 615 warplanes from Curtiss, Douglas, Martin and North American for more than $60 million. Engine orders for the planes were placed with Wright Aeronautical and with Pratt & Whitney. Nor were the British and French the only buyers. The Australians, Belgians, Canadians, Iraqis (who later became Axis allies), Norwegians and Swedes also ordered military aircraft for their own forces. And in the same year, almost $1 million worth of planes went to the Russians.

The importance of these orders can't be overstated. They arrived at a time when industry was about to start layoffs for lack of major contracts, and they increased the employment instead. They spurred factory management into thinking in terms of large-scale production to meet increased needs. They were the direct reason for the development of high-rate production tooling, and for increased training of employees in new processes and production techniques. Finally, they had a very positive psychological value; if somebody wants to buy your products, those products are perceived as excellent.

When war broke out in 1939, the United States had to follow the letter of the law in its own Neutrality Act. Deliveries to France and Great Britain dropped substantially, because they now were belligerent powers and as such, were disqualified from buying arms in the United States.

But Congress changed the law to permit belligerents to buy. In November 1939, the "cash-and-carry" legislation was interpreted to mean that belligerents could buy, pay cash, and move the goods in their own ships.

Within a month, France and Great Britain had ordered 2,500 military aircraft. Industry's backlog at the end of 1939 was $630 million, of which $400 million represented foreign sales. By March 1940, British and French orders alone accounted for 8,200 aircraft in progress. And by mid-year, the two countries were receiving 70 percent of the output of military engines from Wright and P&W.

Clearly this was a problem. On the one hand, foreign sales were paying for the growth as well as the products of American industry. On the other hand, those very products were urgently needed by the American forces themselves, for their own rearmament.

But after the fall of France, Dunkirk, and the Battle of Britain, policy decisions were made at high levels of government. The immediate need to help Britain defend herself was more important to meet than the latter need to build American forces.

It was not a one-way street. One very important by-product of the Allied contracts for American aircraft

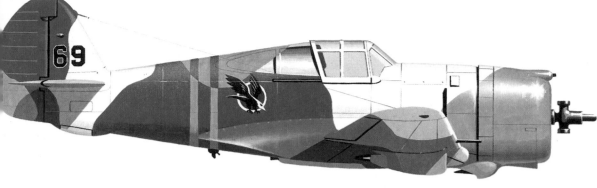

The P-36A was the main production variant of this Curtiss fighter, some 178 being built as part of the U.S. Army Air Corps' largest prewar fighter contract for 210 airplanes valued at $4 million. Camouflage was unusual during this "peaceful" time, and was normally associated with war games.

was the development and production of some of the better warplanes.

The Douglas A-20 series, one of the best light bombers ever operational, started from French interest. The Douglas Model 7B, which had crashed and injured a French officer in early 1939, was ordered in production quantities by the French. Their initial contract called for 100 of the swift attackers.

The best-known example is, of course, that paragon of pursuits, the speedy North American Mustang series. The British, who eventually bought the Mustang first, really wanted to buy more Curtiss Model 87A-1 pursuits, the export equal of the P-40D. But they were concerned that Curtiss did not have enough production capacity to meet British and American needs, and so they approached North American's J. H. Kindelberger in April, 1940. The British came to the point: they wanted North American to build the Curtiss plane.

"Hell," said Kindelberger, "We can build you a better airplane than that!"

The British, desperate for any military planes, agreed but made Kindelberger guarantee delivery of the prototype within 120 days after the date of the contract, which was May 4, 1940. The U. S. had no objection to the deal, but stipulated that two early production aircraft had to be delivered to the AAC for testing.

The NA-73 prototype was finished, though engineless, 117 days later, because its Allison V-1710-39 engine hadn't arrived. The plane first flew October 26, 1940, and the rest—as the cliché goes—is history.

After the fall of France, some of that country's contracted aircraft went to the British. Between July 1940 and December 1941, the U. S. aircraft industry produced more than 22,000 military planes of all types. The Air Corps took delivery on less than half; the British got 6,756, or about 31 percent of the total.

There is a misconception existing today that somehow the United States "gave" those airplanes to the British and the French. Not so; those airplanes, engines, and other weapons of war were paid for, often in dollars, and when the numbers were added at the end of the war, they were impressive. The British and French investment in engine factories alone was $84 million, in the days when that was a huge sum of money.

It is perfectly true to credit the French and the British with providing the impetus that made the United States the efficient, large-scale producer of aircrft that it was.

The fall of France, the evacuation at Dunkirk, and the Battle of Britain were triple traumas to Americans. Few remained isolationist after those three events, which polarized most Americans more than any other happening of the years of the ascendency of the Third Reich.

The floodgates holding back the flow of money for air power finally were opened. During the three years before the attack on Pearl Harbor, the Air Corps was told it could spend close to $8 billion dollars to increase its strength, and to earmark enough of that to buy almost 37,500 planes.

One of the characteristics of war is that it speeds the development of weapons. In combat, the deficiencies of any design rapidly show; if they produce enough fatalities, something is done quickly to improve the situation. War spurred the development of protective armor, of self-sealing tanks that could be bullet-riddled and still hold gasoline. That old standby, the .30-cal. Browning machine gun, soon gave way to the .50-cal., the 20-mm. cannon, and the 37-mm. cannon. Bomb designs proliferated. Engine horsepower increased. Novel design concepts, like tricycle landing gears, took form in experimental shops and on production lines.

The Air Corps sent observers to Europe to learn what they could about the problems of operating military aircraft in modern wartime environments, and to report on the kinds of design improvements that the British were rushing into production aircraft.

In concentrating so much effort on the development of the heavy bomber, Air Corps leadership had almost ignored fighter development trends. Bomber technology, pre-war, was far in advance of fighter technology in the United States. The contemporary of the early B-17s was the Boeing P-26, an open-cockpit, wire-braced low-wing monoplane, and it couldn't catch the B-17 in a flat race.

That kind of bomber performance lent strength to the argument of its proponents that the bomber would always get through. And that, in turn, led to ignoring the concept of the escort fighter. The bomber's speed and gunnery would get it to the target. That was the official argument, and as one result, fighter design languished. It was to cost the bomber forces dearly.

Whether the British saw the possibilities inherent in the Mustang when they first ordered it, or had to find out later, is immaterial. What does matter is that the North American design, which became the pre-eminent long-range escort fighter of the USAAF in later years and numerically dominated the fighter force, was the

A fabulous picture of a BT-9 basic trainer, with R-975 Whirlwind engine and fixed slats, of the 46th School Squadron in 1939. This was a time of rigid colour schemes and tail designators which a year later had been swept away by new schemes.

Exports Pay for Expansion

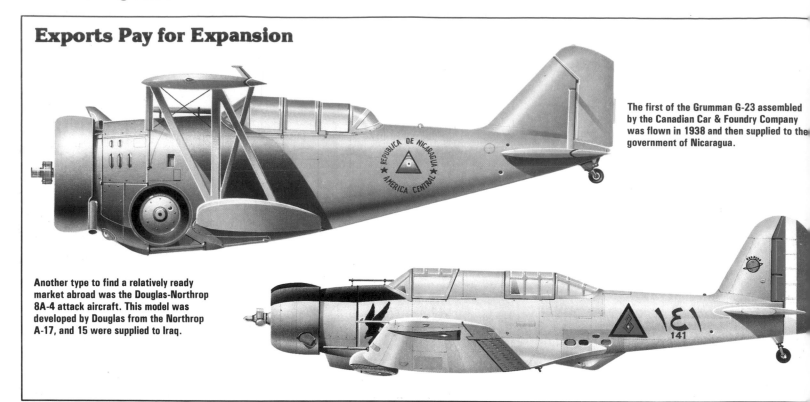

The first of the Grumman G-23 assembled by the Canadian Car & Foundry Company was flown in 1938 and then supplied to the government of Nicaragua.

Another type to find a relatively ready market abroad was the Douglas-Northrop 8A-4 attack aircraft. This model was developed by Douglas from the Northrop A-17, and 15 were supplied to Iraq.

Like Britain's Oxford, the Curtiss AT-9 —far more often called the Jeep than by its official name of Fledgling —was built by the thousand, trained tens of thousands of aircrew, and then vanished with hardly a mention in the history books. Though nominally simple, and powered by 280 hp R-680 Lycomings, it had a wing much smaller than a P-47 and was quite a hot ship. Masters of the AT9 could with confidence tackle any of the big bomber or attack types.

direct result of British interest, British contracts, and British operational experience.

With very few exceptions, and the Mustang is the best known example, the American airmen would fight the war with the airplanes that were in production before the war.

The Flying Fortress had been in production of sorts since 1936. Its counterpart, the Consolidated B-24 Liberator, lagged it by almost four years, but was in production before the U. S. entered the war. Both the North American B-25 Mitchell and the Martin B-26 Marauder entered production in 1941. The Lockheed P-38 Lightning, Bell P-39 Airacobra, and Curtiss P-40 Kittyhawk were in production in 1940, and the Republic P-47 Thunderbolt joined them a year later.

Reorganization Yet Again

When Roosevelt made his 1939 request for funds, the Army air strength was split into the Air Corps, which was a training organization essentially, and the GHQAF, which was a mobile, tactical air force. In March 1939, GHQAF was assigned to the command of the Chief of the Air Corps, Gen. Arnold. Airmen hardly had time to get used to the new arrangement when it was changed again. GHQAF was given a separate status, but under the commander of Army field forces. To soften the blow, perhaps, Arnold was named Acting Deputy Chief of Staff of the Army, and was in an excellent position to coordinate all air power.

It was another one of the innumerable steps that airmen kept hoping would lead to independence. In March, 1941, Robert A. Lovett, one of the Navy's original pilot cadre in World War 1, was named Assistant Secretary of War for Air. He reorganized the air once again and it became the United States Army Air Forces (USAAF) by Regulation 95-5 dated June 20, 1941. Arnold was named Chief of the AAF, and was given the responsibility for plans and policies for aviation. He reported directly to the Army Chief of Staff, and also kept his position as Deputy Chief.

Reorganizing was only a cosmetic solution to the real problem: how to expand for war rapidly and efficiently.

The Air Corps began with a program that had been developed in the spring of 1939. The goal then was to

have 24 combat-ready groups of tactical aircraft by mid-1941. In May 1940, that plan was revised upward to a new goal of 41 combat-ready groups. Before July 1940, it was 54 groups. One year later, the Air Corps projected a need for 84 groups by mid-1942. In a little over two years, the planned tactical force had been virtually quadrupled.

Expanding a military force requires increases in numbers of weapons, personnel and facilities. All of these physical accoutrements of expansion were lacking in the years before Pearl Harbor's destruction.

The flying training program had been turning out about 300 pilots each year, a leisurely gait that kept pace with the small deliveries of aircraft in the pre-1939 time period. The first major incremental improvement was planned in 1939; the 24-group program would require about 1,200 pilots per year, it was estimated. In June, 1940, when the group goal was raised to 41, the training plans suggested that 7,000 pilots per year would suffice. In July 1940, that figure was raised to 12,000. And by Feburary 1941, all pretense at restraint had been dropped, and the Air Corps was talking in terms of 30,000 pilots per year, a hundred-fold increase over its plans of two years earlier.

Planes also require mechanics. In 1939, the Air Corps was graduating about 1,500 per year from its technical training schools. By March 1941, that figure was scheduled to be 110,000, another increase of staggering proportions.

Facilities were hardly adequate. The pre-war Corps lived and operated from 17 air bases and four depots, many of them left over from World War 1 or earlier, and most of them showing signs of their age. There had been no major improvement programs, and the bases suffered from poor maintenance because of budget restrictions. Happily, buildings and runways and barracks can be built more rapidly then complex aircraft. By the end of 1941, those 17 bases had grown to 114 major installations inside the continental United States; 14 more were to be built under pending legislation, and 14 were to be rehabilitated.

This is not to suggest that the coming hordes of airmen would live well everywhere during their training in the United States. Some did; but most didn't. The bases that were developed on a hurry-up basis during the early years of the expansion left much to be

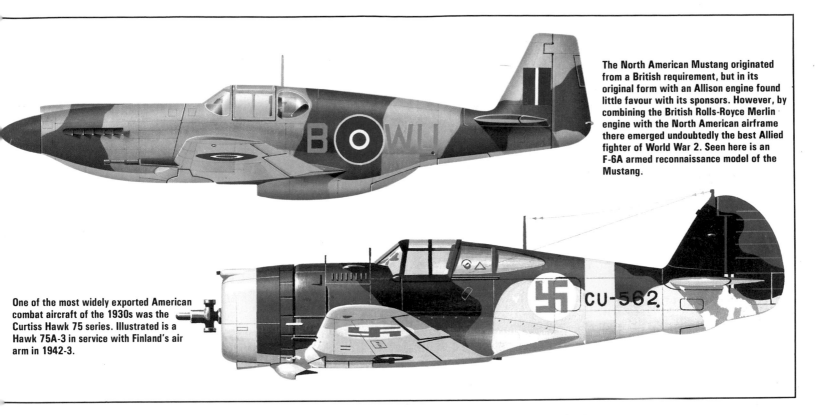

The North American Mustang originated from a British requirement, but in its original form with an Allison engine found little favour with its sponsors. However, by combining the British Rolls-Royce Merlin engine with the North American airframe there emerged undoubtedly the best Allied fighter of World War 2. Seen here is an F-6A armed reconnaissance model of the Mustang.

One of the most widely exported American combat aircraft of the 1930s was the Curtiss Hawk 75 series. Illustrated is a Hawk 75A-3 in service with Finland's air arm in 1942-3.

desired. A tarpaper-covered airmen's barracks in the deep South's summertime has to be experienced to be believed.

Evolution of Strategy and Plans

The defeat of France made the point, and the Tripartite Pact signed in Berlin in September 1940 provided the emphasis. Europe was Germany's; Japan was on the move in Asia, and there was a possibility that the United States might have to face a very hostile world alone, except for help from Canada and Latin America.

Arnold, showing his prescience, established a Strategic Air Intelligence Section in 1940. It was the first American atempt to develop economic, industrial and social analyses that would aid in target selection. Information came from unexpected quarters. The German electrical power grid, their petroleum industry and the synthetic oil plants had been financed in a major way by American banks. The conservative bankers had wanted to see what they were backing, and the Germans obligingly had furnished drawings and specifications, which were still in American bank vaults. That information also was valuable as a trading card; the British needed it.

The trade was made; the British got U. S. data, and the U. S. got about one ton of British intelligence on the German aircraft and engine industries, transportation systems, and the Luftwaffe.

Early in 1941, British and American staff personnel had a series of informal talks. ABC-1, the report on those talks issued March 27, 1941, summarized the common strategy that had been worked out in principle between Great Britain and the United States during those talks. The assumption by the U. S. was that it would be facing Germany, Italy and Japan in any war. The prime American task would be defense of the Western Hemisphere; of Britain, the defense of the United Kingdom.

Since Germany was the predominant enemy, the main effort would be made against her in Europe and the Atlantic. That effort would include a sustained air offensive. The air forces mission was to achieve superiority, and especially in the long-range striking forces. U. S. bombardment units were to work closely in a combined offensive with the Royal Air Force, and their joint targets were to be found primarily in Germany.

Arnold had established an Air War Plans Division in July 1941, drawing on a handful of the best officers he knew. Under Col. Harold L. George, the group included Lt. Col. Kenneth N. Walker, and Majors Heywood S. Hansell Jr., and Laurence S. Kuter. Hansell had just come back from England where he had been collecting target data and the RAF's battle experience. All five officers had been associated closely with the Air Corps Tactical School, and all five were active proponents of air power. Arnold had chosen well.

They produced a first plan, AWPD/1, in seven days between August 4 and 11. It concentrated on the European theater, laid out the target objectives, calculated the force necessary to destroy them, and estimated the requirements for pilots and total personnel strengths necessary to accomplish the plan.

It was a hectic week, and when the plan was done, it was briefed to higher authorities and accepted. Perhaps nobody at War Department level read it too carefully, because one of the features of the plan was a tacit assumption that the USAAF was co-equal with the Army and Navy.

AWPD/1 called for the disruption of the German electrical power system, the transportation system, and the oil/petroleum system, particularly two targets: the synthetic oil complex and the refinery complex at Ploesti. The intermediate objective was to neutralize the Luftwaffe.

Outwardly, the United States Army Air Forces were able to face the prospects of war with a brave front. It had a planned strategy, a planned collaboration with a strong and war-experienced ally, new facilities, filled classrooms, and busy training fields. Industry was in full production, and would deliver about 20,000 planes during 1941. USAAF itself was a reorganized command, more able to deal with the problems facing it. Things looked good.

The facts are otherwise. The country and its armed forces were hardly any more ready for war than they had been in 1917. The same problems were arising, the same mistakes were waiting to be made. And thousands of airmen had to die in hundreds of wasted airplanes, before there would be a real feeling of accomplishment and a measure of success.

North American Aviation and licensees made almost 20,000 trainers with this general shape, but these happen to be Army Air Corps BT-14s, at Randolph Field, Texas. The BT-14 was one of the first of the family to have blunt wingtips and triangular fin. The engine was an R-985 Wasp Junior.

A Quiet and Pleasant Sunday

Admiral Isoroku Yamamoto, Commander in Chief of the Japanese Imperial Navy, was right. His plan had worked, and would give Japan breathing time to win some important victories. From that position of strength, his country then could negotiate with the Western powers for a settlement of the war.

Yamamoto's plan was only a temporary solution. He knew that his Navy could not long stand against the combined strengths of the West, that eventually Japan would go down to defeat. Hence his strategy: strike the main American naval base in Hawaii and do as much damage as possible. If the plan worked, it would give the Japanese military about one year to consolidate their gains in Asia, and to win other battles.

And so, on the morning of December 7, 1941, a quiet and pleasant Sunday in the Hawaiian Islands, a wave of Japanese carrier-based bombers and fighters roared in over Oahu and attacked the Navy's base at Pearl Harbor and the Army Air Forces' main station, Hickam Field.

There were two waves of attackers, and they spent almost two hours over their targets. When the last Japanese plane pulled away from the verdant island and headed north towards rendezvous with its carrier, the U. S. military installations were a shambles.

The Navy was hardest hit. It lost 2,086 personnel killed or dead of wounds, and the heart of the Pacific Fleet: proud warships, now blazing ruins where they lay along Battleship Row. The Army Air Forces lost 206 men killed or missing, and 64 of their 231 Oahu-based aircraft were destroyed. Hickam, Wheeler and Bellows Fields were heavily hit, either by bombing, or strafing, or both.

There had been no action alert for the USAAF, only an alert against sabotage. The planes were parked closely to simplify guard procedures, and—in their state—required a four-hour notice to be prepared for flight.

Somehow, six AAF planes did get airborne about a half-hour after the attack began; during the furious bombing, Army pilots flew 25 sorties against the Japanese, and claimed ten shot down.

Into the middle of the furore flew a dozen B-17s from the 38th and 88th Reconnaissance Squadrons, on their way from Hamilton Field, Calif., to the Philippines. They had no ammunition aboard; their guns were stowed and covered with a protective finish; their armor had been detached and moved forward to balance the planes. In a remarkable collective demon-stration of airmanship, the bombers evaded the Japanese fighters as well as American anti-aircraft, and landed wherever they could find a place, including on a 1,200-foot runway at Haleiwa and on a golf course. One was hit badly enough to be written off, and three others were badly damaged.

About two hours after the attack ended, the first reconnaissance aircraft took off from Oahu to find the carriers. It was a useless mission; Yamamoto's fleet was long gone, headed back after a most successful surprise attack.

In the Philippines, word of the Pearl Harbor debacle had alerted the air commanders, but they delayed any possible effective counterstrike against Japanese positions within range. They did send their aircraft into the air on patrols. Their B-17 units then were ordered to strike the Japanese on Formosa, and they came back to Clark Field, near Manila, to refuel and rearm. They were on the ground when a flight of Japanese bombers flew over and devastated Clark Field and the B-17s. Other strikes against American air installations were the same. A few fighters got off the ground and downed some Japanese bombers, but the

Facing page: The attack on Pearl Harbor on that fine Sunday morning was by far the greatest military shock ever suffered by the United States. This Japanese reconnaissance photograph shows capital ships burning after the attack. The land is Ford Island and the large vessel almost certainly the battleship USS Nevada.

Two of the stricken BBs lie blazing in Pearl Harbor immediately after the attack. Hit by six torpedoes, BB-48 West Virginia settles low in the water, while beyond her, next to the Ford Island shore, BB-43 Tennessee is in little better shape. Both ships lived to fight again; West Virginia supported the landing at Lingayen Gulf while Tennessee supported the Marine assault on Iwo Jima.

In Navy-commanded areas, such as Pacific theaters, old-type rudder stripes were restored in January 1942. Various camouflage schemes were then in use, but this B-17C (BG unspecified) was plain olive drab and neutral gray. Soon the red center to the insignia was omitted to avoid any possible confusion with the enemy's hinomaru (Rising Sun).

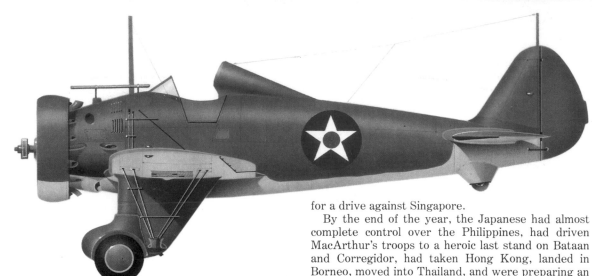

Though scarcely operational, this Boeing P-26A was still on the strength of the 18th Pursuit Group at Wheeler Field on December, 7, 1941. By this time the effective strength of the group was composed of 62 Curtiss P-40Bs and 11 P-40Cs, neither type having an official U. S. name at that time. A handful from this group managed to become airborne and scored the first-ever battle victories of the U. S. Army Air Corps.

A sight all too common on U.S. overseas bases in the first weeks of World War 2 was numbers of airplanes destroyed on the ground by marauding Japanese airplanes. Seen here is an early model Boeing B-17 knocked out at Wheeler Field in the Hawaiian islands on December 7, 1941.

battle was one-sided. When the attackers left after two days of intermittent bombing and strafing, they had achieved effective air superiority over the area for the Japanese forces. A dozen B-17s were left operational, along with 22 Curtiss P-40s and eight Seversky P-35s.

It was the auspicious start of a Japanese sweep of the Far East that lasted only about six months.

The initial successes were on an unprecedented scale. The entire Far East seemed to collapse all at once after the destruction at Pearl Harbor. In 72 hours of war, Japanese forces had destroyed or disabled the U. S. Pacific Fleet's battleships, and had sunk the British warships *Prince of Wales* and *Repulse*. Their bombing had blasted most of the U. S. air strength in Hawaii and the Philippines. They were attacking Hong Kong and Manila, and it was only a question of when they would fall. And they had assembled their forces for a drive against Singapore.

By the end of the year, the Japanese had almost complete control over the Philippines, had driven MacArthur's troops to a heroic last stand on Bataan and Corregidor, had taken Hong Kong, landed in Borneo, moved into Thailand, and were preparing an invasion of Burma and the Malay States that would end in the capture of Rangoon and the fall of that "impregnable fortress", Singapore.

The contrast was strong between this lightning war waged by the Japanese and the relatively conventional pace of the seesaw war in the Middle East and above Europe, and it forced a harder look at the Pacific theater. The United States and Great Britain hardly were strong enough to wage war on one front, let alone two. The best hope was for a holding defensive action in the Pacific, and the building of a powerful offensive force in Europe to defeat Germany. For when the final analysis was made, Germany posed a greater threat to what both the Americans and the British thought of as the civilized world, namely, their immediate areas. Thus it was that the emphasis in building the USAAF was placed on heavy bomber strength in England, to be launched against Germany in support of a planned

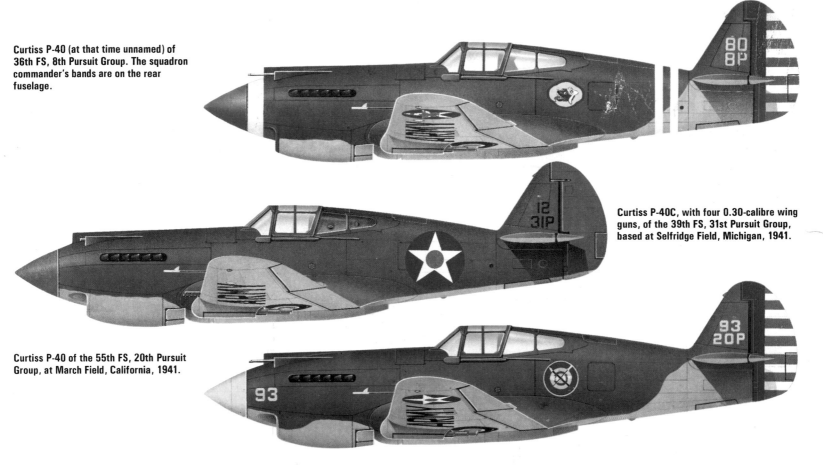

Curtiss P-40 (at that time unnamed) of 36th FS, 8th Pursuit Group. The squadron commander's bands are on the rear fuselage.

Curtiss P-40C, with four 0.30-calibre wing guns, of the 39th FS, 31st Pursuit Group, based at Selfridge Field, Michigan, 1941.

Curtiss P-40 of the 55th FS, 20th Pursuit Group, at March Field, California, 1941.

landing in France in late 1942 or early 1943 (Code name: *Bolero*).

It was a conscious decision: Europe first, and do only what had to be done in the Pacific. It is probable that no Allied military or government leader ever thought, in his darkest private moments, that the Japanese would ever move so far so fast. When they did, the major concern was how to get some forces to the Pacific to blunt the Japanese assaults that were proliferating.

The Pacific was to be a Navy show for several years. Carrier-based air power was used effectively by naval operations officers to soften the beachheads before invasions by the Marines and the Army. Carrier air pounded the best of the Japanese fleet units and commercial shipping, sinking an enormous tonnage and contributing in large measure to the eventual defeat of the Empire.

But the USAAF had its moments in that theater, also, bad ones at first, then gallant and costly defenses, and finally a vindication of the concept of strategic bombing. But at the end of December, 1941, that was only a future hope.

USAAF Strikes Back

The immediate objective was to hit Japan somehow, somewhere. From a number of sketchy concepts, one emerged: an AAF bombing raid against the home islands, launched from a Navy carrier offshore and recovered in mainland China. The idea coalesced from a number of vague thoughts.

Capt. Francis S. Low, a Navy submariner on Adm. Ernest J. King's staff, gets credit for the basic plan: he thought that Army B-25s or B-26s could be flown off a Navy carrier and directed against Japan. Navy Capt. Donald B. Duncan, King's air operations officer, did the analysis, chose the *Hornet* as the carrier, laid out a plan of action, and suggested that modified North American B-25 medium bombers be used. Arnold agreed, and asked Lt. Col. James J. Doolittle to oversee the modifications and train the crews.

The strike was planned as one part of a five-part operation that would eventually establish the Tenth Air Force in Burma. The B-25s would go on strength with the Tenth Air Force after their successful recovery in China.

Doolittle drew the planes and crews from the 34th, 37th, and 95th Bombardment Squadrons of the 17th Bombardment Group (Medium), and from the 89th Reconnaissance Squadron. They trained at Eglin Field, Florida, learning how to snatch the B-25s off the ground at liftoff speeds far below the ones that had been drummed into their heads during transition to the type. Late in March, 1942, they left Eglin for McClellan Field, Calif., for a final inspection of their fleet by technicians at the Sacramento Air Depot. On March 31 they made the short flight to the Naval Air Station at Alameda, watched their B-25s loaded aboard a carrier, and sailed with the task force when it left on April 2.

Doolittle's planes—the mission was his also, after he had volunteered himself to Arnold—had been modified

Taken at about 08:25 on April 18, 1942, this historic picture shows one of the B-25B Mitchells of the special Doolittle force accelerating at full power down the unfamiliar deck of USS Hornet. Steering was assisted by a broad white stripe for the left main gear, with a thin stripe for the nosewheel. Amazingly, all 16 bombers got into the air successfully.

with long-range fuel tanks, reduced armament, and the addition of black-painted broomsticks masquerading as tail guns in the hope of fooling Japanese fighters, at least on the first pass. They were loaded with three 500-lb. demolition bombs, and one 500-lb. incendiary cluster, and their assigned targets were in Tokyo, Yokohama, Nagoya, Osaka and Kobe.

The launch had been planned for April 17 at sunset; but the American force was spotted by the Japanese early that morning and at 8:00 AM, Adm. William F. Halsey, commanding the force, ordered the planes off.

Doolittle was first. Engines roaring, the B-25 rolled straight along the white lines painted on the carrier deck as wheel guides, rotated, and clawed its way into the air at 8:20. The last of the raiders left the *Hornet* at 9:20 AM. Ahead lay 600 miles of flying to the coast of Japan.

On the basis of cold statistics, the daring raid was a dismal failure. Damage to targets was slight. All of the airplanes and some of the crews were lost. Doolittle was despondent. But viewed psychologically, the mission was a tremendous success.

For months, the war news had been bad. The U. S. was being beaten badly; the Philippines had fallen and the survivors of Bataan had been moved to prisons on the infamous "Death March". Doolittle's raid was the first good news in a long time. But more importantly, it was the first bad news for the Japanese. Their government had promised that they were invulnerable; they weren't, and the government had lied. The Japanese people never recovered from the shock of that raid; it presaged what was to come, and from then on, they sensed the doom of their Empire.

The first cause for cautious Allied optimism came early in May, in the Coral Sea, the waters off the northeast coast of Australia. The Japanese were driving toward Port Moresby, on the southeast coast of New Guinea, from which their naval forces could control the Coral Sea and threaten Australia, perhaps even support an invasion.

The Battle of the Coral Sea raged for several days after the first engagement May 4, when U. S. carrier-based air groups hit and hurt a Japanese invasion force sent against Tulagi, in the Solomon Islands. The rest of the battle was fought entirely in air engagements; the opposing fleets never got to Port Moresby.

That campaign blunted, Yamamoto headed toward Midway Island, west-northwest of the Hawaiian group. In his hands it would be a useful base from which to threaten the central Pacific basin and Hawaii. But the U. S. had broken Japanese naval codes, and knew every detail about the task force steaming northward toward Midway.

About mid-May, the 7AF went on alert, expecting enemy action against Midway Island. The Seventh, formerly the Hawaiian Air Force, sent 16 B-17s to Midway, and with them went four Martin B-26s of the Fifth Air Force. On June 2, with nothing happening, six of the B-17s returned to Oahu. They just missed the start of a good fight.

The next day, nine of the Midway-based B-17s struck five Japanese ships close to 600 miles offshore, in a warmup for the main event. On June 4, the four B-26s sortied with an accompanying force of six Navy Grumman TBF-1 torpedo planes, some Marine Douglas SBD-3s, and 14 B-17s, all led by a formation of Navy Consolidated PBY Catalina patrol bombers. The Marauders were on an unusual mission; each carried a standard Navy torpedo slung under its belly, and they were going to attack with the Navy's TBFs in low-level drops of the steel fish. They came in as low and as fast as they could, but Japanese anti-aircraft and fighters got two of the B-26s and five of the TBF-1s. No torpedo scored a hit.

The B-17s bombed a Japanese task force about 150 miles off Midway, claiming hits on some carriers. Other

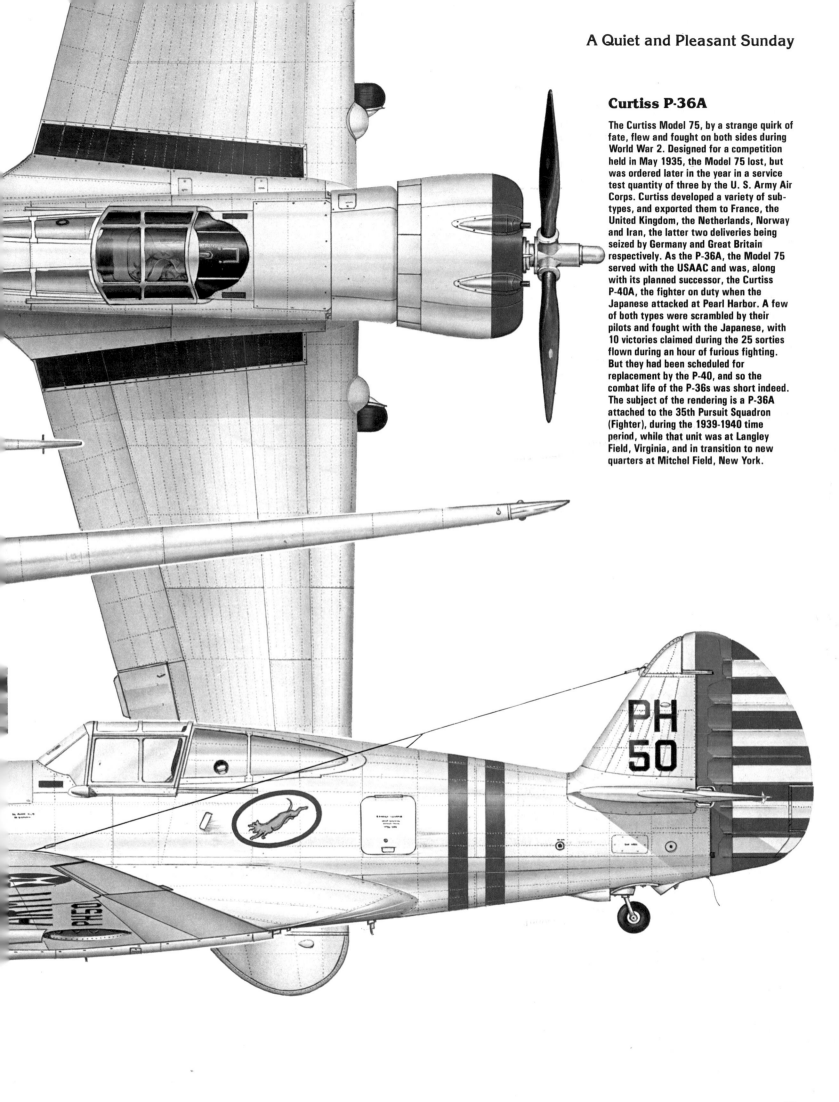

Curtiss P-36A

The Curtiss Model 75, by a strange quirk of fate, flew and fought on both sides during World War 2. Designed for a competition held in May 1935, the Model 75 lost, but was ordered later in the year in a service test quantity of three by the U. S. Army Air Corps. Curtiss developed a variety of sub-types, and exported them to France, the United Kingdom, the Netherlands, Norway and Iran, the latter two deliveries being seized by Germany and Great Britain respectively. As the P-36A, the Model 75 served with the USAAC and was, along with its planned successor, the Curtiss P-40A, the fighter on duty when the Japanese attacked at Pearl Harbor. A few of both types were scrambled by their pilots and fought with the Japanese, with 10 victories claimed during the 25 sorties flown during an hour of furious fighting. But they had been scheduled for replacement by the P-40, and so the combat life of the P-36s was short indeed. The subject of the rendering is a P-36A attached to the 35th Pursuit Squadron (Fighter), during the 1939-1940 time period, while that unit was at Langley Field, Virginia, and in transition to new quarters at Mitchel Field, New York.

B-17s claimed hits on ships that day, and six B-17s that were headed to Midway from Oahu dropped on the *Hiryu*, a Japanese carrier, and claimed hits.

The Japanese fleet turned during the night, and began a retreat. During the following day, the B-17s made 19 sorties, and claimed hits on two heavy warships and two cruisers. Midway Island was safe.

But USAAF activity was only peripheral to the main body of the battle, which was the U. S. Navy's victory. It was a major and decisive defeat for the Japanese, psychologically as much as in reality. Yamamoto would not leave his cabin after the battle, hiding there until his flagship, the giant battleship *Yamato*, had docked. He realized the result of that battle. The Imperial Navy was on the road to defeat.

The Battle of Midway reopened the old arguments about bombers and battleships. The USAAF heavy bombers had dropped more than 150,000 pounds of bombs on the Japanese from altitudes between a few thousand feet and the normal operational ceiling. Their total claims included 22 direct hits on heavy ships, one destroyer sunk, three torpedo strikes on two carriers, and 10 Japanese fighters downed.

These claims were greatly exaggerated, when checked later against Japanese records. But that factor aside, Midway showed that battleships, steaming in tight maneuvers at flank speed and defended by anti-aircraft and fighter cover, could be sunk by bombing. But the bombers that did the sinking were Navy dive bombers, swooping to within a few hundred feet of their targets before loosing their weapons.

The First Ploesti Raid

Halverson Project No. 63 was another unit that had been scheduled to become part of 10AF in Burma, but fate rearranged things. Col. Harry A. Halverson led a detachment of 23 brand-new Consolidated B-24D Liberator heavy bombers on a route that was planned to start in Florida and end with the bombing of Tokyo. They were to be based at airfields around Chengtu, in China's Szechwan Province, and operate from forward bases around Chekiang, from where they stood a better chance of making the round trip to Japan.

They were held at Khartoum on route, waiting for orders, because Japanese advances after the Doolittle raid had become a threat to the Chekiang region. It was early June, 1942, and Congress had just gotten

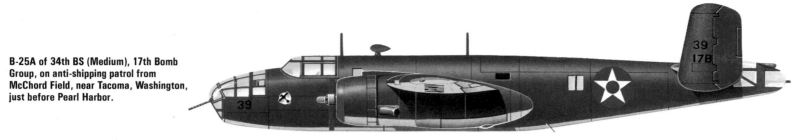

B-25A of 34th BS (Medium), 17th Bomb Group, on anti-shipping patrol from McChord Field, near Tacoma, Washington, just before Pearl Harbor.

around to declaring war on three of the lesser Axis partners: Bulgaria, Hungary, and Romania. The biggest oil refinery available to Hitler's armies, a superlative target for a bombing strike, was in Ploesti, Romania.

Halverson's Project (HALPRO) got the assignment; they never did get to China. They moved from Khartoum to Fayid, on Egypt's Great Bitter Lake, to train and equip for the raid. It was a round trip of at least 2,600 miles and the planes were to recover at a base in Iraq. They would fly at night, over territory for which no charts were available, and where no lights would be showing. The B-24s had not seen combat with any USAAF units. The crews had never fired their guns or dropped their bombs in anger, and had never seen enemy air opposition.

The Royal Air Force at Sayid did all it could, helping with briefings, with supplies for the aircraft and crews, and with the fueling and arming. The Russians never responded to official requests for permission to land in their territory after the attack for refueling.

HALPRO took off late at night June 11, 1942, on the first USAAF mission against any European target. A dozen of the 13 planes that took off reached and bombed Ploesti. There were no losses in personnel or aircraft. And there was no publicity after the attack, leaving Halverson's men puzzled and somewhat miffed. To this day, there is little known about the mission. But one thing is known: HALPRO was first to bomb in the European theater.

The HALPRO and Doolittle raids were symbols, and they were messages to the Japanese that the United States had not been defeated at Pearl Harbor. Those missions also were apart from the main thrust of the USAAF strategy. *Bolero* was still the primary objective, and all forces were building toward that mission as a first priority. There were to be no other ground operations in Europe or North Africa before that landing in France, except in the case of a severe emergency.

Knowing that the Pacific arena was also a scene of heavy action, a military decision was made to send whatever force was available to that region to deal with crises.

Churchill, who never saw much beyond the immediate needs of the British Empire, pushed for an invasion of North Africa, to take pressure off his armies there. It would be easy, he argued, and would not delay the buildup towards *Bolero*. His arguments convinced Roosevelt, who agreed that the United States would land a force in North Africa before the end of July 1942.

By mid-1942, the 8AF had just begun to establish its administrative echelons in England, and was in no position to send any of its planes or crews off on any substantial missions against the continent. Only a handful of American airmen and their planes had arrived, and the closest to combat was the 15th Bombardment Squadron (Separate), training on Douglas A-20s (Boston IIIs) with 226 Squadron, RAF, at Swanton Morley. A crew from the 15th became the first USAAF airmen to fly from England against continental targets. On June 25, 1942, squadron commander Capt. Charles C. Kegelman borrowed one of the Boston IIIs and with his crew, joined a gaggle of 226 Squadron's planes on a low-level raid against rail-road yards at Hazebrouck in northern France.

For publicity purposes, the first "official" combat sortie by 8AF crews had been scheduled for July 4, America's holiday of Independence Day. Six Boston IIIs carried Kegelman's crew and five others, again in company with a number of planes from 226 Squadron. They hit four airfields in the Netherlands. Kegelman's plane was slammed by anti-aircraft fire and damaged badly, but he brought it back. It was a small beginning.

July 4 also was a special day on the other side of the globe. USAAF was scheduled to induct the pilots, planes and ground crews of the American Volunteer Group, familiarly known by their nickname of "Flying Tigers". They were a remarkable group of mercenaries, who had more than money as motivation, and their story has been told many times.

They had been formed as an independent unit to fly and fight in China under the leadership of Brig. Gen. Claire L. Chennault, a great air tactician. Chennault was one of the few air power advocates who believed that the bomber didn't necessarily have to get through, and that a dynamic defense could stop an air strike.

The AVG pilots, like other Americans flying with foreign air forces, were offered the option of joining

Almost silhouetted against the flames and smoke from another unit's target, a group of B-24D Liberator bombers surges on toward its own target area after the long haul from North Africa. Hammered by flak and fighters, the survivors then faced the long haul back to base.

their own country's units after the U. S. declared war. Once inducted, the AVG would become part of the China Air Task Force, and would continue to serve under Chennault, assigned to 10AF. Most pilots elected not to make the transfer; some had better jobs waiting, some wanted to rejoin the Navy or the Marines, their original outfits, and some couldn't pass the AAF physical requirements. Only five decided to move, along with a few ground crew personnel. But in a typical display of their morale and their ethics, about 20 AVG pilots agreed to stay around and fight until they were adequately replaced.

The final score those soldiers of fortune achieved was impressive. They destroyed about 300 Japanese planes at a cost of nine of their pilots and about 50 of their aircraft, Curtiss P-40Bs. They left an outstanding combat record as a goal for their successors, and they gained a place in history.

Finally, the First B-17 Raid

Two weeks after the 8AF's official first combat sortie, American and British military and political leaders met in London to discuss the planned invasion of North Africa (Code name: *Torch*). By then, it was beginning to look more and more like a major operation, and not quite the sideshow Churchill had implied it would be.

Lt. Gen. Dwight D. Eisenhower, then commander of the European Theater of Operations (ETO), assigned a mission and a deadline to 8AF: attain air superiority over western France by April 1, 1943. Three days later, the Joint Chiefs of Staff effectively counter-manded that order with a statement that 8AF would supply heavy and medium bomber groups from its strength for transfer to the *Torch* operation. Further, 15 of its combat groups were to be transferred to the Pacific, where there was an emerging and critical need.

The 8AF, hardly established in England, was rocked by the JCS statement. Lt. Gen. Carl Spaatz, commanding USAAF In Europe, protested the planned drawdown of his forces and wondered just how this could be done while attaining air superiority against the Germans at the same time.

His bomber forces were not yet at strength, and his fighters had yet to become operational in the theater. The RAF stepped into the gap with a promise; it would furnish fighter escort for 8AF bomber strikes, using squadrons of Spitfire IXs developed for high-altitude fighting. Eight days later, August 5, 1942, VIII Fighter Command sent its first fighter force over France.

Eleven Spitfire Vs, then equipping the 31st Fighter Group based at Atcham and High Ercall for training, were flown across the Channel on a practice run. The 31st, formerly equipped with Bell P-39A Airacobra fighters, had left them in the U. S. and had gone to England by sea. They normally would have flown across the North Atlantic, ferrying their own aircraft to war, and shepherded there by B-17 "mother hens". But a series of checkerboard moves jumped bomber units around to the West coast and to the Far East, and the "mother hens" were unavailable.

The pilots of the 31st FG were inexperienced in the ways of combat, and in the theater environment; they needed more than a few hours of local flying. They started training June 26, under the watchful eyes of experienced RAF personnel, and were declared operational in mid-August and assigned to RAF No. 11 Group.

The very first tactical aircraft flown to the United Kingdom by an American crew arrived July 1. It was a B-17E, and it was the total heavy bomber strength in the USAAF in Europe for a short while. By July 27, the 97th Bomb Group, back from the West coast and first of the heavies to arrive in the ETO, was available but hardly ready for operations. It had been sent from the U. S. as soon as the crews were ready to make the ferry flight, and before their training had been completed.

The list of deficiencies was appalling. Crews were in-experienced in high-altitude flying and in formation flight, the basis of the bomber attack. The radio operators could neither send nor receive Morse code well. Most of the gunners had never shot at a towed target, let alone an enemy fighter, and some of them had never operated the B-17 turrets in the air.

They trained at a fast pace, and were alerted August 9. The weather cancelled the first alert, and did not let up until the 16th, when the forecast for the next day promised clear skies.

The target for the August 17 mission was the huge railroad yard at Rouen-Sotteville, in northern France. A dozen B-17s from the 340th, 342nd, and 414th Bomb Squadrons were the strike force, and another six were to fly a diversionary sweep along the coast of France.

The lead aircraft was piloted by Col. Frank A. Armstrong, Jr., group commander of the 97th. In the pilot's seat of the lead ship, second flight, was Brig. Gen. Ira C. Eaker, commanding VIII Bomber Command. His B-17E was named "Yankee Doodle."

They lifted off the runway at Grafton Underwood beginning at 3:12 PM, formed up and flew to rendezvous with four Spitfire IX squadrons from the RAF, who escorted them to the target. The B-17s dropped about 37,000 pounds of bombs, and half of them landed within the target area specified.

They returned safely with no losses for the mission, covered on the flight home by five Spitfire IX squadrons, again from the RAF. They landed just after 7:00 PM.

The value of the raid was in its demonstration of a principle: high-altitude precision bombing. Fortun-ately, the bombing accuracy was high on that first strike; there were no desparate Luftwaffe pilots making daring attacks to break the formation and pick off individual planes.

Historians who have written about World War 2's vast panorama have called 1942 the year when the tide turned. But the tide did not turn in the skies over Europe or the Pacific that year. With the first B-17 raid out of the way, the demands for units to support *Torch* increased, and there were serious doubts raised at 8AF about its abilities to wage any kind of an effective air war.

But the Rouen-Scotteville raid did mark a turning point, and it gave future historians a most convenient place to halt their narratives and to consider separate theaters of war from then on.

When the 8th AF arrived in England in 1942 its heavy equipment looked like this. The B-17F was uniformly olive drab, and the formations had yet to build to the state-sized armadas of two years hence.

Tactical Air Power Matures

Field Marshal Erwin Rommel, the Russian defense of Stalingrad, heroic Free French fighters, faulty German grand strategy and American supply lines to the Far East are tied together in an untidy package that was called the Desert War. Fought along the coastline of North Africa from Morocco to well inside Egypt, the Desert War saw the development of hard-hitting tactical air power to become a major factor in the eventual Allied victory there and later in Italy.

In 1941, Rommel's Afrika Korps and the British played a deadly game of cowboys and Indians across the sands of the desert wastes, in short sharp tank engagements and clashes of infantry. In early 1942, from his position at El Agheila, on the southern tip of the Gulf of Sidra in Libya, Rommel began a drive toward the Suez Canal, more than 800 miles to the East. Tobruk, chosen by the British as a place to stand and defend, fell June 20 to Rommel's army. Now he saw a larger prize. Originally, his goal was to take Malta, Britain's supply station in the Mediterranean, but the Suez Canal now was only 500 miles away, and

Hitler agreed it was the priority target. It was a strategic blunder.

But it was a frightening threat to Britain. Egypt, key to the Middle East, was vital to the continuation of their war. And by then, it also was vital to American interests.

With the loss of Guam and Wake Islands in the Pacific to the Japanese, supply routes from America to the Far East had swung around the globe in the other direction. They crossed the South Atlantic, and moved through northern Africa and the Middle East to India. Those lines had to be kept open to supply the Burma and China theaters, and to send weapons and food to the Russians.

Churchill had requested more aid, and particularly more air aid, for the British forces in the Middle East. The RAF, Middle East, was doing a superlative job; but it needed reinforcements. Faced with the need to keep its own lines open, and the British request for more air power, the USAAF had only two alternates. One was to reinforce the RAF in the theater with a

With 9,816 built, the B-25 was by a short head the most important of all the AAF medium bombers, and certainly the most versatile and widely used. By 1944 the most numerous model in the European theatre was the well-defended B-25J, two of which, without nose package guns, are seen winging their way to attack Kesselring's forces in Italy in 1944. Their unit was the 321st BG of the 12th AF.

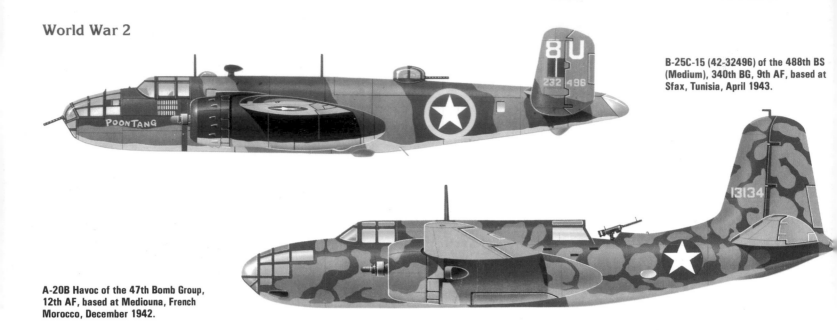

B-25C-15 (42-32496) of the 488th BS (Medium), 340th BG, 9th AF, based at Sfax, Tunisia, April 1943.

A-20B Havoc of the 47th Bomb Group, 12th AF, based at Mediouna, French Morocco, December 1942.

Excellent bombing off Bizerte (Bizerta), Tunisia, in late 1942. A direct hit has exploded a supply vessel that was obviously carrying munitions. Fragments are falling over a wide area.

transfusion of aircraft and supplies, at the expense of USAAF needs in Europe. The other was to send in USAAF combat units. Both were costly endeavors. USAAF chose the latter, and planned an orderly schedule for the build-up, trying to match the short-term needs of the Middle East with the requirements for supporting *Torch* and the pre-invasion air operations over Europe.

The first reinforcements to arrive in the Middle East were unexpected. The HALPRO detachment staged through Egypt for its Ploesti raid June 11. The crews that got their B-24Ds back to Fayid stayed there waiting for orders. Then Maj. Gen. Lewis H. Brereton

flew in from India with a detachment of nine beat-up B-17s from the 9th Bombardment Squadron, all that 10AF could spare from its meagre strength. On June 28, Brereton activated the United States Army Middle East Air Forces (USAMEAF) with his own and Halverson's detachments as the nucleus.

The fighters and medium bombers of USAMEAF were attached to the RAF's Western Desert Air Force. Commanded by Air Vice Marshal Sir Arthur Coningham, WDAF became one model of air-ground co-operation for the USAAF to emulate.

WDAF and the British Eighth Army had joint head-quarters on the premise that air and ground strike

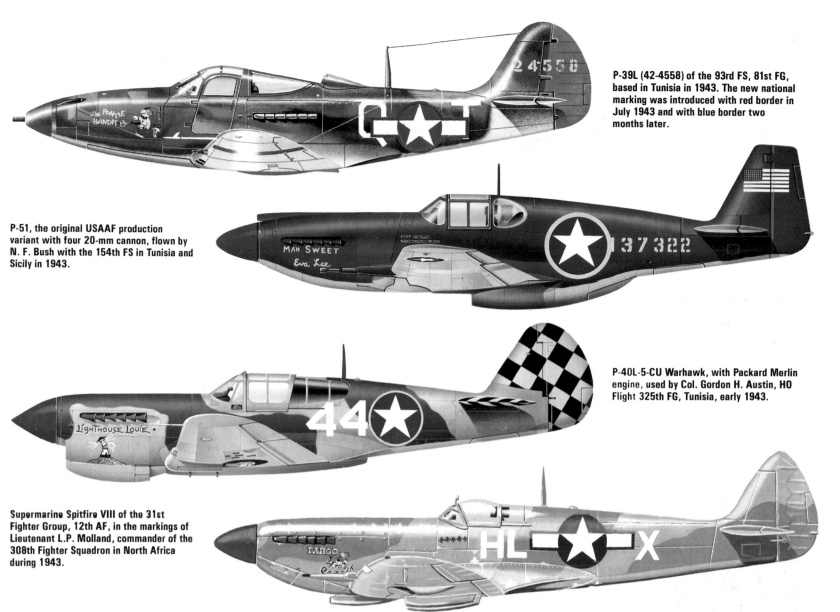

P-39L (42-4558) of the 93rd FS, 81st FG, based in Tunisia in 1943. The new national marking was introduced with red border in July 1943 and with blue border two months later.

P-51, the original USAAF production variant with four 20-mm cannon, flown by N. F. Bush with the 154th FS in Tunisia and Sicily in 1943.

P-40L-5-CU Warhawk, with Packard Merlin engine, used by Col. Gordon H. Austin, HO Flight 325th FG, Tunisia, early 1943.

Supermarine Spitfire VIII of the 31st Fighter Group, 12th AF, in the markings of Lieutenant L.P. Molland, commander of the 308th Fighter Squadron in North Africa during 1943.

forces were co-equal. It was a professional and personal relationship between airmen and soldiers that made the system work; each strove to understand the others' problems, and to do what could be done to ease them.

WDAF was a mobile, tactical air force, with its own radar controllers, a detachment of engineers to build and maintain airfields, and anti-aircraft and light armored cars to defend those fields. Its main strength was a combination of fighters and light bombers— Hurricanes, Spitfires, and some Gladiators from Britain, and American-built Boston and Maryland light bombers. The fighters often doubled as fighter-bombers.

The British retreat stopped at El Alamein, deep inside Egypt, at a gap between the sea and the Qattara Depression, an impassible area of deep canyons with steep walls. British morale was boosted by a leadership change: Gen. Bernard Montgomery was placed in command of the Eighth Army. They held, and then dug in to prepare for a counter-attack.

Coningham sent his pilots out on an air offensive to gain air superiority in the skies over Montgomery's army. The RAF had 813 aircraft in commission, and USAMEAF contributed another 130. Against those 943 Allied planes were ranged just over 600 German and Italian combat aircraft with an estimated service-ability rate of 50%. They had no spare parts, no replacement items for their operations; heavy Allied air strikes against Axis supply lines had seen to that.

Montgomery ordered the Eighth to the attack October 23, and by November 5, Rommel's drive had been turned back. Air support had been with Mont-gomery all the way, pounding the Germans and bombing their supply ships in the Mediterranean.

After El Alamein, Torch

Torch was planned as an Allied, largely American, invasion of North Africa at three points: Casablanca, in French Morocco, and Oran and Algiers, in Algeria. It was a co-ordinated attack to remove the threat of German and Italian ground forces in North Africa. The American landings on the west coast would move toward the British Eighth Army in the East, and trap

Just 20 of the 527 P-38F Lightning twin-engined fighters were completed as F-4A unarmed reconnaissance aircraft, and two of these rare birds are seen here in Tunisia in January 1943. Serving with the 90th Photo Reconnaissance Wing, they were among the first Lightnings to operate in the European theatre.

B-25C-20 of the 81st BS (Medium), 12th BG, 12th AF, operating from Gerbini, Sicily, in August 1943.

Facing page: Vertical shot of Messina, Sicily, on May 8, 1943, during an attack by B-17s of the 15th AF. The B-17F pictured belongs to the 414th Bomb Squadron, 97th Bomb Group.

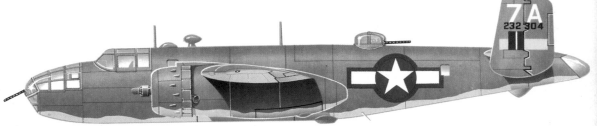

B-25C-10 of the 487th BS (Medium), 340th Bg, 12th AF, operating from Catania, Sicily, in September 1943.

Below right: During World War 2 a very small number of combat units were manned by black flight personnel, one being the 332nd Fighter Group of the 15th AF. Here the CO of one of the 332nd squadrons, Capt. Andrew D. Turner (left) post-flights with "Lucky" Lester whose P-51B is seen behind.

Below: "Desert Warrior" was an exceptional B-25 whose crew was made up of representatives from each of the four squadrons of Col. Ed Backus' "Earthquakers" group, plus (on this occasion) a Canadian radio operator. Its battle record fills the left side of the nose.

the enemy in the middle.

Primary air support was the responsibility of the newly-established 12AF, cut from the heart of 8AF strength. Gen. Doolittle assumed command September 23, 1942, and within a few days the first combat units began arriving. They were to consume more than half of the available strength of 8AF, and a quarter of its combat-experienced units.

The D-day landings November 8 were essentially unopposed, although the French did put up some resistance. There was little air action for 12AF; most of the support came from carrier-based fighters and bombers that ranged inland. The 31st Fighter Group, arriving by way of Gibraltar in its Spitfire Vs, was jumped by a half-dozen Vichy French Dewoitine D.520 fighters, and claimed three shot down in the brief combat that followed. The 60th Troop Carrier Group, its C-47s moving paratroopers to seize key airfields, lost a few of its planes to French fighters and French anti-aircraft.

Algiers fell on D-day, Oran on November 10, and Casablanca and the Vichy French forces surrendered November 11. But not Tunisia. The Germans had enough troops there to control the country, and so it had to be conquered by force.

The Germans reinforced their garrisons by ship and air, with as many as 50 Junkers Ju 52 transports landing each day at Bizerta. They based their fighters along the east coast of Tunisia, and sent them and bombers from Sicily and Sardinia against American and British ground forces. By mid-December the Allied drive had stalled; the winter rains had arrived and Tunisian mud brought air and ground operations to a halt.

Montgomery continued to move west, enjoying better weather. Tripoli fell January 23, 1943, and released bombers from close support tasks to concentrate on the ports that were the key to the African campaign: Naples, Messina, and Palermo.

The Casablanca Conference, held January 14 between Roosevelt and Churchill, produced a new command structure in the theater. As part of it, two air strike forces were created: Northwest African Air Forces (NAAF), including 12AF, WDAF, and the RAF's Eastern Air Command, and Middle East Air Forces (MEAF), including the RAF, Middle East, and 9AF.

The development of tactical air power happened, day by day, as the airmen learned how to work with ground troops. North Africa offered a wide opportunity to learn tactics. There was shipping to strike, armored columns to bomb and strafe, troop concentrations and supply dumps to bomb. While the bomber forces were hammering ports and shipping, the fighters and light bombers were working down close to the sands, hitting anything that moved or shot back.

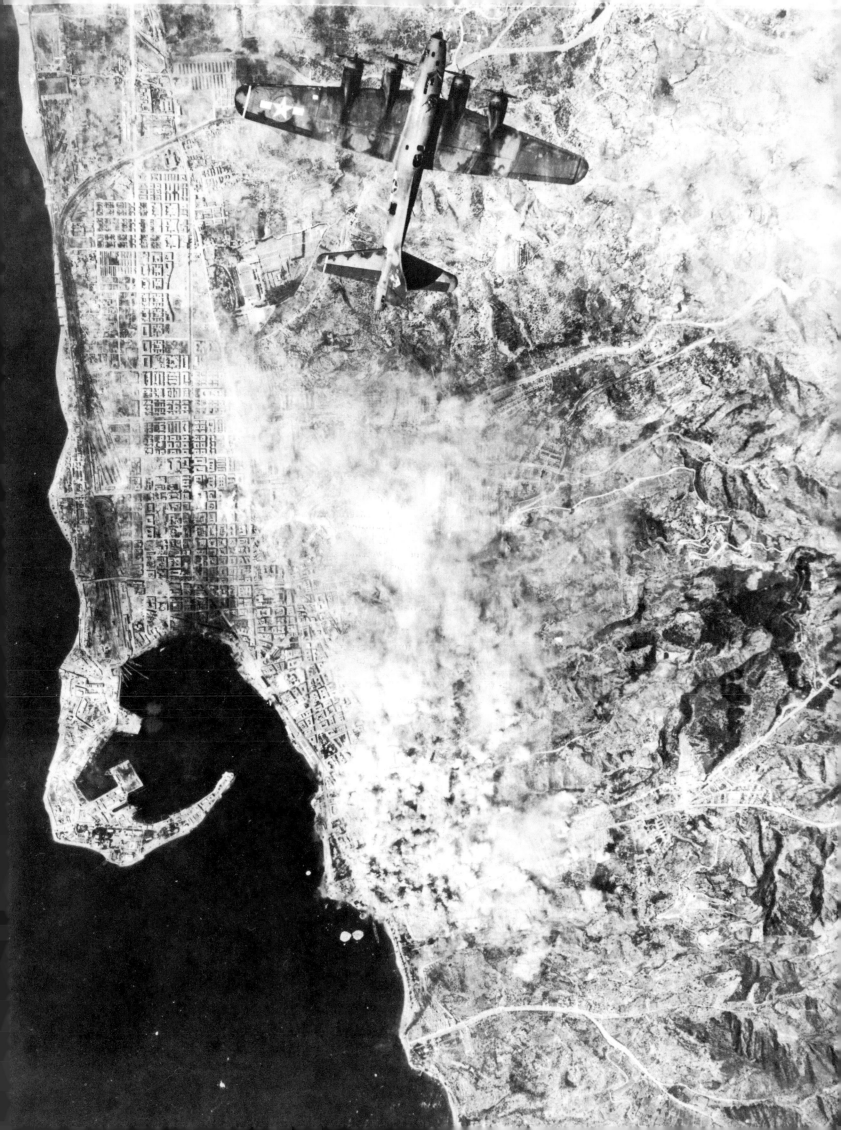

B-25Js of the 12th AF at an Italian base in 1944. The aircraft in the foreground had flown 103 missions at that time.

altitude to drop their bombs on the German positions. The offensive was broken, and the Germans continued their retreat toward Cap Bon, their only remaining escape route. Tactical air power chased them, and sunk their ships and flamed their supply aircraft on the runs from Italy.

American fighter units, now on the east coast of Tunis around Sousse, monitored all the air and sea convoys to Cap Bon by radar. Like wolves, they harried the slow-moving ships and planes. On April 18, 1943, they caught a large air convoy of tri-motored Ju 52s on their way back to Italy after having unloaded in Bizerta. Four squadrons of P-40s from the 57th Fighter Group, 9AF, with a top cover of Spitfires, ripped into them. When the "Palm Sunday Massacre" was over, about 60 transports and 16 of their escort of Bf 109 and Bf 110 fighters had been downed. Four days later, RAF Spitfires and South African Air Force P-40s caught another convoy, this time of giant Messerschmitt Me 323 six-engined transports, and shot down 21 of them. It was the end of German attempts to fly in supplies by day.

The heavy bombers kept up a relentless attack against ports and airfields, reducing docks and loading cranes to tangled steel and iron, and cratering the runways and flattening airport buildings. On April 10, a force of 24 B-17s found and sank the Italian heavy cruiser *Trieste*. She was anchored in a cove at La Maddalena, Sardinia, protected from torpedo attack by an anti-submarine net. But she had no protection from bombs dropping from 19,000 feet. She was hit, burned and sank.

The heavy bombers were in a type of war that gave no indication of the very real problems they would have later in Europe. The B-17 defenses were not yet fully probed and countered by the German fighters that attacked them on the few occasions when the Luftwaffe intercepted a raid. During the entire North African campaign, only 24 B-17s were lost in combat, and only eight of these were charged to Italian or German fighters. The rest were accounted for by flak or "other causes".

Rommel retreated westward for almost three months, moving his battered force over more than 1,700 miles. Near the end, he and his staff were ordered home; his men were faced by both British and Americans, and were penned on Cap Bon peninsula just across the straits from Sicily and freedom.

It was denied. The Sicilian coast had been bombed, its ferries destroyed, and its ships were sunk or burned. Rommel's proud Afrika Korps began surrendering in early May, in small numbers first and then in hordes. Hundreds of thousands had been lost to death or injuries during the adventure, and about 250,000 were left to capitulate.

The long and bitter campaign—almost three years of it—had finally ended. Mussolini's dream of a new Roman Empire stretching across the North African coast was dead, and Hitler's armies had been beaten there and before Stalingrad.

From the viewpoint of history, *Torch* was a diversion for the USAAF. It cut the heart out of 8AF combat strength, forcing a postponement of *Bolero* and the invasion of Europe. Yet the alternate was impossible.

USAAF participation in *Torch* paid off. In short time and at very low cost in lives and planes, USAAF learned the lessons of close air support, of interdiction, and of ground-air cooperation. In short, they learned about tactical air power. The instructors were the Royal Air Force, Middle East, and particularly the WDAF under Coningham.

Today, when you listen to a briefing about the USAF's Tactical Air Command, the briefing officer starts by describing the roots of TAC philosophy. The experience in North Africa heads the list.

The continual hard usage of the fighters produced new problems that the P-38 force was the first to feel. The Lightnings had been pulled from 8AF and sent to North Africa because they had range, endurance and versatility. But they were kept in the air by expedients; cannibalization was not uncommon, and squadron strengths were below the authorized level. When "Hap" Arnold heard about the situation at the Casablanca Conference, he ordered the last available units of Lockheed P-38s, held in reserve by 8AF, to come down to the fight.

It was tiring and dangerous work, flying belly to the sand. But that task, combined with the methodical advances of the infantry, gradually forced the Germans north in Tunisia. They mounted one last major offensive against raw American troops dug in at Kasserine Pass. It panicked them, and weakened the British and Free French positions on the line of battle. It threatened the airfields at forward operating locations; they were abandoned with the loss of stored gasoline, supplies and some disabled aircraft, all of which were burned or destroyed to keep them out of German hands.

Everything with wings was thrown into the fray at the Kasserine Pass. Heavy bombers howled by at low

Sunny Italy was a joke to over a million alternately frozen and drenched infantry in 1943, and the Allied air forces fared little better. This 15th AF B-24D is needing almost full power to taxi through floodwater.

Across the Strait of Sicily

Pantelleria was one of a group of fortified islands held by the Italians in the Straits of Sicily. Oval in shape, rocky and hilly, it was called the "Italian Gibraltar". It was something less, although formidable enough to require reduction before the planned invasion of Sicily could go forward.

Its airfield could handle four-engined bombers. Its underground, 1,100-foot long hangar could support a force estimated at 80 fighters. There were more than 100 gun emplacements around the island, and a garrison of about 10,000.

Strategically, it dominated the strait, and could observe and influence the movements of ships and aircraft in the area.

NAAF was given the job of softening the island. About 1,000 operational Allied aircraft were available against about 1,300 Axis planes operational. But beginning May 8, the air battle went only one way.

Between that date and June 11, when British troops went ashore to receive the surrender, Allied aircraft flew 5,285 sorties; the fighter-bombers and bombers dropped 6,200 tons of bombs. The largest share of the work was shouldered by USAAF components in NAAF; they flew 83% of the sorties, dropped 80% of the bombs.

It was the first time that a surrender of a land area had been forced by air. The invasion only placed troops ashore for the formality of the signing. Then the Allies cleared the airfield and based the 33rd Fighter Group there to support the invasion of Sicily.

A triangular island kicked by the toe of the Italian boot at Messina, Sicily is barren and mountainous. Field Marshal Albert Kesselring had 300,000 troops to defend and hold the island. The Axis had 31 air bases on its rugged terrain, populated with a full force of operational aircraft and bolstered by additional forces based on mainland Italy. Perhaps 1,600 planes were available to Kesselring.

The pre-invasion objective was to destroy that air strength. During June, NAAF bombed the airfields, and destroyed about 1,000 aircraft. During the first ten

A-36 attack Mustang, with Allison engine, of the 27th FB Group on the Italian front, 1944. Note the 190 mission symbols.

P-51B of the 318th FS, 325th FG, 15th AF, on the Italian front in late 1944.

Major Herschel H. Green of the 15th AF poses on his P-51D in Italy.

Bombs away over Italy for a mixed group of B-26 Marauders of the 12th AF. Aircraft "90" is a B-26B-10 and the others B-26s, B-25s or B-50s, each carrying a full load of eight 500-pounders.

days of July, just prior to the invasion, they flew 3,000 combat sorties.

The assault on July 10, 1943 opened with large-scale airborne operations; the paratroopers of the 505th Parachute Infantry were carried to battle by Douglas C-47s of the 51st Wing, NAAF Troop Carrier Command. Tactical aircraft from NAAF were busy over the heads of the invasion fleet and ahead of the assault, flying 5,000 combat sorties during that phase. The Allies had seized and held air superiority; the Luftwaffe had evacuated what they had left to the mainland, and there was not a single serious air attack on the invaders.

Patton's Seventh Army and Montgomery's Eighth landed under air cover that was part of a model campaign. Before the landing, Allied air power had reduced enemy resistance, pounded his airfields, destroyed most of his aircraft, and cut his lines of communications. During the assault, tactical aircraft patrolled above the fleet and protected the beachheads, while the transports moved the paratroopers to their landing zones. Then the task turned to support of the invasion, bombing and strafing ahead of the troops, and flying interdiction missions to cut lines of communication and isolate the battle.

Sicily fell in 38 days. The beaten Germans had been harrassed every foot of the way back to the ferries and across the Strait of Messina into their mainland retreats.

Now, On to Rome!

Montgomery had led his Eighth Army into Italy and was working his way up through Calabria under heavy air cover. The Americans had planned a landing farther north, at Salerno, south of the Bay of Naples. Under the code name *Avalanche*, the U. S. launched the Fifth Army, commanded by Gen. Mark W. Clark, against Salerno and its German defenders.

On D-day, September 9, 1943, the Americans landed under heavy ground fire, but with little trouble from enemy air power. By September the Axis air strength had been sharply reduced by the NAAF tactical forces. The once-aggressive Luftwaffe was a shadow of its former power. Captured German documents showed later that only 82 fighter and 26 attack sorties were mounted that day by the Luftwaffe.

But German ground troops made Salerno a fierce fight, and by September 14 were so much in charge that Clark asked the Navy to consider withdrawal plans. That day, and the days before it, every available combat plane was in the sky above Salerno, pounding German artillery, strafing vehicles, bombing armored troops. During the first days of the invasion, NAAF flew 3,400 sorties, and the bombers dropped a massive load that averaged 760 tons per square mile. On a more understandable level, that is about equal to dropping a single 1,000-pound bomb in the center of every backyard in a typical American suburban housing development.

By the next day, the German defense was broken. Troops started to withdraw towards Naples, Clark's men following. The Germans stopped long enough to destroy the docks, and to level and burn everything within a quarter-mile radius, and then moved out of Naples headed north. Clark's troops poured into the grateful city October 1.

To that point, the air war for Italy had been the testing ground for concepts of tactical air power that had been developed in North Africa. The landings in

This B-26B-40 was operating from Decimomannu, Sardinia (today a NATO base) in 1944, with the 444th BS, 320th BG. The formation on the facing page may well be from the same Bomb Group.

Sicily had set the pattern; the landing at Salerno refined it. The Allies had unequivocal air superiority; the Axis had been driven from the skies. The Germans could muster only 29 bombers in the Mediterranean theater by December, 1943.

On January 22, 1944, the Allies landed an invasion force on the resort beaches of Anzio and Nettuno, south of Rome. The purpose was to relieve pressure on the main ground offensive moving slowly toward Rome. The weather lifted long enough to permit strong air support for the Anzio assault.

A few days later, some sporadic German air activity began. But it was quickly beaten out of the skies. Allied fighters claimed 28 victories on January 27, and 21 on the following day. By the next morning, German air opposition was very weak, and on the 30th, no German planes were spotted over the beaches.

The Germans counter-attacked in early February, and followed with a major counter-offensive in mid-February that called out the heaviest Allied air action of the Italian campaign up to that time. The Germans almost broke through to the beachhead; air power helped blunt their drive.

Clearly the landings at Anzio and Nettuno were not doing what they had been planned to do: relieve pressure on the main Allied thrust north along the west coast of Italy.

The Allied drive north stalled at a killing ground around Cassino, strongpoint of the German Gustav Line across Italy from Gaeta on the Tyrrhenian Sea to Pescara on the Adriatic. On nearby Monte Cassino stood St. Benedict's abbey, source of the Benedictine Order and a most sacred spot to Catholicism. The Germans either were, or were not, using the heights and the abbey itself for observation, communications and sniping. The argument still is open, even though it became only of academic interest after the destruction of the abbey February 14, 1944.

A force of 254 bombers—B-17s from 15AF and B-25s and B-26s from 12AF—roared over the sacred site, dropped 576 tons of bombs, and smashed the heritage of centuries. The next day, P-40 fighter-bombers from 12AF worked over the ruins in an attempt to pave the way for ground troops on the advance. Again the next day, close support for the troops was flown by 12AF A-36 aircraft in additional sorties against the rubble.

Monte Cassino was in ruins. Only St. Benedict's cell and his tomb remained under the pulverized stones. And the advance was still stalled.

Military leaders had been nurturing a plan for a massive air assault heavy enough to break the stalemate at either Anzio or Cassino. Bad weather had held up such a strike, but it promised to clear around mid-March. Cassino was the chosen target.

Some airmen, notably Lt. Gen. Ira C. Eaker, commanding the recently organized Mediterranean Allied Air Forces (MAAF), argued unexpectedly against the big strike. They pointed out that such an assault could actually be a hindrance to forward movement of troops, especially armor. They were argued down.

The entire tactical force of 12AF was flung into the

battle order, along with almost 300 B-17s and B-24s from the 15AF. They dropped 1,000 tons of 1,000-lb. demolition bombs against Cassino. The blasts shattered every building, ripped the earth beneath and between them, blew bricks and stones and mortar and wood into a fine powder, and left a lunar landscape where the town had stood.

The infantry took over an hour to move into town through the rubble, and the Germans met them. Eight days later, the battle still unresolved and the air forces grounded by foul weather, the Allied ground forces

A stepped-up forward echelon of P-38J Lightnings of the 15th AF in Italy in late 1944. One of the quietest fighters of all time, the P-38 was pleasant and long-ranged, and a valued bomber and reconnaissance platform. Low rate of roll was a handicap in dogfighting.

Above: Among the final missions by the 12th AF fighter-bombers were strafing runs by P-47s along the roads to the Brenner Pass near Verona in 1945.

Right: There are few more difficult targets than a railroad bridge attacked at 90° to the tracks, but this bridge at Anastasia, Italy, was knocked out by one bomb run by B-26s.

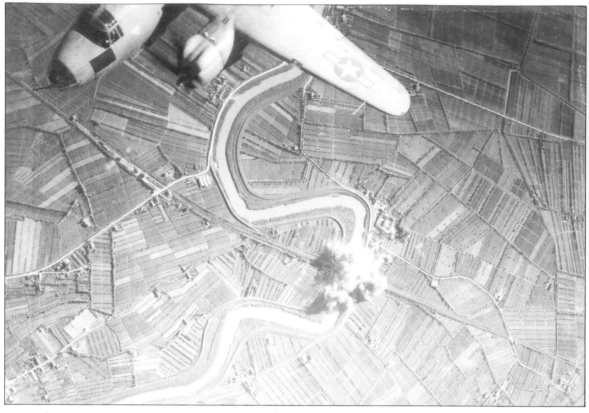

One of the classic air war pictures of all time, this records the death of a 15th AF B-24H hit by flak over northern Italy in the final year of the war. Getting out of a stricken B-24 was always difficult even with both wings intact; only two men made it from this one.

pulled back to regroup. Weather was the best Axis ally; "sunny Italy" was a hollow joke. Rain, mud and a raw winter slowed the advance to a crawl.

From September 1943 through all of 1944, flying weather was rarely good. Even Italy's usually beautiful spring and fall months were marred by long periods of unfavorable weather. Air operations often were cancelled. Once airborne, bombers often failed to find their targets under the thick cloud cover; fighters and bombers missed rendezvous points. And because war in Italy was a war that depended on air support, it hurt not to have it.

Strangling the German Forces

The major problem in Italy was the continuing stalemate of the ground war. Tenacious holding actions and determined counter-offensives marked the German front. The Allied drive had gone to ground south of Cassino and on the beaches at Anzio and Nettuno.

There appeared to be one useful way to help: Use air power to cut off the supplies flowing south to the defenses of the Gustav Line.

The spiny geography of Italy has forced the construction of its railways into constricted areas close to both coasts. There are crossovers from one side to the other, but they are lines that were routed through mountain passes, demanding many bridges, viaducts and tunnels. The railroad system was a tempting target, and had already received its share of attention from the heavy and medium bombers of 15AF and 12AF. But now there was a new air plan in the making, one that would build a bottleneck across Italy and then plug the bottle. No rail traffic would move south to the Gustav Line if it worked. It was appropriately named: Operation *Strangle*.

The front had stabilized at Anzio and Cassino, and was relatively quiet on both sides. The bad weather that had hampered air operations for so long showed signs of breaking. Tactical air was relieved of its obligations to support the ground fighting, and on March 19, 1944, went off on its special war against Italian railroads.

The purpose was obvious: draw two lines across Italy, from coast to coast, and stop all rail traffic between them. One line ran through Pisa to Rimini, and the other was south of Rome. Strategic, tactical and coastal air forces were turned loose, each with assigned missions.

There was a different concept to the attacks this time. When the fighting was in southern Italy, attacks on the marshalling yards were the best use of air power tactically, because most of the supplies headed for the battle area passed through only a few major yards. But central and northern Italy, the industrial heart of the country, had too many yards to keep knocked out of action.

Bombing statistics from earlier interdiction strikes against railroads showed that it took more than 400 tons of bombs to put the average yard out of action, but less than half that would destroy a bridge. Further, it was easier to lay track and repair yards than it was to rebuild or replace a bridge.

And every important rail line had them by the dozen, often in isolated regions and with little oppor-

Late-series P-47D of the 86th FS, 79th FG, based at Fano on the Italian coast south of Rimini, in February 1945.

tunity to bypass them either with temporary construction of another rail line, or with a road.

It was a new approach to the use of tactical air power in two ways. First, it used fighter-bombers extensively, and tested their abilities to prepare the way for a ground offensive. Second, previous interdiction strikes had been against a class of targets, such as bridges, or marshalling yards. Now the target was a transportation system, whole segments of railroads, with their yards, bridges, tunnels, maintenance and repair shops, and rolling stock. With that out of action, the fighter-bombers could turn to the roads; find and destroy the vehicles that the Germans would certainly use to replace their lost rail transportation. And hit coastal shipping, small effort though it was; it still moved some supplies.

Strangle kicked off March 19, 1944. Within five days the medium bomber force had cut every rail line that supplied the German front. They were kept cut until the end of the campaign. The XII Air Support Command flew more than 4,200 sorties against communications between April 1 and May 12, and the

Desert Air Force flew night interdiction attacks, using two squadrons each of their Douglas Bostons and Martin Baltimores.

By mid-April, 27 major railroad bridges had been dumped into the valleys below. Between Rome and Florence, all the main bridges had been cut well before the ground offensive began in mid-May.

Massive attacks by heavy bomber forces hit the rail yards of the north. On March 28, a combined force of about 400 B-17s and B-24s from 15AF bombed the marshalling yards at Verona and Mestre. The next day, they attended to yards at Bolzano, Turin and Milan. On April 7 they hit the Mestre yards again, and also the installations at Treviso, Bologna, and Ferrara. Bad weather slowed the pace, but on April 30, 500 heavies went out against several of the yards.

This was accomplished in the face of foul weather. The medium bombers had been grounded, or had their missions aborted by weather about half of the time. They managed to rack up 200 missions only because some crews flew multiple strikes on some days.

The Luftwaffe was hardly in evidence. A raid on the

A clutch of fragmentation bombs drop from a B-17G of the 15th AF over Kesselring's troops facing the 8th Army in Northern Italy in late 1944.

Republic P-47D

The massive Republic Thunderbolt, designed around a turbo-supercharged engine as an interceptor, found its true role as a long-ranging, hard-hitting ground attack aircraft. The type roved the low skies above German installations, bombing, rocketing and machine-gunning anything that looked even slightly unfriendly. More than 12,000 of the P-47D models were eventually built and, during their production, the clear-view hood was designed and introduced as a standard item. Their range at first suited them for the job of escorting Fortresses, Liberators, and the medium bombers on raids over the Continent; fitted with drop tanks, they could take the bombers close to Berlin, but not far enough for the deep penetration of German industrial bastions further south and east. "Rabbit" was one of the aircraft of the 527th Fighter Squadron, 86th Fighter Group, that fought its way north out of Africa through Sicily and Italy. It was a P-47D-25-RE, built at Republic's Farmingdale, New York, plant. The red-and-white tail striping was a features of 86th FG aircraft.

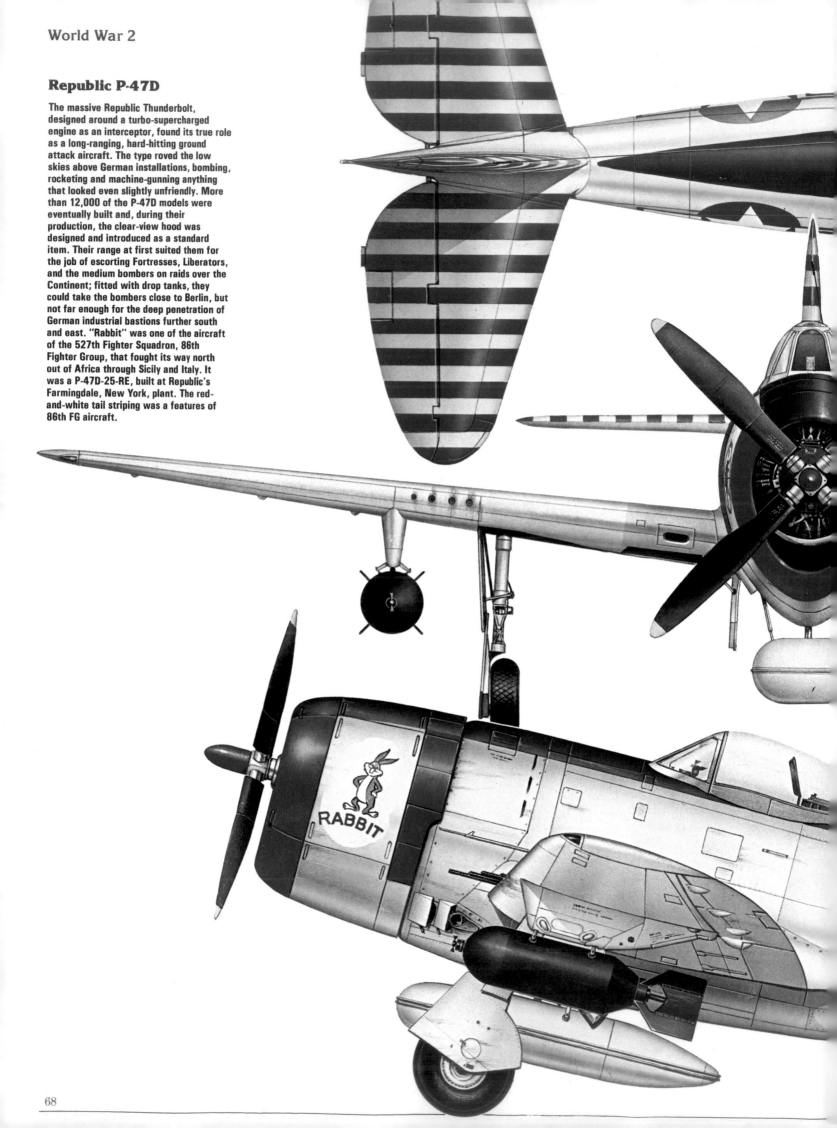

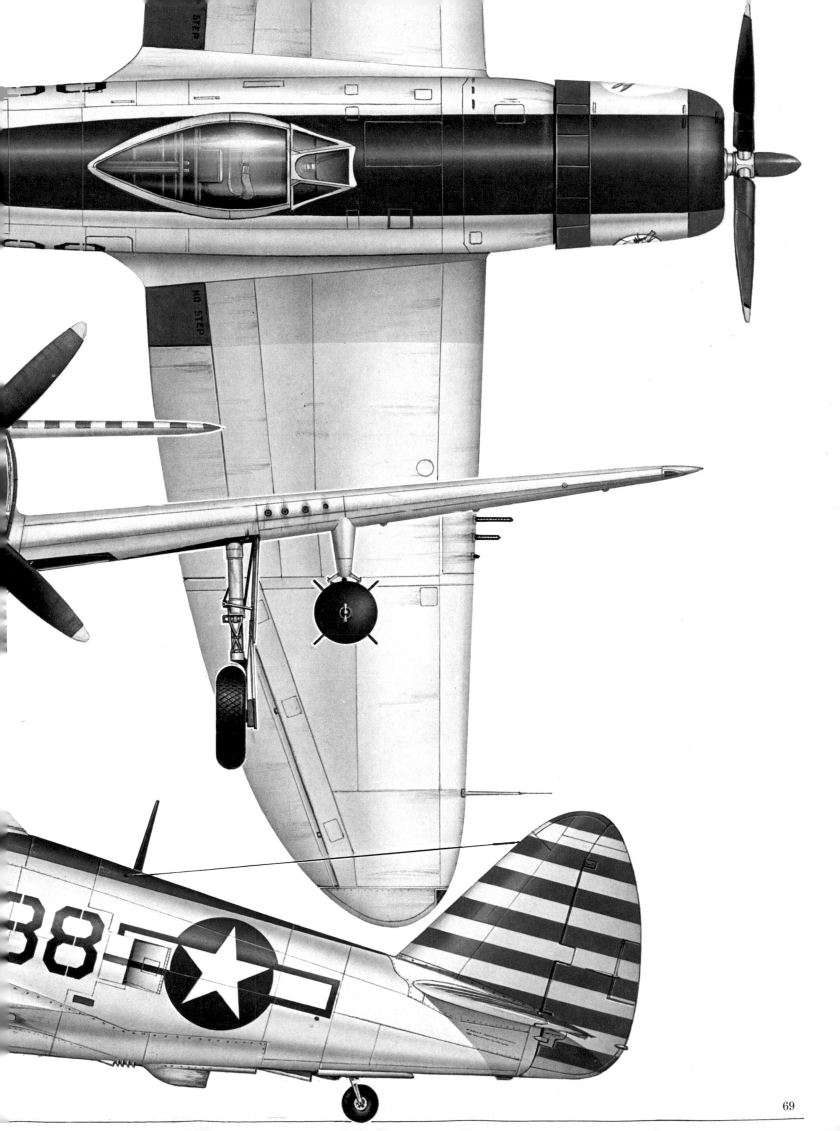

Left waist-gunner's view of the Alps and 14 of a force of 15th AF B-24H Liberators droning towards Germany, and flak.

A B-24 going down after being hit by flak over Munich. This was a 15th AF raid on Hitler's rail network.

day before *Strangle* was kicked off, flown by the heavies, had caught most of their aircraft on the ground. The Luftwaffe bases at Udine, Villaorba, and three other locations, were hit by 373 heavies carrying 43,000 twenty-pound fragmentation bombs.

When the results were in *Strangle* were judged a success. No rail traffic had ever moved closer than 50 miles to Rome. Collaboration between heavy and medium bombers, and fighter-bombers cut the bridges and kept them cut, and effectively closed 19 ports along the coasts.

The desperate Germans shifted from rail to motor transport, as expected, and their vehicles then were targets for every low-flying aircraft around. They sent supplies by coastal shipping, which was promptly strafed, bombed and sunk by Coastal Air Force. Then it was horse-drawn wagons and feet that finally moved the Germans north. It began as an orderly withdrawal; *Strangle* turned that retreat into a shambles and then into a rout.

On May 11, ground forces broke out on a major offensive that was intended to break the Gustav Line and end the Italian campaign. That day, 730 B-17s and B-24s dropped thousands of bombs on tactical targets in support of the offensive. The next day, 670 heavies pounded marshalling yards; on the next, 700 bombers repeated the performance.

On May 18, Cassino finally fell. On June 4, 1944, the Allies entered Rome. And there is where most histories leave the Italian campaign. The invasion of Normandy was about to steal the scene, and to attract the reporters and photographers. But the task of the soldiers and airmen was not over; they were to spend almost another year before the Germans surrendered in Italy.

In early September, air units attacked troop concentrations in the Po Valley. The Germans were building still another defense, the Gothic Line, and air power was called on to support the Allied drive to break it. By now it was routine. The Germans would form a strong defensive line, and the Allies would attack it. Allied air power would fly interdiction strikes against railroads and supply movements behind the German lines, and would bomb and strafe German troop concentrations and gun emplacements closer to

the front. Day after day the fight wore on, well into October.

MAAF celebrated Columbus Day that year with a massive strike of heavy bombers from 15AF. Seven hundred of them carpeted the marshalling yards at Bologna with high explosives, and then the weather took over for the rest of the month, grounding almost all air action in Italy.

By mid-November, the Germans were beginning to withdraw from northern Italy into the Balkans. Aircraft hit their trains and their trucks, cut railroads in the Brenner Pass to Austria, blasted Bologna time after time, dropped thousands of bombs in the Po Valley.

Finally in April 1945 the Germans had enough. They were in full retreat, harrassed along the way by MAAF fighters and fighter-bombers, by medium and heavy bombers that were relentless when the weather was right.

On April 15, Operation *Wowser* was dispatched. Every flyable heavy bomber in 15AF was sent to support the Fifth Army in its drive to clean the Germans out of Italy once and for all. B-17s and B-24s, 1,142 of them, escorted by P-38s and P-51s, attacked German troops on the highways out of Bologna, hit rail bridges, ammunition factories and dumps. It was the largest raid mounted by 15AF during the war. And although 15AF was primarily a strategic force, let it be noted that they flew *Wowser* against tactical targets and performed a classical mission of tactical air power.

From then on, all air operations were aimed at plugging the retreat gaps in front of the panic-stricken German soldiers. On April 29, 1945, the remaining Germans surrendered unconditionally, effective May 2. Six days later, the war in Europe was over. Hitler was dead, and victorious Allies met in drunken celebration at the Elbe River.

In all, an even dozen German generals surrendered their troops at one time or another in Italy. Eleven of them said that air power was chiefly responsible for their defeat.

The early lessons learned in the North African desert had paid off. Tactical air power had been forged in those wastes and tempered in the skies over Sicily and Italy. It had been a major component of Allied victory in the forgotten war.

Bomber Buildup

There was absolutely no doubt in their minds who'd win the war. Their fathers and uncles had landed in France in 1917 with the same certain knowledge and the same cocky attitude. The young pilots of the newly established Eighth Air Force bomber squadrons knew they'd win the war, and they knew exactly how they'd win it.

Their Flying Fortresses would bomb in broad daylight from high altitude, hitting the pickle barrel from 30,000 feet, and shooting down any Luftwaffe pilots foolish enough to tangle with a bomber bristling with .50-cal. machine guns.

Those untested crews reflected popular opinion back home, and a simplistic view of the air war against Germany that was held by their commanders, and even by most high-level brass in England and in Washington.

The success of their first mission against the railway yards at Rouen-Sotteville reinforced their opinions. Later missions further emphasized the ease with which the B-17s flew to the target, dropped their lethal loads, and flew home again. They were escorted part of the way to the target, and partway home, by RAF Spitfire squadrons, because they lacked their own escort fighters. But they'd gone to Abbeville and Amiens, Courtrai and Meaulte and Rotterdam, in eight missions with no losses, and even the skeptical RAF officers observing their operations seemed to be coming around to the American way of thinking.

From the dozen B-17s dispatched against Sotteville, their strength had grown to 37 on the second mission to those yeards. Two B-17s, their first combat losses, were shot down by German fighters on the September 6, 1942, mission against the Potez factory at Meaulte. They went back again October 2, with more than 400 escorting fighters, and this time got off loss-free.

It began to look relatively easy. The post-strike photos showed fair to good bomb patterns; losses were low, and the weather cooperated.

There appeared to be some truth in the bombast. But Air Marshal Arthur T. Harris, commanding the RAF's Bomber Command, was not convinced. He was inclined to believe his own experience.

The Royal Air Force had gone to war in 1939 with much the same attitude that the Americans brought to England in 1942. RAF bombers flew unescorted daylight raids, trusting to speed and defensive armament to fight off the Luftwaffe. Neither was adequate. The

Three Strategic Air Depots in England channeled the vast output of B-17 and B-24 bombers to the operational 8th AF Bomb Groups to make good attrition. This 1944 photograph shows the immense scale of the task. Within 48 hours all these B-17Gs probably wore the insignia of a recipient BG.

Probably the most famous U. S. fighter group in the ETO—only the 4th could rival it—the 56th FG was the original and outstanding exponent of the mighty Republic P-47, arriving with their P-47Cs in January 1943. This echelon comes from the group's 62nd FS.

Virtually every bomber in every theater had its own name, selected by the crew. Occasionally they picked a name already in use. This B-17F got in ahead of a B-26B of the 322nd BG which had to settle for "Idiot's Delight II".

Germans battered Bomber Command beyond its ability to recover rapidly. Daylight raids quickly gave way to night missions. In the first heavy night strike against Ruhr Valley targets, the 99 bombers dispatched came through with negligible losses. From then forward, Bomber Command struck at night.

The Luftwaffe countered. The Kammhuber Line, an in-depth defense, was established; it used radar tracking to guide interceptors to the RAF bomber stream. On one raid to the Ruhr, Bomber Command lost 21 percent of an attacking force. To add insult, a study of post-strike photographs of the raids showed that nine out of ten crews were dropping their bombs more than five miles from the targets.

By the end of 1941, the Luftwaffe had regained air superiority at night over the Continent. Bomber Command's performance was disappointing, and Prime Minister Winston Churchill suggested they spend the coming winter months gathering strength for a spring offensive.

In March 1942, Bomber Command bounced back with a devastating strike against the Renault factories at Billancourt, near Paris. The plant was out of production for four months, and the Wehrmacht lost deliveries equivalent to the tank and transport requirements of five fully motorized divisions.

Air Marshal Harris, commander since February, was responsible for the revitalization. He also was responsible for what came to be called the "thousand-plane" raids. By drawing in every operational aircraft and crew, including some in training units, Bomber Command was able to send 1,046 aircraft to Cologne on the night of May 30, 1942. They dropped 1,455 tons, and left the city burning fiercely, with more than 45,000 homeless and 250 factories destroyed.

The second 1,000-plane mission sent 956 bombers against Essen. They did little damage to the city, and none at all to the Krupp works, the primary target. The third such mission was mounted against Bremen; 904 bombers dropped on its industrial heart, severely damaging one of the Focke-Wulf factories. Those three missions were the only giant raids for a while; Bomber Command's strength would permit no more on that scale. But a large force still could be mustered, as on the night of July 30, when the RAF sent 630 bombers against targets in Düsseldorf.

So it was that before the USAAF had dropped a single bomb on a European target, the Royal Air Force was consistently sending a force of several hundred bombers against major industrial cities. Harris was demonstrating his concept of strategic bombing. It had to be done at night, by large numbers of bombers, with cities as targets, and with the simplistic goal of burning the Germans out of their homes and, not incidentally, killing as many as possible.

It was a doctrine on a collision course with American plans for the employment of their bombers.

Experiment in Doctrine

The mission assigned to the Eighth Air Force and its VIII Bomber Command was experimental. The command was told to destroy carefully selected targets. The missions were to determine the bombers' ability to hit pinpoint targets in daylight, to defend against fighter attacks, and to evade anti-aircraft fire. Underneath the boasts, there were some doubts about the doctrine, held by others than Air Marshal Harris.

The first shock came on October 9, on a mission against steel, locomotive and freight-car works at Lille, in France. Eighth AF dispatched a mix of 107 B-17s and B-24s, but only 69 of them reached and bombed the primary target. Three B-17s and one B-24 were lost; bomber gunners claimed 56 Luftwaffe fighters shot down. But only nine bombs fell within 500 yards of the aiming point, and the Luftwaffe actually lost two planes.

The cockiness began to fade. Europe's historically bad weather cancelled eleven missions on the twelve days after the Lille raid. The planned invasion of North Africa (*Torch*) took one-third of Eighth AF strength to another theater. The less-experienced crews left behind were sent on a series of fruitless attacks against the nearly impregnable German U-boat pens. To top it all, the Luftwaffe had analyzed the bomber defenses and found the weak spot: the nose. Now, German fighters slashed into the bombers in head-on attacks, and the losses began to rise.

By the end of 1942, the Eighth's offensive had slowed to a near-halt. Only about two dozen missions had been flown since their first, more than four months earlier, and they had yet to make their first drop on a target within German boundaries.

This also annoyed Churchill. He thought it better if the USAAF would join the RAF in night bombing, which by then was producing good results. But Gen. Eaker convinced the Prime Minister otherwise, when the two met at the strategic Casablanca Conference in January 1943. Eaker said that the RAF by night and the USAAF by day could " . . . bomb the devils around the clock." Churchill liked the phraseology as much as the idea, and changed his mind about the best use of the USAAF.

The concept of a combined bomber offensive against Germany, flown by both the RAF and the USAAF, was endorsed during the conference. Its goals were defined and the planning was begun. Details, including target selection and priorities, became the responsibility of a group of USAAF officers, primarily for two reasons. First, the RAF already was fully occupied with its own version of a bomber offensive. Second, much of the plan centered on the buildup of the USAAF bombing force and its best employment in the combined operation.

The plan was evolved, reviewed, changed and finally approved by the Combined Chiefs of Staff, to take effect June 10, 1943. It was given the code name of *Pointblank*.

On January 27, 1943, VIII Bomber Command sent 91 bombers on the first American mission against a German target. But only 58 aircraft bombed the submarine construction yards at Wilhelmshaven. It was a poor show; and three bombers were lost.

Up to this time, American bombing technique had been static; but the next few months saw a development of tactics and equipment that led to a major improvement in the effectiveness of the force.

The B-17s and B-24s had been bombing in elements of three aircraft, until crews discovered the defensive advantage of grouping a pair of these elements. This squadron formation evolved into a combat box, a group of three squadrons stacked in space in a way to give the best forward fields of fire to the top and bottom turrets.

The 1st Bombardment Wing, under Brig. Gen. Lawrence S. Kuter, carried it one step further and derived the combat wing, consisting of two or three combat boxes, each box being made up of aircraft from a single bomb group. That seemingly random scattering in space of up to 54 bombers became the maximum defensive formation and a standard for the command. It was later to be modified as conditions dictated: opened out, when flak was the primary enemy; bunched together even tighter when the Luftwaffe threatened.

Bombing was a cooperative effort between bombardier and pilot, the former calling out course corrections to the pilot, who held altitude and airspeed as nearly constant as possible. The famed Norden bombsight was an analog computer that solved the geometry of bomb ballistics with cranked-in data for airspeed, altitude, drift and heading. Human instruction and reaction time, fraught with possibilities for mistakes, linked bombsight and flight path.

Early in 1943, a new bombing aid arrived in the European theater. AFCE (Automatic Flight Control Equipment) linked bombsight and autopilot; with it, the bombardier actually flew the airplane during the bomb run, directing its course by adjustments to the bombsight, and eliminating a human source of confusion and error.

Also early in 1943, some of the bomb groups tried a technique they believed would improve the bomb pattern. They put their best bombardier in the lead aircraft of the combat box; when he toggled his switches for the drop, so did every other bombardier in the formation. The result was a near-simultaneous drop and a tight bomb pattern. If the lead bombardier was really good, the results of the drop were extremely satisfying.

The first time all these came together was on the

Behind the long and courageous day missions of the VIII Bomber Command were millions of man-hours of toil in the night. Much of this was devoted to aircraft and engine maintenance, but the sheer labour of loading the bombs was, by any standards, tremendous. Here armorers prepare GP 500-pounders for a B-24 of an unidentified BG. The unique roll-top-desk bomb doors slid up the outside of the fuselage.

March 18 mission against the submarine construction yards in Vegesack in northwest Germany. Among those on the mission was the 305th Bomb Group, commanded by Col. Curtis E. LeMay, a tough, innovative and brave leader. LeMay had been at the forefront of these new ideas to improve defensive formations and bombing accuracy. The unit turned in an outstanding performance. Using AFCE and dropping on signal from the lead bombardier, they put more than three-quarters of their bombs within 1,000 feet of the target.

Increasing the Effort

The first VIII Bomber Command mission to dispatch more than 100 heavy bombers was sent against the Fock-Wulf factory at Bremen on April 17. Sixteen of the 115 B-17s dispatched were lost, further emphasizing the need for a long-range escort fighter. The bombers, it seemed, could not fight their way to the target and back with acceptable losses.

Republic P-47 Thunderbolt fighters, designed as interceptors but used for escort, had been in the theater since December 1942. But continuing engine and radio trouble had kept them out of action. They finally joined the May 4 raid to Antwerp, going all the way to the target and back with 65 heavy bombers. There were no losses.

May was another benchmark month. Four more heavy bomber groups became operational, and the available force took an upward leap. On May 14, more than 200 bombers were sent against targets at Kiel, Antwerp and Courtrai, and 198 bombed their primary targets.

The missions became riskier, as the crews were sent more often to bomb Germany's industry supporting the Luftwaffe. They still were making the trips without the long-range fighter escort—the P-47s had about the same combat radius as the "short-range" Spitfires—and with a force that included four bomber groups that had been operational only about one month.

By then, the Luftwaffe had developed a whole string of anti-bomber tactics. They had added cannon and rockets to their armament. They had tried air-to-air bombing of large formations, and had developed coordinated attacks, with determined waves of fighters vectored in by plan, or by a radar-guided flight controller on the ground. Their single-seat fighters had been augmented by two-seaters, with heavier armament and improved gunsights.

There was an abortive attempt by the USAAF to develop a long-rang escort fighter quickly: The YB-40, a B-17E modified to carry more guns, one pair in a "chin" turret under the nose. Twenty were built to prove the concept and most were sent to VIII Bomber Command. Few completed their missions; their performance was so inferior to that of the bombers because of their greatly increased weight. But their

One of the lesser-known types was the Vultee A-35B Vengeance, designed as a dive bomber but usually employed as a station 'hack' such as this example at an 8th AF base in England in 1944.

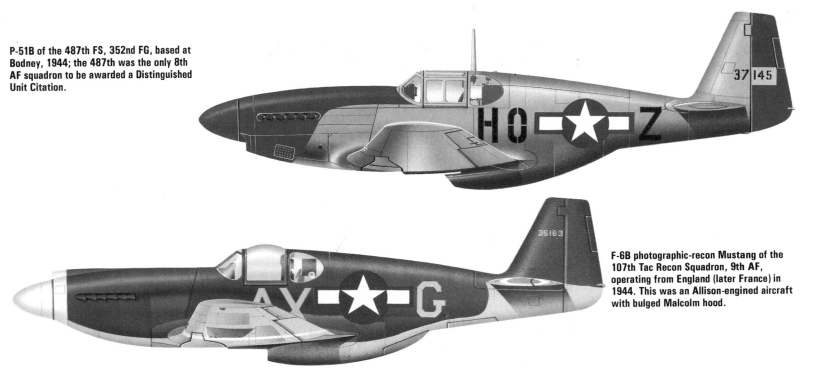

P-51B of the 487th FS, 352nd FG, based at Bodney, 1944; the 487th was the only 8th AF squadron to be awarded a Distinguished Unit Citation.

F-6B photographic-recon Mustang of the 107th Tac Recon Squadron, 9th AF, operating from England (later France) in 1944. This was an Allison-engined aircraft with bulged Malcolm hood.

chin turrets were kept and added to the standard B-17 line to produce the "G" model of that famed bomber.

The P-47 escort range was increased by the addition of a droppable fuel tank, one of the most valuable tactical innovations of the war. On July 28, they aided a force of more than 300 bombers; they met them 260 miles from the English coast, and shot down nine Luftwaffe fighters out of the estimated 60 that attacked. But the bombers' performance was miserable. Out of 302 dispatched, 95 bombed targets. The division that went to Kassel lost 22 out of 49 aircraft; the other groups, hitting Oschersleben and targets of opportunity, escaped loss.

That mission, the deepest penetration of Germany to date, was one of a group of six in one week. It included the USAAF's then-longest mission, a 1,900-mile round trip to targets in the Trondheim, Norway, area on July 24. Other targets were Hamburg and Kiel,

One of the unlucky medium bombers was ship 43-10129, a Douglas A-20J Havoc which burned after being hit by flak on a daylight mission in 1944; already much of the rudder and elevator fabric has gone. This model was a lead-ship with bombardier nose.

Boeing B-17F

If there was a Queen of the Skies over Europe during World War 2, it was the Boeing Flying Fortress, the product of equal parts of technology, an inflexible concept of strategic bombing, and a superb public relations campaign. She finally became effective as a bomber once her crews had developed the tactics to drop bombs on target and to survive the trips in and out. But as to her flight characteristics, there were differing and highly emotional opinions. And more than one crew threatened to strangle the designers who located the armor plates so that they only protected against attacks from the rear. "Fast Woman" was a B-17F-40-BO, built by Boeing in Seattle, and attached to the 303rd Bomb Group's 359th Bomb Squadron. She is shown as the Group's aircraft probably looked when they began their assaults on German targets late in January, 1943, flying from their base at Molesworth, in England's Huntingdonshire. The F model was greatly improved over earlier Forts; more power, more and better armament, more fuel and increased gross weight and payload made her a tough attacker.

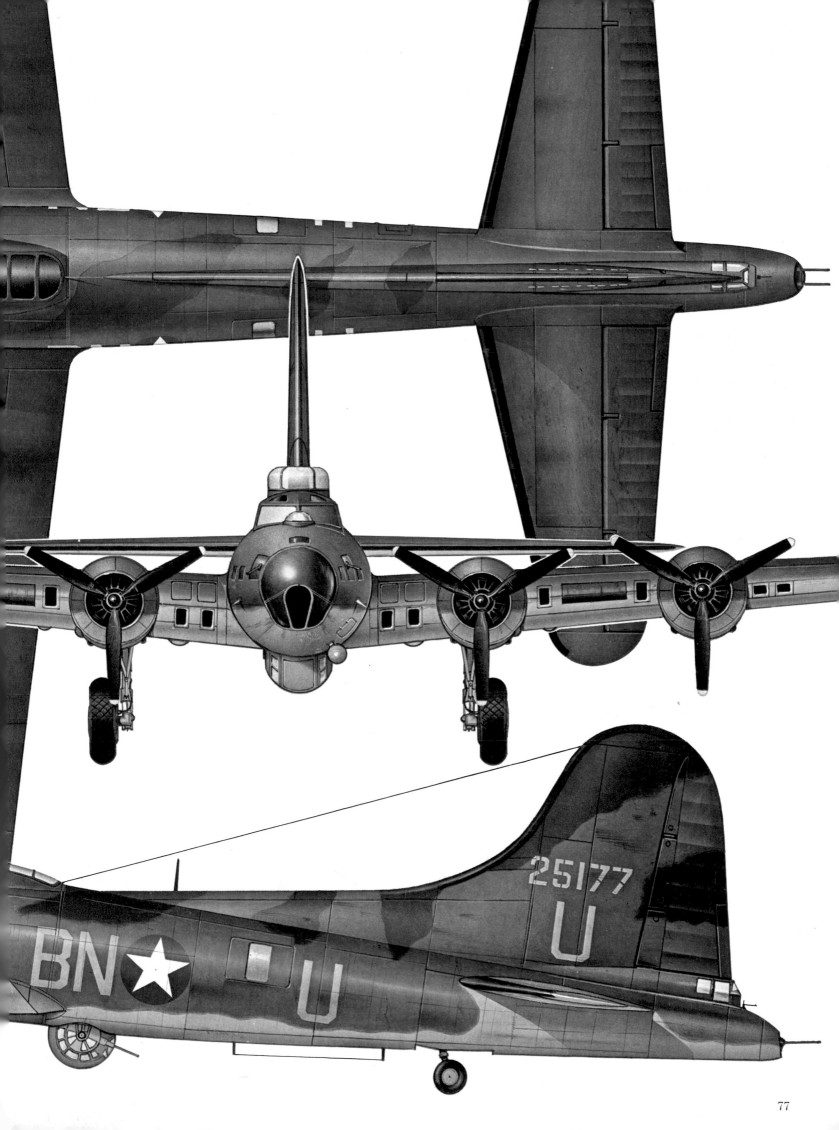

One of the very first B-17s to go into action with the VIII Bomber Command had its rudder, and parts of the tailplane (horizontal stabilizer) and rear fuselage, chewed to pieces by a propeller of a Fortress immediately astern. This happened during one of the early raids, almost certainly by the 97th Bomb Group on St. Omer, France, on October 2, 1942.

Over the notorious Merseburg oil refinery on November 2, 1944 this B-17G of the 486th BG had its entire nose torn off by heavy flak. The No. 2 engine was also blown off, and its propeller can be seen spinning away.

July 25; Hannover and Hamburg, July 26; Kiel and Warnemünde, July 29; and Kassel again, July 30.

They lost 88 bombers and their crews on those missions, and other crewmen killed and wounded. More airplanes were fit only for scrapping when they had reached home. The first four missions had dispatched more than 300 heavies each; the fifth sent out 249, and the sixth could muster only 186. Overall losses averaged above eight percent. The brief offensive against Germany ended after the second mission to Kassel.

Double Trouble

It was August 17, 1943, and Eighth Air Force was about to celebrate the first anniversary of its first bombing mission with a planned double strike. The selected targets were the ball-bearing factories at Schweinfurt, and the huge Messerschmitt complex at Regensburg, source of 200 Bf 109 fighters every month.

The plan involved precise timing, massive fighter escort support, diversionary sweeps, attacks against Luftwaffe bases along the route, and three B-17 task forces, totalling seven combat wings.

The 4th Bombardment Wing, commanded by the recently promoted Brig. Gen. LeMay, was to lead the attack. It had 146 B-17s available; they would draw the heaviest German opposition against their leading position, and so were assigned the larger force of escorts. Their target was the Messerschmitt factory. After bombing it, the wing was to continue south over the Alps and recover the aircraft at Telergma, about 100 miles inland from Bône, on the Mediterranean coast of Algeria.

Brig. Gen. Robert B. Williams commanded the 1st Bombardment Wing, assigned to strike the bearing factories of Schweinfurt. They were to leave ten minutes after LeMay's force, and were expected to find much less opposition. The Germans were expected to have tangled with the 4th BW and to be preoccupied with landing, refueling, and rearming.

The escorting force included 18 squadrons of P-47s from VIII Fighter Command, and 16 squadrons of RAF Spitfires. Martin B-26 Marauders from the VIII Air Support Command were detailed to hit Luftwaffe bases at Bryas-Sud and Poix in France; their cover would be more RAF Spitfires. RAF Hawker Typhoon fighter-bombers were sent against Poix also, and against the bases at Lille-Vendeville and Woensdrecht. Two forces of RAF Mitchell (North American B-25) medium bombers, escorted by Spitfires, were to create diversions by striking railway marshalling yards at Calais and Dunkirk.

LeMay's wing got off on schedule; weather delayed the departure of Williams' force for about five hours, a very costly delay. There was a mix-up in escort force rendezvous; LeMay later wrote that they "... never saw a P-47 or a Spitfire. Our fighter escort had black crosses on their wings!" But he was in the lead plane, a B-17F of the 96th Bomb Group, and may not have seen the escorts from that forward position. The planes reached their bombing altitudes between 17,000 and 20,000 feet about 20 minutes before they left the coast of England.

The 4th BW arrived at the target with 127 of its B-17s still in formation, and dumped their mixed loads of 500-lb. general purpose bombs and 250-lb. British incendiaries within 19 minutes. The 300 tons of bombs smothered the buildings, hitting every one, and

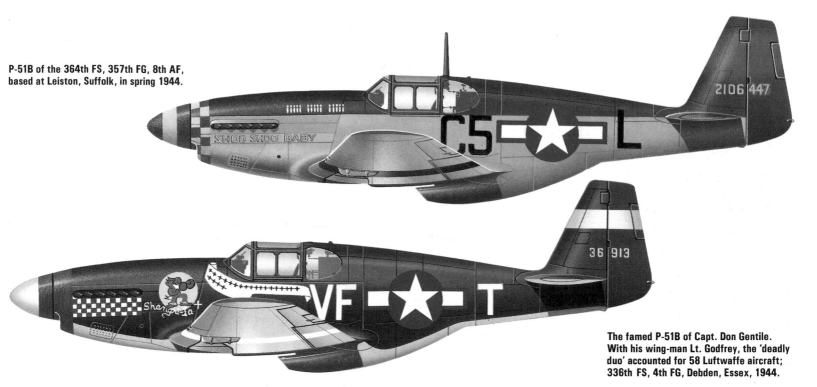

P-51B of the 364th FS, 357th FG, 8th AF, based at Leiston, Suffolk, in spring 1944.

The famed P-51B of Capt. Don Gentile. With his wing-man Lt. Godfrey, the 'deadly duo' accounted for 58 Luftwaffe aircraft; 336th FS, 4th FG, Debden, Essex, 1944.

nearly demolishing five of the six main structures.

The Regensburg raiders continued south, crossed the Alps, and the Mediterranean, and landed at Telergma to find a nearly deserted base with most of its support equipment gone. The plan to turn around there, carefully developed by LeMay on an earlier trip specifically for that purpose, had been completely forgotten in the moves of war in North Africa. So the crews turned to, aided by the few local technicians still on station, and readied their reduced fleet for the return trip to England.

The Schweinfurt force of 230 dispatched Fortresses fought their way to the target, got 183 B-17s over the primary, and dropped about 425 tons of mixed incendiaries, 500-lb. and 1,000-lb. GP bombs in about 12 minutes.

Then they turned toward England, picking up their escorts on the way back. But the fighters were badly outnumbered by an angry and well-directed Luftwaffe, and the toll was heavy.

LeMay's crews managed to get 85 bombers headed back home from North Africa a week later. They had been assigned a mission for the return flight: bomb the aerodrome at Merignac, near Bordeaux, because it was the base for the Luftwaffe's Fw 200 long-range bombers that preyed on Atlantic convoys. Besides, it was on the way back. But only 58 bombed the target; three were lost, and the rest of the force made it back to England.

Schweinfurt had been hit, but not destroyed; its production was off during the following weeks, but a shortfall of ball bearings never developed in the German industry. They had dispersed the industry, and also had developed other sources in neutral countries.

Regensburg, on the other hand, was badly hit. A postwar survey of the Messerschmitt complex conducted by a USAAF Air Technical Intelligence team, reported thus:

. . . up to the time of the first air raid on 17 August 1943, (Regensburg) was able to stay consistently ahead of its schedule. Through July 1943 it had produced 2545 Me-109's against 2089 scheduled. After this raid, and during the period of dispersal which followed it, the group was unable to get back to scheduled monthly production until January 1944.

The double raid had decimated four bomb groups. Sixty B-17s had been lost; more importantly, 600 crewmen were gone. Thirty planes were abandoned in North Africa because of battle damage; 28 of the planes that got home received major damage. The Luftwaffe had, in effect, put 100 bombers out of action, for a loss of 25 fighters. The raids were not followed up, either by the AAF or the RAF. Combat crews received no extra time off after their mauling, and their morale sank. It was time to fall back and dress the deep wounds inflicted by the German defenders.

Fortunately, the weather cooperated. On 18 of the 30 days of September, German targets were almost obscured by heavy cloud. On 12 of those days, the meterorologists predicted clearing conditions; twice it actually cleared. Only 11 missions were flown in September, and only one of them went to Germany. That was a shallow penetration against Emden, in the first tentative use of a radar bombing system by the VIII BC. All the rest of the targets were considered "easy".

This P-51B, "Shangri-La", was among the most famed fighters of the Second World War. It was the aircraft in which Capt Don S. Gentile (pronounced 'Jen-tilly"), seated on the wing, scored the last 16 of his 21 confirmed air victories in early 1944. Unit: 336th FS, 4th FG, based at Debden. Photo taken 10 April 1944.

Ploesti and the Oil Campaign

The heroism of the crews that flew the August 1, 1943, low-level raid against Ploesti shines so brilliantly that almost everything else about the mission is remembered only dimly in comparison.

That specific mission was a tactical failure. It did not knock the Romanian refineries out of action, and it did not set German fuel availability back. It was the second of 22 missions flown by the USAAF against Ploesti, by forces ranging in size from the dozen B-24Ds of the HALPRO detachment to an armada of 761 heavies from the Fifteenth Air Force that struck it June 23, 1944. It was hit from high-altitude flight, from one low-altitude assault, and from dive-bombing attacks by brave P-38 pilots.

In many ways, Ploesti was a typical strategic target. Its eight refineries processed about ten million tons of fuel annually, including the high-octane aviation gasoline that helped keep the Luftwaffe airborne.

Ploesti had been specified as a strategic target in January 1942. HALPRO struck it June 11 that year, six days after the U. S. had formally declared war against Romania. It lay at a great distance from USAAF bases. The Eighth AF was more than 1,300 miles away in England. The Northwest African Air Forces (NAAF) was based almost 1,000 miles to the south. It was a well-defended target; by the time of the later strikes, Ploesti was the third-best defended enemy area, ringed with anti-aircraft sites, concealed by smoke screens, and protected by German, Romanian and Bulgarian fighter units.

Five heavy bombardment groups, all equipped with the slim-winged, slab-sided Consolidated B-24s, were chosen for the mission (Code name: *Tidal Wave*). The 44th Bombardment Group (Heavy), Col. Leon Johnson's "Eight Balls", was a veteran Eighth AF unit. Along with the 93rd BG(H), Col. Edward Timberlake's command that called itself "Ted's Traveling Circus", the 44th was taken from Eighth AF strength and sent to Benghazi, on the eastern coast of the Gulf of Sidra, in Libya. Timberlake was grounded by higher headquarters after planning to lead his group on the raid. Lt. Col. Addison Baker took over.

From NAAF came Col. John Kane's 98th BG(H), the "Pyramiders", and Col. K. K. Compton's "Liberandos", the veteran 376th BG(H). The fifth group, Col. Jack Wood's 389th "Sky Scorpions", had been scheduled to go to the Eighth AF and was diverted to the Ploesti raiders.

For this strike, the planners decided to attack at low level, hoping to catch the defenders by surprise. The planes were modified: bombsights were replaced by a simple mechanical sight; top turrets were altered to fire straight ahead; extra .50-cal. machine guns were installed in the noses. Bomb bays held two auxiliary fuel tanks to raise the normal 2,480-gallon fuel supply to 3,100 gallons.

They trained across the desert wastes, roaring wingtip to wingtip a few feet above the sands, dropping dummy bombs on an outline of the refineries they had been briefed to attack. Instead of working with conventional vertical reconnaissance photos, the pilots memorized detailed, accurate sketches of their targets as they would look on the run-in from treetop level.

And at 7:00 AM local time on sunday morning, August 1, the lead Liberator lurched under the full power of its four engines, rumbled and rolled down the

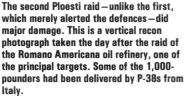

The second Ploesti raid—unlike the first, which merely alerted the defences—did major damage. This is a vertical recon photograph taken the day after the raid of the Romano Americana oil refinery, one of the principal targets. Some of the 1,000-pounders had been delivered by P-38s from Italy.

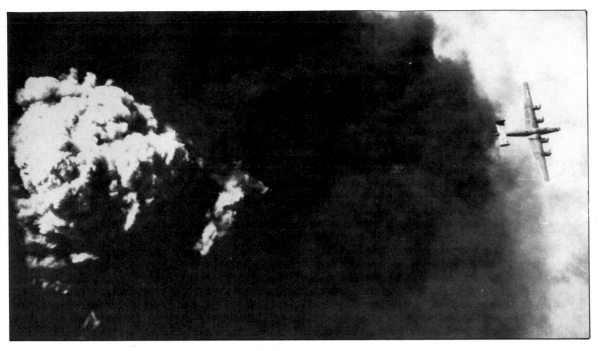

Strangely, the assault on Ploesti began with a modest raid that merely ensured the refineries would be heavily defended in future, and built up to a devastating crescendo in the last weeks before the area was captured by the Allies. One of the big raids in the last month Ploesti was in Axis hands took place on August 10, 1944, when this B-24 of the 15th AF's 451st BG was photographed over the target.

One of the fine photographs taken during the 761-bomber attack on Ploesti on June 23, 1944 shows this B-24H of the 718th BS, 449th BG over the burning Astro Romano refinery. Curiously the aircraft does not appear to be aligned with the target, but course-changes and wind could provide an answer.

runway and struggled into the air, followed by 176 more. One remained, a burning wreck following an engine failure on takeoff, a turnback, and a crash.

The force headed north for the island of Corfu, where they would turn in toward the northeast and Ploesti. It was an experienced group; many of the airmen had completed more than 25 missions, and the commanders were seasoned battle leaders. The Germans were waiting. One of their signal interception units near Athens, having cracked the code, had been reading Ninth Air Force message traffic. They intercepted a message from the Ploesti-bound bombers alerting friendly forces that a large number of B-24s had taken off from Libya. It was intended as a "Don't shoot!" warning to friendly anti-aircraft gunners, but it was one of several clues the Germans got that morning. The Athens station broadcast the news to all defense units, and the hunt was on.

The bombers encountered haze; in spite of the experienced crews in the formations, the mass of planes began to separate into its five groups. Different commanders flew different formations, had taught different power settings. Then they had to climb to 11,000 feet to clear the Pindus mountains of Albania; clouds were between the raiders and the mountains. Getting through again became a matter of group practice, and two stayed under the clouds for a while, and three went into them in the climb.

They came out of clouds and over the mountains, down the other side of the Pindus, over the Danube and the fertile plains beyond, letting down for their runs to the three initial points northwest of Ploesti. But the leading 376th made a wrong turn, mistaking another town for its IP; the 93rd, maintaining formation discipline and radio silence, followed. They flew directly toward Bucharest, and were nearly there before discovering the error. They swung back toward the northeast, now far off course, with the attack plan destroyed and with the defenders both alerted and informed of the target.

Only six B-24s from the 376th hit their assigned targets; the rest and the 93rd dropped on targets of opportunity, most of which had been assigned to other groups. The 44th and 98th made their bomb runs, one on each side of a railroad, and were hit hard by heavy and accurate fire from a German flak train that was steaming at full throttle along the rails. Kane and Johnson led their groups into an exploding target array, identified and bombed their own targets amidst the flames and blasts of erupting tanks of fuel. The

389th reached its target with all of its force intact, and destroyed the refinery at Campina with accurate bombing.

It was a Hell. The refinery tanks, bursting in spectacular gouts of flame, scorched the paint on the low-flying B-24s. Heavy smoke hid key reference points, concealed factory chimneys, power lines and other obstacles. Fighters harassed them. When they came off the target and headed for home, they were a badly mauled force.

Forty-one bombers had been lost in the action over the targets, and another 13 on the way in or out. About 42 percent of the refinery capacity was destroyed. It was far from enough; Ploesti had been running at about 60 percent of capacity for lack of crude oil. It took the Germans a few days to repair some pipes, open some valves, and get the fuel flowing again.

When this raid had been planned, it was believed that the low-level strike, followed by eight conventional bombings from high altitude, would put the refineries out of action. Not so. Ploesti continued to operate, untouched, for more than eight months following the August 1 strike. During that time, the USAAF and the RAF argued long and often bitterly about the best way to stop the Germans. The Americans wanted to bomb the oil production and storage system; the British wanted to hit transportation. When Eisenhower finally bought the transportation concept, the USAAF obediently went after railway marshalling yards, and some were in the Ploesti area. By strange coincidence, bombs often fell short or long of the yards, and hit refineries.

The Ploesti "yards" were hit April 5, 15, and 24, 1944; May 5, 6, 18 and 31; and June 6. But the deception was no longer necessary, if it ever was. The legitimate targets included oil, and Ploesti was being bombed for what it was.

On June 10, the strange strike force was 46 Lockheed P-38s from the 82nd Fighter Group, each bearing a single 1,000-pound bomb. Their escort was 48 P-38s of the 1st Fighter Group. They left their home base at Vicenzo, Italy, for a dive-bombing assault specifically aimed at the Romano Americano refinery. They did some damage, but lost 22 Lightnings. It was not tried again.

On June 23, 761 heavy bombers, the largest of the forces sent against the Romanian target, hit the refineries. On June 24, 377 went back again. On July 9 and 15, both raids were led by pathfinder planes, directing the bomb drop with the relatively new H2X system. More strikes followed: July 22, 28 and 31; August 10, 17, 18 and 19. On August 24, Ploesti shut down. The Russians captured the city August 30.

The striking forces dispatched almost 7,500 bombers against Ploesti over 26 months of attacks. The considerably lesser number that reached the target dropped 13,469 tons of explosives and incendiaries. Perhaps as many as 12 per cent of the bombs never detonated, a chronic problem that plagued both USAAF and RAF. Ploesti's death throes cost 350 heavy bombers.

Of bravery there was no lack on August 1, 1943, or on the missions that followed. All the participating bomb groups in *Tidal Wave* received Distinguished Unit Citations. Lt. Col. Baker, 2nd Lt. Lloyd Hughes, Maj. John Jerstad, Col. Johnson and Col. Kane received the Medal of Honor, the United States' highest award. And on the July 9, 1944, strike against the same durable target, 1st Lt. Donald Pucket earned his Medal of Honor. Baker, Hughes, Jerstad and Pucket died at Ploesti, four of the many.

Crewmen in the bomb groups called Ploesti the graveyard of the Fifteenth. It was; but it was also a symbol of living and individual heroism on a grand scale. If that is any comfort, these many years later, then remember Ploesti for that alone.

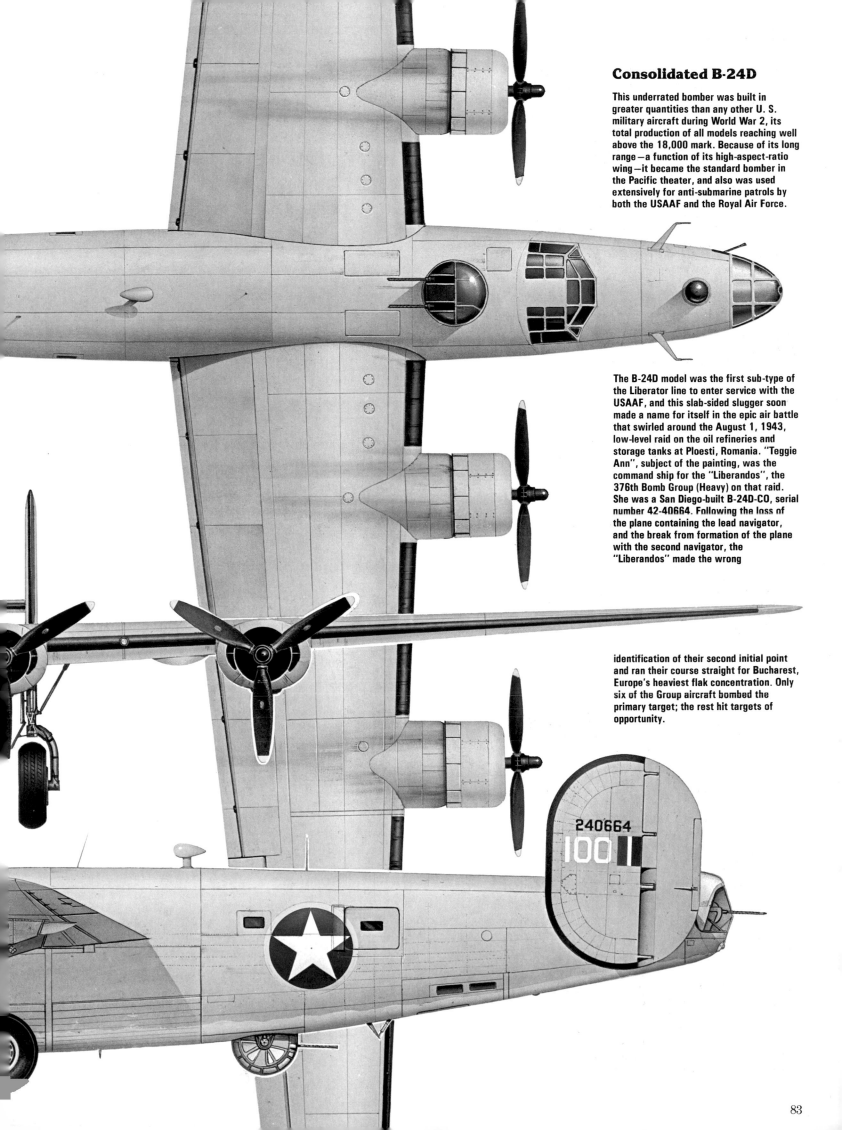

Consolidated B-24D

This underrated bomber was built in greater quantities than any other U. S. military aircraft during World War 2, its total production of all models reaching well above the 18,000 mark. Because of its long range — a function of its high-aspect-ratio wing — it became the standard bomber in the Pacific theater, and also was used extensively for anti-submarine patrols by both the USAAF and the Royal Air Force.

The B-24D model was the first sub-type of the Liberator line to enter service with the USAAF, and this slab-sided slugger soon made a name for itself in the epic air battle that swirled around the August 1, 1943, low-level raid on the oil refineries and storage tanks at Ploesti, Romania. "Teggie Ann", subject of the painting, was the command ship for the "Liberandos", the 376th Bomb Group (Heavy) on that raid. She was a San Diego-built B-24D-CO, serial number 42-40664. Following the loss of the plane containing the lead navigator, and the break from formation of the plane with the second navigator, the "Liberandos" made the wrong

identification of their second initial point and ran their course straight for Bucharest, Europe's heaviest flak concentration. Only six of the Group aircraft bombed the primary target; the rest hit targets of opportunity.

Lockheed P-38s being unloaded from a freighter at Queen's Dock, Liverpool, England, January 9th, 1943. They were to play an important role in escorting the bomber forces over long ranges.

An unusual combat-camera shot showing not only a Messerschmitt Bf 110G twin-engined fighter but also a friendly P-47D. Two P-47 pilots went for the Messerschmitt, and Maj. Everett Stewart (355FG) scored hits (as shown here) on the left wing. Lt. Coleman then cut in front and Stewart had to stop firing and watch Coleman finish the job.

October Crisis

In October, 1943, the Luftwaffe drove the USAAF out of German skies in a classical demonstration of the importance of seizing and holding air superiority. Four major raids were mounted by Eighth AF from October 8 and 14. The bombers fought their way through to the targets each time, but the cost was unacceptable. Within that single week, Eighth AF lost 158 B-17s and their crews. Many other bombers were mangled so badly they had to be scrapped. Coming less than two months after the heavy losses of the double mission, it was a hard blow and a decisive one.

The early October missions once again underscored the pressing need for long-range escort fighters that could go the distance with the bombers. The P-47, then predominant in escort flights, had a 300-mile operational radius when it was carrying droppable wing tanks. But the Luftwaffe knew just where the P-47s had to drop out of formation and return home on the deeper missions to targets that lay 400 or more miles inside the Reich. Within minutes, black-crossed fighters would swarm over the bomber formations.

The most notorious victims were the 100th Bomb Group, forever after called the "Bloody Hundredth". On the October 10 mission against Münster's railroads and waterways, they were low lead group of the combat box. German fighters stood off, lobbed rockets into the group, and broke it up. Then they picked off the Fortresses, one by one, downing an even dozen in seven minutes.

The Luftwaffe repeated the tactic against the second mission to Schweinfurt on October 16. Just after the P-47s turned back above Aachen, the Luftwaffe showed in force. The attackers lost 28 B-17s before they reached the target, but 229 of the 291 dispatched dropped their bombs in the most damaging of the 16 missions eventually flown against the ball-bearing factories.

Second Schweinfurt cost the Eighth 600 men and 60 bombers; 17 more B-17s were scrapped, and 121 were damaged and needed major work. The Germans paid 38 fighters for that particular victory; the bomber gunners claimed 186 destroyed.

It was the end of clear-weather deep penetrations of German air space for the rest of the year. The Luftwaffe now held undisputed control of the daylight skies over Germany.

But there was more to the October crisis. The continued bombing effort of the combined forces of the USAAF and the RAF was not decimating German aircraft deliveries, nor destroying the German morale. In retrospect, we know why.

First, German production capacity had been underestimated consistently, by as much as 30 percent in the case of fighters. Second, the claims of German aircraft destroyed by bomber gunners were consistently exaggerated. Third, the need for repeated attacks against a single target complex within a short time span was not appreciated.

The strength was available, it seemed; Eighth AF had a daily average of nearly 900 bombers and 650 crews on hand. But during September and October, the maximum number of planes over the targets never exceeded 360. And Germany was bombed only once in September.

Part of the problem was the weather, which often was responsible for cancelling planned strikes just before scheduled takeoff. Another reason was an operation codenamed *Starkey*, a combined British and American attack on the Pas de Calais area. It drew off

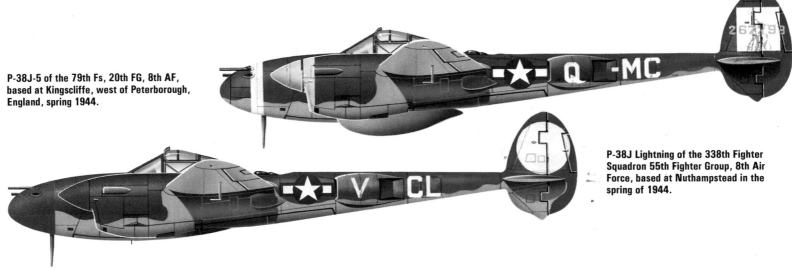

P-38J-5 of the 79th Fs, 20th FG, 8th AF, based at Kingscliffe, west of Peterborough, England, spring 1944.

P-38J Lightning of the 338th Fighter Squadron 55th Fighter Group, 8th Air Force, based at Nuthampstead in the spring of 1944.

683 sorties by VIII BC during August and September, almost one-third of the total flown during those months.

There seemed to be no way to increase markedly the number of sorties flown from England. There was a finite number of bases, with little or no room for more. Traffic control was becoming difficult; bomber forces were assembling over the North Sea to clear the skies over the bases. There were persuasive arguments for organizing another heavy bomber force in a less crowded area with better weather, and the planners seized upon Italy and the Foggia area as that locale. The Fifteenth Air Force was established November 1, 1943, drawing its heavy bomber units from the Twelfth Air Force, which then became a tactical air organization. The plan was to use Fifteenth AF to supplement the attacks by Eighth AF and the RAF, to put more weight of bombs on German targets. The Fifteenth AF bombers would hit from the southeast while Eighth AF crews sortied out of the northwest.

The beginner's luck still held for the USAAF. On the first mission flown by Fifteenth AF, one day after its establishment, the bombers pounded the Messerschmitt assembly plants at Wiener Neustadt. It was the most damaging of all the strikes against that target; production fell from 218 aircraft in October to 80 in November and 30 in December.

But Italian weather was not that good, either, and the weather over the targets didn't change because the attack came from a different direction. After that first raid, Fifteenth AF was called away to support the ground war in Italy; its first raid was its last for the year against German industry.

Combined Bomber Offensive

Pointblank had begun in the spring of 1943 as an offensive planned to reach a zenith just before the invasion of Europe. Its goal was to help make that invasion possible through the destruction of German military, industrial and economic strength, and the demoralization of the German people.

It was conceived as a closely knit operation, with coordinated RAF night raids and USAAF daylight missions. But the two comrades-in-arms had different ways of reaching their goals, and "round-the-clock" bombing of specific targets remained a catchy phrase rather than an ongoing program.

The intermediate objective of *Pointblank* was the defeat, preferably by destruction, of the Luftwaffe, the Reich's shield against the bomber forces. The German domination of the air demanded a serious offensive to break that grip. The plan was code-named *Argument*, but the campaign has been known more familiarly as "Big Week", since its primary need was for about one week of clear weather. In November 1943, when *Argument* was first detailed, that blue-sky spell was almost three months in the future.

Meantime, two developments were occuring that would upgrade the performance of the existing bomber forces. The first was the availability, at long last, of a long-range escort fighter that could go deep into Germany.

Lockheed's elegant P-38 had arrived in the theater in mid-October 1943, with the 55th Fighter Group. The twin-boomed fighters were able to carry a 75-gallon drop tank under each wing; so equipped, they could escort out to more than 500 miles, 200 miles further than the P-47 escorts could go. That radius covered most of the German strategic targets, but left little fuel for combat at the extreme limit of the escort. And, in a one-to-one dogfight with a Bf 109 or an Fw 190, the P-38 was not the most maneuverable of aircraft.

The Cinderella story subject was North American's P-51 Mustang, whose fighting potential was first realized by the British. It had the promise of greater range and maneuverability than anything before it. Compared to the P-38, the P-51 cost less to build and to maintain; it had half the number of engines, for one thing.

In September 1943, Gen. Arnold suggested to the RAF that it would be a nice gesture were they to make some of their Mustang squadrons available to escort the heavies of VIII Bomber Command. Air Chief Marshal Sir Charles Portal agreed, and assigned four squadrons to the task, beginning in January 1944.

One AAF P-51 unit, the 354th Fighter Group, had landed in Europe, fitted itself into the Ninth Air Force structure, and was waiting assignment. They drew escort on a December 5 mission, taking a bomber force

On November 3, 1943 B-17s of the 40th Wing bombed Wilhelmshaven. Part of the escort was the freshman 55th FG with P-38s but another important section was the veteran 56th FG with P-47s. One of the 56th's squadrons was photographed moments before peeling off in flights of four to go on the mission.

to Poix, south of Amiens, as their baptism of battle. On December 13, they went with the big birds to Kiel, some 430 miles away.

They might have done the trip on internal fuel only; the Mustang could escort out to about 475 miles from home that way. With two 75-gallon wing tanks, it had a 650-mile escort radius. With two 108-gallon wing tanks, the combat radius became a phenomenal 850 miles.

The second development that improved bomber performance was the use of radar blind-bombing systems. It was, like so many of the developments of that war, a British concept. They called it H2S, and made some sets available for combat trials in a few B-17s of the 482nd Bomb Group for the Emden raid in September 1943. The results were impressive. U. S. radar development also was well along, but H2S offered a quick solution to an immediate need. The Radiation Laboratory of the Massachusetts Institute of Technology, assigned to improve the system for American production, hand-built a pre-production run of 20 sets, enough to equip a dozen B-17s and provide adequate spares.

Those B-17s, now sporting the U.S.-built H2X system in a "double-chin" nose geometry, also joined the 482nd and went on their first big practice mission against Wilhelmshaven November 3. Nine pathfinders using the H2X system, and two still equipped with the British H2S led 539 attackers to the German port, an easily identifiable radar target. They dropped more than 1,400 tons of bombs, damaging the aiming point, and lost only seven heavies. Beginner's luck again, as events were to prove.

The early results of radar bombing encouraged the Eighth to go and bomb when they would otherwise have stayed grounded by target weather. In December, VIII Bomber Command off-loaded 13,142 tons of bombs, for the first time exceeding the monthly weight totals of RAF Bomber Command.

Most of the bombing during the early winter of 1943 was done by H2S or H2X, and most of the attacks were directed against easily read radar targets: the port cities of Bremen, Wilhelmshaven, and Kiel. Early radars were able to "see" and present the sharp differences between land and water far better than they could distinguish different kinds of terrain, or define an inland city shape.

It was a temporary, probably inadvertent, abandonment of precision bombing, and a step into area bombing for the Eighth AF crews. In no way could the radar-directed drops have been called pinpoint bombing. The high explosives smashed docks and houses indiscriminately, rather than neatly tumbling a single shipyard into ruin. From October 15 through December 15, a total of 151 combat boxes bombed those three ports. Only six managed to place their bombs within one mile of the aiming point.

Weather Break for Big Week

Finally, the weather forcasts were favorable. It would be clear for about one week beginning February 20. As usual, there were some last minute doubts; the night before the mission was cloudy. But the word went out to go; the skies cleared, and off the bombers roared.

Filling in details of B-17Gs and their crews ready for the mission by the 379th BG on 29 January 1944. The column on the extreme right gives details of previous attacks. At VE-Day the 379th had dropped a bigger tonnage of bombs (26,459·6) than any other in the AAF. Today neither the control board nor the ops room exists, and Kimbolton is no longer an airfield.

The first day's offensive was the grand opener. VIII Bomber Command dispatched more than 1,000 heavies, of which 941 were to be credited with combat sorties. They were escorted by 33 fighter groups from VIII Fighter Command, Ninth AF and the RAF. A dozen targets has been chosen: assembly land component plants for the Luftwaffe's best day and night fighters. Most were in the area between Brunswick and Leipzig, about 500 miles from the English coast. The attacks had been started by the RAF the night before; they hit Leipzig hard, and the tired defenders were still in the streets, trying to restore order, when the AAF armada hit.

That night, the RAF went out again, hammering Stuttgart. The AAF day raid, on a smaller scale, struck the plants at Brunswick, German airfields and storage parks. On February 22, the USAAF hit six targets, including both Schweinfurt and Regensburg. The next day, only the Fifteenth AF flew, sending 102 sorties against Steyr, in Austria, and its ball-bearing factories.

On February 24, the Eighth went back to Schweinfurt, and sent other strikes to Gotha and Steyr. That night the RAF raided Schweinfurth again, guided by the fires still burning from the American attack. On the next day, the USAAF bombers blasted Messerschmitt plants at Regensburg, Augsburg, Stuttgart and Fürth. Then the weather closed in, and "Big Week" was over.

The German aircraft producers lost about two months of badly needed fabrication time, and they also received an urgent directive to disperse. That made the industry a more elusive target and a more difficult one, but the act of dispersing strained the already overloaded transportation systems and further disrupted the economy.

The AAF lost about 2,600 crewmen to all causes, and 226 bombers and 28 fighters. They dropped about 10,000 tons of bombs, almost equal to the tonnage of the whole first year of Eighth AF operations. The RAF dumped another 9,198 tons in their five raids of *Argument*, losing 157 bombers in the campaign.

But most importantly the Luftwaffe had been beaten. After the assaults of *Argument*, the German air arm never again opposed a daylight strike with a major force that dogged the bombers from entrance to exit. Their losses were close to 600 aircraft, and a large number of the last classes of well-trained and experienced pilots. They were to hit hard again, on a number of future missions, but for the time being certainly, and for the rest of the war almost certainly, they had lost control of the air to the Allies.

On to Berlin

The next step in AAF strategy was to force the Luftwaffe to come up and fight, so that the remaining strength could be destroyed. Berlin was the logical target to tempt them with; if they would defend any city, it should be that one.

The opening gun made a tiny report. Weather forced the recall of the March 4, 1944, mission, except for one combat wing that didn't receive the communication. They flew over the southwest suburbs of Berlin and dropped bombs from 31 B-17 bomb bays. They and their Mustang escort got home safely.

The crew of the B-17 "Tom Paine" prepare for a mission. The airplane was named for one of the most celebrated sons of Thetford, near which the crew were based.

Asked to pick one picture to represent the U.S. Air Force, few would quarrel with this photograph taken in 1944 over the small, irregular fields of England. The unpainted B-17Gs—part of the greatest aerial armada in the history of the world—are from the 8th AF's 381st BG.

Lockheed P-38J

A poem was written about the P-38 Lightning and, in contrast to much of the wartime verse, it was complimentary. Its words included lavish praise for ". . . an escort of P-38s . . ." And that's where the twin-tailed fighter made its reputation. It had the range and other performance attributes to take the big bombers to their targets deep in Germany. The sight of a formation of those elegant aircraft scissoring the deep blue air above them must have cheered many a B-17 and B-24 pilot. The P-38 was an advanced design for its time, with a full-vision canopy, tricycle gear, turbo-superchargers and centerline armament of formidable striking power. Strap on belly or wing tanks, and she had the range; drop them, and she could fight. "Jeanne" was a P-38J-15-LO, serial number 43-28430, assembled at Lockheed's plant in Burbank, California, and sent to join the 55th Fighter Squadron of the Eight Air Force's 20th Fighter Group. She was based at Kingscliffe, Northants., in Great Britain, and at one time her placarded nose recorded one enemy aircraft destroyed, along with two locomotives and a torpedo boat, plus participation in nine fighter sweeps, two bombing raids, and 30 escort missions.

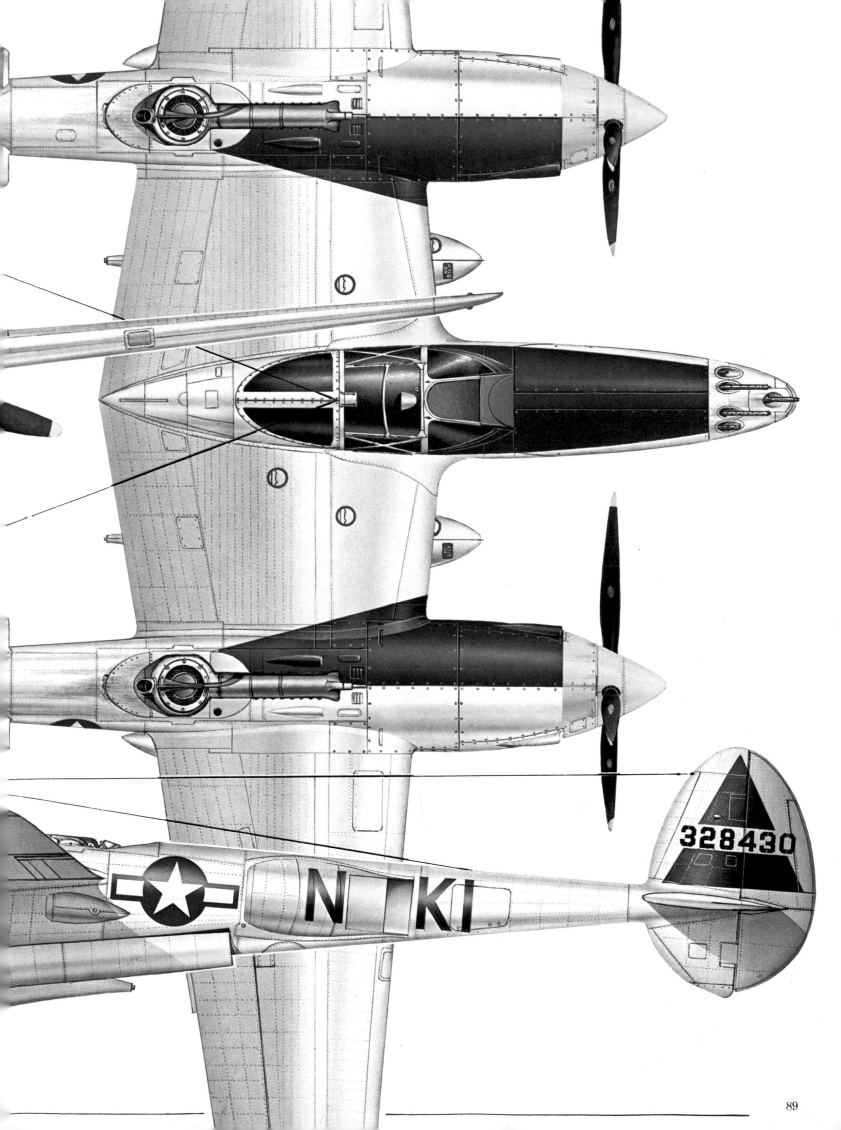

Another wartime base that no longer exists, RAF Great Dunmow throbbed with activity on April 11, 1944. A 9th AF base, it housed the 386th BG, some of whose officers are chatting on the control tower with the topmost brass: Maj-Gen Lewis M. Brereton, Gen Dwight D. Eisenhower and Maj-Gen Carl A. Spaatz.

Two B-17Fs of the 91st BG, one of the pioneer Bomb Groups of the 8th AF, in olive drab with medium green blotching along the edges. The 91st, based at Bassingbourn, had the highest losses of any AAF group in the war, but also the highest claims for enemy aircraft destroyed (420).

The second Berlin mission on March 6 was no more productive. Bad bombing by 658 heavies scattered explosives and incediaries all over the greater Berlin area. The planners were right; the Germans did defend their capital, and very well indeed. The attackers lost 69 bombers to the Luftwaffe, the highest single day's loss by the Eighth to that date.

It was the start of a long campaign against the Reich capital and it became a turning point in the air war. After March, the rate of USAAF bomber loss to enemy aircraft decreased sharply. The Messerschmitt menace had been overcome.

There was one more major offensive that spanned 1943 and 1944, and it drew in all available aircraft. Some strangely shaped structures had been spotted in French forests, laid out on a site shaped like a ski, and pointing toward England. The British were understandably concerned.

Daring reconnaissance missions, flown by both British and American pilots, brought back photographic coverage of a 150-mile wide belt southeast of London. Photo-interpreters ticked off one ski site after another, identifying 75 of them during December, 1943.

There were differences of opinion about the best way to destroy the structures. The British held out for heavy bombers. The Americans thought fighter-bombers at low altitudes could do the job best. They had tests made at Eglin Field, Florida, against replica ski sites, to back their beliefs. But they were overruled, and the heavies were sent out against the forest sites in Operation *Crossbow*.

On the day before Christmas, 670 aircraft from VIII Bomber Command dropped 1,700 tons of bombs on 23 different ski sites, with good results. The commanders continued to send out the heavies, subtracting their striking power from the *Pointblank* campaign. Perhaps to hedge their bets, they also dispatched forces of medium bombers and fighter-bombers.

Crossbow attacks lasted until D-Day, June 6, 1944. An estimated 83 out of the 96 discovered sites had been put out of action. It had taken 25,150 bombing sorties that dropped 36,200 tons of high explosives. The cost was 771 airmen and 154 aircraft.

The best estimates of the campaign's effect agree that it delayed the V-1 buzzbomb attacks on London by about three to four months by destroying the launching ramps. It had taken, on average, 436 tons of bombs for each ski site hammered into rubble. And somewhere in the files, there still is a report of the Eglin Field tests, in which fighter-bombers dropped thousand-pounders with delayed-action fuses and destroyed replica ski sites for an expenditure of about one ton per site.

When the Combined Bomber Offensive had been first established, it was given a finite life span. The end date was April 1, 1944; on that day, the CBO officially and legally ceased to exist. A few more missions were flown against *Pointblank* targets, but for all practical purposes that part of the air war was over.

The United States Strategic Air Forces, consisting of VIII Bomber Command and Fifteenth AF, were placed under Supreme Headquarters, Allied Expeditionary Force (SHAEF), commanded by Gen. Dwight D. Eisenhower. They were joined by RAF's Bomber Command, and by the Allied Expeditionary Air Force, a tactical organization consisting of the RAF's Second Tactical Air Force and the USAAF's Ninth Air Force.

Now the task that faced them was the final drive on behalf of *Overlord*, the invasion of Europe. They had only a few weeks left to accomplish that mission.

Prelude to Götterdammerung

Air power made the invasion of the Continent possible. Consider whatever other factors you will, in the final analysis that statement withstands the most reasoned criticism.

The planners spelled it out in the requirement list for *Overlord*. Photograph the beaches and inland avenues of the assault. Blast the beach defenses. Destroy the German radars. Weaken the Luftwaffe so that their fighter-bombers could not slow Allied troop movements. Transport and drop one British and two American airborne divisions. Maintain air superiority above the invasion fleet and over the beaches.

In short, preparations for *Overlord* included as a necessary item the concentrated, versatile, unique and successful application of air power.

About that there could be no argument. But about the best form in which to apply air power there were many arguments, differences of opinions, and clashes of egos.

There was, for example, a major difference of opinion about the best way to immobilize German reserve units that would be moved to the battle front. Eisenhower's team at SHAEF generally favored hitting the Belgian and French railroads, including their bridges, key yards and maintenance facilities. That would, they argued, create a "railway desert" in northern France. That would prevent, or at least hamper, the German troop movements. These officers wanted to use all available Allied air strength for the job, drawing them from their assigned tasks against

Eight 500-pounders string out from a B-26G of the 9th Bombardment Division during one of thousands of attacks on the German rail network in 1944. This run was made through almost solid cloud cover.

From early 1944 thousands of USAAF fighters roamed German airspace, often attacking targets of opportunity after escorting bombers. Here P-51s have started several fires on a train laden with army trucks. Occasionally there were cataclysmic explosions dangerous to the attackers: one train was laden with dozens of flying-bomb warheads.

By March 1945 the Luftwaffe hardly dared to show its face. Here 13 of the once-feared Ju 87 "Stukas" were caught lined up at Lippe about to try to demolish the vital Remagen bridge over the Rhine, captured intact. They were caught on the ground by P-47s of IX Tac Air Command.

strategic targets deep in Germany. The expected bonus was that the Luftwaffe probably would come up to fight and could be further weakened in the resulting combat.

Ranged against this concept were three officers with their own ideas about stopping the Germans: Spaatz, Eaker, and the RAF's "Bomber" Harris. They wanted to hit Germany with their heavy bomber fleets until about three weeks before the scheduled landings, and then go after the railroad system. If they could concentrate their bombs on German oil processing and storage facilities, Spaatz argued, it would deny badly needed gasoline to the Luftwaffe and Wehrmacht. The German air force probably would fly to defend these raids, and then could be defeated in the air.

Spaatz also had a further concern; he was on record against mass bombings with their needless casualties, and he saw the strikes against the railroad system as very costly to Belgian and French civilian employees. He wanted no part of that kind of killing for the United States Army Air Forces.

The final choice had to be made by Eisenhower. He took a month to weight the alternatives, then chose the attacks on the transportation system as the better of the two from his viewpoint of assuring a successful invasion. The question of civilian casualties bothered him, also. But in the cold equations of war, that was acceptable as an unpleasant, but necessary, factor.

Building Tactical Air Power

A major part of the pre-invasion task was the building of the Ninth Air Force. Its mission: support and assist the invasion landings, and then work with the advancing armies on their drive to defeat and occupy Germany.

The decision for a separate air force, rather than an expansion of the VIII Air Support Command, the tactical arm of the Eighth Air Force, was Gen. Arnold's. He moved Ninth AF from the Middle East to Europe, along with its commander, Lt. Gen. Lewis Brereton. The Ninth's initial cadres were the VIII ASC and the VIII Tactical Air Service Area Command, but by early 1944, personnel were assigned directly from the United States.

There was severe competition between the Eighth and the Ninth for new fighter groups scheduled for European operations. Both organizations needed fighters; both wanted them to be P-51 Mustangs. The Eighth won that competition at first; later, as Mustang production poured from the U. S., both air forces got a large share.

Fighter strength of the Ninth just before the invasion was 13 full groups of P-47s, plus three of P-38s and two of P-51s, a total of about 1,500 assigned to IX Fighter Command. IX Bomber Command had eleven groups equipped with Martin B-26 medium bombers and Douglas A-20 light bombers. IX Troop Carrier Command had 14 groups of air transports.

As part of the pre-invasion assignment, the Ninth also struck targets in the *Crossbow* and *Pointblank* folders. Its medium bombers were sent on diversionary and primary attacks against German-used airfields. Its fighters also escorted the big birds of the Eighth. During "Big Week", Ninth AF mediums supported the Eighth AF heavies with assaults on German airfields, and IX Fighter Command dispatched the major share of the escort force for those raids on strategic targets.

By April, 1944, the Ninth was an operational tactical air force, ready to turn to direct support of the invasion. In addition to strikes against *Crossbow* sites, IX BC hit railway marshalling yards, and the 67th Tactical Reconnaissance Group photographed more than 160 miles of French coastline and two inland belts about 120 miles long.

It should be noted that these specific reconnaissance missions, like many other pre-*Overlord* sorties, were only part of the total number of missions flown. There was danger of alerting the Germans to the prospective use of a particular stretch of beach. So for every mission in the invasion area, one or two more were flown against a similar target geographically distant, to deceive the Germans.

Within a few short months, the Ninth built from a new organization to the largest tactical air arm in the war. By the date of the invasion, Ninth AF had on hand about 4,500 tactical aircraft of all types and about 2,700 gliders.

The air attacks in support of *Overlord* began on schedule, fifty days before the landings. The primary target was the Luftwaffe. A vitally important second-

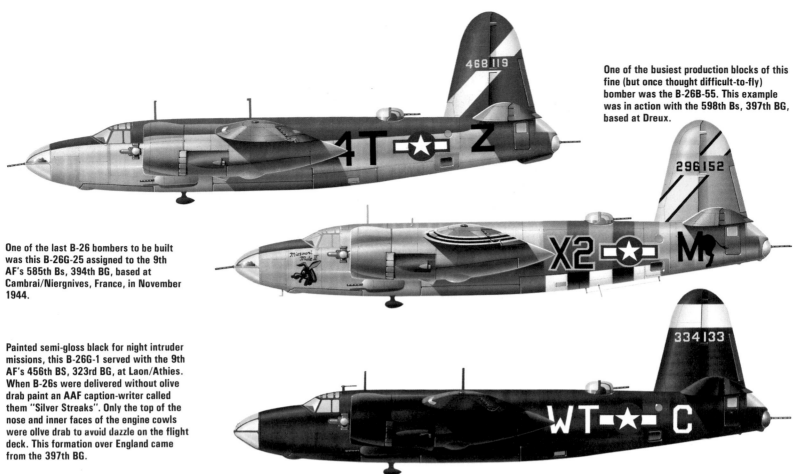

One of the busiest production blocks of this fine (but once thought difficult-to-fly) bomber was the B-26B-55. This example was in action with the 598th Bs, 397th BG, based at Dreux.

One of the last B-26 bombers to be built was this B-26G-25 assigned to the 9th AF's 585th Bs, 394th BG, based at Cambrai/Niergnives, France, in November 1944.

Painted semi-gloss black for night intruder missions, this B-26G-1 served with the 9th AF's 456th BS, 323rd BG, at Laon/Athies. When B-26s were delivered without olive drab paint an AAF caption-writer called them "Silver Streaks". Only the top of the nose and inner faces of the engine cowls were olive drab to avoid dazzle on the flight deck. This formation over England came from the 397th BG.

ary mission was a thorough photo-reconnaissance of the coastal aras. Then on D-Day minus 30, the target list was expanded to include the transporation networks, the coastal defenses, and potential Luftwaffe bases within a 130-mile radius of the landing beaches.

The Ninth AF was most heavily involved; the other air forces were still employed against strategic targets deep in the Reich, and against the *Crossbow* sites. As the target list grew, the Ninth was joined by the Eighth and by the RAF, whose Second Tactical Air Force was a powerful addition to the air strength.

By the end of April, a dozen major rail centers had been blasted into a rubble of twisted steel, mangled rolling stock, and demolished buildings. The Germans countered by concentrating their anti-aircraft artillery at the railheads, and by fast repair of trackage breaks. By the end of May, although even more railway junctions had been put out of action, the expected breakdown of the system had not yet been achieved.

Strafing moving trains had not been condoned because of the danger of killing civilians. But the trains had to be stopped, so the fighters were turned loose. The first of these *Chattanooga Choo-Choo* missions on May 21 sent 763 AEAF fighters over northern France and 500 Eighth AF fighters over Germany, with orders to shoot up any train anywhere. Within a few days, daylight train movements stopped dead, halted by the simple interdiction tactic.

Its early service life marred by an unusually high accident rate resulting from the type's heavy wing loading, the Martin B-26 Marauder soon developed into an effective if unforgiving light bomber and attack aircraft. Seen here is a formation of B-26B models, the most widely produced variant.

A Bf.109 is caught in the
sights of a P-47 and dies in flames over
France.
**By far the most important transport of the
Allies was the ubiquitous Douglas DC-3,
called, in military guise C-47, C-53, R4D,
Dakota, Skytrain and by many other
designations. More than 2,000 assembled
in Britain in the first half of 1944 as seen
here, until they almost jammed the
airfields and even surrounding farmland.
This group seen in the June sunshine were
assigned to the IX Troop Carrier Command.
Within hours they were to be painted in
invasion stripes, ready for action.**

On May 26, Ninth AF B-26s struck for the first time at
the bridges on the Seine. Before the invasion forces
landed, every span downstream of Paris had been cut,
in a major contribution to stopping the movement of
German reinforcements.

Airfields were a more difficult class of targets. There
were more than 100 usable fields within reach of the
Normandy invasion coast. Further, forward airfield
repair is easily and quickly done. Thus a large number
of targets had to be hit heavily, and at the last possible
moment. It was done by the mediums and light
bombers of Ninth AF primarily.

By mid-April the Ninth turned its attention to the
Atlantic Wall, the Wehrmacht defense line along the
Channel coast. RAF Bomber Command and Eighth AF
heavies joined the fray later. Together they damaged
about half of the coastal gun batteries behind the
beaches. The RAF's Second TAF sent its Hawker
Typhoon fighter-bombers against the German radars;
they either destroyed or made inoperable almost
every installation in the area. On D-Day the Germans
were radar-blind.

At least eight reconnaissance missions were flown
each day before the invasion to photograph the changing appearance of the beaches. Pilots of Second TAF
and IX Fighter Command shared those missions, and
for deception photographed two sites elsewhere for
every Normandy location.

Most dangerous of the recon sorties were eleven
flown at extremely low level by pilots of the 10th Photo
Reconnaissance Group, Ninth AF. Roaring above the
beaches at about 15 feet altitude, these "Dicing"
missions brought back very detailed information about
the German beach defenses. The 10th PRG received a
Distinguished Unit Citation for its work.

Meantime, very satisfying results were being obtained in the strategic bombing campaign against oil
production and processing, at least at this stage of the
assault. Germany drew about half of all its production
of fuel from a combination of synthetic gasoline plants
and crude oil refineries that had been unwisely concentrated in three areas: Ploesti, Silesia, and the Ruhr.

Early missions against oil were experimental; not all
Allied leadership was convinced of the strategic
benefits that Spaatz and the Americans argued would
accrue from bombing German oil processors. Proof
came soon. The Eighth sent 935 heavy bombers, well
escorted, to the Ruhr May 12. More than 800 reached
and bombed the primary targets. All were damaged,
and some were hit heavily. There was an unintentional
bonus; one of the buildings hit at Merseburg-Leuna
contained the laboratory where heavy-water experiments were being done as part of Germany's nuclear
weapons research. Aggressive attacks by more than
150 Luftwaffe fighters shot down 46 bombers and ten
fighters, but lost many of their own in the combat.

By striking at the production of refineries and
synthetic fuel plants, the USSTAF drew the Luftwaffe
up to fight, and to lose. By then, every single loss was
critical to the Germans, because in mid-May, for the
first time, Luftwaffe pilot losses exceeded the available replacements.

Normandy Landings

Last-minute activity reached into the late hours of
June 5, 1944. Broad black-and-white wing and fuselage
bands, "invasion stripes", had been painted on fighters,
light and medium bombers, and gliders. Bombs had
been loaded, engines checked, ammunition boxes filled,

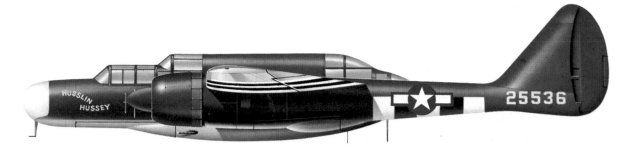

P-61A-5 "Husslin Hussey" of 422nd NFS,
Scorton, 1944.

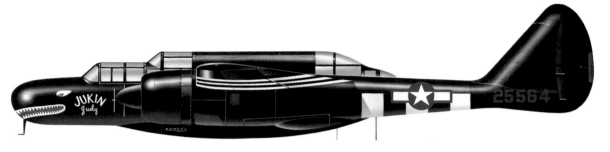

P-61A-5 "Jukin Judy" of 422nd NFS,
Scorton, 1944.

guns boresighted.

At midnight, the port propeller of a Douglas C-47 turned, urged by a whining starter. The engine caught, coughed and roared into life. Its sound was echoed again and again in the minutes that followed. Engines warmed, the pathfinder planes trundled out for take-off. Aboard were the drop teams who would mark the landing zones for the airborne assault.

The RAF was out that night with its heavy bombers, pounding the coastal batteries with almost 6,000 tons of high explosives. At 1:45 AM on the morning of June 6, IX Troop Carrier Command began the takeoff and aerial assembly of 813 transports, holding paratroopers

of the 82nd and 101st Airborne Divisions. On other bases, 237 RAF transports were lifting into the night skies carrying the British 6th Airborne Division.

By early light, the invasion fleet of thousands of boats and ships of all types was off the beaches under the cover of 171 fighter squadrons. Supporting fire from warships was greatly augmented by the heavy bombers of the Eighth AF, unloading more than 2,700 tons of high explosives on the shore defenses. The bombs were fused to burst on contact, so that cratering would be minimized and Allied tank movements would be least hampered by the terrain.

That single day, the USAAF flew 8,772 combat

Paratroops of an airborne division fill the sky over newly won France as the USAAF 9th Troop Carrier Command's C-47s practise for the Rhine crossing in late 1944.

sorties and the RAF flew 5,676. The Luftwaffe was hardly to be seen; it had been overwhelmed, and managed to get only a few dozen sorties over the beaches. Eisenhower had predicted just that; he had told his troops the night before not to worry if they saw any aircraft, because they'd be Allied.

It was a costly landing, but far less so than it would have been without the effective air support and the complete domination of the air by the USAAF and RAF. The Allies had landed eight divisions, two of them dropped behind Utah beach to help cut off the Cherbourg peninsula. The Luftwaffe was denied air bases within striking distance; 67,000 tons of bombs neutralized potentially useful airfields. Rail centers and bridges had been hit with 76,000 tons, and German reinforcements were cut off from their normal transportation to the front. They started to walk; some troops confiscated bicycles and automobiles from the French. Straggling Wehrmacht troops were still heading north to battle ten days to two weeks after the invasion.

June became a "Big Month"; the USAAF flew 82,369 combat sorties. That's a daily average of 923 heavy bomber missions, 297 light- and medium-bomber sorties, and 1,692 fighter flights.

Five days after the landings, the Allied forces had put 16 full divisions ashore, equipped and manned. Tactical air units were moving into new bases in Normandy, and now were only a five-minute flight from the front.

Frantic Bombing

June also saw an abortive attempt at American cooperation with the Russians in Operation *Frantic*, which was aptly named. It was conceived as a shuttle-bombing program, with the heavies hitting targets in eastern Germany and then continuing onward to recover at Russian bases. It was one of those ideas that seemed good at the time, particularly since the Allies were concerned about keeping the Russians in the war and preventing them from making a separate peace with the Germans.

Today, *Frantic* is not remembered for its frustrations, which were many, or its successes, which were minimal. It is celebrated as the best bit of bombing the Luftwaffe ever did. On June 21, a lone Heinkel 177, an otherwise undistinguished airplane, tracked a large formation of B-17s headed in a generally easterly direction. It shadowed the bombers and got a fix on their destination. That night, the Luftwaffe bombed the Russian airfield at Poltava, destroying 43 dispersed B-17s and 15 Mustangs. German bombs hit an ammunition dump, and a fuel dump, and almost a half-million gallons of aviation gasoline brightened the night sky.

Frantic was short-lived, and strategically was of zero value. In theory, it was to have some diplomatic advantages, which have long since proved useless and forgotten.

The concept of carpet bombing—saturating an area ahead of a battle line with concentrated bomb drops—was an appealing one to ground commanders. But often, their air counterparts argued against it, as Eaker had done at Cassino. Plowing the battlefield, they pointed out, often made it impossible for armor and troops to advance at a normal pace, and gave the surviving defences too much time to reorganize.

But a commanders' conference decided to try it to aid the breakout of the Allied forces from the beachhead area. Operation *Cobra* called in all Eighth AF heavies, and all Ninth AF fighters and medium bombers. The fighters, loaded with bombs, rockets and full ammunition, hit an area 250 yards by 7,500 yards just ahead of Allied troops outside St.-Lo. Medium and heavy bombers saturated a one- by five-mile area just

Douglas C-47A

Developed from the immortal DC-3 commercial transport, the Douglas C-47 cargo carrier served with the United States Army Air Forces as an all-purpose hauler of anything or anybody that could be loaded aboard or towed behind. It also flew in the air arms of Allied countries, notably the United Kingdom and Russia, in which latter the type was built under license. C-47s — and other model numbers that described only minor differences from the basic design—hauled gliders fro the invasions of the southwest Pacific and Europe, carried paratroops to battle, flew out the wounded and the refugees, brought supplies and medical aid to remote outposts equipped with primitive landing strips of truncated length. More than 10,000 military versions of the basic C-47 were built. The specific plane shown here is a C-47A-65-DL, serial number 42-100558, built at the Long Beach, California, plant of the Douglas Aircraft Company and marked in the livery of the 81st Troop Carrier Squadron, 436th Troop Carrier Group, that participated in the airborne assaults on Normandy, southern France, Holland and Germany.

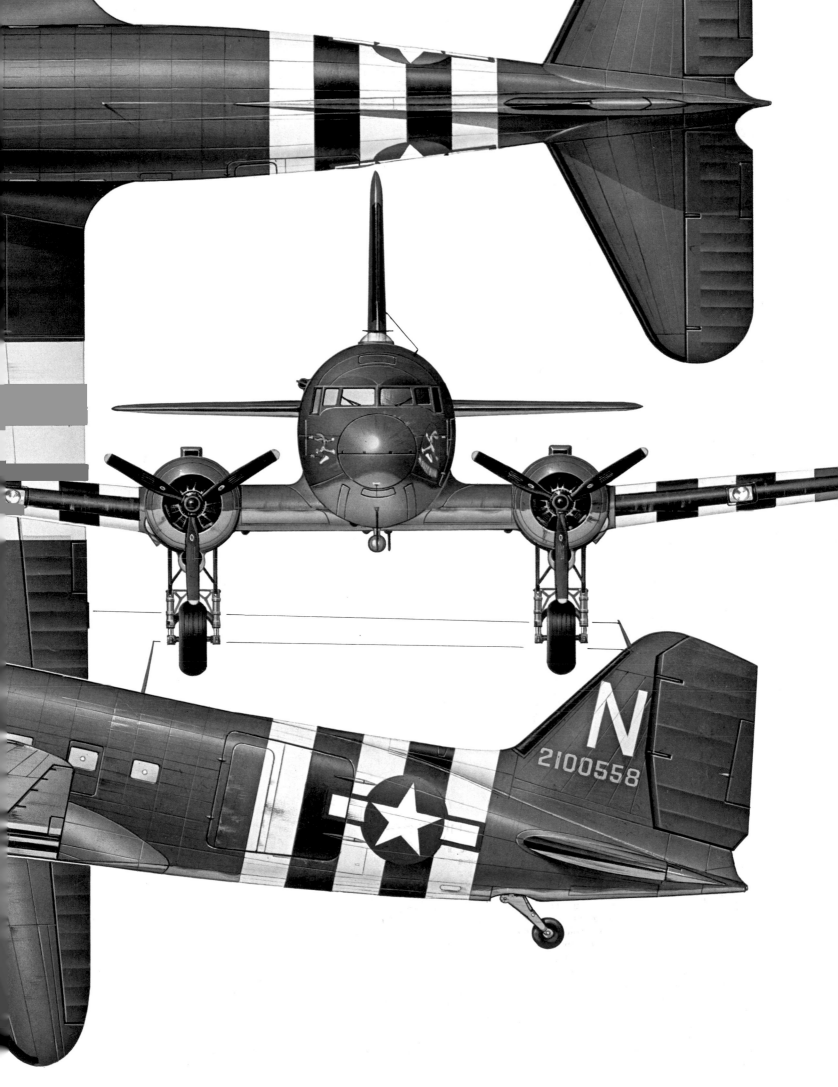

P-38J of the 401st FS, 370th FG, 9th AF, based at Florennes, Belgium, in November 1944. (Today Florennes is home to an F-16 Fighting Falcon squadron.)

Below right. By D-Day (6 June 1944) the large and powerful P-61 Black Widow night fighter was operational with the 9th AF in Europe. This aircraft, of the 422nd NFS at Scorton, in northern England, was one of the early P-61A-1 batch with dorsal turret, here hidden behind the fin.

Plan view of a formation developed by the 9th AF for day high-level bombing with P-38s, all releasing their bomb or bombs (one or two 1,000- or 2,000-pounders) when their pilots saw the lead-ship do so. The lead-ship had to be a droop-snoot with bombardier and Norden sight.

beyond the fighter-bombers' target.

The first fighter dove to the attack at 9:38 AM July 25, and the last bomber pulled away at 12:23 PM. In the three hours between, the areas were smothered with almost 4,200 tons of bombs, and struck repeatedly by rockets, machine gun and cannon fire, and some napalm. More than 1,500 heavies had dropped, in addition to 380 medium bombers and 559 fighters.

Some bombing was very inaccurate, and U.S. forces took casualties. But one German panzer division was shattered; those not immediately killed or wounded were deafened, in shock, and demoralized completely. *Cobra* had won the battle of St.-Lo; but Eisenhower said it should not be done against because of the inherent possibility of friendly casualties.

Air and armored units set up a team approach, with pilots attached to ground units to call in attacks according to immediate tactical needs. Armored column cover became a new operational mission; four aircraft per column of advancing armored troops flew armed reconnaissance and protected the column.

The Ninth AF, fully geared to its primary task of ground support, bombed and strafed the retreating Germans. On July 29, they caught a boxed-in German armored force on a road between two small French villages. From mid-afternoon to late in the summer evening, P-47s of the 405th Fighter-Bomber Group systematically smashed the three-mile long column. They were aided by artillery and tank gunfire from ground forces blocking both ends of the road.

It was devastating; the road was made impassable. The attack destroyed 66 tanks, 204 vehicles and 11 guns, and damaged 56 tanks and 55 vehicles which were abandoned.

Racing with Patton's Third Army

Now the flamboyant Lt. Gen. George S. Patton began his dash through France. Swinging in a giant arc hinged on Caen, his Third Army armor rumbled across France, headed for the German frontier. The danger in a rapid advance is that it may leave the flanks uncovered. Flanking attacks, taught to military students early in their careers, can be most successful; they punch into an advancing column and cut it. Patton, himself a competent amateur pilot and aircraft owner, sensed what air power could do. He asked Brig. Gen. O. P. Weyland's XIX Tactical Air Command to cover his southern flank. It was a brilliant concept, and proved a successful, and historic, use of the capabilities and strength of aircraft.

A German counterattack across the southern region of the Cotentin peninsula was slowed by air, blunted

and turned by the GIs, and converted into a retreat. Patton chased them toward Argentan, while Montgomery moved his British and Canadian armies toward Falaise, planning to trap the Germans between the two Allied forces. The pincer never met; the Germans got out through the gap between the towns. But it cost them heavily; Ninth AF and RAF Second TAF fighter-bombers worked over the roads in the gap and decimated the German columns.

During this period, tiny Piper L-4s, the military models of the immortal Cub, began flying "horsefly" missions, acting as forward air controllers and calling in strikes against targets designated by ground units. It was another example of the air-ground teamwork that moved Patton to comment that the cooperation between Third Army and XIX Tactical Air Command was " . . . the best example of the combined use of air and ground troops that I have ever witnessed."

In August, a second invasion of France echoed on a smaller scale the landings of June in Normandy. It was preceded by concentrated bombing by strategic heavies of MAAF, hitting naval facilities at Toulon and other Mediterranean ports. The target list was expanded, just as at Normandy. One mission was unique to the area: air drops of weapons and supplies to the Maquis,

Despite taking time out to strafe ground targets, the escort fighters usually got home long before the heavies. Here P-47s of the 78th FG cool off while B-17s circle to land at an adjoining base, probably Bassingbourn, home of the 91st BG.

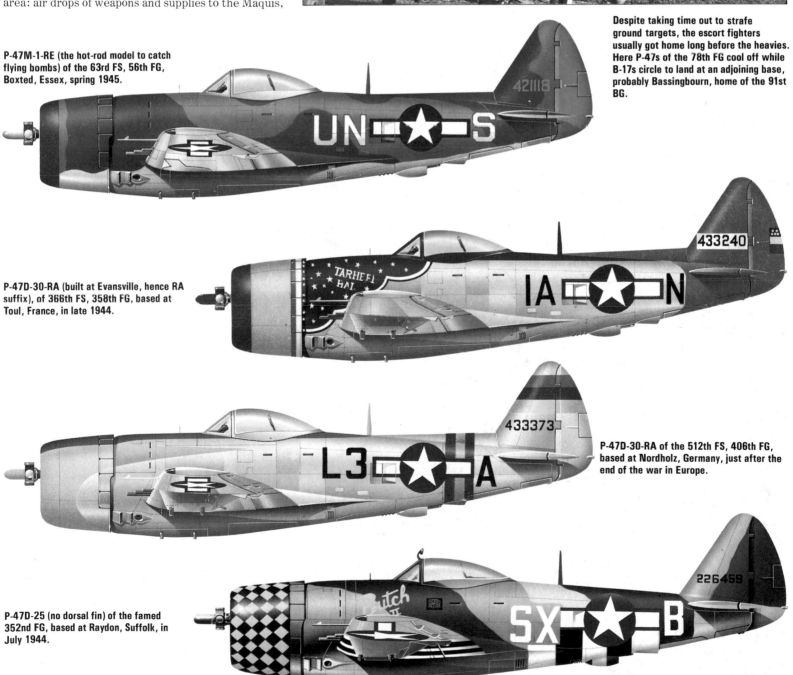

P-47M-1-RE (the hot-rod model to catch flying bombs) of the 63rd FS, 56th FG, Boxted, Essex, spring 1945.

P-47D-30-RA (built at Evansville, hence RA suffix), of 366th FS, 358th FG, based at Toul, France, in late 1944.

P-47D-30-RA of the 512th FS, 406th FG, based at Nordholz, Germany, just after the end of the war in Europe.

P-47D-25 (no dorsal fin) of the famed 352nd FG, based at Raydon, Suffolk, in July 1944.

Baby Bumps II

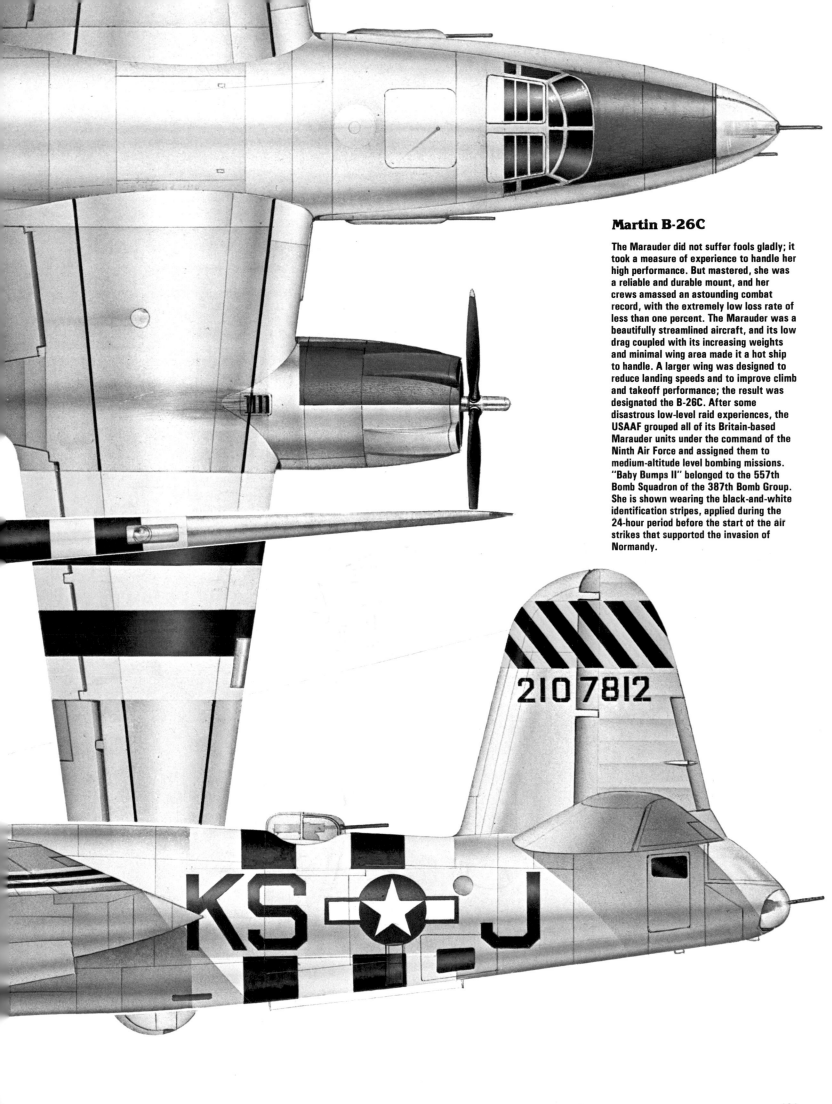

Martin B-26C

The Marauder did not suffer fools gladly; it took a measure of experience to handle her high performance. But mastered, she was a reliable and durable mount, and her crews amassed an astounding combat record, with the extremely low loss rate of less than one percent. The Marauder was a beautifully streamlined aircraft, and its low drag coupled with its increasing weights and minimal wing area made it a hot ship to handle. A larger wing was designed to reduce landing speeds and to improve climb and takeoff performance; the result was designated the B-26C. After some disastrous low-level raid experiences, the USAAF grouped all of its Britain-based Marauder units under the command of the Ninth Air Force and assigned them to medium-altitude level bombing missions. "Baby Bumps II" belonged to the 557th Bomb Squadron of the 387th Bomb Group. She is shown wearing the black-and-white identification stripes, applied during the 24-hour period before the start of the air strikes that supported the invasion of Normandy.

P-51B of the 374th FS, 361st FG, 8th AF, based at Bottisham, Cambs, in June 1944.

the French underground that contributed so much to the war by harrassment of the Germans and destruction of their facilities.

The invasion force landed August 15, in the face of light opposition, and took few casualties. More than 5,000 paratroopers were dropped a few miles inland from almost 400 planes of the Provisional Troop Carrier Air Division; others were landed during the day by parachute and by glider.

The beachhead was seized, expanded and consolidated, and the drive north began up the Rhone valley. Seventh Army outran its supply train, necessitating air drops of supplies. Within a week the Germans were in full retreat, heading for Belfort, where they stood long enough to organize a withdrawal and to establish a defense line.

Every foot of the way, XII Tactical Air Command had supported the invasion and the northward drive. From late August, it was almost the only air strength the Allies had in the area; the rest had been drawn back to try to finish off the war in Italy.

These rapid movements consumed supplies at an abnormal rate; spot shortages began to appear and

then broaden. First Army needed 571,000 gallons of fuel each day; Patton's Third was burning a million gallons every 24 hours. Air supply was tried. During one ten-day period, IX Troop Carrier Command flew in 2,500,000 gallons of fuel; it met about 16 percent of the total requirement. Even Eighth AF heavy bombers were pressed into tank-car service; B-24s toted 200 five-gallon jerry-cans of gasoline in each bomb bay.

Paris was liberated August 25, and France was free soon after. Patton's Third, still at full throttle, reached Nancy and the outskirts of the Siegfried Line in mid-September and there ground to a halt, out of fuel.

By then, the Allies had established a continuous front from the Channel to Switzerland.

Nickels and Carpetbaggers

The special abilities of aircraft were used in a number of non-combat, although risky, missions. One was "nickeling", dropping leaflets over occupied areas. Hundreds of millions of these propaganda sheets were cast into Europe, at first in loose bundles tossed out a hatch or gunner's window. Technology took over, and a

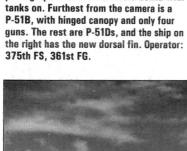

Three species of P-51 are visible in this photograph of escorts outward bound with tanks on. Furthest from the camera is a P-51B, with hinged canopy and only four guns. The rest are P-51Ds, and the ship on the right has the new dorsal fin. Operator: 375th FS, 361st FG.

leaflet bomb was devised, dropped in the usual manner. A small explosive charge broke open the package after it was well clear of the aircraft.

Underground operations, particularly by the French Free Forces of the Interior (FFI, or Maquis), contributed much to the success of Allied arms. But they needed supplies: weapons, explosives, ammunition and medicine. Third Air Division took on the task, and organized several mass drops with as many as 324 B-17s unloading their bomb bays on seven drop zones.

Other supplies were delivered by "Carpetbagger" squadrons, four B-24 outfits that flew modified aircraft on many trips to the Continent, delivering agents and ammo, guerrillas and guns, medicine and leaflets. The shiny black Liberators, their belly ball turrets replaced by an open hatch called the "Joe-hole"—from which agents, known in orders only as "Joe" or "Jane" parachuted—had begun their clandestine flights early in 1944, well ahead of the invasion. By mid-September, with France and Belgium liberated, they turned to Norway on additional missions.

Other B-24s, augmented by C-47s from Troop Carrier Commands, operated in the Balkans and northern Italy, aiding partisan units. C-47s once rescued Yugoslavian leader Tito and his staff just ahead of a German assault that surely would have captured them and changed history.

These missions, whether dropping leaflets or agents, were risky. No crew could be certain that the signal lights below were genuine, or that the radio message was coming from a guerrilla band and not from its German captors. Night flying, even in the later stages of the war, was an uncertain art. Radio location was only relatively accurate. And every underground unit, with reason, was both suspicious and trigger-happy.

The results were intangible. "Nickeling" or inserting an agent never produced the satisfaction that seeing a good bomb pattern on target could. Yet, in their way, those missions helped speed the victory.

Hitting the Sources of Fuel

Two days after the Normandy invasion, Spaatz had issued an order to the Eighth and Fifteenth Air Forces: first priority of the heavy bomber forces, from then on, was to deny fuel to the enemy. Legitimate battlefield emergencies would be dealt with as they arose, but the primary goal was the strategic objective Spaatz had long argued for.

The Eighth was to strike the synthetic fuel plants of central and eastern Germany, and to bomb the refineries near Bremen, Hamburg and Hannover. The Fifteenth was to continue to work over the Ploesti complex, along with other crude-oil refineries near Vienna and Budapest. They also were assigned synthetic-fuel plants, in Poland, Silesia and the Sudetenland.

Harris and the RAF made a major contribution to the campaign. The RAF's 205 Group, based in Italy with the Fifteenth AF, had been quietly mining the Danube, main transportation route for fuel from Romania. Barge after barge was blown out of the water by the RAF's work. Bomber Command continued to make night runs to the Ruhr valley, bombing synthetic-fuel plants there.

Spaatz had more than 3,300 heavies to assign, and Harris about 1,100. During the summer of 1944, they sent the bombers against oil, industry, the *Crossbow*

sites, and often a tactical target designated by a ground commander.

The Eighth flew on 78 of the 92 days of June, July and August, and dropped 154,000 tons of bombs. The Luftwaffe seldom sortied; but it posed a new threat in the form of small, streaking interceptors, the potentially deadly Me-163 rocket-powered aircraft. They were first sighted in late July in a raid on the very durable target at Merseburg-Leuna. On August 16, a half-dozen of the little jets attacked a formation of heavy bombers, doing no real damage. But their impressive performance left more than one crew badly shaken and very apprehensive about the next mission in that area.

If the fighters were less of a menace, the flak was much more. Concentrations were dense, gunners good. Bomber losses mounted; in the summer months, the

With bombs still in the bay, this A-26B was hit by flak seconds before the release point. In fact this superb new attack bomber suffered a lower loss-rate in action than any other type of bomber in the AAF—and it was to go on in the thick of American wars until 1970, by which time most were older than their pilots!

This Douglas A-26B-15, built at Tulsa, was based at Beaumont-sur-Oise in April 1945, serving with the 552nd BS, 386th BG. For most of the war this had been a B-26 outfit.

North American P-51D

The Mustang was every fighter pilot's dream aircraft. Its speedy lines, smooth surfaces and superb finish marked it as the top of the breed. What matter that its highly touted laminar-flow, low-drag wing produced neither laminar flow nor low drag? It looked simply elegant, was elegantly simple, and under its caressed contours it carried the wallop of a heavyweight boxer in the frame of a light-footed ballet dancer. Packed with fuel, it had the range to escort bombers to the deepest targets in the Third Reich. Based on Iwo Jima, Mustangs escorted the very long-range B-29s in their raids on the Japanese homeland. They could tangle with anything the Germans of Japanese could put into the air, and win most of those contests. The painting shows an unnamed P-51D-NA, serial number 44-13926, attached to the 375th Fighter Squadron, 361st Fighter Group of the Eighth Air Force. The squadron got its Mustangs while based at Bottisham, Cambs., beginning in May, 1944; the unit later moved to Little Walden, in Essex, and continued its fight from there. The squadron code, partially hidden by the port aileron, was E2.

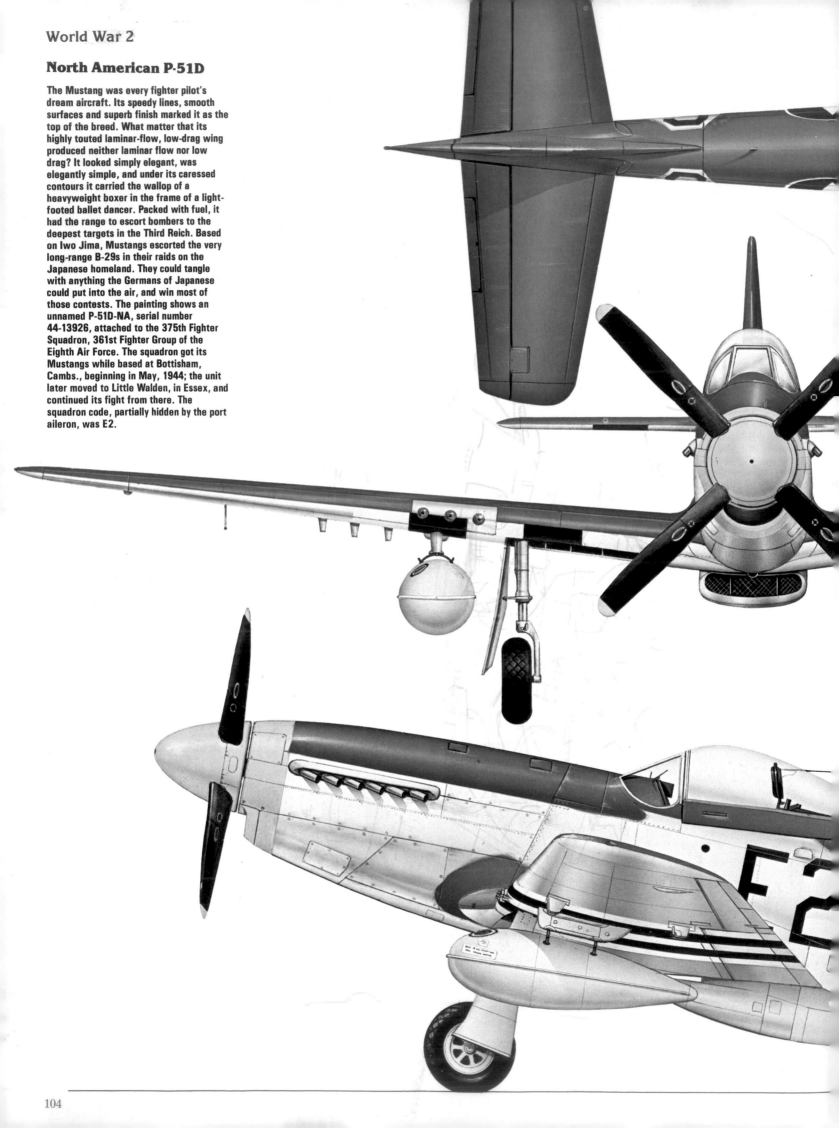

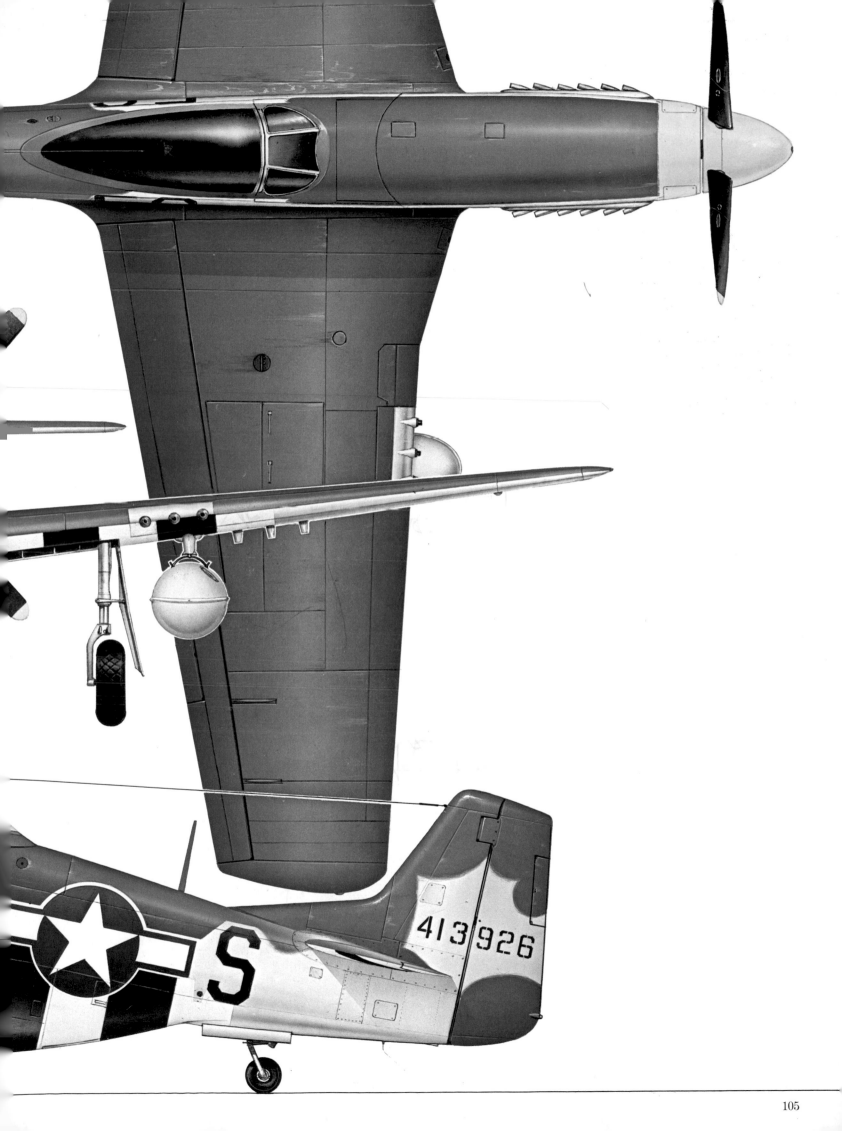

413 926

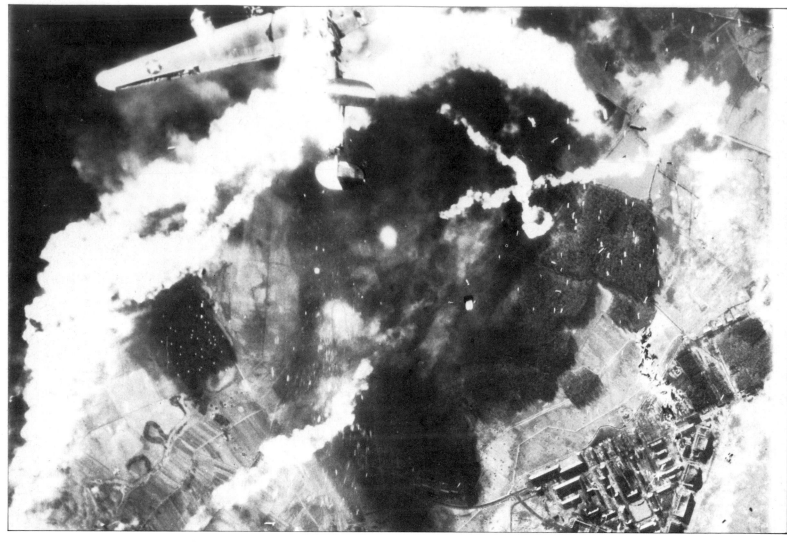

Tuesday December 12, 1944 brought a welcome break in the cloud that had covered Germany, and bombardiers took visual sightings on the marshalling yards at Hanau and Aschaffenburg. One of the losers was this B-24 of 489 BG.

The Dora-9, the 'long-nosed' Fw 190D-9, was one of the most formidable fighters of the entire war. This one was nearly hit by the bombs from a 9th AF B-26 in a mission which read: losses, nil; enemy fighters destroyed, one.

Eighth lost 922 heavies out of its operational force, most to flak, some to weather, few to fighters.

But the bombing was working. By September, German fuel production was down to about one-quarter of its normal quantity. That throttling was felt deeply by the Luftwaffe; its fighters were parked in vast arrays on the ground, out of fuel even for taxiing to a dispersal site. They were most appealing targets for any wandering fighter or bomber, and the Luftwaffe was losing them at the rate of 500 each week.

Paradoxically, German aircraft production never had been higher. The factories, many dispersed and some underground or in mountain caves, churned out complete fighters faster than they could be ferried away.

The heavies kept hammering at the oil targets; even one-quarter of normal production was too much to allow to the Germans. The resiliency of the targets was impressive. Ploesti took multiple missions before its shutdown. The vast synthetic fuel plant at Merseburg-Leuna was another durable target. It was hit 22 times by USSTAF and twice by Bomber Command; they flew 6,550 sorties and dropped 18,328 tons of bombs on that single plant before they knocked it out for good.

The smarter Germans knew what was happening, and tried to make the point with Hitler or his staff. Albert Speer, the architect who became a production genius, said about the first raid against the synthetic-fuel plants: "It meant the end of German armament production."

Operations Market/Garden

Now Montgomery's task was to drive toward the Zuider Zee, crossing the Rhine and outflanking the Siegfried Line defenses. In support, he was assigned a huge airborne operation: *Market*, which would land about half the combined strengths of the British 1st and the American 82nd and 101st Airborne Divisions.

Market was preceded by heavy air strikes against German flak defense by Eighth AF and RAF heavies. Then on the morning of September 17, the troop carriers and glider trains took off: 1,546 aircraft, and 478 gliders. Losses in their drop and landing zones were minimal, and the Luftwaffe was hardly in evidence. a day later, a second aerial fleet dropped and landed reinforcements from 1,306 aircraft and 1,152 gliders.

But the British drop zone was in front of two strong German panzer divisions, and *Garden*—Montgomery's ground operation—became a disaster. The Germans were not yet beaten on the ground, and *Market/Garden* did nothing to speed the defeat.

Maintaining a flow of supplies remained a problem. The ground armies had halted against the Siegfried Line because they were low on supplies. Eisenhower made the point: an additional deep-water port to the north was " . . . an indispensable prerequisite for the final drive into Germany." Antwerp was the logical choice, and the ground campaign to reduce its defenders and capture it was supported all the way by tactical air strikes. So were subsequent drives against Aachen and other German towns on the invasion route to the Ruhr.

It was desperate, heavy ground fighting all the way. The Germans had brought up every possible reinforcement. They dug in and held, taking terrible losses, but not giving much territory in exchange. Air power was doing all it could, as 1944 ground toward its end. The Allies had air superiority over the battlefield, and

held it. The Luftwaffe was rarely seen, and German soldiers grew increasingly bitter as they wondered where their air support was hiding.

The Final Offensives

U. S. Strategic Air Forces and RAF Bomber Command rearranged their target priorities September 23. Oil headed the list; second were ordnance, armored fighting vehicle and motor vehicle factories.

The strategic offensive against oil was beginning to show both progress and problems: progress, because the full production flow had slowed greatly; problems, because it hadn't stopped. The Germans had mastered rapid repair, and also had a vast force of slave labor available for the jobs. Between successive raids they were able to produce significant quantities of fuel.

There were also disturbing indications that the Luftwaffe wasn't quite as defeated as had been hoped. German fighters did not harass bomber raids all along their routes as they had done, but they often did attack in force in a single pitched air battle. So the USSTAF went back to the German aircraft industry again, specifically targeting those plants where jet fighters were being produced. But it was not to be a successful campaign.

By careful hoarding of gasoline, the Luftwaffe was able to mount some telling blows. On November 2, almost 400 fighters blitzed an Eighth bomber strike, and shot down 26 heavies. Once again, USSTAF reacted, bombing Luftwaffe operational bases. It was no more effective than the attacks on the aircraft, ball-bearing and armored-vehicle industries had been.

The relative ineffectiveness of the campaigns against such strategic targets was a cause for considerable

concern. It was, after all, a tenet of faith in the USAAF that strategic bombing was the way to win a war; but strategic bombing was not, apparently, winning that one at that time. USAAF wanted to know why.

Part of the reason was that bombing technology still had not advanced very far. Radar bombing was inaccurate; nearly half of the blind-bombing missions were near-failures. The Eighth had an unenviable score on its radar missions; its average CEP (Circular Error Probable, the radius of a circle within which one-half of the bombs fell) was two miles. The Fifteenth was only half as bad, with a one-mile CEP.

Even daylight drops in clear weather were not always accurate. Further, there was little known about the best combinations of bomb type and fuze setting. A significant percentage of the bombs dropped, on or off target, never detonated.

By December the Luftwaffe was stronger than it had ever been, numerically. The bomber force had been reduced drastically and its pilots transferred to fighters in home defense squadrons around the Reich. New jet and rocket fighters were beginning to hit the Allied bomber formations. Armed with new weapons, and changed tactics, the German air defenses were again a potential danger.

Their acceptance of battle alternated with periods of stand-down. One of the latter occurred during the early part of December, and it was only one of many clues that the Allied forces had that something was in the offing.

Reconnaissance pilots had begun reporting major troop and supply movements on the German side of the lines. Stockpiles appeared, camouflaged in fields and along roads. Trains moved heavy equipment toward the front, and armored columns were spotted, lost and

This B-24H, "Burma Bound" of a 15th AF unit, was pictured limping home on three R-1830s after an attack on Munich in December 1944.

Loading 0.50-calibre belts into the eight vast ammunition bays of a P-47 was a skilled task. These 56th FG armorers never muffed it, and the pilot, Gabby Gabreski, became top-scorer of the AAF in Europe with 28 air victories.

then seen again closer to the battle lines.

It all coalesced in the early morning hours of December 16, when a German offensive roared into the Ardennes region, driving a deep bulge into the Allied front. The Wehrmacht was back at the top of its old form: Blitzkreig. Armored units slashed into the outnumbered and outmaneuvered Allied defenses, overran the battlefield and pushed about 50 miles to the West. It was a desperate attempt to buy time with the slim possibility of destroying several American divisions and perhpas even recapturing Antwerp, with its mountains of supplies and tanks of fuel. It was a brilliant stroke, and it was geared to a long spell of bad weather that grounded most of the Allied counter-air action.

Finally the weather cleared, and a massive counter-offensive began. On the ground, determined drives by American troops started the inexorable retreat of the Germans. The pathetic attempt by the Luftwaffe to seize control of the air was a miserable failure. Allied strategic and tactical air units pulverized rail transport west of the Rhine, halting the forward movement of German reinforcements. By the end of the month, the Wehrmacht was in retreat, and eventually got away without the loss of a single major unit.

The German New Year gift was the final coordinated offensive by the Luftwaffe, the one big blow that Gen. Galland and other Luftwaffe commanders had discussed for so long. They assembled a task force of 700 to 800 fighter-bombers and sent them on a two-hour strike against Allied airfields. Designated Operation *Bodenplatte (Baseplate)*, it was planned as a damaging assault against tactical air strength. It backfired, and gave the Luftwaffe one of its worst days. Sources vary on the extent of German losses; but any losses were punishing at that time. Pilots could not be spared, and the 36 U. S. fighters that were destroyed out of the total Allied loss of about 150 were not worth the cost to the dying Luftwaffe.

The Combined Chiefs conferred at Malta January

Strategic Bombing over North West Europe

The purpose of the U.S. strategic bomber forces in the UK was to bomb Germany's industry to destruction with pinpoint day bombing. However, the B-17 crews at first suffered operational problems with their airplanes and the European weather, and then from the attentions of the German fighters. But better B-17s and tactics, combined with the advent of the Mustang escort fighter to permit the 8th AF to fulfill its task.

1. Briefing before a mission by AAF bomber crews from an English airbase (note base plan in background).

2. A B-17G of U.S. 8th Air Force (possibly the 381st GB) being marshalled to a halt after a mission.

3. One of the most famous 8th AF bombers, "E-rat-icator" was an olive-drab B-17G (AF No 42-39930) assigned to the 730th BS, 452nd BG at Deopham Green.

4. B-24H "Little Warrior" died over Quakenbruck, Germany, on 29 June 1944; the 493rd BG aircraft took a direct flak hit.

5. Possibly the only aircraft to reach the AAF already named, "5 Grand" was the 5,000th B-17 built by Boeing, and thousands of employees signed their names on it.

6. Frames from Lt Lee G. Mendenhall's combat camera show a victory over a Bf 109G, which in the final picture has hit a tree and cartwheeled into snow.

7. Douglas A-20 Havocs were important light bombers of all Allied air forces in the ETO; these 9th AF A-20G and J models were heading for France.

8. High over Germany, P-47Ds of an 8th AF Fighter Group dive to engage the enemy. Bomber crews appreciated the escort.

9. The scene ahead of a B-24 co-pilot, as the sky fills with ice crystals in contrails from a 15th AF Bomb Group.

1

3

2

4

30, and decided to give the Russians a hand by sending heavy bombers against targets selected by the Kremlin. Fine, said the Russians; hit the transport centers in eastern Germany: Berlin, Chemnitz, Cottbus, Dresden and Leipzig among others.

One of those raids took the Eighth to Berlin in a massive February 3 strike. About 1,000 B-17s hit the capital, and another 400 B-24s pounded Magdeburg. Skies over Berlin were clear; the bomb drops were accurate and devastating in the government-building area. About 25,000 civilians died. On the night of February 13, the RAF slammed Dresden, with 772 heavies dropping their huge loads on that city. Next day, 311 B-17s of the Eighth hit Dresden with a second blow. About 35,000 died there; for propaganda reasons that figure was inflated greatly by the Germans and later used as fact by some historians and writers.

There was little left to do for the strategic force and for tactical air as Germany crumbled in those last months. Gen. Spaatz sent an April 16 message to Eaker

and Doolittle which began: "The advances of our ground forces have brought to a close the strategic air war . . . "

The last raid against a strategic target was flown by the Eighth, as they had flown the first. On April 25, they hit the Skoda armament works in Pilsen, Czechoslovakia. Then the Eighth turned to supply drops, evacuating prisoners of war, and taking 30,000 sightseers—the hard-working ground crews of the heavy bomber squadrons—over the lunar landscape that German cities had become.

The Allied armies joined at the Elbe; Russians, French, British and Americans shared confiscated wine in a few moments of mutual respect and delight that the war was, for them, over. They had survived, the single most important fact of their lives.

Germany was dead. The Third Reich expired in a Götterdammerung of its own choice and its own devising. Its residual government surrendered May 7, 1945.

The war in the Pacific was a hard-fought tactical campaign fought largely by the Army, Navy and Marine Corps, with powerful USAAF support. Finally, though, the B-29 strategic bombers of the Air Force were in a position to unleash a rain of death on Japan's hapless cities.

Sixty North to Twenty South

Between the great land mass of China and the huge island that is Australia lie archipelagos with exotic names dimly remembered from primary school geography: Sumatra, Borneo, New Guinea, Celebes. Where were Yap, Salamaua, Wakde, Morotai? Who lived in the Caroline or the Gilbert and Marshall Islands?

They lay in the massive Pacific basin, dotting dozens of smaller seas, stepping-stones that the Japanese trod in their expansion. They were rich in resources, like the oil at Balikpapan in Borneo, or in strategic position, like the port of Rabaul or the island fortress of Truk.

Far to the north lay the remnants of a land bridge that, eons earlier, had connected Asia and North American. Now a wind-swept and forbidding string of islands reaching in a great arc from Alaska toward the Kamchatka Peninsula, they also were of strategic importance. Their names were spoken in another of the myriad of strange tongues of the Pacific: Kiska, Attu, Unimak, Adak.

These faraway places were the jungles and tundras, mountains and savannas that American military strength would fight for, because—as they led outward from Tokyo—they also led back to the heart of the Japanese empire.

It was a war theater of unique parts, tropical islands with bare-breasted beauties and sandy beaches in one region, a consuming jungle in another, and permafrost in a third. Into that theater of operations moved seven separate American air forces, each with a difficult almost impossible mission. Each was at the absolute end of the supply and communication lines, knowing with certainty that the planners in Washington and London considered them to be of secondary importance, to be supplied after the European theater got all it needed.

They started with small cadres and aging airplanes. Their fighters were the Bell P-39 and the Curtiss P-40; their bombers the early North American B-25 and the Douglas A-20. A handful of heavy bombers and some Douglas C-47 transports completed the fleet. With that

The Pacific foams under bombs and ·50-calibre fire as B-25s of the 345th BG (see p.115) attack a Japanese frigate off the Indo-China coast in early 1945. Twenty years later the USAF was to be at war again in this theater.

111

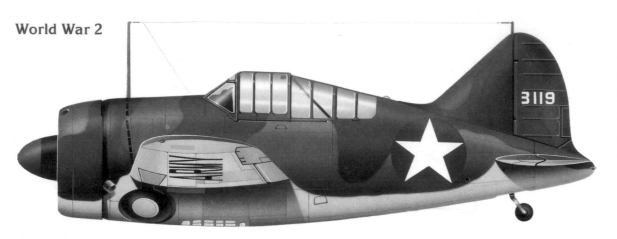

The Brewster F2A, named Buffalo in British Commonwealth service, was a portly Navy fighter that fared badly at the hands of the Japanese. This example, a B-439, was one of a batch of 20 for the Dutch East Indies which were taken on charge by the USAAF before being passed to the RAAF to help defend Australia in mid-1942.

strength, commanders were told, keep the Japanese at bay until Hitler is beaten.

The Fifth Air Force, moving back toward the Philippines with Gen. Douglas MacArthur, began at the nadir of his retreat to Australia. The Seventh Air Force left an idyllic life in Hawaii, and set out for another assemblage of islands, and another, and another.

The Tenth in India and the Fourteenth in China struggled in strange environments to hold and beat back the Japanese. When they needed support, it was the China-India Wing of Air Transport Command that flew its C-47s and C-46s over the treacherous air routes of the "Hump", to move precious cargoes nearer the front.

The Jungle Air Force, the Thirteenth, began in the lush greenery of New Caledonia, and moved through the Pacific with the Marines and the Navy, rolling back Japanese forces. And in the frozen north, the Eleventh tussled with the toughest weather imaginable, fought their battles in defense of U. S. territory, and finally presided over a beaten Japanese invasion attempt.

Then, just about when the world began to notice these unheralded heroes of the hinterlands, the Superfortresses of the Twentieth Air Force came in, and proceeded to make the final surrender of Japan inevitable. In the doing, they drew much of the attention, and nearly all of the glory.

Think in these perspectives. The Pacific is a monstrous theater of war, a vast water mass four or five thousand miles in diameter. Yawata, Japan's Pittsburgh, was 1,500 miles from the closest forward bases in China, and Tokyo was 2,000 miles away. From Australia to Balikpapan was more than 1,000 miles. You could fly northwest from Australia for 1,000 miles and still be over New Guinea. Sumatra, Java and the Philippines are all 1,000 miles long. From Saipan, Tinian and Guam it was 1,600 miles to Tokyo, one-way.

The first task in the Pacific was to contain the Japanese, the second job was to roll them back and seize their bases, and the third was to hit Japan itself. It had to be done in that order.

The American 'island hopping' campaign in the Pacific in World War 2 was greatly aided in the tactical way by considerable softening up of each target just before the invasion. Here Consolidated B-24 Liberator heavy bombers prepare to take off from the crushed coral strip on Funafuti Island in the Ellice group to unload on Tarawa island.

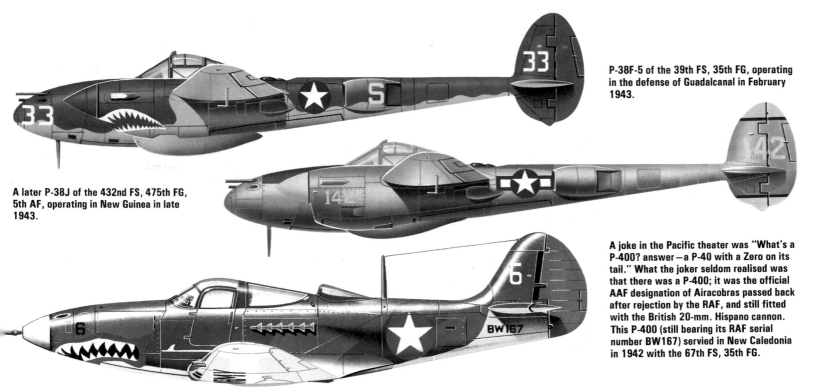

P-38F-5 of the 39th FS, 35th FG, operating in the defense of Guadalcanal in February 1943.

A later P-38J of the 432nd FS, 475th FG, 5th AF, operating in New Guinea in late 1943.

A joke in the Pacific theater was "What's a P-400? answer — a P-40 with a Zero on its tail." What the joker seldom realised was that there was a P-400; it was the official AAF designation of Airacobras passed back after rejection by the RAF, and still fitted with the British 20-mm. Hispano cannon. This P-400 (still bearing its RAF serial number BW167) servied in New Caledonia in 1942 with the 67th FS, 35th FG.

North from Australia

The Japanese were well-established on the northern coast of New Guinea and had begun a summer, 1942, offensive to drive across the mountains and take Port Moresby on the southern coast.

Maj. Gen. George C. Kenney, MacArthur's top air commander, organized the Fifth Air Force in September 1942, and gave it a single immediate mission: seize and hold air superiority over New Guinea.

Hitting the enemy bases at Buna and Lae, Douglas A-20 light bombers roared in a few feet above the water, dropping a new weapon: the parafrag bomb. It was a 23-lb. fragmentation bomb with a rudimentary parachute attached, and an instantaneous fuze. It dropped nose first, hit, and exploded in a steely scythe that sliced into Japanese aircraft.

It was one of several innovative field adaptations of existing weapons by Fifth AF. A-20s were modified to carry four .50-cal machine guns in their noses for strafing. The B-25s were altered to carry eight of the same weapons. Thus armed, a light or medium bomber could attack airfields or shipping, the two major targets for Fifth AF, drop its bombs, and swing back to strafe.

On March 1, 1943, Kenney's airmen, augmented by Royal Australian Air Force pilots flying Bristol Beaufighters, caught a 16-ship Japanese convoy in the Bismarck Sea. For three days, bombers and fighters of the Fifth and the RAAF worked over the vessels. Only four escorting destroyers managed to get away. Hundreds of survivors were left clinging to rafts and floating debris. On the fourth day, the planes came back and ruthlessly hunted down and strafed the hapless Japanese troops. It was the end of attempts to supply Lae by organized convoys.

In October, the Fifth hit Rabaul, giving Adm. William Halsey an assist with his assault on Bougainville. Navy and Thirteenth AF planes pitched in, and together they destroyed enemy air power in New Britain. Early in 1944, a sustained air offensive knocked Rabaul out of action, and the Fifth turned its attention to Hollandia. A three-day attack, started April 1, 1944, devastated the place.

Pre-invasion strikes against the Philippines began in August, 1944, with attacks on Mindanao Island. But MacArthur decided to go directly for Leyte. Fifth AF destroyed 314 Japanese planes in that campaign for a loss of 16 of their own. Luzon Island was next.

The Japanese had little chance to get into the air. On January 7, 1945, Clark Field near Manila was blasted

Eyed professionally by the pilot of a Vought F4U Corsair fighter-bomber, a North American B-25 Mitchell light bomber takes off on a strike.

The Douglas A-24 was the AAF model of the Navy SBD Dauntless carrier-based dive bomber, differing in such things as electric system voltage and tire size (for soft fields). This A-24B served with the 312th BG (Dive), Makin Island in the Gilbert group, December 1943.

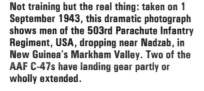

Not training but the real thing: taken on 1 September 1943, this dramatic photograph shows men of the 503rd Parachute Infantry Regiment, USA, dropping near Nadzab, in New Guinea's Markham Valley. Two of the AAF C-47s have landing gear partly or wholly extended.

by nearly 8,000 parafrags, dropped by 40 B-25s and 97 A-20s. All the B-25s and 20 A-20s screamed across the field in a broad line abreast. That strike was followed by the rest of the A-20s, running in from the opposite direction to catch the defending gunners, if any, from behind. The Japanese counted 60 burned and battered aircraft; the Fifth lost one B-25 and four A-20s.

But on the same day, the Fifth also lost Maj. Thomas B. McGuire, 431st Fighter Squadron, after his 38th victory. McGuire and Maj. Richard I. Bong were rivals for the top score in the theater. Bong had been first to pass Capt. Eddie Rickenbacker's 26-victory tally from World War 1; he did that April 8, 1944, while a Captain attached to Headquarters, V Fighter Command. He was promoted to Major and sent home on temporary duty; but he came back, and raised his score to 40, ending the war as the USAAF's top-ranking ace. Both Bong and McGuire won Medals of Honor for their exploits, as did eight other airmen of the Fifth.

Col. Neel E. Kearby, commanding 384th Fighter Group, was one of them. He led four P-47s on a routine reconnaissance flight October 11, 1943, in New Guinea, saw a Japanese "Oscar" (Nakajima Ki-43 fighter) and shot it down. Minutes later, he spotted a formation of a dozen bombers escorted by 36 fighters. Outnumbered 12 to one, Kearby led his flight into action. He shot down three more "Oscar" fighters and a single "Tony" (Kawasaki Ki-61 fighter). For six in one flight, Kearby was awarded the Medal of Honor.

He was one-upped January 11, 1945, by Capt. William A. Shomo, 82nd Tactical Reconnaissance Squadron, famed as "The Flying Undertaker". Shomo, in his black-trimmed Mustang, was on a reconnaissance flight to Aparri with wingman 2nd Lt. Paul Lipscomb, when they saw a single "Betty" (Mitsubishi G4M bomber) escorted by a dozen "Tony" fighters. Shomo and Lipscomb ripped into the formation; Shomo shot down the bomber and six fighters within the 15-minute time span of the battle. Lipscomb got three more fighters. Shomo received the Medal of Honor.

After Manila was captured in March 1945, the Fifth moved to Okinawa for its final build-up preceding the planned invasion of Japan. From that island base Fifth AF launched strikes against targets on Kyushu, Japan's southernmost island, and against shipping and the Chinese coastal ports held by the enemy.

Republic P-47D-20-RA, one of the "Razorback" models built at Evansville, with the 19th FS, 318th FG, on Saipan, July 1944.

The Fifth was on Okinawa when the war ended; they had been a vital part of MacArthur's brilliant campaign.

Island Hoppers

The Hawaiian Air Force was first to see air combat in World War 2, when a few of its fighters fought against the Japanese armada that December morning. On February 5, 1942, Hawaiian Air Force became the Seventh Air Force.

Its first major action was in the June 3 Battle of Midway. Heavy and medium bombers, staged through Midway Island, sortied against the Japanese fleet with poor results.

The first major air offensive for the Seventh was part of Operation *Galvanic*, the amphibious assault of the Gilbert Islands. The Seventh moved to the Ellice Islands in August, leaving six of its fighter squadrons on Hawaii for the defense of the islands. Heavies from Seventh AF supported the task force in the invasion that began November 20, 1943.

Operation *Flintlock*, an amphibious assault directed against Kwajalein atoll, began January 31, 1944. The Seventh AF heavy and medium bombers helped soften Japanese air installations on Maloelap and Wotje. Part of the Seventh's weaponry for those engagements was a 75-mm. cannon mounted in the nose of some of its new B-25Gs.

The overwater missions required the range of medium and heavy bombers, and so Seventh sent its single-engined equipment back to Hawaii in March and April.

The Marianas campaign was next; Saipan, Tinian and Guam were needed as bases for the Superfortresses, and Seventh AF was assigned to the pre-invasion support task. It began with a thorough photo-reconnaissance of Saipan. On June 15, 1944, the first wave of American troops hit the beaches, with the P-47s of Seventh AF flying in close support alongside Marine and Navy fighters. The Japanese defended the island from an extensive network of caves, pillboxes, trenches, and other strongpoints. Thunderbolts of the 318th Fighter Group were first to use napalm in battle; they bowled their fire bombs into Japanese defense on Tinian Island.

Late that autumn, Seventh AF sent strikes to the Volcano and Bonin Islands. Iwo Jima, the island selected as an emergency base for B-29s because it was about halfway between Saipan and Tokyo, was invaded February 19, 1945. When the island was declared secure March 16, VII Fighter Command moved to Iwo to escort B-29s on their missions. The first was flown April 7; 108 P-51s went with the big birds to Tokyo, shot down 21 intercepting fighters, lost one of their own. But by then the B-29s had begun flying unescorted night incendiary raids, and there was little demand for daylight escort.

So VII Fighter Command went out on its own long-range sweeps, hitting targets in Tokyo, Nagoya and Osaka that were more than a 1,200-mile round trip distant. VII FC flew 51 long-range missions between April 7 and August 14. Thirteen of them were B-29 escort flights; the rest were fighter sweeps. The longest was a 1,600-mile round trip flown August 14 by 48 P-47Ns of the 507th Fighter Group. They left their base on Ie Shima and flew to Keijo, in Korea. About 50 defending aircraft met them; the P-47s fought at that extreme range for about a half-hour, shot down 20 of the enemy and lost only one. That action won the group a Distinguished Unit Citation, the only such battle honor awarded to a P-47 unit in the Pacific.

The Seventh was another of the small Pacific air forces, whose statistics were overshadowed by the larger numbers of the European war, and by the superior publicity generated by the Navy fast carrier task forces, their fighter and bomber squadrons, and the Marine Corps.

The Jungle Air Force

Thirteenth Air Force was just unlucky enough to spend its fighting career adjacent to the jungles of the South Pacific islands. It grew out of a welter of command problems and inter-service rivalries in the theater that centered on the proper use of the available B-17s. Navy, with overall command in the area, wanted to use the sea search capability of the Fortresses; AAF thought they should be out bombing. It seemed as if the only solution was to create a new and separate air force, and so the Thirteenth was born.

Soon after its establishment in the New Hebrides and New Caledonia islands, its combat units moved to Guadalcanal with the Marines, and began a long series of campaigns against Japanese strong points in the Pacific. Thirteenth AF pilots were comrades-in-arms with Marine and Navy fliers, and with the airmen of the Royal New Zealand Air Force.

With Guadalcanal finally secured, the Navy-commanded amphibious task forces moved on up the Solomon Islands, taking New Georgia, Munda, Vella Lavella, and Bougainville, then reducing the Japanese stronghold of Rabaul, on the tip of New Britain.

By mid-1945 a quarter of the globe was a graveyard of smashed Japanese war materiél. This A6M Zero died at Munda Island, New Georgia, in the Solomons.

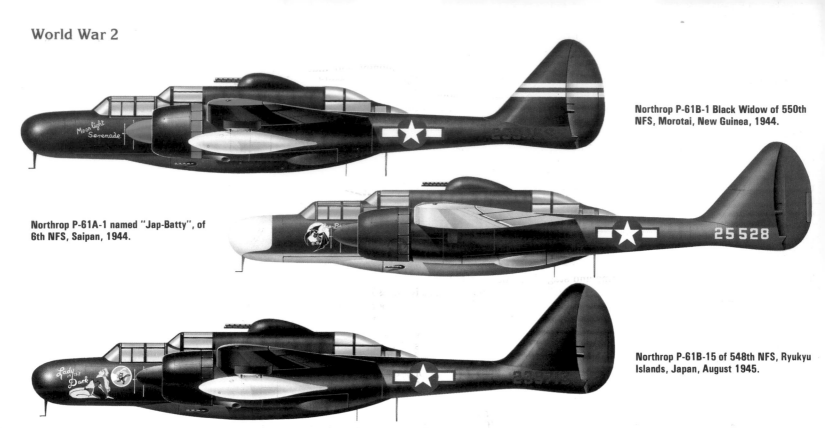

Northrop P-61B-1 Black Widow of 550th NFS, Morotai, New Guinea, 1944.

Northrop P-61A-1 named "Jap-Batty", of 6th NFS, Saipan, 1944.

Northrop P-61B-15 of 548th NFS, Ryukyu Islands, Japan, August 1945.

The Thirteenth made three unique contributions to the war. First, 18 P-38s from three XIII Fighter Command squadrons intercepted and shot down the aircraft carrying Japanese Admiral Yamamoto. Second, the 868th Bomb Squadron (Heavy) pioneered low-altitude radar night bombing of enemy shipping, and did so much damage that Japanese attempts to resupply troops by that means were abandoned. Third, the long-range XIII Bomber Command heavies hammered Japanese fortresses at Truk, Yap and Palau, in unescorted overwater missions of 1,400- to 1,800-mile lengths, fighting off determined Japanese interceptions and dodging very heavy flak concentrations.

On New Guinea after those campaigns, Thirteenth AF became a part of Far East Air Forces, along with the Fifth, and began the Philippine offensive. Its heavies helped wreck the oil processing facilities of Balikpapan, and supported the invasions of Palawan and Borneo.

It was a difficult war for the Thirteenth, compounded by command complexities and concepts. But Thirteenth AF was part of a team, and it never let the side down.

The Generalissimo's Lifeline

China was captive, its eastern coast and southern land borders blocked by the Japanese. Only one supply route remained; it led from Assam, in northeastern India, to the Chinese cities of Kunming and Chungking. For almost three years of the war, every single item that reached either the American forces in China, or the armies of Generalissimo Chiang Kai-shek, got there by air. Bulldozers and typewriters, toilet paper and gasoline, shoes, rifles and medicines were airlifted to China in one of the most hazardous and difficult flying missions ever attempted.

The airlift portion was only part of a 1,300-mile tortuous supply trail. Cargo was unloaded at the Indian port of Calcutta, moved to Assam by slow train, was loaded on air transports and flown to Myitkyina, in Burma. There it was transferred to barges on the Irrawaddy river and floated downstream to Bhamo, where it was offloaded and trucked to Kunming over the winding Burma Road. In May, 1942, the Japanese seized the airfield at Myitkyina, and cut that route.

Only a direct air link between Assam and Kunming remained as a possibility. It was a 500-mile run above some of the worst terrain and in some of the worst weather in the world. Between the two terminals lies the Santsung Range, an extension of the Himalayas known to pilots as "The Hump" or "The Rockpile". Its peaks topped 16,000 feet and its passes were above 14,000. Thunderstorms, 100-mph. winds, frightening turbulence, and icing at every level above 15,000 feet combined to make the route a pilot's nightmare.

It was begun with Douglas C-47s of Tenth AF, valiant but out of their depth in the fierce conditions of the Hump route. Airfields were totally inadequate, from any viewpoint. The Hump region was uncharted, and any other navigational aids were non-existent. Living conditions were as bad as anywhere in the world; civilization, in the GI sense, had not reached the upper Assam valley. The Japanese bombed the airfields; there were only about 40 Tenth AF fighters for defending the bases, and escorting the transports on the Hump run.

The accident rate was appalling. Veteran pilots referred to the run as "The Aluminum Trail"; there was a wreck for almost every mile of its length, more than 450 planes downed. Maintenance had to be done at night, when the aircraft were cooler. To touch their

Probably taken at Kunming in 1943, this shows the two most important Curtiss aircraft of the AAF, with a C-46A Commando arriving after its long haul "over the hump" and a P-40K Warhawk fighter of the 23rd FG (the famed Flying Tigers, American Volunteer Group, actually part of the Chinese AF).

metal skins during the day produced second-degree burns. Spare parts were in great demand, and short supply. When new planes did arrive, crews got the impression they had been hastily assembled and never checked out; they required much too much time in maintenance.

Air Transport Command took over the Hump operation in December, 1942. The tonnage began to rise steadily, only interrupted for causes like monsoon rains that turned the bases into mud sloughs. And each time that things seemed to be going well, another customer had an urgent need for air cargo.

In March, 1944, British units defending against an enemy drive into Assam urgently needed air resupply. In May, Lt. Gen. Joseph Stilwell began his Burma offensive and became another airlift customer. The Twentieth AF moved its B-29s into China and staged raids from forward bases near Chengtu, China; they also drew on ATC air supply.

And always, Generalissimo Chiang and his representatives in Washington pressed for increased tonnages of supplies, reminding U. S. leadership of the precarious position of loyal Chinese troops.

Late in the war, the single air lane across the Hump had broadened to a 200-mile wide air corridor through which about 650 planes moved every day. The Burma Road never carried more than 6,000 tons of supplies in any month, a figure exceeded routinely by planes from several of the Assam bases. The record performance was set August 1, 1945; Hump pilots flew 1,118 round trips, carrying 5,327 tons of supplies without a single accident or incident.

It was a prodigious accomplishment, ferrying 650,000 tons of freight by air across a treacherous stretch of mountains. It consumed men and planes, ruined health

and careers, wasted money and materiel. Yet the offensive war in that theater could not have been waged without it; it was the only way to go.

But the true return on the awful investment came later. The experience gained at such cost was the foundation of worldwide strategic airlift operations, and on that foundation the Berlin Air Lift would be built three years later.

On the Road to Mandalay

The Tenth Air Force seems to have been expected to handle the complete air situation in the China-India-Burma theater. It set up shop in New Delhi in May 1942, and was told to defend Burma, assist the British in the defense of India, and protect the air route from India to China.

To do that massive mission, Tenth had almost no air strength. Its heavy bombers had been taken away and sent to the Middle East in June, 1942, along with its first commander, a dozen badly needed transports, and the accoutrements of a headquarters. By December that year, Tenth AF had all of 32 heavy bombers on its roster, with ten of them non-operational; 43 medium bombers; and 184 fighters, of which 24 were useless for combat.

What it lacked in equipment, the Tenth made up for in effort. It began the airlift to China over the Hump, with all the problems that mission entailed. It spun off two Air Task Forces, one to China and the other to India. It was primarily an interdiction force, hitting tactical targets: shipping, port facilities, maintenance and repair yards for locomotives, and railroad bridges and junctions.

Its B-24s bombed Rangoon's docks and port facilities

Sgt Elmer J. Pence adds, with the help of his pet monkey, another Rising Sun to a P-40 (probably a P-40E) of the 26th FS, 51st FG, of the 14th AF in China in 1944.

Most of the fighters in China were P-40s but this P-51B was in action there (unit unknown) in 1944, together with numerous other aircraft of the 14th AF. Camouflage schemes were often non-standard, and like the P-40s this fighter appears to have British-style "dark green and dark earth" with gray underside.

regularly, flying unescorted missions until some P-38s arrived as new equipment. The missions were about 1,500 miles round trip, considerably farther than the distance from British bases to Berlin and back.

The Tenth participated in a joint air offensive in late November, 1943, with the RAF and a heavy bomb group detached from Chennault's Fourteenth AF. The results were only mediocre. But the crews gained back some confidence in two attacks on Bangkok, December 19 and 23. The 2,000-mile round trips took 14 long hours, much of it at night, but the bombs hit the docks and there were no losses among the heavies.

Eastern Air Command was formed December 15, 1943, from the Tenth AF and the RAF's Bengal Command, merging Tenth AF units into two new air forces: Strategic and Third Tactical. Like so many of the multi-service organizations that flourished during the war years for political reasons, EAC had shortcomings. So it was reorganized June 20, 1944, and the Tenth again became a separate combat command, one of six component units of the new EAC. With one fighter group and one fighter-bomber group, plus supporting troop carrier and combat cargo squadrons, the Tenth moved into the upper Assam valley to assist Stilwell's drive to retake Burma. He brought off his remarkable victory in large measure because of Tenth AF support. The Burma campaign ended May 3, 1945.

The Tenth was transferred to China soon after, opening headquarters at Kunming July 23, with hardly two weeks remaining in World War 2.

Once a Tiger . . .

Maj. Gen. Claire L. Chennault is remembered as a brilliant strategist and tactician. As commander of the American Volunteer Group, a three-squadron air force that operated from Burma and China, Chennault

planned basic tactics for the "Flying Tigers" that enabled them to score heavily against their Japanese opposition. Then, as commander of the China Air Task Force, Tenth AF, Chennault again showed his special skills. When CATF was absorbed as the nucleus of the Fourteenth Air Force, he was given a single mandate: strike the Japanese wherever and whenever they were found.

The Fourteenth was a small force, even by Pacific standards. It began with a single fighter group, one bombardment group of heavies and a squadron of mediums, totalling an official 356 aircraft, but with far fewer available for operations. When the war ended, the peak strength of Fourteenth AF was five fighter groups, still one heavy bomber group, and a single medium bomber group, an authorized strength of 798 aircraft.

With that relative handful of planes, Chennault defended half of China, protected one terminus of the Hump routes, ferried much of his own supply requirements, and sent offensive missions as far east as Shanghai, as far southeast as Haiphong, and as far west as Burma. His fighters and bombers were the only consistent air support force the Chinese armies had.

Chennault believed that China could be defended by the proper application of air power, and he tried his best to get what he saw as necessary. He was promised a build-up of Fourteenth AF strength, but it came too late. He never had enough supplies, and often most of the Fourteenth was grounded, out of fuel.

The Fourteenth also was a tactical force; even its heavies were used in that role. Chennault and his commanders understood strategic bombing, but they never got enough aircraft, bombs or fuel to sustain an offensive. The heavies often had to be pressed into ferry service, flying back to India for supplies.

Chennault had based some of his strength at forward bases in eastern China. From those fields, Fourteenth AF bombers pounded coastal shipping, denying the Japanese the supplies that followed the shipping lanes along the coast of China and Indo-China. So the Japanese began a major offensive to drive down through China from above Hankow to Indo-China, to establish a land route for supplies between northeastern China and the south. It would also cut off the advance base network being used by the Fourteenth.

By late autumn, 1944, the drive had overrun Fourteenth AF bases in the east, and the American units pulled back to Kunming, the headquarters of the Fourteenth. The Japanese had gained 1,500 miles in eight months of ground combat, had isolated the southeastern segment of China, and gained their supply routes. Hardly five months later, they began a pullback; troops were needed desperately to defend Japan, and the gains of the offensive in China were given back.

By May 1945 there was little left for the Fourteenth to do. They had supported the Chinese ground armies, hit shipping, and defended the Hump. The war was winding down and with it the mission of Fourteenth AF. Today, it is one of the forgotten air forces, except by its loyal alumni. But it was once a tiger.

Allison-engined P-51A flown by Col Philip Cochran, commander of 1st Air Commando Group, Burma, 1944.

Deep-Freeze Fighting

It was cold, to begin with. It had the williwaw, a brisk wind of about 100 mph. There was neither a calm nor a dry season, and it was possible to have both thick fog and high winds simultaneously. The weather was good perhaps eight to ten days each year. "If you can see for a hundred feet, it's a clear day," said the pilots.

That was the daily condition in the Aleutian chain, where the frozen war was fought by the freezing Eleventh Air Force. It was in action early. Admiral Yamamoto, in his planned attack on Midway in June 1942, sent a diversionary force spearheaded by two carriers to the Aleutians, hoping to convince the U. S. that it was a serious threat against the northern approaches and so dilute the possible opposition at Midway.

The Eleventh was forewarned through intelligence

messages. It mustered its handful of heavy bombers, its mediums, and a few squadrons of fighters. Augmented by U. S. Navy patrol boats and three Royal Canadian Air Force squadrons on temporary transfer with the Americans, they set out to defeat the foe. The Japanese bombed Dutch Harbor, at the Alaska end of the Aleutians, and landed occupation forces on Kiska and Attu, at the opposite end of the chain. When the offensive ceased, it had cost the defending forces 78 men and 14 planes.

The Eleventh then was given the task of striking the Japanese shore installations, which were well and cleverly defended. The enemy had about 50 "Rufe" (Nakajima A6M2) floatplane fighters. They had set up anti-aircraft batteries of several calibers. They had surveyed the routes by which any U. S. attackers might come, and had strung cables across the mountain

Officers and men of the 74th Fighter Squadron, 23rd Fighter Group, pose on a Curtiss P-40 fighter at a base outside Kunming on February 1, 1943.

B-25J Mitchell of the 498th BS "The Falcons", 345th BG, San Marcelius, Luzon, Philippines, April 1945.

B-25J-32 of the 499th BS (Medium) "Bats outa Hell", 345th BG, operating against Japan from Ie Shima, July 1945.

Allison-engined Curtiss P-40E of the 11th FS, 343rd FG, Aleutians, 1942.

passes they might use in the approach. On the first raid, a conventional high-altitude bombing mission, the Americans were pounded hard by the defenses, and lost one of the heavy bombers. On the second raid, they came in low with B-17s, surprised the Japanese and bombed well, they thought. But post-strike photo-reconnaissance showed no hits at all.

The Eleventh began a serious program of getting at the Japanese. They learned how to attack very low above the water, how to operate in foul weather, how to navigate in the extreme North latitudes. Slowly their force built. But the real enemy was the weather. More aircraft and crews were lost to the raging Arctic winds and fogs than to the Japanese.

There was never a solid strategic offensive by either side in the theater. There were a few fierce fights, like the one of September 14, 1942. A dozen Liberators, escorted by 14 P-38s and 14 P-39s, headed for Kiska from Adak. It was, curiously enough, a clear day; the Japanese spotted them miles off and began firing at ten miles. The force came in at 50 feet, fighters and bombers alike. The heavies sank two ships and set three more afire. Three midget subs were slammed

into twisted metal. Six flak batteries were knocked out of action. More than 200 troops were killed or wounded. The P-38s took on the waterfront, machine-gunning floatplanes while the P-39s shot down five that managed to get in the air and attack. Two of the P-38s were lost in a mid-air collision, but the U.S. force retired with no other casualties.

The Eleventh routinely bombed the Japanese after that, then supported Operation *Landgrab*, the recapture of Attu in May, 1943. There the defenders were wiped out after a foolhardy final charge. The Kiska defenders were evacuated under the cover of fog two weeks before the Americans put 30,000 armed troops on the island August 15 to retake it.

Without a Japanese presence in the Aleutians, there was little mission left for the Eleventh. They sent bombers against the Kuril Islands north of Japan, and demonstrated another advantage of air power in so doing. Their threat contained two major Japanese garrisons: 34,000 men on northern Hokkaido Island, and 41,000 in the Kurils, plus more than 400 aircraft. In the last analysis, that was the major contribution of the Eleventh toward winning the war.

Three 14th AF crewmen of the B-24 "The Goon" pose by part of their lethal payload in China. The fuselage tallies indicate 24 bomb missions and 16 Japanese airplanes destroyed.

The Decisive Bombardment

Finally, the United States had a strategic bomber capable of carrying sufficient bomb tonnage over great enough distances to produce significant results. It was the Boeing B-29 Superfortress, and its deployment to the Pacific theater forced the surrender of Japan before a single enemy soldier had set foot on her shore.

Original plans for B-29 deployment called for operations from bases in Northern Ireland and Egypt; from those two flanks they would carry out a huge aerial pincer movement against Germany. With Hitler defeated, the bombers would move to the Pacific and support the surface forces that were to invade Japan from the east coast of China and from the southwest Pacific. Gen. Arnold saw the single flaw in that plan, from his viewpoint: the word "support". The plan saw the B-29s only as a tactical strike force; not a word was written about a strategic air offensive.

Arnold proposed the only course possible under the conditions that existed when he attended the Quadrant Conference at Quebec in August 1943: base the B-29s in India, and stage them through forward bases in China for the attacks on Japan. It was a totally inadequate plan; but it was the only plan conceivable in Arnold's mind at the time, and he clung to it. At the Cairo Conference in December that year, Generalissimo Chiang agreed to build the bases in China.

The Cairo Conference was the first official recognition that the B-29s would conduct an air offensive. Second, the British agreed to construct bases in India for the B-29s. Third, the Joint Chiefs of Staff agreed upon the capture of the Marianas islands to serve as B-29 bases in the Pacific theater.

Command and control problems immediately arose, because of the multi-headed, multi-national organizational structures in that region. Generals MacArthur, Stilwell and Chennault wanted B-29 operations either under their command or their control; Admiral Nimitz thought the Navy ought to have a first claim; Generalissimo Chiang saw the B-29s as an important factor in his war against the Japanese. The issue finally was

The sequential salvoing of bombs from this 6th Bomb Group B-29 forms a figure-eight pendant in the sky. This characteristic pattern can be seen in many photographs of Superfortresses after bomb release. The aircraft carry the Circle-R identifier and the red-tipped vertical tails of the 6th BG. The closer B-29 is numbered 55; the farther is aircraft 51.

Before starting the engines from the flight engineer's position, the props have to be wound through some turns by hand. And so the ground crew, their hands protected against the coral-roughened edges of the prop blades, take turns man-handling the blades through their slow revolutions.

A dozen Superfortresses from the **444th Bomb Group** hold formation off the starboard wing of another B-29. The diamond on the vertical tail is the identifier for the **444th**; numbers inside the diamond varied within the squadrons. The single B-29 finished in the early olive drab top and gray belly camouflage scheme is a **B-29-1-BW**, the **37th** plane off the Wichita, Kansas, production line.

settled the way the Army Air Forces had settled things before: a complete new air force was created, to be commanded and controlled directly by Gen. Arnold from Washington.

The Newest Air Force

The Twentieth Air Force was activated April 4, 1944. It brought under its umbrella both the XX Bomber Command and the XXI Bomber Command. XX BC had been formed November 20, 1943, to include originally the 58th and 73rd Bombardment Wings (Very Heavy) that were the pioneering B-29 users. XXI Bomber Command had been created later when it became apparent that the 58th was going to India and the 73rd to the Marianas, and that the distance between them required separate command structures.

Each wing was based on a seven-aircraft squadron, four squadrons to each group, and four groups to each wing. Two 11-man crews were formed for each plane. Thus a complete B-29 wing, early in 1944, would deploy 112 aircraft and 2,464 crewmen.

The 58th headed for Calcutta and a complex of bases to its west. They had been British bomber fields, expanded by thousands of Indians working under the direction of Engineer Aviation troops. The first B-29s arrived there in April, 1944.

The Chinese bases were built near Chengtu by local peasants drafted for the labor force, numbering perhaps a quarter of a million. In three months, the Chinese had drained the rice paddies chosen for the airfield sites and converted them to operational, if primitive, B-29 bases. All four were ready by May 1, 1944.

Now the problem was to supply the Chinese bases.

Gasoline, bombs, bullets, spare parts, tires, and the thousand-and-one necessities of operational deployments had to be moved by air to the Chengtu bases. By stripping the Superforts, they could be adapted to carry about seven tons of fuel in auxiliary tanks. It was not an efficient way to move gasoline; two gallons of fuel had to be burned at a minimum for each gallon delivered to a forward base.

The supply route also was flown by Air Transport Command, as part of the Hump lifeline to China. XX Bomber Command included a number of Consolidated C-87 cargo transports, modified B-24 bombers, and these were used to augment the logistics lines.

The first mission was not successful. XX Bomber Command dispatched 98 B-29s against railroad shops at Bangkok on June 5, 1944. The planned four-plane diamond formations never assembled completely; weather forced the B-29s to run on the target individually or in paired elements. After 14 aborts at the start, others failed to find the target; it was bombed by 77 of the Superforts, more than half dropping by radar indications from altitudes between 17,000 and 27,000 feet.

Five were lost on the return trip. A dozen landed at bases other than their home fields, and 30 landed at bases that weren't even part of XX Bomber Command. Post-strike photos showed that about 17 bombs had fallen in the target area.

The second raid was worse. On the night of June 15, 68 B-29s were dispatched against Yawata. Fifteen bombed the target visually, and 32 used radar. The rest of the fleet had aborted. One B-29 was lost in combat, six to non-combat causes, and 55 crewmen were killed or missing. The bombing was atrocious; a single hit was scored on a powerhouse three-quarters

of a mile away from the aiming point. Nothing came closer.

For his own political reasons, Arnold was pushing the B-29s; he wanted them to be out hitting strategic targets. At that time, neither the bombers nor the crews were ready for long-range strikes against difficult targets, by day or night. Arnold demanded more than they could give, and would not ease off the pressure to produce.

He sent Gen. LeMay to take over August 29. LeMay went through the XX Bomber Command as he had done earlier in Europe, observing first, then evaluating, then correcting. He abandoned the four-plane diamond in favor of a 12-plane combat box, gave up the night raids, asked groups to select lead crews, and established a school for lead bombardiers. Within a month he had reorganized the command. The 58th Wing was disbanded on paper, and shuffled; its planes and personnel were dealt out to new groups of three squadrons each, with ten aircraft per squadron. Maintenance and bomb squadrons were combined.

The subsequent missions were the real training program that the crews had never had. Gradually they gained confidence in themselves and their aircraft.

But Where Are the Targets?

The XXI Bomber Command had been organized and was waiting its move to the Marianas. Its commander, Brig. Gen. Haywood S. Hansell, Jr., was called to a meeting with Chief of Staff Gen. George C. Marshall in early October, 1944. Marshall told him about plans for the early stages of the campaign against Japan, and that the first strike was being planned as a joint Navy and AAF mission. Hansell liked the idea, because it meant that Navy fighters would be available in the target area for defense of the B-29s. Marshall wanted some assurance from Hansell that the B-29s could make the first raid sometime in November. Hansell, knowing that he couldn't say no, said yes. As he wrote later, "It would involve an attack from bases which were 6,000 miles away, which we had never seen but hoped were ready, against targets whose locations we did not know."

The assigned targets were aircraft and engine factories. They were suspected of being somewhere around Tokyo and Nagoya, but nobody knew exactly where. They were pinpoint targets, and would have to be hit using precision bombing techniques in daylight. The B-29s would have to fly formation to the target for self-protection; there would be no escorts.

It was a complete turnaround for the 73rd Wing, then the only component of XXI Bomber Command. The wing had trained in radar bombing techniques; now it had to retrain on optical systems. It totally revised its operations, flight formations, and gunnery tactics.

When Hansell led the advance elements of the 73rd to Saipan, the situation was worse than they might have suspected. They had expected to find two finished bases, operational with four paved runways, all the facilities, and 100 hardstands on each base. They found one half-finished base with a partly finished runway and 40 hardstands. There was a gasoline storage area and a bomb dump, but no other facilities. The second base existed in part, but a large hill at one end of its main runway eliminated for B-29 operations.

Hansell faced a formidable task: complete the base, organize the headquarters and the wing, bring in 120 Superforts, and send some of them out on a mission against Japan. All of that carried a one-month deadline.

One stroke of good fortune eased the task. A crew from the 3rd Photo Reconnaissance Squadron arrived with their B-29, and decided to fly a reconnaissance mission to Tokyo. Hansell considered grounding the crew for rest; they had flown all the way from Kansas

with stops only for refuelling. But the crew was eager, and Hansell was persuaded. They found crystal-clear skies over Japan, and cruised over the islands for three hours. They returned with superb photo coverage of the areas where targets were expected, and the photo interpreters were able to spot them easily.

Meantime the Navy found itself in a major sea battle in the Leyte Gulf, supporting MacArthur's return to the Philippines, and cancelled its share of the first Tokyo strike. Adm. Nimitz recommended that the B-29s be grounded until the Navy could support them properly. He also suggested that the B-29s be used to mine the Japanese sea lanes, rather than sending the big planes off on strategic bombing missions.

Then Gen. Kenney chimed in with a letter to Arnold saying that the B-29s could not do the job from Saipan, because they lacked the range, and that even if they could, the Japanese fighters would destroy them at will. His basic argument—range—was a touchy issue. Air Transport Command, which controlled worldwide movements of all military aircraft, had refused to let the B-29s fly in squadron formation from San Francisco to Hawaii, just 2,400 miles distant. ATC's argument was that the Superforts didn't have the range for formation flight over that distance. The irony was that once the B-29s got to Saipan, their main mission was to fly in squadron formation for more than 3,000 miles, while loaded with bombs.

Arnold took a consensus of his top air commanders, who agreed with Kenney, and sent that news to Hansell. With it was a personal note that said, in effect, if you still think you can get away with it, good luck!

The final input came from Brig. Gen. Emmett O'Donnell, commander of the 73rd Wing, who told Hansell they were in no position to carry out the planned mission, and suggested that it be changed to a night attack. Hansell saw that whole coalescence of events as pivotal to the future of strategic bombing. If he agreed with Nimitz, it was an admission that the B-29s could not operate without Navy support. If he agreed with Kenney, it would probably mean that the Twentieth Air Force would become another component of Far East Air Forces. If he agreed with "Rosey" O'Donnell, it meant that primary targets could not be attacked, raising questions about the need for the specialized force of the XX and XXI Bomber Commands. The political and strategic implications were many. Hansell weighed them, and gave the order to go as planned. Mission San Antonio I was dispatched as scheduled.

The strike camera of the 500th Bomb Group B-29 catches its opposition rising to do battle. Framed almost dead center in the picture is a twin-engined Nakajima J1N Gekko, codenamed Irving in the Pacific theater. But its performance was just not high enough to make the Gekko an effective interceptor, and the chances are that the airplane shown here never made more than one pass against the B-29 formation before falling behind and below it, never to catch up.

Oh, there your are, Little Friends! Boy, I like to see you guys right out there; we just might need all the help we can get. We're headed for Japan and a hot target, and they're going to have everything they've got in the air to meet us at the IP (Initial Point, the first of several reference points for a bomb run). The Mustangs have joined the Superforts near Iwo Jima, and will fly with them to the islands and back, escorting the big bombers to the target and back home again until the fighters peel off for their own base on Iwo Jima.

One thing you could do in a B-29 was to see forward, and sometimes it was a Hell of a feeling with just some glass between you and a Japanese fighter. On the other hand, maybe all that framing would help if he started shooting. The super-secret, in-the-pickle-barrel-from-30,000-feet Norden bombsight stands naked in the bombardier's position for all to see.

The low-angled sun is just off our five o'clock position as we run in to the target, bomb bay doors open, gunners alert for an attack. Down below the rice paddies look green and rich; once we get beyond this second belt of them, we start the drop, walking the incendiaries across the city. Part of it already is burning, off there at two o'clock, and we'll set the rest of it off. Damn! Don't these people know when they are licked? We've burned everything worth burning and they still won't quit. Goddamn, here comes one of the bastards now! Gunners, watch your seven o'clock! Watch it!

The First to Go

The target was the aircraft engine plant of the Nakajima Aircraft Co. Ltd. at Musashino, near Tokyo. On November 24, 111 B-29s took off, led by O'Donnell in "Dauntless Dotty", lead ship of the 869th Bomb Squadron. They were joined by a few Boeing F-13As, the photo version of the B-29, to drop "rope"—longer and heavier strands of the foil used to confuse ground radars—and to photograph the effects.

That mission ran afoul of the jet stream, then an unexperienced phenomenon. A high-altitude wind, roaring along at a ground speed of nearly 150 miles per hour, carried the bombers along at well over 400 mph. Bombing accuracy suffered; the ballistics tables had not allowed for such speeds. Two dozen Superforts hit the primary and 64 dropped bombs on the docks and on Musashino. About half the bombing was done by radar. The F-13 photographs showed 48 bomb hits in the factory area. Casualties among the Japanese were 57 killed and 75 wounded. The 73rd lost one bomber in combat, with its 11-man crew listed as missing, one crewman dead and four wounded.

The first mission did accomplish two things. It had proved the point; the bombers had found and hit a major, heavily defended target in bad weather, and had sustained minimum losses. Bombing accuracy would improve things later. Second, the Japanese had just learned they were no longer safe at home in the island chain.

Three days later the bombers returned to Musashino, and left the target undamaged. In their absence, Japanese bombers raided Isley Field, the Saipan base, and destroyed four Superforts in two strikes that day. It became a serious threat; Japanese bombers would fly in low from Iwo Jima, and hit and run. Before they were temporarily stopped by a heavy combined raid by B-29s and Seventh AF B-24s, they had destroyed 11 Superforts, severely damaged eight, and had done minor damage to 35. The raids had killed 45 Americans and wounded more than 200.

On December 13, the bombers hit the Nagoya engine plant of Mitsubishi Heavy Industries Co. Ltd. and destroyed about one-fifth of the factory area. Only after the war was it learned that damage was so severe that it halted parts machining, forcing subsequent reliance on inventory and outside suppliers. It also forced the Japanese to start dispersing their plants. Nagoya's dispersal program was so poorly managed that no engines were assembled at the remote site.

A number of only mediocre missions followed, and Arnold began to get restive. He had no decisive results that he could use as examples of air doctrines and concepts. He had decided to swallow the bitter pill; the India-China operation just wasn't at all effective, and would have to be moved to the Marianas. LeMay was available, and he had stirred things up in India, improving them; why not send him to replace Hansell and do the same on Saipan?

The irony of events: the last mission from Saipan under Hansell's command was a spectacular success. The B-29's losing streak was broken in a raid on the Akashi plant of Kawasaki Aircraft Engineernig Co. Ltd., a major producer of engines and twin-engined fighters. Sixty-two B-29s pounded it out of the war. The plant was closed; what was salvageable was moved to a dispersed site.

The next day, January 20, 1945, LeMay relieved Hansell. Five days earlier, XX Bomber Command had flown its last B-29 mission from the Chinese bases. They flew a few more from India against closer targets, generally tactical ones chosen by theater commanders. On March 29, they made a last low-level strike, against the oil facilities in Singapore, and called it a day. Some of their number were already on Saipan, and within a few days, the remainder of the command was headed there also.

Faced with almost insuperable difficulties, XX Bomber Command had dispatched only 49 missions during its ten-month stay in India and China. It averaged about two combat sorties for each aircraft per month, hardly an outstanding record.

LeMay Takes Over on Saipan

LeMay began, as usual, by observing. He rode some of the missions to Japan. Most of the raids he dispatched were standard, high-altitude precision daylight or radar bombing strikes against point targets. In between, he tried some fire raids, using incendiary bombs instead of high explosives. Two were flown, and the results were carefully analyzed by Arnold's staff.

On February 19, 1945, a new target directive gave LeMay redefined priorities. Aircraft engine factories were first, as before; in second place were two items of equal priority. Incendiary attacks on cities shared the spot with the bombing of aircraft assembly plants.

The most successful test of the fire raids occurred February 25. The 73rd, 313th and 314th Bomb Wings struck Tokyo with a combined force of 172 B-29s bombing the primary. They left 28,000 buildings in ashes, and a smoldering square mile of inner city.

The Superforts went back to Musashino for the eighth time March 4. The weather again defeated the attack. That mission marked the tacitly accepted end of any attempts to continue with precision bombing by visual means from high altitudes during the daylight hours. The eight trips to Musashino had put 835 aircraft over the target, but had destroyed less than four percent of the roofed area of the factory. It was a miserable performance, and it was high time to find out what was so wrong.

In the final analysis, it was the weather. Between the high-altitude winds of the jet stream, which threw out all the existing techniques of bombing, and the frequent thick cloud cover over the targets, there was little hope of accurate bombing. To hit the pickle barrel, somebody had pointed out, you first must be able to see the pickle barrel.

There were other factors. The engines did not perform as expected at altitude. The bomb load was smaller than it should have been. Fighter interception was determined and often strong. Anti-aircraft reached easily to the bombing altitudes.

LeMay kept coming back to the same concept: bomb

with incendiaries, from low levels, at night. The winds were lighter, clouds were thinner or above the bombers' path. Engines would operate cooler, last longer, and burn less fuel. By flying in a stream and not a formation, more fuel could be saved. Japanese night fighters were few and poorly handled, so the defensive systems of the B-29 could be cut back to the single tail gunner, and all the ammunition weight and turret poundage could be saved. Trade all that weight for bombs. Trade the fuel saved for more bombs.

LeMay made the decision. The missions would be flown at altitudes between 5,000 and 8,000 feet by stripped B-29s carrying almost all of their bomb load as incendiaries. They would drop on fires set by pathfinder B-29s. And, if things worked out right, they would set Japan ablaze from end to end.

Fireball in the Night

The first mission was scheduled for March 9, 1945. Each aircraft was loaded with about six tons of bombs. The main force carried two dozen M69 500-lb. incendiary clusters; the pathfinders were loaded with 180 M47 napalm bombs each. The orders dispatched 334 Superforts. They struck a target area of about 12 square miles in Tokyo. Their fires were spread by the wind from house to house across tiny alleys and narrow streets, burning bamboo and paper and the resinous cedar wood frames. A fire storm was generated.

The damage was far worse than in any other raid on Japan, including the two atomic bomb strikes at Hiroshima and Nagasaki. A million Japanese no longer had homes; 84,000 were dead, 41,000 injured, primarily from burns. A quarter of Tokyo was blackened, smoking rubble. It cost 14 B-29s.

March 11: Nagoya hit by 285 B-29s, and burned. March 13: Osaka hit by 274 B-29s and burned. March 16: Kobe burned. March 19: Nagoya burned again. Then the fire blitz died, out of incendiaries. It had been an outstanding campaign, and it was a complete abandonment of the traditional doctrinal use of daylight, precision, high-altitude bombing.

For a few weeks, the Superforts were diverted to hit tactical targets in support of the costly invasion of Okinawa. Bomb dumps were replenished with incendiary stocks during that series of missions, and in mid-May the fire raids began again. In a month of fire-bombing, concentrated, devastating, terrifying, Japan's six leading industrial centers—Tokyo, Nagoya, Kobe, Osaka, Yokohama, and Kawasaki—were incinerated.

The smaller cities came next; on average, two fire raids per week hit them. There were little or no defenses, and B-29 losses were small. In late July, LeMay began dropping warning leaflets over Japan, listing the cities on his target list. The effect on the Japanese has been recorded; it created a sense of terror, or of inevitable death. Whichever reaction it provoked, it broke the will of the Japanese home front.

LeMay's leaflets listed the target cities, and warned that some of them would be bombed on the night following the leaflet drop. The raids eventually destroyed another 57 secondary industrial cities.

Meantime, an unheralded B-29 operation—originally unwanted—was setting some major marks of its own. The 313th Bomb Wing, operating out of Tinian's North Field, was mining Japanese waters. The sea lanes supplying the islands had been blocked by naval actions and the flow of commerce to Japan had been severely curtailed. Only one significant water

There are two 8,500-foot parallel runways at Tinian's West Field, and one of them is now the active for aircraft 62, of the 444th Bomb Group, easing in for a landing, power reduced and flaps down. Waiting for her to clear the runway is another B-29, with its flaps extended to the takeoff position and its huge props flailing at the warm Pacific air.

By day and night, the raiders hit the home islands of Japan, destroying by fire one city after another. Residents were notified by dropped leaflets just which cities had been selected for targeting during the next few days, and—in effect—were given notice to leave.

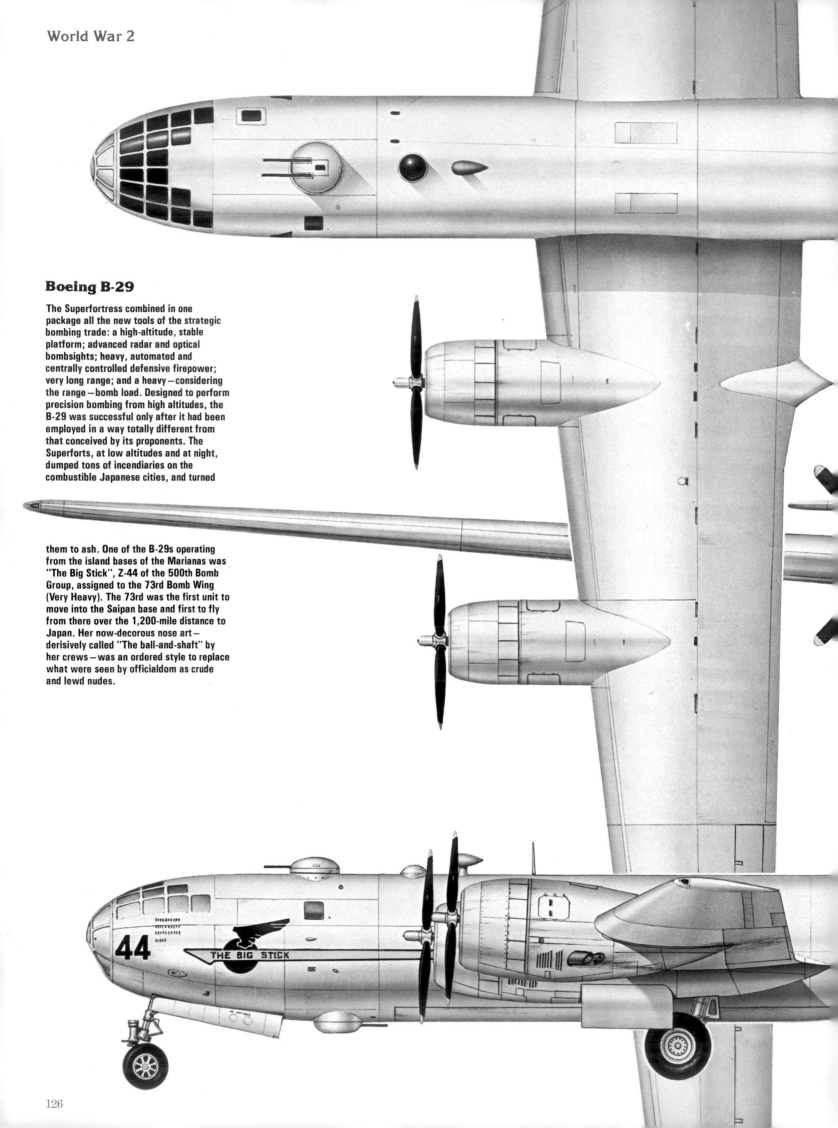

Boeing B-29

The Superfortress combined in one package all the new tools of the strategic bombing trade: a high-altitude, stable platform; advanced radar and optical bombsights; heavy, automated and centrally controlled defensive firepower; very long range; and a heavy—considering the range—bomb load. Designed to perform precision bombing from high altitudes, the B-29 was successful only after it had been employed in a way totally different from that conceived by its proponents. The Superforts, at low altitudes and at night, dumped tons of incendiaries on the combustible Japanese cities, and turned

them to ash. One of the B-29s operating from the island bases of the Marianas was "The Big Stick", Z-44 of the 500th Bomb Group, assigned to the 73rd Bomb Wing (Very Heavy). The 73rd was the first unit to move into the Saipan base and first to fly from there over the 1,200-mile distance to Japan. Her now-decorous nose art— derisively called "The ball-and-shaft" by her crews—was an ordered style to replace what were seen by officialdom as crude and lewd nudes.

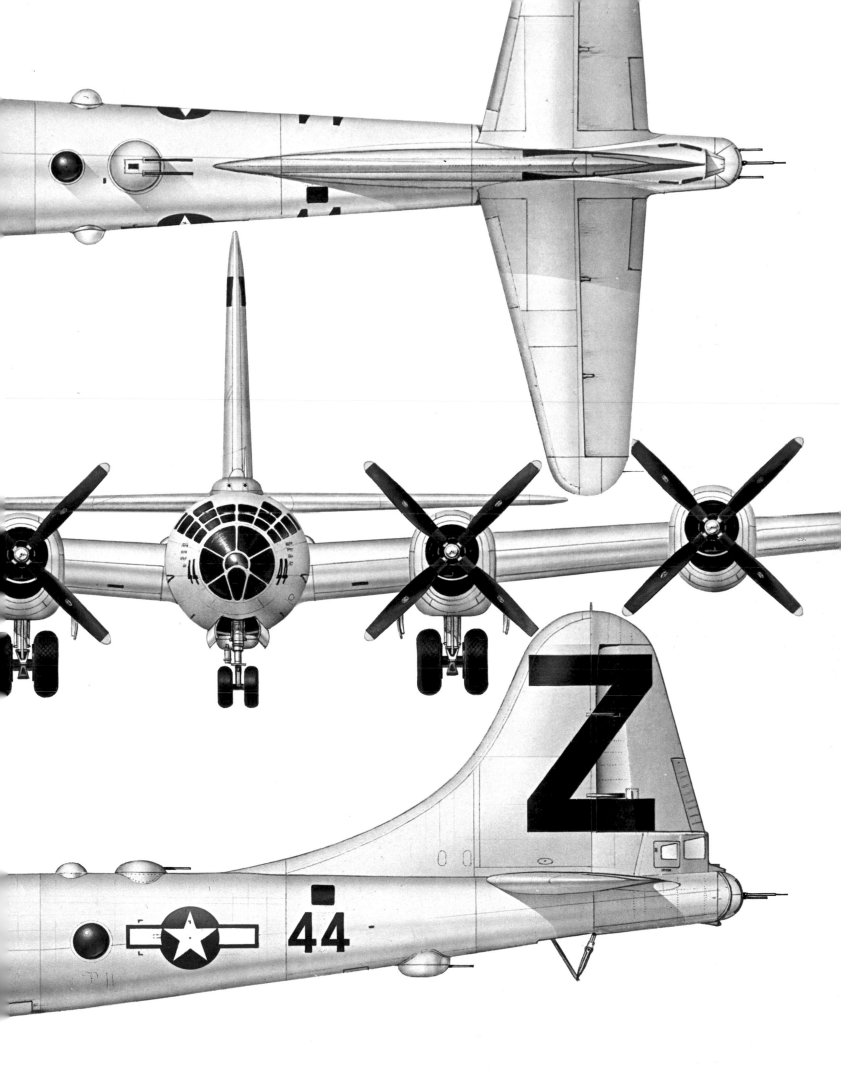

If there was a single B-29 that is remembered from the war, it is the "Enola Gay", dropper of the first atomic bomb. Here she is, training at Wendover Field, Utah, for that memorable mission. The unbroken lines of her belly underscore her special role; she carried only the tail turret for defense.

There are four parallel, 10,000-foot runways that handle the air traffic generated by B-29 operations at North Field, Tinian. The 313rd Bomb Wing and the 509th Composite Group, trained with the atomic bomb, were based here. This photograph, taken during the last days of the war, shows more than 200 B-29s on hardstands; three are on the runways, in various stages of their takeoff runs, and at least six more wait on taxiways for the runways to be cleared so that they can roll to the ends, rev up the engines, and go.

route remained open, and it approached the Inland Sea through the Shimonoseki Strait at its eastern end. It was a narrow channel, eminently suitable for mining. The Navy had been after Arnold for months to divert some of his air strength for that job, and he finally acquiesced.

Missions were flown at relatively low levels, using APQ-13 radar and Loran for finding the target area and dropping the mines. The first attack was flown the night of March 27, 1945, by 92 B-29s; on March 30, another force of 85 bombers sowed a second batch of mines and sealed the strait and its approaches. The only Japanese counter was mine-sweeping, a hazardous task in the presence of acoustic and magnetic mines. No Japanese warship larger than a small destroyer got out of the Strait after those first two weeks. Destroyers tried to clear the waters when they were ordered to Okinawa to try to assist in the defense against the American amphibious assault; but four of them were blown out of the water by the mines. By the end of April, the toll was 18 ships either on the bottom or permanently disabled in the strait.

LeMay ordered that one bomb group concentrate on the mining missions unless needed elsewhere for a top-priority strike against a ground target. The 505th BG (H) became the specialist unit; they flew a flurry of 14 missions in less than a month, mining ten major shipping lanes in the Sea of Japan and the Inland Sea.

The record mining mission was flown by a 6th BG B-29 from Tinian to the Korean port of Rashin, 2,362 miles distant. It dropped its mines in the harbor approaches and flew home. It was airborne for 19 hours 40 minutes, and had covered 4,724 miles non-stop.

It was a very productive use of the bombers. The 12,000 mines they sowed destroyed more than ten percent of all the merchant shipping that Japan lost from late March, 1945, until the end of the war.

Lesser results came from the precision bombing by radar of Japanese oil storage and refining facilities. The 315th BW(H) arrived at Northwest Field, Guam, in May and June, 1945, equipped with late-model B-29Bs. They were specialized planes that had no top or belly turrets; only the tail gunner's position remained for defense. Their bellies were painted a glossy black to defeat the searchlights. And just below the belly was mounted what looked like a small wing, the radar antenna of the APQ-7 "Eagle" system, a new and more accurate blind-bombing radar.

The 315th flew 15 missions using the "Eagle" system. They were able to carry larger-than-standard bomb loads, because of the weight saved by the elimination of turrets and fire-control system. On later strikes, the bomb loads were close to ten tons.

But Japan was too far gone for these missions to have had any but secondary effects. The oil came in from overseas, primarily, and blockades and mining had dried up the supply that might otherwise have been stored and refined in the targets that the 315th struck.

One Bomb, One Metropolis

On June 11, a group of B-29s began to arrive at Tinian's North Field, and parked its aircraft in a guarded and sequestered section of that sprawling complex. Combat flight training started for the 509th Composite Group June 30. On July 20, the group began a string of a dozen strikes against carefully chosen Japanese cities, flying the missions with two to six planes and dropping single bulbous bombs.

Gen. Spaatz, commanding U. S. Strategic Air Forces, received a secret order July 24. It informed him that the 509th CG would drop its first special bomb on any one of four cities: Hiroshima, Kokura, Niigata, or Nagasaki. The attack would be made as soon as weather permitted visual bombing, but not before August 3.

The special bomb was, of course, the first atomic weapon, "Little Boy", ready since July 31. The weather had been bad for a spell; it looked good for August 6, and LeMay issued the orders for Special Bombing Mission 13. Hiroshima's urban industrial area was the primary target; secondary was Kokura and its arsenal; tertiary was the urban area of Nagasaki. Mission details were very specific: bomb altitude was to be between 28,000 and 30,000 feet; speed, 200 mph; both pilot and bombardier had to see and agree on the target; bombing had to be by visual means.

The rest of the story has been told time and again in many contexts. There is one important point: Hiroshima was blown out of existence on August 6, 1945.

Kokura was the second primary target chosen for the follow-on strike; bad weather saved it and fate decreed that Nagasaki would die in its stead. On August 9, just before noon, the blinding light of a thousand suns flashed in the skies above that city and in one primordial blast leveled its buildings, seared its vegetation, boiled its canals and streams, and killed its people.

The war had only days to go, and the B-29s continued their raids on Japan. On the night of August 14, 160 Superforts were out burning Kumagaya and Isezaki; 132 hit the Nippon Oil Company in a 3,650-mile non-stop mission from the Marianas. Mines were sown by 39 more B-29s. On the way home, they heard the news of the surrender.

The B-29s had dropped more than 91 percent of all the bomb tonnage that struck the home islands of Japan, destroying its industrial and urban heart as thoroughly as the B-17s and B-24s had destroyed German cities and factories. In military terms, the losses were light; 343 B-29s were lost in combat.

Japan surrendered to the devastating effects of air power, with a home defense force of more than two million combat-ready troops and 9,000 kamikaze airplanes waiting for the invasion that was never needed. Some will point out that Japan was already defeated by blockade; its major food and fuel sources had been denied the country. They will further point out that there may well have been 9,000 kamikaze planes, but where were 9,000 kamikaze pilots going to come from? And finally, the composition of the home defense forces, as in Germany, must have included the elderly, the infirm, and the invalided, and could not have been considered seriously as a fighting force.

Those arguments have a partial truth about them. The B-29s did not win the war. In the end, it was a team effort, joining the Army, Navy, Marine Corps, Coast Guard, and a hard-working home labor force with the new strength of the USAAF. That combination won a part of the war. There were other nations involved, for far longer and at far greater cost, and it is important to remember that.

Air power did not win World War 2. But it did make a decisive contribution to the final victory and the war would have been much more costly, and would have dragged on for much longer, had it not been for the tactical and strategic air power employed so effectively by the British Empire air arms and by the United States Army Air Forces.

On 23 July 1945 the Allied Combined Chiefs of Staff discussed the effect of using the newly developed atomic bomb. The dropping of two of these weapons (incidentally, of two different types), on Hiroshima on 6 August and on Nagasaki two days later, swiftly brought the war to an end. It halted the move to the Far East of thousands of American and British bombers from the European Theater, and not only avoided the need to drop a planned 1,051,000 tons of conventional bombs but also made a bloody invasion of Japan unnecessary.

The mushroom cloud rises above the devastated Japanese city of Nagasaki after the second atomic bomb was dropped on the hapless population on August 9, 1945.

Independence for the USAF

The war was over, with unexpected suddenness. The abrupt ending found invasion plans still in the making, and production lines still turning out aircraft and tanks and trucks. Millions were in uniform, scattered all over the world. Germany and Japan lay in ruins; the countries they had cruelly conquered were at least as badly, and perhaps worse, off. The wartime momentum of the offensive had to be slowed and stopped.

The easiest thing to shut off was the flow of the industrial production of war materiel. Corporate management received notice by telegrams; next day, guards at the gates turned the employees away. The plants were closed; half-finished aircraft, raw materials, jigs and fixtures were sold for scrap. Overnight, thousands were out of work. Rosie the Riveter was sent back to the kitchen, there to wait decades for a comparable social force that would recognize the importance of women in the ranks of labor and management.

The United States Army Air Forces had been the direct cause of the sudden armistice. Two nuclear bombs finally ended the long sentence of slow death by fire that the B-29s had imposed on Japan. And the USAAF, like the other services, was faced with the need to do several equally important tasks as soon as possible.

First, political and popular pressures were on to "... get the boys home". Second, the last months of the war had spawned new technologies and a new generation of air weapons. Sweepback, the jet engine, radar, and guided missiles obviously were the new wave, and any air force that neglected them would do so at its own peril. And third, the USAAF, having staked out a claim to equality among its sister services, was facing a political battle to get that claim recognized in the face of opposition.

Bring the Boys Back Home

The USAAF had about 2,200,000 men and women in uniform at the end of World War 2, and possessed about 64,000 airplanes of all types. About ten percent of the personnel were regular Army, and could be expected to stay on in the postwar service. But the other nine-tenths were ex-civilians and their families wanted them back home as soon as possible.

This, of course, is one of the characteristics of citizen soldiers. They fight for the duration; once the war is ended, they want to get back immediately to whatever they were doing, even if it was only loafing around the corner store. Gen. George Washington faced the problem first, with farmers who wanted to get back for the spring plowing and the fall harvests. Pershing faced the same issues after November 11, 1918. And here it was again, to torment the leaders of the powerful and worldwide air force.

It was done, somehow. Not without the usual number of foul-ups, but it was done and the USAAF was drawn down to a slim shadow of its one-time greatness and strength. By the end of April, 1946, the USAAF numbered less than a half-million; a year later, it had shrunk to 303,000. In less than two years, the military strength of the United States Army Air Forces was back at its pre-Pearl Harbor level.

There were more than 413,000 aircrewmen by the end of the war; less than two years later, the number was 24,000. Maintenance personnel, the core of any military service, also shrank by about 90 percent. With fewer airplanes to fly, and fewer maintenance people, one might expect things to even out a bit, and operational efficiency not to suffer too much. That was not the case. During the war years, the overall availability of combat aircraft was about 50 percent; that is, one out of every two airplanes was ready to go and fight. Little more than one year after V-J Day, availability was down to less than one plane out of five.

The powerful USAAF, ruler of the skies above Germany and Japan, had achieved that position with more than 218 combat groups of aircraft. In December, 1946, the combat-ready strength of the USAAF was just two groups that had survived the immediate postwar drawdown.

The Technological Revolution

Spurred by the pressures of war, a technological revolution had occurred that set the style and pace for postwar aircraft and missile design and development.

The end of World War 2 brought peace to the millions, but great and largely imponderable new problems to the strategic planners. As the victorious U.S. Air Force contracted like a burst balloon, such factors as jet propulsion and the atomic bomb made it essential to re-equip the front-line squadrons with new aircraft. None of the new designs was more breathtaking than Northrop's XB-35, a monster all-wing bomber which made its first flight in 1946. (This is the third XB-35, with single propellers instead of contraprops, first flown in 1948.) The newly formed USAF Strategic Air Command had to make crucial choices at a time when, in general, piston bombers were too slow and jet bombers lacked range. The all-wing concept appeared to offer a good compromise.

The new generation takes over. This photograph was taken over the Bavarian Alps in 1947 when the F-80 was beginning to replace the P-47 throughout first-line fighter groups.

Today when the Air Force has to fight for funds for each new aircraft it is nostalgic to recall 1945 when the AAF had a problem wondering what to do with 60,000 surplus aircraft! They were jammed on to airfields around the world; this field at Erlangen, Germany, was somewhere to put a few B-17Gs.

The 1939 orders of battle contained biplane fighters; Great Britain, Italy and Russia still had them in front-line units, although the monoplane was fast replacing them. The primary armament for air-to-air combat was a battery of small-caliber machine guns; the gunsight was a simple optical type, often no more refined than the bead-and-ring type used in the first World War. Bombers were short-range, low-capacity monoplanes; some had a good turn of speed and could outrun many contemporary fighters. That fact, unfortunately, became part of doctrine in high places and was responsible for the deaths of many bomber crewmen and the failure of many bombing missions later in the war.

By the end of the war, some fighters were powered by jet propulsion, and had sweptback wings for reduced drag at their high operational speeds. Primary armament was a battery of heavy, rapid-firing cannon, or multiple mounted large-caliber machine guns. Fighters were equipped with wing strongpoints to carry ordnance: bombs, rockets, napalm tanks. Although some air combat utilized radar sighting, most gunsights still were optical although they had been considerably refined. The bombers had become tonnage haulers, particularly in the RAF, and were often dropping with fair precision on targets the crews never saw except as an indication on a radar scope.

Night fighting had become a rudimentary art, and German, British and U. S. pilots and radar operators made kills under control of ground radars and their own airborne equipment for finding and sighting on the quarry.

The first use of guided missiles in warfare had served notice of a new generation of weapons. As poor as the V-1 and V-2 were, as inaccurate and unreliable, they did do horrendous damage and additionally were responsible for a reduction in the bomber offensive against Germany, because many heavy bomber sorties were dispatched against them instead. Anti-aircraft missiles, happily too late to see combat use by the Germans, also presaged the future. Air-to-surface weapons, like the Fritz-X used by the Germans against Allied shipping, and the Bat, used by the U. S. Navy against Japanese shipping, also were the forerunners of weapons to come.

Electronic warfare was born in those short years. It began with the unsophisticated, but effective, radars that could detect aircraft movements. The first counter was a simple and direct one: bomb the radar sites. More subtle countermeasures were developed, such as the use of "window" or "rope" to saturate the return

and produce a bright blob on the enemy radar scope. Later, electronic jamming and deception entered, to be countered by equally tricky ideas.

A majority of these new technological steps had been taken by the Germans. The AAF was extremely interested in finding out about them for two reasons: First, the classical military one of knowing the enemy's weapons so that counter-measures could be prepared; second, using enemy technology as a building-block for advanced developments of similar weapons for the AAF.

One of the reasons the United States lagged behind the Germans, and the British to a lesser extent, was that advanced research and development for the military had not been a well-organized, continuously funded program in America. During World War 2, it was a stated policy that military research and development ought to be confined to improving existing aircraft, ships, tanks and artillery. But the leaders who were building toward an independent air force had other ideas.

In September, 1944, as Dr. Theodore von Karman told it later, Gen. Arnold asked him to form a scientific group that would develop guidelines for future aeronautical research, looking toward long-term programs. Arnold was particularly interested in the future of jet propulsion and of such guided missiles as the V-1 and V-2. He emphasized that interest in his first meeting with von Karman's group, when he said that the Air Forces had always been built around pilots, but that the next Air Force was going to be built around scientists.

Von Karman's committee began to see some progress from its meetings by early in 1945. And in March that year, Arnold suggested that von Karman and a selected team go to Germany and find out what they could about aeronautical research and development. Much of Germany was in Allied hands by then, and already technical intelligence teams were finding and acquiring the weapons data of the Third Reich.

One of the early discoveries was a previously unknown research institute, named after Hermann Göring, well hidden in a forest near Brunswick. Part of the documents found there was a collection of data on sweepback, including the results of a series of systematic wind-tunnel tests. A quick glance showed that they confirmed the value of sweepback for drag reduction at high speeds. One of the von Karman team, a Boeing engineer named George Schairer, saw an immediate use for the data. Several American companies were designing advanced military aircraft for transonic performance, and sweepback was one of the obvious keys to solving the problems of rapid drag increases near the speed of sound. Information gathered by von Karman's group was forwarded to the United States and distributed throughout the aircraft industry as rapidly as possible. Schairer added his personal endorsement in his correspondence with Boeing.

Other interesting data found at Braunschweig was a wind-tunnel test series to determine the optimum location for a jet engine nacelle. The Germans built a wind-tunnel model of a wing that could mount a nacelle at various locations above and below the wing, and at different fore-and-aft locations. Noted at the time, and distributed by the group, those results later provided valuable input to the Boeing designers.

The sweepback data found its first tangible expression in the North American XF-86, which was redesigned with a swept wing in November, 1945, and first flew October 1, 1947. Both sweepback data and nacelle position information were useful in the design of the Boeing XB-47, which first flew December 17, 1947. Both aircraft set the style for fighters and bombers that followed.

In August, 1945, von Karman's group submitted a

secret report, "Where We Stand", comparing German and American wartime aeronautical science and technology. But since the original mission was to develop a long-range research plan, von Karman's team prepared a second report, "Toward New Horizons", which became, with a companion volume called, "Science: The Key to Air Supremacy", the major impetus for basic scientific research in the USAF.

Von Karman's report underscored his belief that the Air Force was the pre-eminent defense arm and that to maintain that position required a continuing input of science and technology. It was a most important document, and it served as a guiding outline for many years afterward.

Unification and Separation

The establishment of a separate, co-equal Department of the Air Force was an idea suggested many times before, and attempts had been made to obtain legislation to that end as far back as 1916. By the end of World War 2, the United States Army Air Forces were, for all practical purposes, an independent service. Neither of the senior services challenged that position, nor would they have done so, given the exigencies of the wartime situation. The USAAF, in turn, was wise enough not to push too hard and too fast for the recognition it had long sought. The war provided the opportunity for all the services to concentrate on a single goal most of the

Most numerous of the first-generation straight-wing jets, the P-84 (later F-84 — Thunderjet was also the chief Allied fighter-bomber in Korea. These were three of the first P-84Bs to reach the newly created U.S. Air Force (49th Fighter-Bomber Wing).

The third and last of the Bell XP-59A Airacomet prototypes, the first US jet aircraft, as painted in summer 1943 whilst testing at Lake Muroc (later named Edwards AFB).

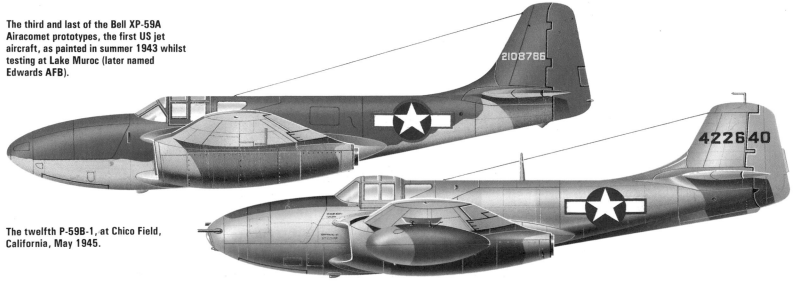

The twelfth P-59B-1, at Chico Field, California, May 1945.

time, and gave them a chance to learn how to work together in combined operations that tested all their resources and skills.

But this gentlemen's agreement was due to end, legally, six months after the end of the war. The USAAF would, like Cinderella, transform into its old status when time ran out.

Most of the support for a co-equal Air Force came from the Army, and most of the opposition came from the Navy. Both of those services had studied the problem, informally and formally, and had come up with different conclusions. The Army endorsed the concept of a single unified service structure in a formal plan to Congress in March 1944. The Navy said that was not the way to go.

The next move was made by the Joint Chiefs of Staff who appointed a committee of senior Army and Navy officers and charged them with the task of evaluating three variations on the overall organization of the national defense. Their final recommendation, dated March 1945, was for a single Department of Defense,

An outstanding design in all respects, the Lockheed P-80 Shooting Star flew in January 1944, and in an enlarged and more powerful form entered service in 1946. These were P-80Bs, with a thinner but thicker-skinned wing; many served in Korea.

subdivided into three co-equal services: Army, Navy and Air Force. The committee also suggested that action be taken soon, because of the six-month limitation on the legality of the wartime status of the USAAF.

The Navy did its own study later that year and found that there ought to be three departments, one each of War, Navy and Air, but not a single Department of Defense. The Army weighed in with its own report in October, 1945, recommending a single Department of Armed Forces.

Congressional hearings on legislation introduced during 1945 to the same basic end produced a parade of witnesses, pro and con, and a failure to report out a single bill by the end of the year.

President Harry S Truman finally got action. In a message to Congress December 19, 1945, he asked for new legislation to establish a single department of defense under which the air arm would be co-equal with the other services. He synthesized several suggestions made in earlier reports, borrowing liberally from the JCS and the War Department, tossing in some Navy ideas, and blending the mix. The first attempt by Congress to produce the suggested bill failed when the Navy resisted. The service resented the fact that it would be in a minority position against the Army and Air Force, and that no longer would the Navy be regarded as the first line of defense.

Truman called in the Army and Navy Secretaries and told them to iron out their differences. They couldn't; so Truman put together a compromise, and the Senate Committee revised the bill accordingly. The Navy still disliked and opposed the bill. It was never reported out of committee for a vote on the floor of the Senate.

By January 1947, when the Eightieth Congress began deliberations, a final version of the bill was ready. But it, too, was subjected to the additions, modifications and deletions that are standard for any major legislation in Congress. What finally resulted was the National Security Act of 1947, and it became a law July 26 that year. It established the single Department of Defense, and three military departments—Army, Navy and Air Force—under civilian control. It also established the National Security Council, the Central Intelligence Agency and the National Security Resources Board.

The functions and roles of the three services were detailed in Executive Order 9877. The Air Force was, under its terms, to organize, train and equip air forces for a variety of operations, to develop weapons, tactics, technique, organization and equipment of Air Force combat and service elements, to provide missions and detachments for foreign service, to provide means to coordinate air defense among all services, and to assist the Army and Navy in their missions.

It took time to transfer authority from the Army to the Air Force, and to organize for action. Consequently, although the National Security Act took effect late in July it was not until September 18, 1947, that W. Stuart Symington was sworn in as the first Secretary of the Air Force. That date is the official birthday of the United States Air Force.

The Legal Basis

Under U. S. law, the Congress must authorize the size and general organizational structure of the military services, as well as appropriating and authorizing the funds they are seen to need. Existing legislation already applied to the Army and Navy; but the newly created Air Force, after September 18, no longer was covered by similar law. It left the USAF with pretty much of a free hand, initially, for organizing its headquarters and its field commands.

The background for the USAF organization was the

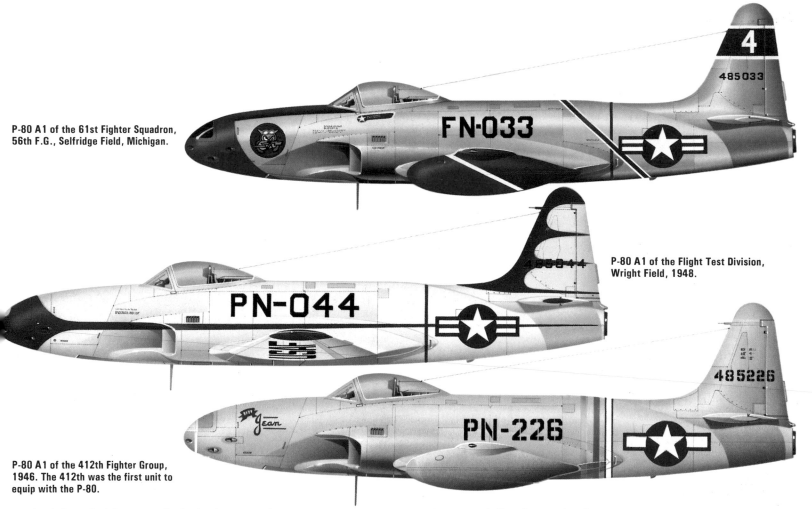

P-80 A1 of the 61st Fighter Squadron, 56th F.G., Selfridge Field, Michigan.

P-80 A1 of the Flight Test Division, Wright Field, 1948.

P-80 A1 of the 412th Fighter Group, 1946. The 412th was the first unit to equip with the P-80.

work of Gen. Carl Spaatz, who had taken over from Arnold as Commander, Army Air Forces, on February 15, 1946. Spaatz had an Air Staff study recommanding a specific reorganization, and he put it into effect. The basic structure was 70 combat groups and 22 specialized squadrons, plus a support force. The Staff recommended changes in the headquarters and field organizations, also.

Spaatz created three functional combat commands: Strategic Air, Tactical Air, and Air Defense. Those three major units, born March 21, 1946, stayed as the basic organizational building blocks for the last year of the USAAF and for 32 years of the USAF. Only in 1979 did the fundamental structure change, when Air Defense Command was absorbed by Tactical Air Command.

Five support and five overseas commands also were set up at the same time, with most of the foreign-based air strength concentrated in United States Air Forces in Europe (USAFE) and Far East Air Forces (FEAF). It should be noted that theater commands, such as FEAF, were operating commands that "owned" no combat airplanes. Their strength was in the deployed or detached units drawn from one of the combat commands.

The headquarters organization charts looked like one for any large corporation. The Chief of Staff, who also had several staff officers, had four deputy chiefs: operations, materiel, personnel & administration, and finance. The operations deputy included directorates of plans and operations, training and requirements, and intelligence. Two staff officers to the deputy headed the guided missiles group and the air communications group.

The deputy for materiel included four directorates: research and development, procurement and industrial planning, supply and services, and air installations, with a single staff officer in charge of the special weapons group.

Each of the commands, whether functional or theater, shared an equal level in the overall organiza-

tion of the USAF. Each reported directly to a headquarters deputy charged with supervision of the specific command.

Now the USAF had an organization, and had inherited a doctrine for guidance. It had few people, and fewer planes, but it was beginning to formulate the outlines for the legislation it hoped Congress would pass to make its status legal.

And then, almost overnight, the United States took on new responsibilities as a protector of the free countries of Europe, devastated by war, and the Air Force was faced with a new challenge of overwhelming responsibility.

The North American B-45 Tornado was the U.S. Air Force's first four-engined jet bomber, and resulted from the air force's desire to gain operational experience with an interim type (turbojet engines in an airframe that reflected piston-engined technology) before moving onto more advanced types. The Tornado entered service in 1949, and found its real niche as a reconnaissance bomber.

With the F-86 Sabre the USAF received what was unquestionably the best fighter in the world in the late 1940s.

The North American F-82 Twin Mustang long-range escort fighter. This type was developed by the relatively simple expedient of marrying two Mustang fuselages and opposite wing panels by a common centre section and stabilizer.

Out of Isolationism

World War 2 marked the transition of America from an isolationist country to an international power. The country had waged war on continents and oceans, and had sent millions of men and women to all points of the compass. Many of them came back changed by the experience.

The prime mover was a blunt, unsophisticated politician from midwest America, the very stronghold of isolationism: President Harry S Truman. Communist-supported uprisings were racking Greece and Turkey, and Truman asked Congress in his message of March 12, 1947, to furnish $400 million in military and economic aid to the governments of those two countries, and to send Americans to both to assist in the distribution of that aid.

It was the first element of what later was called the Truman Doctrine: "Totalitarian regimes imposed on free peoples, by direct or indirect aggression, undermine the foundations of international peace and hence the security of the United States."

Truman's call for aid to Greece and Turkey was answered by Congress, and later echoed and expanded at Harvard University's graduation exercises June 5, 1947. The speaker was Truman's Secretary of State, former Chief of Staff George C. Marshall, and what Marshall suggested in his speech was a program of U.S. financial aid to European countries to help them rebuild their economies and industries that had been shattered by the war.

Marshall's European Recovery Plan, known everywhere today as the Marshall Plan, was quickly put into action. In August that year, 16 European countries sent representatives to a Paris meeting where they worked out final details of the American aid program $17-billion plan.

With the Truman Doctrine and the Marshall Plan, that was to be their road back to normalcy: a four-year, the United States became formally a world power. And with world power go world responsibilities. At that time, the ultimate way to carry out America's new role as protector of the Free World was with air power and the threat of the atomic bomb.

Air Bridge to the East

It was a strange question, and the listener wasn't quite sure what he had heard. It was repeated: "Can you transport coal by air?"

"Sir," said Maj. Gen. Curtis LeMay, "The Air Force can deliver anything."

LeMay completed the conversation, hung up the telephone, and started thinking. He had just been asked by Gen. Lucius D. Clay, the U. S. military governor of Germany, to start an aerial supply line from the U. S. zone of occupation to Berlin, bringing in the necessities of life to a city of two and one-half million people. It was a formidable challenge, but LeMay must have been used to such tasks by then.

Nobody from President Truman on down expected that LeMay's USAFE command could meet the requirements. At best, they hoped the Air Force would be able to deliver enough so that the Berliners could get by for a while on those deliveries plus inventories, and that the airlift would buy time for negotiations with the Russians. They had underestimated LeMay and USAFE, and the organization that would grow out of their initial efforts.

The Geography of Berlin

Berlin stood alone, surrounded by the Russian-occupied zone of Germany. The Russians permitted only specified rail and auto routes for access, plus three air corridors 20 miles wide that led westward to the British, French and U. S. zones. Russian checkpoints marked every approach or exit route on the surface; Russian fighters patrolled the areas adjacent to the air corridors. A Russian air traffic controller was one of four, each from one occupying power, in a joint air traffic center that monitored all plane movements in and out of Berlin.

Russian harassment of transportation had been a frequent occurrence since the occupation began. Early in 1948, it began to increase; the Russians were using it as a visible sign of their opposition to the proposed currency reform backed by the Western powers. On March 31, the Russians announced that road and rail traffic to Berlin would be subject to inspection by their guards beginning the following day. The Western allies refused to submit, and cancelled their surface transportation with the exception of food trains.

Berlin, like most metropolitan centers, was dependent on outside food, fuel and supplies. There was no space in the city for farms, or even inadequate private gardens. What Berliners ate moved into the city by rail or road. The threat of blockade—siege, really—was potentially very dangerous to the existence of the city.

France, Great Britain and the United States decided to proceed with currency reform; new Deutschmarks would be issued, one for every ten Reichsmarks. The Russians reacted immediately, with a proclamation that protested the reform and prohibited circulation of the new money in the Russian zone and in Berlin. Immediately afterward, the Russians ordered all passenger train and all motor vehicle traffic between Berlin and the West stopped at midnight, June 18, 1948.

Six days later, they dropped the other shoe. Food trains had continued to run over the line from Helmstedt to Berlin, and had not been stopped by the Russians. Now the line had developed "technical troubles", the Russians said, and would have to be closed for repairs. They tore up about 100 yards of track to guarantee no passage of rail traffic.

The Western powers had two choices. They could stay and starve, or they could evacuate their own people and leave Berlin to the gentle mercies of the Russians. The Berliners had had one dose of that treatment, and wanted no more. The Western powers correctly saw what would happen if they pulled out, and vowed to stay in Berlin somehow.

Careful calculations showed that the 2.5 million people in Berlin, excluding those in the Russian zone, could be kept alive on about 4,500 tons of food and other essentials each day. There was only one way to deliver that amount: By air, through the corridors to Berlin.

LeMay had available a total of 102 Douglas C-47 and two Douglas C-54 transports. The C-47s could haul

When the Russians suddenly closed every road, railway and canal linking Berlin with the outside world in June 1948 they thought such bullying tactics would make their Allies back down and get out. They never thought the city could be supplied from the air, but the Berlin Airlift—called Operation Vittles by the USAF and Plain Fare by the RAF—built up until by May 1949 some 8,000 to 10,000 tons was flown in daily, and it was the Russians who backed down and removed their barriers. A major force on the airlift were 200 USAF C-54 Skymasters, two of which are seen refuelling at Wiesbaden.

Millions of travellers familiar with Berlin-Tempelhof will be intrigued by this picture taken during the Airlift showing C-47s being unloaded. Crated goods were in fact much less common than the staple commodities of food, coal and other bulk loads.

Operation Vittles had to be backed up by a furiously expanded USAF training and maintenance organization. These pupil aircrew and instructors are watching the 'crab' of a Link Trainer (early flight simulator) on a navigational exercise. Soon they will be heading for Berlin 'for real'.

three tons at best; the C-54s, ten. The daily requirements of Berlin would demand the equivalent of 1,500 C-47 flights. There was one airport in the American zone at Templehof, and one in the British zone at Gatow. The Royal Air Force had a handful of C-47s, but the combined force was far below the need.

By scraping together every available plane and crew, USAFE was able to fly 80 tons of supplies into Berlin on Sunday, June 26. Two days later, the RAF began its ferry runs to Gatow. For a couple of weeks, this force flew the corridors, carrying essentials to Berlin. The Russians began making aggressive passes at the transports, and a threat appeared to be building.

The USAF reacted by adding the two remaining B-29 squadrons of the 301st BG to the one already at Furstenfeldbruck for rotational training, and deployed two more B-29 groups—60 bombers—to British bases. Then USAF announced that a wing of Lockheed F-80 fighters would be moving from the Canal Zone to Germany in August. And on July 20, 16 F-80s from the 56th Fighter Group, Selfridge AFB, Michigan, landed in England on their way to take up station at Fursten-feldbruck, near Munich in the U. S. zone.

By then, the "LeMay Coal & Feed Delivery Service" had passed the 1,000-ton daily delivery mark. But there was a belief in higher headquarters that the operation ought to be taken out of LeMay's hands and given to the Military Air Transport Service. The organization was the airlift specialist, by charter, and LeMay's forte was combat operations. If the Russians were to make an overt move, he would have his hands full with the fighting, and the airlift operations would necessarily have to take second place.

On July 23, the Airlift Task Force was established by MATS on orders from USAF Headquarters. MATS dispatched eight squadrons of C-54 Skymaster transports to Germany; 72 planes, with three crews for each. The airlift was about to change markedly.

Maj. Gen. William H. Tunner was director of the ATF, and immediately organized a staff and went to Germany to take over from LeMay. "I expect you to produce," said LeMay. Said Tunner, never at a loss for a pithy statement, "I intend to."

Tunner later described the situation he had inherited as " . . . a real cowboy operation." Flight and ground crews were unscheduled. The C-47s were in poor shape. Utilization was low. Maintenance time was high. The air routes were very restrictive; Templehof and Gatow were four minutes apart by air, and seven Russian airfields surrounded Berlin. There was no

room to maneuver; holding patterns were overhead at each field. Templehof had no runways; the Germans had flown from the sod field, and pierced steel planking had been laid down later for USAFE operations.

The key, Tunner knew, was high utilization. It was much easier operationally to use a smaller number of larger planes and make the maximum number of trips with them. It simplified traffic control and ground handling. But it added to the maintenance load, because the increased number of takeoffs and landings was bound to raise some Hell with engines and tires. No matter; that could be handled. Go for utilization.

The corridor from the U. S. zone to Templehof was longer by more than half than the two others available to the Western allies. The RAF bases at Fassberg and Celle were a 160-mile flight from Berlin; Templehof was 290 miles from Rhein-Main in the U. S. zone. Two planes based at Fassberg could do the work of three at Rhein-Main. Tunner approached the British about a combined action. By August 21, American planes were loading at Fassberg. On October 15, the USAF and RAF operations officially merged into the Combined Air Lift Task Force. Tunner was commander, with Air Commodore J.W.F. Mercer as his deputy.

The C-47s were replaced as rapidly as possible with C-54s, which became the workhorse of the fleet. About 275 of the four-engined craft came from various USAF bases around the world. The Navy element of MATS sent along two squadrons—24 planes—of R5Ds, their equivalent to the C-54, and stayed with the airlift to the end. One Douglas C-74 made one recorded trip, and five Fairchild C-82s were used to move some specialized large vehicles.

For a brief period, the British carried salt to Berlin aboard Short Sunderland flying boats. They had been designed for open-seas operations, and had superb anti-corrosion protection. They were well suited to carry salt, which would have ruined other aircraft. The big boats were flown to and from the Havelsee, near Spandau, a suburb of Berliln.

The final fleet size varied, but stayed fairly close to a composition of 300 C-54s, with about 225 involved in the airlift at any time, and the remaining 75 in maintenance. The British had about 100 aircraft of several types; they worked them hard and did, in true RAF style, more than they were asked to.

Operations

Start with a C-54 at Wiesbaden, loaded with supplies for Berlin. All eastbound flights carried a code name of "Easy"; westbound flights were "Willie". C-54s were "Big Easy" or "Big Willie". The supplies, if civilian, were "New York"; "Chicago" was a military cargo for the U. S. forces. For the French, supplies were "Paris". If it was a load of equipment to maintain runways or build something, it was "Engineer".

The crew of a "Big Easy" with "New York" on board was given a specific departure time, to the second. They knew the radio call signs and tail numbers of the three planes that would precede them in the corridor and the two behind. They had gotten a weather briefing that was updated every 30 minutes, and which included en-route reports from radiomen in every seventh airplane going to Berlin.

They started their engines, taxied out and began the takeoff roll on the dot. They climbed out at 500 fpm., and started the first steps of the standardized procedure that would ease them into the approaches to the single corridor they would share with planes dispatched from nearby Rhein-Main.

They overflew Darmstadt and Aschaffenberg, turned on a heading of 033 and flew towards Fulda, the last checkpoint in the U. S. zone. Over the Fulda range station, each pilot broadcast the number of his plane so that pilots behind him could check their watches and

monitor their separation. From Fulda the corridor led straight to the Templehof range station; the flight was made at exactly 170 mph. At the Templehof station the pilot turned left to the beacon at Wedding, starting his letdown procedure on that leg. At Wedding he turned downwind, and continued a specified approach procedure to 1,500 feet altitude as he turned onto final approach. The letdown continued to the decision height at 400 feet.

When the plane landed at Templehof, it was met by a "Follow-Me" jeep and spotted on the ramp. The crew came down the steps to be greeted by an operations officer with a return clearance and a weather briefing. A German Red Cross jeep pulled up, operated by the loveliest girls in Berlin, to dispense coffee, doughnuts and snacks. Meantime, the unloading crews of Germans and displaced persons were moving the cargo off the plane and into trucks.

The total turnaround time was thirty minutes, and that short stop was attributable to a couple of things. First was Tunner's insistence that the crews stay with the airplanes, instead of going into the terminal building for snacks, briefings, clearances and line-shooting with friends. The services were brought to the plane instead. Second, the unloading crews were the very people who stood to benefit the most from the aerial bridge, and therefore understood why quick turnaround was an essential part of the total operation.

In low visibility, the dispatching and receiving airports used GCA (Ground-Controlled Approach) radars, which incidentally were the oldest units then in use. Templehof also had high-intensity approach and runway lights; that field was surrounded by tall apartment buildings and the final approach slope was steeper than normal.

Navigational aids were standard for the time: Low frequency homing beacons, low frequency radio range stations, and VHF voice communication.

Standardization

MATS and Tunner were great believers in standardization. If everything was standardized, there was little room for mistakes. It started with a standardized training course for replacement pilots at the "Little Corridor" school at the Great Falls, Montana, base. Every C-54 had a standardized instrument panel. A standard crew was three men: captain, co-pilot and flight engineer. Departure procedures from the main bases, the flight through the corridors, and the approach procedures to Templehof or Gatow had been standardized.

So were the weather limits: 400-foot ceiling and one mile visibility at Templehof, because of the apartments that lined the field; 200 feet and one-half mile at Gatow, because of the flatter approaches possible. A missed approach became a departure procedure to an alternate, generally the home base. There were no go-arounds, no second chances. There was no stacking in bad weather, and there were very few missed approaches, even in the worst weather.

Planes were dispatched on a three-minute headway; the runways at Templehof and Gatow were in use every 90 seconds for alternate takeoffs and landings. In the corridors, the planes maintained constant airspeeds and headings, and were assigned cruise altitudes with a 500-foot vertical separation between successive aircraft in each group of three. Typically, the first would be flown at the low cruise altitude of 2,000 feet; the second C-54, three minutes behind,

Operation Vittles in full swing, 24 hours a day: light blazes from the Wiesbaden AB maintenance hangar while streaks of light are left on the time-exposed film by C-47s taxiing out for takeoff.

Air traffic controllers have to be made, a task taking at least a year. Many come from the ranks of aircrew (especially during wartime) but these were new trainees at Great Falls, AFB, Montana, in late 1948.

would be at 2,500 feet; the third, another three minutes downstream, would be at 3,000, and the fourth would be back down at 2,000 again.

All flight speeds were predetermined and controlled from the ground at all times, even during the approach and landing.

As expected, engines and tires were taking a beating. The design mission of the C-54 had been long-range transport: Normal takeoff from a smooth runway, followed by a long flight at cruise power to a distant terminal. Then, after having burned off most of its fuel load, the C-54 would make a relatively light-weight landing.

The MATS C-54s took off at a gross weight of about 72,000 pounds, and landed at about 71,000 pounds. In contrast, the approved landing weight for civilian operation of the same airplane was only 63,500 pounds.

With a higher ratio of landings per flying hour than normal, and with most of them being made on the rough pierced steel planking of the temporary runways, the tires suffered. With a higher percentage of the engine life being spent at takeoff power, the engines suffered. At one time, Tunner had to fly spare tires in from the U. S. on a priority mission. Meantime, supply officers were out scrounging engines to add to their very limited stock of spares. They came across a batch of a similar model, and whipped them into the pipeline, choosing to ignore the fact that those engines had lower ratings.

The C-54s were being worked hard, flying eight and one-half hours a day as an average. They badly needed routine maintenance for all the other systems—electrical, cabin conditioning, hydraulic—as well as new tires and spare engines. And there were not enough people to install the 90 engines a month before their expected change time, or to mount 23 new tires every day.

Tunner got permission to recruit ex-Luftwaffe mechanics to work on the planes at Templehof. It was initially difficult, because of the non-fraternization policy of the occupying powers. A Luftwaffe major general was found who had served in air transports, knew the problems and spoke English; Hans Detlev von Rohden supervised the translation of the technical manuals into German, and the new mechanics began to arrive. By the end of the airlift, German mechanics outnumbered their American counterparts.

After a C-54 had logged 200 hours in the airlift, it was flown to the USAF depot at Burtonwood, England, for an inspection. After four of these, it was loaded with a cargo of reparable engines and flown to the United States by a MATS ferry crew. The first U. S. stop was Westover AFB, Mass., where its cargo was off-loaded; the plane then was ferried to one of the four civilian overhaul facilities handling airlift planes and was cycled through a 44-day major overhaul. At the end of that time, the plane picked up a cargo of spare parts, overhauled engines and similar items and took off for Germany.

Operation Little Vittles

The big airlift was called Operation *Vittles*, that latter word being a rural Americanism for victuals. There was also an Operation *Little Vittles*, and it came about because Lt. Gail Halvorsen got along well with kids. He got to know the children who watched the planes come in at Templehof, and he occasionally passed candy and chewing gum out on his sightseeing trips around the base. Then he began waggling the C-54 wings when he was on low finals over the kids' heads. The children waved back, and Halvorsen decided the next time he'd drop some candy to them. He made small parachutes from handkerchiefs, and his crew chief slung them out of the door on the final approach.

Like other humanitarian gestures in wartime, it

caught on. The children increased in number, and Halvorsen became the unwitting founder of Operation *Little Vittles*. People in the U. S. sent bundles of handkerchiefs; packers carefully cut time-expired parachutes into squares. Aircrews donated their gum and candy, and Halvorsen and fellow pilots made the candy run part of the airlift.

It was exactly the kind of gesture Americans are known for, and it was great public relations for the USAF. Today, people remember Operation *Little Vittles*, and call the big one the Berlin Airlift.

Airlift tonnage continued to increase; the curves climbed steadily. The French came into the operation; they had no transport fleet to offer, but they did have another airport in Berlin, at Tegel, and they made it available. There was an approach hazard; a radio tower, operated by the Russians, presented a menace to instrument approaches. The British and Americans decided to negotiate with the Russians for its removal; the Russians refused. The stories vary a little from that point on, but in any event, it was the French who solved the problem. They gave a party at Tegel to celebrate the opening of the field, and invited the RAF and USAF contingent. The *joie de vivre* of the occasion was interrupted by the muffled sound of an explosion. The Russian radio tower had been demolished, perhaps by the French; but certainly, the British and the Americans could not be held to blame because they were, after all, attending a party, were they not? The Russians griped, but did nothing.

Perhaps the message had begun to penetrate. Berlin was not going to be taken by siege and starvation. In fact, rations actually had been increased during the airlift. Berliners had coal for the winter, milk for their children, medicines for the afflicted, and food for all. The Russians backed down. On May 9, 1949, the USSR military governor announced that the blockade would be lifted at one minute past midnight, May 12.

The airlift continued after, to augment the stocks carried in once again by rail and road, and just in case the Russians changed their minds. The phase-out was gradual until the official ending September 30.

In terms of the times, the statistics were impressive. The aircraft of the USAF and RAF, together with about three dozen civilian charter planes out of England, had brought almost one ton for every Berliner in the beleaguered city. With the exception of one 15-hour period in November, 1948, the month of the "great fog", the airlift had been a round-the-clock operation, seven days a week. In mid-April, 1949, the "Easter Parade" delivered almost 13,000 tons of supplies in 1,398 flights, a record day for the airlift, The original delivery goal of 4,500 tons daily was raised, and met, to 5,620 tons daily in October, 1948.

The total delivered was 2,325,000 tons, with 1,783,000 hauled by the USAF and the remainder by the RAF and the civilian aircraft.

It was, and remains, a major achievement of air power. But one nagging question lingers: What if the Russians had tried to interfere with the corridor traffic? They did use harassment, sometimes buzzing the transports, often flying alongside and then peeling off with a flourish. But nothing worse than that.

Did the USAF hold air superiority over Germany and the corridor routes then? Only implicitly, in the strength of the B-29s in England and the fighters in Germany. It may be argued that the potential of the atomic bomb monopoly was too powerful a deterrent for the Russian military to have made any serious attempts to interfere in the air.

But that monopoly was to be short-lived. It was lost forever, sometime in the weeks just before the end of the airlift. President Truman made the ominous announcement September 23, 1949: There was evidence that the Russians had recently exploded an atomic bomb.

Another picture of intensive Operation Vittles training at Great Falls AFB, this shows radio officers busy with plain language and Morse classes. Today communications radio (background) is much more capable and about one-hundredth as large.

Shattering of the Morning Calm

The North Korean army slashed across the 38th parallel and sliced through South Korean defenses. Battered and in full retreat, the Republic of Korea needed help. Only the United States was in a position to offer it.

Word of the attack got to Headquarters, Far East Air Forces, at 10:00 Sunday morning, June 25, 1950, six hours after the border crossing. The immediate task for FEAF was to assist in the evacuation of Americans; airlift was assembled by mid-afternoon.

Next morning, Gen. Douglas MacArthur, now commander of United Nations forces, ordered Fifth Air Force chief Maj. Gen. Earle E. Partridge to cover the Inchon embarkation of departing Americans. Partridge called in the North American F-82Gs of the 4th, 68th, and 339th Fighter (All-Weather) Squadrons (FAWS) from their Japanese base. The U. S. Air Force was at war again.

What made the Korean conflict different was the single fact that the U. S. atomic bomb monopoly had been broken. The Russians had the weapon, and certainly would use it if attacked. Kim Il Sung's North Korea, and Mao Tse-Tung's China, then just a few months old, were client states of the USSR. Would the Soviet Union take action in the event of a certain defeat for North Korea, or a threat against China? Nobody could be sure.

Hence, the limited war in Korea, the first fought by U. S. forces. Hindsight, so liberally applied by conservative spokesmen, decries the actions taken then. But in June, 1950, the view forward was not clear at all. Besides, the USAF was a weak reflection of its wartime greatness.

The Republic of Korea (ROK) air force would be no help; the 16 trainers and liaison types had not a single bomb rack or machine gun mount among them. Fortunately, the North Korean AF was weak; it numbered 62 Il-10 attack craft, about 70 Yak piston-engined fighters, and some supporting planes. Its first combat was its first defeat; five Yaks struck Kimpo about noon June 27. In less than five minutes, three were burning on the ground. The first USAF kill was credited to Lt. William G. Hudson, 68th FAWS. An hour later, eight Il-10s made the same mistake, and four were flamed by four Lockheed F-80Cs of the 35th Fighter-Bomber Squadron.

That evening, President Truman told MacArthur to send the USAF and Navy to battle. MacArthur ordered Fifth AF to hit targets between the battle line and the 38th parallel. First on the offensive were a dozen elegant Douglas B-26 light bombers (in World War 2, designated A-26 attack aircraft). The 8th Bomb Squadron, 3rd Bomb Group, hit the rail yards at Munsan early June 28; at dusk, four 19th Bomb Group

In the first year of the Korean war the F-51 Mustang flew more combat missions than any other Air Force type, usually laden (as here) with bombs and rockets. This F-51D in the hands of Capt William K. Hook was photographed around midnight during August 1950.

During World War 2 the AAF never had a really effective air/sea rescue aircraft, and in the ETO tended to rely on the ASR organization of the RAF. By the Korean war the Grumman SA-16A Albatross had changed all that. This example was based at Okinawa during B-29 missions, and like its sister-ships served for the next 20 years.

Strategic bombing in Korea was a major operation, which for the first time saw large precision-guided air/surface missiles, such as the 12,000-lb VB-13 Tarzon. Even free-fall bombs were effective in large enough quantity, and many major targets received almost as many as had Krupps a few years previously. This 6 November 1950 picture shows how the B-29s left the Chosen nitrogen-fertilizer and explosives plant at Hungnam.

B-29s sailed in and hit roads and railroads north of Seoull.

Next day, nine more B-29s flew from their base at Kadena, Okinawa, to hit Kimpo airfield, now in enemy hands. On June 30, Truman authorized the use of available land forces in the fight; the Navy took up positions to blockade North Korea, and the war escalated.

The 22nd and 92nd Bomb Groups (Medium), equipped with B-29s, were deployed from SAC's Fifteenth AF in the U. S. to operational control of FEAF. Together with the 19th BG and the 31st Strategic Reconnaissance Squadron, they were formed into FEAF Bomber Command, under Maj. Gen. Emmett O'Donnell.

The NKAF was obliterated in less than one month, and the USAF had control of the air. Now the need was for ground support, but available Korean airfields could not handle the Lockheed F-80C fighter-bombers. Six squadrons converted backwards, trading their F-80s for F-51s.

The ground-air team established in World War 2 to coordinate air strikes with Army needs was not working well in the rugged and dangerous Korean hills. Field liaison officers with Eighth Army, Task Force 77 and the USAF set up an informal control system; they borrowed a pair of North American L-17s assigned to the 24th Infantry Division. Two USAF lieutenants flew the first Korean airborne FAC missions and called in about 20 flights of F-80s their first day on the job.

Ground War a Determinant

The objectives and use of air power were in large measure determined by the movement of the ground war, once the brief strategic bombing campaign was closed out. The momentum of the initial North Korean invasion carried its forces forward, pushing the retreating Americans and the remnants of the Koreans into the Pusan area. There, behind a defensive perimeter, the Eighth Army dug in and held.

That stubborn defense, coupled with a massive air offensive flown by Mustang fighter-bombers from Japan staging thorugh Taegu, bought time. The ROK Army regained some strength, reinforcements arrived for the Eighth, and the NKA drive was halted and turned. MacArthur's landing at Inchon followed, under an umbrella of complete air superiority and preceded by B-29 interdiction strikes, Navy fighter sweeps, USAF and Navy ground attacks to support the invasion, and Marine Corps close support.

On September 17, the Eighth began its drive northward, gathering momentum as it moved. B-29s flew ahead, destroying bridges on the route of the retreating NKA, and blasting their troops in a carpet-bombing attack running a mile along the Naktong river. Seoul was recaptured and by October 1 the ROK army was crossing the 38th parallel, moving as fast forward as it had earlier retreated.

By then, the Chinese were committed to fight, and had moved ground and air units into the area just north of the Yalu river. On November 26, they launched a major offensive and drove the UN forces back down the peninsula to a line of resistance south of Seoul, where the war began its long stalemate. The UN forces countered in early 1951, and moved forward to a line roughly equivalent to the 38th parallel. Truce talks began July 10, 1951, and the armistice was signed July 27, 1953.

To describe a war like the Korean conflict in limited space allows no room for endless narratives of hammering machine guns and exploding MiGs, as pertinent as they are. Instead, consider the air war as three different, though related and simultaneous operations: the strategic bombing campaign, a short-lived attack against short-listed targets; the interdiction campaign, which isolated the battlefield, cut supply and communication lines, and supported the advance or covered the retreat of the UN ground armies; and the air-superiority campaign, that pitted Sabres against MiGs in an aerial gunfight at the OK Corral.

The Strategic Bombing Campaign

North Korean industry helped the Japanese during World War 2, and now was supplying not only its home country but also Manchuria. The Japanese-built Korean hydroelectric projects, among the world's largest, exported power. But the main source for NKA war materiel was Russia. The decision had been made not to provoke that country, and so strategy in Korea had to stop at the Yalu river border with Manchuria.

There were four major industrial centers on the northeast coast and one on the west, typical strategic targets. Because they were crowded together in complexes, the basic decision was to hit them by areas and not by target systems. For area bombing, incendiaries were the weapon of choice; a backup plan based on the use of demolition bombs and precision bombing tactics also was offered.

The strategic campaign started July 13; the 22nd and 92nd groups flew their B-29s against the rail center at Wonsan. The dust had hardly cleared before MacArthur demanded their return to support the Eighth Army. The campaign had opened and closed, temporarily, with a single attack.

The Joint Chiefs of Staff chafed at the delay. North Korea was contributing to the strength of Russia in the Cold War. Its chemical industry was supplying some of the radioactive elements the USSR was using in its nuclear weapons research. To guarantee the bombing offensive, the JCS authorized two more B-29 groups, with the proviso that they be used only in the strategic campaign.

The kind of bombing the JCS had in mind was demonstrated in three successive missions flown against the complex of explosives and fertilizer factories at Hungnam. With no guarantee of good weather, the ability to bomb by radar was necessary, and the 19th BG did not have the AN/APQ-13 radar installed. FEAF sent the 22nd and 92nd groups out against Hungnam, an easily discerned target for World War 2 radar equipment.

Mission Nannie Able was flown July 20 by 47 B-29s; they bombed by radar, and all bombs hit the target. Nannie Baker, on August 1, was a visual bombing exercise for 46 B-29s; they hit the fertilizer factory and produced a very destructive explosion. On August 3, Mission Nannie Charlie sent 39 B-29s against Hungnam with good results. The three strikes neutralized the complex.

By then, the 98th and 307th Bomb Groups were on their way to the theater; they left the United States August 2 and 1 respectively. The 98th flew its first combat strike August 7, and the 307th August 8, underlining the mobility concept that SAC had been advocating and now was demonstrating.

The mission of August 8 marked the start of the sustained strategic bombing campaign. It was planned to be a maximum effort every third day, using two groups; by August 20 it was expanded to a three-group effort with a two-day standdown between attacks for crew rest and aircraft repair and maintenance.

The bombing pattern was leisurely. With complete air superiority, the limiting factor was air traffic control from Kadena and Yawata, Japan. Interdiction strikes and fighter sweeps were dispatched during the same time frame the bombers used, and the crowded skies posed a real threat to safety, particularly in bad weather.

It was fortunate the North Koreans had no air defenses worthy of the name. Bombing by squadrons at lengthy intervals could have resulted in decimation of the B-29s if there had been a strong fighter defense or even powerful anti-aircraft batteries. Bombing accuracy was assessed later by ground parties advancing through North Korea. Pyongyang, the North Korean capital, was almost untouched by bombs except for its industrial complexes which were gutted. That was typical.

By September 15, there was little left on the strategic target list. The last strategic mission was dispatched September 26 against the huge Fusen hydroelectric plant near Hungnam. Eight B-29s from the 92nd put it out of action with a well-dropped pattern that cut the main water supply line to the turbines and knocked out the transformers.

After this strike, the Joint Chiefs ordered the bombers to go back to interdiction. But with the ground armies advancing toward the Yalu at a very fast pace, and the Yalu itself as a barrier against any bombing further north, the available target area dwindled daily. The B-29s soon ran out of targets, and were not needed for ground support tasks because the offensive was so successful.

The Superfortresses had obliterated the targets on the list with the single exception of the Rashin area, taboo because of political considerations. One bomber was lost to enemy action. By the end of October, the 22nd and 92nd groups, their task completed, were on their way back to the United States. On October 27, FEAF Bomber Command stood down.

New War, New Rules

The Chinese entry meant that it was a new war, and the UN command immediately adopted new rules. The ban against incendiaries was lifted; the B-29s were sent out on fire-bombing raids against northern cities near the Yalu crossings. The crews were told to fly a two-week maximum effort, and to fly to exhaustion. The attacks were to start at the Manchurian border and move south, with the single exception again of Rashin, still regarded as too close to the border to be

One of very few Air Force aircraft that saw extensive action in World War 2, Korea and Vietnam, the Douglas A-26 (from 1948, B-26) Invader combined good performance with great firepower and long endurance. This picture of a B-26B being rearmed in Korea was taken on 11 September 1950. By this time the nose had been rearranged to take eight ·50-calibre guns, two more than in 1944.

The Fairchild C-119 Flying Boxcar, a much more capable development of the wartime-designed C-82 Packet, arrived in good time for the Korean campaign. Here a "Dollar-nineteen" para-drops rations and gasoline to UN troops on a snow-covered battlefield a few hundred feet below, near Chungju.

On 17 September 1952 the P-51D of 1st Lt David L. Gray of the 18th Fighter-Bomber Wing was damaged whilst on a close-support mission and its landing gear refused to extend. After bellying in, Gray walked away without a scratch.

Though constraints on USAF fighter pilots in Korea were nothing like as severe as those politically imposed in SE Asia some 15 years later, it was still a major achievement to get into firing position behind a MiG-15. This combat camera sequence shows strikes on a MiG's left wing in April 1953.

attacked without risk of hitting Manchurian territory.

To operate near the Yalu, the B-29s would need escort. SAC, then equipped with its own fighters, sent the 27th Fighter-Escort Wing from its home at Bergstrom AFB, Texas, to Korea. The 27th flew its first sorties December 8, from Taegu.

But even escorted missions were dangerous for the B-29s. On March 1, 1951, Superforts of the 98th BG arrived at the rendezvous late and proceeded to attack Kogunyong without fighter escort. Nine MiGs jumped the formation, which closed ranks and headed for Japan. Ten B-29s were shot up, three so badly that they had to make emergency landings at Taegu.

The Sinui-ju railroad bridges were hit April 12 by 39 B-29s, escorted by the 27th FEW as screen and the 4th FIW as high cover. MiGs tore through both screen and cover, got to the formation, shot down two of the bombers and damaged six more. It was an end to B-29 missions near the Yalu until more adequate escort forces were available.

In October, 1951, five of the big bombers were lost in a single week, one short of the total B-29 losses from the beginning of the war. China was showing all the attributes of a major air power, and it was suicidal to fly B-29s in the face of such strong daylight opposition. The decision was made to operate at night, using ground radar and other bombing aids, but primarily trusting to Shoran (an accurate, SHOrt-RANge navigation aid) and developing its use in combat.

The Chinese countered with radar-controlled searchlights and an airborne controller to track the force and call in fighters. After only one of a four-plane B-29 element survived a night attack over Kwaksan on June 10, 1952, the Superfortresses were painted with gloss black lacquer on their bellies to defeat the searchlights.

For a September 12 strike against the Sui-ho hydroelectric plant on a clear night, B-26 light bombers attacked first on low-level searchlight suppression while six B-29s orbited above with electronic countermeasures to defeat the enemy radars. The main force of 29 Superforts dropped 2,000-lb. semi-armor-piercing bombs and blacked out Sui-ho. On a second night strike September 30, three B-29s attacked early, dropping air-burst bombs for flak suppression, then orbited the target using ECM against the radars. Seven B-26s flew searchlight suppression strikes in support. Again the main force, this time 45 heavy bombers, blasted the Namsan-ni chemical plant, last of the strategic-type targets in the north.

The enemy still persisted, and in October 1952 the

B-29 tactics changed again. The bomber stream was compressed to one-minute intervals between elements. ECM was emphasized, and the first "ferret" missions were flown by RB-29s of the 91st Strategic Reconnaissance Squadron, the redesignated 31st SRS, to analyze enemy electronic emissions. A screen of Marine Corps Douglas F3D-2N Skyknight night fighters flew as a forward barrier for the B-29 formations. Later, when the USAF had its own Lockheed F-94C night fighters, the Marines shifted to overhead cover between the initial and breakaway points of the bomb run. Irregular attack schedules were tried, with altitude variations to avoid contrail formation. The dark of the moon was a favored time to bomb. These measures together made the B-29 survivable as the Chinese defense tactics improved.

The B-29 was, by then, badly outdated; but it was the only available bomber that could do the job, and it soldiered on until the armistice. It saw action for the 37 months of the war, missing only 26 days of that period in combat. The B-29s flew 21,000 sorties, and dropped 167,100 tons of bombs, more than was dropped during World War 2 by the several hundred B-29s stationed in the Marianas. And it was all done with a maximum force of 99 Superfortresses.

The Interdiction Campaigns

Four interdiction campaigns were conducted during the first year of the Korean war; in addition, there were innumerable interdiction missions which did not come under the blanket cover of a campaign, but were in response to some immediate tactical need.

Interdiction Campaign No. 1 was a combined effort by FEAF's strategic bombers, Fifth AF tactical aircraft, and Navy planes from Task Force 77. Their mission: halt the NKA advance that was driving the UN forces down the peninsula, and cover the UN retreat. The first strikes were on August 2 by B-29s of FEAF's Bomber Command against rail yards. They knocked out the main rail centers in eight days and then turned to the rail bridges north of Seoul; across those structures moved much of the NKA supply train.

On August 16, the Superforts were pulled away by MacArthur for a massive air strike against suspected NKA positions north of Pusan. O'Donnell, without convincing proof that the NKA was concentrated in the area, didn't favor the strike, but went along with the MacArthur request. So 98 B-29s dropped 1,000 tons of high explosives from a low altitude against a supposed 40,000 NKA troops along the Naktong river, near Waegwan. Post-strike reconnaissance showed no evidence that a single NKA soldier had been hit. The largest "carpet-bombing" attack since the invasion of Europe in 1944 was apparently a complete waste.

In other missions, the light bombers and fighter-bombers in Fifth AF had been hitting bridges, railroads and roads on specific strikes and armed reconnaissance. One group of B-26 crews developed a makeshift night-intruder operation, and scored against truck convoys moving at night.

By September 4, all the bridges on the target list of 44 had been destroyed, except for seven, and those had been rendered impassable. It was the official end of the first interdiction campaign; within a few days, the Pusan breakout occurred and the needs of the ground armies changed.

MacArthur's planners for the Inchon landing wanted massive air support, following the patterns established five and six years earlier. The aim of Interdiction Campaign No. 2, scheduled to begin September 9, was to ready the objective area. Targets were bridges again, north of a line between Pyongyang and Wonsan; they were Bomber Command's, while Fifth AF gave close support to the landing. The campaign lasted into late September, and went as planned except that the

ground troops moved faster than expected. The interdiction moved north, to stay ahead of their advance.

Targets for the third campaign were bridges on both coasts. Bomber Command destroyed many of them, cutting off the retreating NKA forces, but also hampering the advance of the UN armies to some extent.

The fourth campaign was long, bitter, and best in terms of results. Planned before the Chinese entered the war, it was quickly changed to strike at their supply lines during their rapid advance southward. That objective was temporarily cancelled by MacArthur's request for heavy air strikes against troop concentrations, and the towns and villages hiding or supplying the Chinese and North Korean armies. Little interdiction was accomplished during the first month.

But after the first week of January, 1951, all available aircraft were pressed into service. The retreat of the Eighth Army was not turned into a rout because of the close air support given by tireless airmen. USAF air was so active that the Chinese armies could only move by night. Their drive, under the pressure of constant air attacks and the damage of interdiction, began to slow. Their logistics system gave way. Foraging became a necessity. Ammunition and rifles had to be captured instead of being supplied. Reinforcements took as long as four months to reach the front from the Yalu crossings. It was too much to stand, and the Chinese were forced to negotiations.

The Fight for Air Superiority

FEAF began the war with 32 all-weather F-82Gs and 365 F-80Cs. The theater could not support more, and more were not available anyway. There was a stock of North American F-51 Mustang fighters in service

with Air National Guard units in the U.S., and 145 of them were scraped together for Korean service. Out of necessity, FEAF agreed to a step backwards; six of its F-80C squadrons would convert to F-51s.

The early air fighting was sporadic; the NKAF was weak, unskilled, and inexperienced. But the Chinese across the border were aggressive. In August they began firing anti-aircraft at UN planes patrolling the Yalu area.

On October 3, Premier Chou En-lai said that Chinese troops would defend Korea if the UN forces crossed the 38th parallel. In spite of this warning, and of all the signs that the USAF was encountering, MacArthur told Truman at their Wake Island conference October 15 that it was very unlikely that the Chinese would interfere. Besides, he assured Truman, the Chinese had no air force. (FEAF had just submitted new intelligence estimates crediting the Chinese with at least 300 combat aircraft, including jets. Three days later, an RB-29 crew counted 75 fighters on the field at Antung, on the Manchurian side of the Yalu.)

Three Chinese Yak fighters finally crossed the Yalu November 1 and bounced a T-6 and a single B-26; one of the fighters was shot down by the B-26 crew. That afternoon, six MiG-15s attacked another Mosquito and a flight of Mustangs; they all survived.

First blood of the jet versus jet war was let December 17 during a maximum-strength attack against Sinui-ju, near Antung. F-80Cs of the 51st FIW were flying top cover for fighter-bombers, and were engaged by the MiGs. Lt. Russell J. Brown locked onto a MiG and shot the plane down for the first jet-age combat victory.

Within a few days, the Chinese MiGs had shown

An October 1952 picture taken at about 500 knots over Korea's rugged mountains as the F-86E Sabres of the 51st FIW streak north towards the MiGs. The 51st, with the 4th, introduced the swept-wing jet to active service.

A major FAC platform was the T-6 trainer, which usually marked targets with a smoke rocket or phosphorous grenade. This "Mosquito" (FAC) T-6 was photographed in August 1951 flying with the 614th Tac Control Group, 5th AF.

their potential by gaining a degree of air superiority. They stopped all daylight reconnaissance by the RB-29s, outclassed the available Fifth AF fighters, and could destroy the fighter-bombers almost at will. Then the Sabres arrived to fight, and the air situation changed almost overnight.

North American F-86A fighters of the 4th Fighter-Interceptor Wing, deployed to Korea from the U. S., entered action December 15. The wing's pilots were experienced; many of them had been aces in World War 2, and by the end of the year they had flown 234 sorties, gotten in 76 fights, and shot down eight MiGs. They also had developed the tactics for the new fighter, using a "fluid-four" flight, and four flights spaced at about five-minute intervals on their fighter sweeps to the Yalu. They had first gone to battle at cruise speeds, to discover that it takes too long to accelerate to top speed for fighting. After that, they went into combat at high speed, with all the available energy they could store in the airframe. They made their kills from the classical six o'clock position, and they restored UN air superiority.

From then, it was a seesaw battle as the Chinese sought to regain what they had just lost, and the USAF fought to hold the skies. The Chinese plan was simple; they would use the MiGs to regain air superiority, and under that protective umbrella build and rebuild the North Korean airfields under "MiG Alley" and nearer the 38th parallel. That done, they would move in the

MiGs being stockpiled behind the Yalu barrier, and the air war would be theirs.

At the beginning of 1951, the Chinese advance had captured so much of Korea that the Sabres had to leave for Japan, their bases overrun. There they were helpless to aid, because they lacked the range to get to Korea and to fight there. In their absence, Chinese airmen seized control of the air over an area lying between the Yalu and the Chongchon rivers, from the west coast of Korea to roughly the mid-point of the peninsula. They owned that chunk of sky; in recognition, FEAF pilots called it "MiG Alley" and the name stuck.

On the ground, the Chinese were in retreat and once again air bases in Korea were available. The Sabres moved back March 6 and began systematically defeating the Chinese MiGs. The Communists could not hold the skies, and in May they announced that an International Communist Volunteer Air Force would join combat. In came the first team, Russian instructor pilots, who introduced new tactics but were defeated handily anyway. The ground war stopped with the

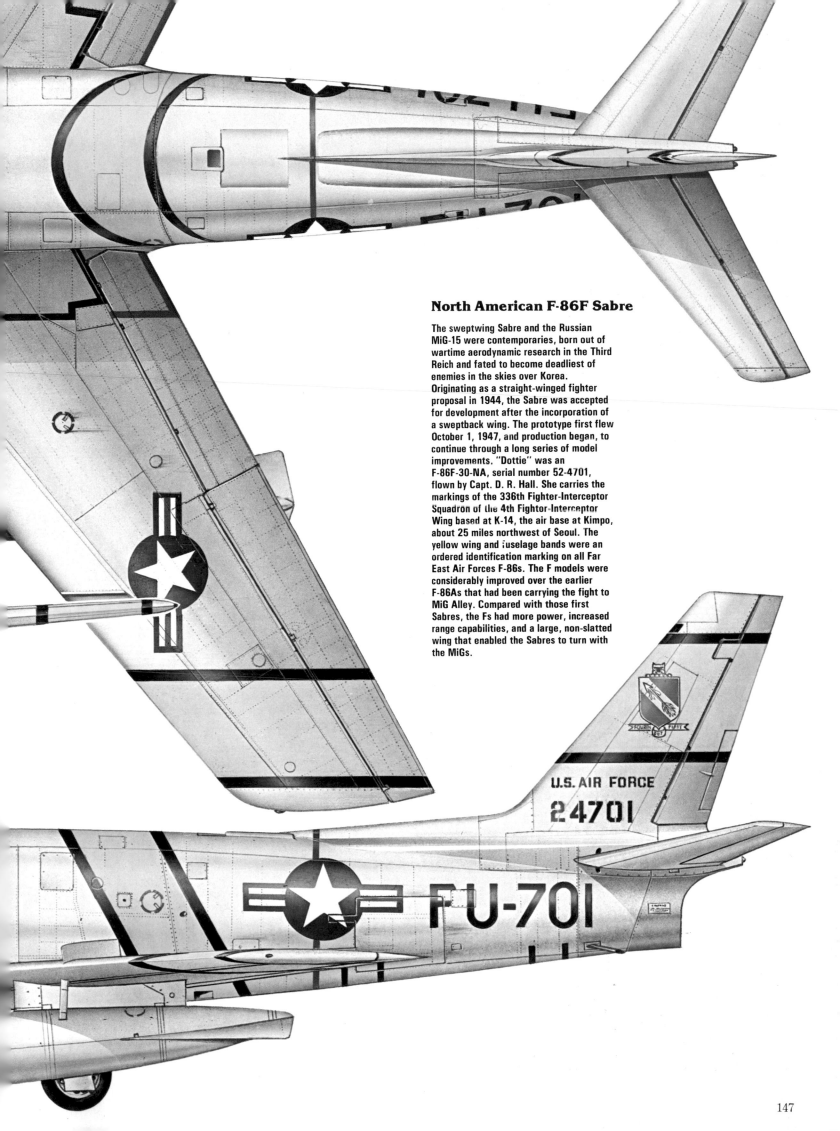

North American F-86F Sabre

The sweptwing Sabre and the Russian MiG-15 were contemporaries, born out of wartime aerodynamic research in the Third Reich and fated to become deadliest of enemies in the skies over Korea. Originating as a straight-winged fighter proposal in 1944, the Sabre was accepted for development after the incorporation of a sweptback wing. The prototype first flew October 1, 1947, and production began, to continue through a long series of model improvements. "Dottie" was an F-86F-30-NA, serial number 52-4701, flown by Capt. D. R. Hall. She carries the markings of the 336th Fighter-Interceptor Squadron of the 4th Fighter-Interceptor Wing based at K-14, the air base at Kimpo, about 25 miles northwest of Seoul. The yellow wing and fuselage bands were an ordered identification marking on all Far East Air Forces F-86s. The F models were considerably improved over the earlier F-86As that had been carrying the fight to MiG Alley. Compared with those first Sabres, the Fs had more power, increased range capabilities, and a large, non-slatted wing that enabled the Sabres to turn with the MiGs.

A gout of flame illuminates the night as the pilot of an F-94B Starfire briefly checks his afterburner before moving out from dispersal on July 27, 1953. The F-94B was the first afterburner-boosted aircraft in USAF service; a radar-equipped night interceptor, it provided escort for B-29s.

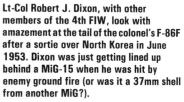

Lt-Col Robert J. Dixon, with other members of the 4th FIW, look with amazement at the tail of the colonel's F-86F after a sortie over North Korea in June 1953. Dixon was just getting lined up behind a MiG-15 when he was hit by enemy ground fire (or was it a 37mm shell from another MiG?).

beginning of the truce talks July 10, and two days later the Communist air offensive quieted down.

Red Stars on the Offensive

By the end of July, the Chinese airfields around Antung held more than 300 MiGs; against them, FEAF had 89 F-86As in the theater, not all combat-ready.

The Communist planes charged into battle in large formations, holding an altitude advantage and outnumbering Sabres by four to one. With no hope of further reinforcement from the U.S., Fifth AF gave up its fighter-bomber strikes in the area under "MiG Alley". The Chinese now were flying the MiG-15bis, an improved model with more thrust, operated from rejuvenated airfields. By the winter of 1951, they had driven the B-29s out of the daylight skies.

In December, the 51st FIW converted to new F-86E models and the Sabres now totalled 127, a number meaningful only on paper. About 45 percent of the planes were out of commission for parts or needed maintenance, the supply of drop tanks had been exhausted, and there were only about 60 Sabres ready to fight instead of 127. But for some yet-unexplained reason, the Communist air offensive turned docile in mid-December. They stopped defending the new airfields, and changed their tactics. It looked as if their high command had made a decision to treat the war as a vast training ground, and to cycle pilot classes through an advanced education.

The Chinese and North Koreans had established a joint operations center at the Antung complex of airfields, and had defended it not only with many MiGs, but with a large number of anti-aircraft artillery batteries of medium and large caliber. Additionally, they had installed more than two dozen early-warning radar sets and about a dozen ground-controlled intercept radars. In May 1952 they began sending MiGs out under GCI direction and the air war heated up again.

The Sabre supply was on the increase, and the first F-86F models began to arrive in June. With more thrust, and the solid leading edge replacing the slotted one of earlier models, the F was a more formidable adversary that could stay with the MiGs in maneuvering. It was tried as a fighter-bomber in Korea, because the straight-winged Republic F-84 Thunderjets just couldn't handle the MiGs consistently, although they did a superb job of delivering their heavy ordnance loads on target.

Two wings of F-86F Sabres, the 8th and 18th FBWs,

were designated to fly fighter-bomber missions, while the 4th and 51st fought for air superiority.

The increased air pressure was felt by the Chinese and, on February 4, 1953, Chou En-lai made it known that his country was ready to consider a cease-fire. Fifth AF, while perfectly willing to accept truce talks, knew the real-world situation and determined to maintain its hold on the air. The aim was to get the MiGs to come up to fight and to be defeated.

The campaign started with leaflet drops, made by B-29s over Chinese ground forces in North Korea, asking where the Communist Air Force was. It had been conspicuous by its absence there, and captured troops had been bitter about the lack of friendly air support covering their movements. That bit of psychological warfare was countered by Radio Pyongyang in a propaganda campaign of its own, accusing the Fifth AF pilots of being gangsters who killed innocent women and children and bombed hospitals. Lt. Gen. Glenn O. Barcus, one of the more colorful characters the war produced, warned the radio station a week in advance that he would attack it on May Day, the biggest Communist Party event and holiday.

Four wings of Sabres took off and headed northwest toward Pyongyang, trying to look like a fighter sweep flying to "MiG Alley". They roared over Pyongyang and then, without preliminaries, rolled over to dive-bomb, strafe and generally ruin Radio Pyongyang. With the debris still settling, Barcus broadcast in the clear from his own F-86 his personal "greetings" to the Communists: "These attacks . . . are our response to your insulting lies . . . This is all now, but we shall be back every time you broadcast filthy lies about the Fifth Air Force." He signed off with rank and name. It was one of the better moments of the sideshow psywar conducted in Korea.

Another clever stroke was the offer of a $50,000 reward for the defection of any MiG pilot with his plane. Deliver it to Kimpo, the leaflets said, and get freedom and fifty thousand. Very soon after that, the best MiG pilots disappeared from the Korean skies. There is no proof, but psywar specialists believe that the Russians pulled their pilots out, rather than risk the international humiliation that would result if one of their own defected. A North Korean pilot made the break, claiming later that he had not heard of the offer. He took the money, though, and headed for California.

The Communist combat crews that were left were not very good, and "MiG Alley" became Fifth AF territory in a series of turkey shoots. During May, 1953, Sabres sighted 1,507 MiGs, and engaged 537 in combat. They shot down 56, lost one Sabre. In June, the Sabres fought 501 of the 1,268 MiGs they saw, shot down 77, probably got 11 more, and damaged 41. No F-86s were lost. July was a repeat, but only 32 MiGs were shot down; Fifth AF lost two Sabres.

Those fierce gunfights above the Yalu kept the Chinese air force out of the skies above the UN ground forces, and away from the USAF, Navy and Marine fighter-bombers and light bombers while they conducted their decisive interdiction strikes. The Chinese lost overwhelmingly; 792 MiG-15s went down, many with their pilots, and they only took 78 Sabres in exchange.

Air superiority was a determining factor in the Korean war. The Chinese finally yielded to it; either they feared an expanding air war, with more advanced weapons from the United States, or they felt the pressure of the existing air strength, or both.

The air forces of the United Nations, and that was primarily FEAF and the Fifth, ruled the daylight skies above the Land of the Morning Calm, throttled the flow of supplies and war materiel, and slaughtered countless numbers of Chinese soldiers where they stood.

It was, finally, a triumph for air power.

Keeping an Eye on the Enemy

"We're eyeball to eyeball, and I think the other fellow just blinked."

Dean Rusk, President John F. Kennedy's Secretary of State, said it softly in the tensed hush of the Cabinet Room of the White House. It was Wednesday afternoon, October 24, 1962, and the gathering had just heard that some Russian ships headed for Cuba had altered course. It was the first indication that the Russians were beginning to ease the pressure of the Cuban confrontation.

It was another of the potential head-on collisions that had marked the post-war years. But it was a far more serious crisis than any before it, because it involved the presence of Russian nuclear tipped intermediate-range ballistic missiles sited in Cuba and capable of blanketing most of the United States.

Their presence had been discovered by daring photo-reconnaissance of the island, one of the means that the U. S. had for keeping an eye on possible enemies.

It was apparent early in the Cold War, if it had not been completely apparent in World War 2, that Russian progress and capabilities in warfare would not be easy to assess. They were reluctant to publish their prowess in aeronautical science or missile technology. They attended no international conferences in science or research. And a long history of national paranoia, going back to the early Czars, added to the difficulty of

Vigilance was the key word during the Cold War and effective long range aerial reconnaissance over unfriendly territory was a critical requirement. One project was to use the B-36 to carry a speedy jet to a heavily defended target and then carry it home again. The Ficon (Fighter Conveyor) project mated the XF-84F and a B-36 either to enable the fighter to make photo-recon passes over distant targets or to use the fighter to defend its mother aircraft. Here the original prototype XF-84F is extended below a GRB-36 strategic-reconnaissance aircraft on a hinged trapeze.

At first a covert spy aircraft operated by the CIA with cover (unwittingly?) provided by the civilian NACA, the Lockheed U-2 moved on in the 1960s to become a legitimate USAF platform packed with sensors for many kinds of mission. This example was one of the first batch to be formally assigned to SAC; later almost all were rebuilt into later versions.

learning anything through open means about the Soviet military might.

Right after World War 2, the United States enjoyed, if that is the right word, the atomic monopoly. Technically, U. S. aircraft were far superior to Russian types. Dealing from that strength, the intelligence gatherers decided to take advantage of the performance of American planes and use them to go look at the Russians, photograph whatever installations could be seen, and monitor electronic transmissions.

The redesignated and reactivated 72nd Reconnaissance Squadron (Very Long Range, Photographic) began operations at Ladd Field, Alaska, in October 1947. It was an unusual unit; its equipment was a dozen Boeing F-13A aircraft, the photo-reconnaissance versions of the B-29, and a half-dozen—the only half-dozen—Boeing B-29F models.

Boeing lists the B-29F as a standard model that was winterized for Arctic tests. The tests were of long-range reconnaissance, and the B-29F was quite a different airplane from the ones that had bombed Japan. In addition to being winterized, and carrying the red-tipped wings and tail Arctic markings, the F models were some 10,000 pounds lighter, and were stripped of all their defensive armament systems and bomb racks. They had additional fuel capacity, and their engines had been hand-picked by conscientious crew chiefs. They could stay in the air for 33 hours, and spent a lot of that time at altitudes around 40,000 feet.

They were among the first to fly surveillance missions near, perhaps over, the territory of the Soviet Union. And there was nothing the Russians could do about it. Their interceptors were helpless at altitude, and the Russian pilots then couldn't handle the weather problems that have plagued Arctic flying since its inception.

As electronic equipment became more capable and more discriminating, it offered an attractive complementary input to photographic reconnaissance. On days when the enemy could not be photographed because of the weather, they could be "seen" by radar, and the scope picture could be photographed. The enemy's radio message traffic could be monitored and analyzed, for further input, as could his radar transmissions.

All this had been done during World War 2 to some degree. As time and equipment progressed, electronic means came to be used more and more for reconnaissance. The most dangerous use of all was in ferret missions.

Ferret missions are a deadly game of electronic warfare, in which real people are killed. The purpose of the game is to fly close enough to an enemy, and threateningly enough, to provoke a reaction. Generally, the first reaction is the use of search and height-finding radars. If the threat appears serious, missile-guidance or anti-aircraft radars may join in. Ground-control interception radars may be brought to bear, and all of this will be accompanied by message traffic, passing orders and observations.

The ferret airplane monitors, records and analyzes the enemy transmissions, sometimes jamming or countering them. It works both ways; the enemy, knowing the way the game is played, also may introduce deception and try to confuse or misguide the ferret. If the ferret can be lured into enemy territory, the enemy may very well try to shoot him down. That stops the missions and, by chance, delivers some new electronic warfare equipment to the enemy.

The first loss in ferret missions along the Russian coastlines was a Navy aircraft, probably a Lockheed P2V, shot down in the Baltic April 8, 1950. On October 7, 1952, a Boeing B-29, possibly from the redesignated (again) 72nd Strategic Reconnaissance Squadron (Photographic) was shot down six miles off Japan's northern island of Hokkaido.

These were the early casualties in the Cold War which often degenerated into a hot engagement. Not only ferret and reconnaissance aircraft were attacked; innocent commercial airliners were attacked, sometimes shot down, by Communist bloc fighters during those years. Air France, British European Airways, Cathay Pacific, El Al, KLM and Sabena all suffered losses ranging from a few casualties to the entire aircraft with passengers and crew.

In 1954 and again in 1955, Navy ferret missions were attacked. MiG-15s shot down a P2V over the Sea of Japan September 4, 1954, and attacked a second near the Bering Strait July 23, 1955. The latter got away to a forced landing in American territory.

In September, 1958, the Russians apparently lured a Lockheed C-130, carrying a crew of 17, off its course in Turkey. It crossed the border into Soviet Armenia, and was shot down near Yerevan.

Ravens over the Barents Sea

The Boeing RB-47E of the 55th Strategic Reconnaissance Squadron, Strategic Air Command, cruised high above the Barents Sea. Its usual three-man flight crew was augmented by three "Ravens"—electronic warfare specialists—in a capsule fitted in the B-47's bomb bay. The plane was on a ferret flight, probing the borders of Russian territory and monitoring the electronic transmissions from radars and communication systems.

Maj. Willard G. Palm's crew had left Brize Norton air base in England on a flight planned to parallel the coastline of the Kola peninsula, reported as the home base of Russian heavy bomber units. It was to turn northeast well off the pointed bill of Kanin peninsula, and turn northwest upon approaching Novaya Zemlya to return to base. The same area undoubtedly had been profiled earlier, and Palm's flight may have been the unlucky one that the Russians decided to use as an example.

At about 50 miles offshore, a pair of MiG-15s formed on the sweptwing Boeing, held for a minute, and then broke off to attack. Cannon fire flamed the B-47's left wing, and Palm ordered the bail-out. Co-pilot Capt. Bruce Olmstead and navigator Capt. John McKone ejected, got good chutes, landed in the sea, inflated their life rafts and were picked up later by a Russian trawler. Palm stayed with the airplane and apparently ditched; his body was recovered and returned by the Russians. The three ravens' bodies were not found.

Olmstead and McKone were released by the Russians January 25, 1961, and returned home.

That incident occured July 1, 1960; a similar incident happened again March 10, 1964, to the crew of a Douglas RB-66A. The light twin-jet reconnaissance bomber was available in at least two versions, one for photographic and the other for electronic reconnaissance.

It was operating out of a French base on a training flight and was heading toward the East German border. Its flight path was monitored by ground radar controllers, and they saw it make a feint toward the east. But it continued to fly eastward long after it should have turned back. The controllers transmitted a return code, but received no acknowledgment. Then they transmitted in the clear, adding a warning that the border was about to be crossed. That also was not acknowledged.

The plane was about 16 miles inside East Germany when it was intercepted by a fighter, probably an East German MiG-17. It hit the RB-66A on the first firing pass, and Capt. David Holland ordered the bail-out. Holland, Capt. Melvin J. Kessler and Lt. Harold W. Welch got out safely and were captured. Welch was returned March 21 because of injuries he had received; the other crewmen were returned March 28 after much negotiating between the U. S. and Russia. The crew was cleared of blame in a USAF inquiry, and the incident was officially claimed to have been caused by a faulty compass. It was a weak story; the RB-66A certainly had two, and probably three, compasses. It was being monitored and possibly directed by ground radars.

It was most probable that the Russians or East Germans, also very capable people, had jammed the communications and given the crew a false radar signal to steer by.

Of all the daring reconnaissance missions flown during those years, the best known and most remembered were the more than 400 sorties flown over the island of Cuba in late 1962. It was a time when the United States and Russia were very, very close to war.

The Cuban Confrontation

Cuba had been a thorn in the side of the U. S. ever since Fidel Castro took power January 2, 1959. The United States broke diplomatic relations with the island, and in April, 1961, encouraged, supplied and then failed to support an invasion by exiles.

The Bay of Pigs fiasco loosed an avalanche of arms from Cuba's new protector, the Soviet Union. Everything from pistols to artillery, MiG-15s to MiG-21s, motor torpedo boats and coastal patrol ships had been delivered. Following a July, 1962, visit to Moscow by Raul Castro, then Defense Minister, there was a noticeable upturn in the volume of shipping reaching Cuba. The harbors of Havana and Mariel were crowded. Strangely, the Russians kept all Cubans away from the docks during the off-loading, and handled the heavy work with their own deckhands and stevedores.

Some Cuban refugees reported seeing things that looked like rockets; others, with some technical skills, were able to make sketches in sufficient detail to confirm what had been only a suspicion. The Russians had brought anti-aircraft missiles to Cuba.

Ever since the break in diplomatic relations, Cuba had been the subject for an occasional reconnaissance flight by one of the CIA's Lockheed U-2 aircraft. The Cubans were able to identify, but not intercept, the

Almost certainly taken in Japan, this beautiful picture shows an RB-47H, one of the five reconnaissance and electronic-warfare models of the famed SAC six-jet swept-winger. One of the H-models was the last of more than 2,000 B-47s in AF service, retiring on December 29, 1967.

gray planes. They knew that a U-2 piloted by Francis Gary Powers had been shot down by a Russian missile on May 1, 1960, and they probably pointed out to the Russian advisers that Cuba ought to have the same opportunity, in order to prevent further incursions of Cuban airspace and reconnaissance of the island.

A U-2 mission was routed over the suspected areas of missile deployment August 29, 1962, and it brought back the first photographic evidence of the missile sites. At least two were positively identified, and six others looked suspiciously like anti-aircraft missile batteries. In a third section of Cuba, the photos showed a short-range coastal defense missile battery, the type used against an invading force or a pre-invasion naval action.

The U-2 overflights were scheduled for September 5, 17, 26 and 29, and October 5 and 7. Each one brought back more information: Three new SAM sites and three more cruise missile sites were spotted. What the U-2s could not photograph was the arrival of offensive ballistic missiles. They reached Cuban ports about September 8, and were off-loaded and moved at night for concealment.

Photo-interpreters scanned the many U-2 pictures and discovered that the SAM sites were part of a familiar pattern. They had seen pictures of the layout before, taken over Russia. It was a launching site for mobile medium-range ballistic missiles, and the SAM sites were located to defend them. Further, the anti-aircraft missiles were on launchers, ready for firing.

It was a new ball game. There was a potential risk of losing a U-2 and another Powers incident. Defense Secretary Robert S. McNamara made the decision to have further U-2 flights made by USAF pilots from Strategic Air Command. It was a fine distinction; the U-2 pilots employed by the CIA were all recent transfers from the military services, and ostensibly civilians.

After a quick checkout in the U-2, Majors Rudolf Anderson, Jr., and Richard S. Heyser, of SAC's 4080th Strategic Reconnaissance Wing at Laughlin AFB, Texas, climbed into the polished gray airplanes October 14. They flew southeast, made their landfalls, and then crossed the island on coordinated flight paths that covered the suspect area around San Cristobal in detail and duplicate. Both were within range of the Cuban SAMs at times, but neither was fired upon.

The U-2s carried back pictures of a medium-range ballistic missile field site. Seven missiles were on parked transporters outside of shelters, and an eighth was parked next to one of the four erectors on the site. Propellant loading equipment was standing by. At a second site, the cameras caught six missile transporters that had been parked in the shade, and a Russian truck convoy moving into the site.

Now the reconnaissance task became two-fold. It had to photograph all of Cuba from high altitude, pinpointing existing sites and at the same time searching for others under construction. When specific objectives had been located by this technique, low-flying reconnaissance aircraft would be dispatched to get detailed pictures.

SAC moved the 4080th SRW to Florida, and both Navy and Tactical Air Command reconnaissance wings were alerted that their services might be required. SAC's deployment was only part of a feverish activity as bomber, reconnaissance and fighter units headed for Air Force bases in Florida. Squadrons of North American F-100s and Lockheed F-104s poured into Homestead AFB, southwest of Miami. More F-100s

Along with RF-8As of the Navy the RF-101 Voodoos of the Air Force flew round-the-clock photo-reconnaissance cover of the island of Cuba during the Missile Crisis of 1962. In this frame from a low oblique film of Casilda port, taken on 6 November 1962, the shadow of the RF-101C can be clearly seen.

and the available force of Republic F-105s headed for McCoy AFB, already crowded with an operational SAC B-47 wing. Air Defense Command deployed some of its Convair F-106A strength to Patrick AFB. TAC's 4th Fighter Wing moved in its entirety from Seymour Johnson AFB, North Carolina, to MacDill AFB, near Tampa, and the 363rd Tactical Reconnaissance Wing came down from Shaw AFB, South Carolina.

The tactical fighters were ordered to stand by for a strike against Cuba, if needed. All of SAC's missile crews went on maximum alert, with 156 ICBMs cocked and ready to launch. Gen. Thomas S. Power, SAC commander, dispersed the B-47 force to 40 civilian airports, and ordered the B-52s to maintain an airborne alert. All the bombers were loaded with nuclear weapons.

SAC U-2s flew 2 sorties between October 14, the date of the first confirmation of the ballistic missile deployment, and October 22. The photography was excellent and frightening. Nine missile siles had been discovered at four separated locations. Mobile medium-range ballistic missiles armed six of those sites, and intermediate-range missiles were slated for the remaining three. The latter were still under construction, and were fixed launch pads rather than the field sites used by the mobile missiles.

Intelligence specialists concluded that the weapons had nuclear warheads, and that they could be launched in an intial salvo of 40 against targets as far west as Wyoming and Montana. They estimated that full operational capability would be reached by mid-December, 1962.

Of lesser, but still significant importance, was a force of Ilyushin Il-28 light jet bombers, which had enough range to attack targets in the southeastern United States with tactical nuclear weapons.

President Kennedy spoke October 22, describing the Cuban situation and detailing the measures against the threat: a quarantine of the island, increased surveillance, and a readiness to retaliate. He announced that U. S. dependents were being evacuated from the base at Guantanamo Bay. He asked the Organization of American States and the United Nations Security Council to meet and discuss the problem.

The next day, low-level reconnaissance flights began, shared by the USAF McDonnell RF-101Cs from the 363rd TRW and Navy Vought RF-8s from Light Photographic Squadron 62. Leaving Florida, they dropped down close to the level of the Gulf waters to stay under the Cuban radar screen, the popped up at the shoreline to roar in just above the treetops, nose cameras cycling. One pilot said he surprised some Russians playing volley ball; he was so low, he insisted, that he almost collided with the ball.

Every two hours either a Navy or a USAF low-level reconnaissance flight sped across the island, photographing the missile sites. The Russian reaction was concealment and the deployment of anti-aircraft artillery. Pilots reported flak bursts, but none was wounded and essentially no damage was done to the hurtling reconnaissance planes.

High-altitude coverage continued to bring back evidence of work progress at launch pads and field sites, and also photos of MiG-21 interceptors parked along the runway at Santa Clara airfield and on the ramp at Camilo Cienfuegos. On the 24th, the first evidence of an easing of tensions came when some of the shipping altered course. The impatient Kennedy told the Russians October 25 that if they continued to emplace the offensive missiles, " . . . further action will be justified."

The action came from the Russians. At 10:15 AM October 27, Maj. Anderson was shot down and killed. His U-2 had been hit by one of the SAMs. That was bad enough; but the situation rapidly got worse. Another U-2, on what was described as a high-altitude sampling flight in the Arctic, became lost and flew into Russian airspace. Red-starred fighters were scrambled to intercept, and the USAF sent fighters from Eileson AFB in Alaska to find the errant U-2 and escort it back home. Instructions were broadcast to the U-2 in the clear, an unprecedented event, giving the pilot specific headings to steer. Fortunately, the U-2 turned back; Kennedy included an apology for the incident in his next message to Khrushchev.

Kennedy's letter was delivered personally to the Soviet Embassy by the President's brother, Robert, who took advantage of the opportunity to remind Ambassador Dobrynin that the U. S. was ready to begin military action early the next week.

Powerful, highly supersonic and long-ranged, the RF-101 Voodoo was a great advance on the RF-84F which it replaced from 1959. Even earlier the RF-101A had engaged in remarkable overflights of China and other Communist territory, some in the hands of Nationalist Chinese. This is one of the more numerous RF-101C versions.

One of more than a thousand reconnaissance photographs taken of the San Cristobal site during the Cuban Missile Crisis, this frame from a low-level RF-101 run on 23 October 1962 shows one of the launch areas with three shelters for SS-4 Sandal MRBMs. Constant coverage showed US intelligence officers hour-by-hour developments.

FISHBEDS WITH MISSILES UNDER WINGS

AA-2 (AAM

Addition of modern MiG-21 ("Fishbed") interceptors with AA-2 air-to-air missiles to the revolutionary Cuban air force was another shock to the United States in 1962, but perfectly legitimate and in no sense a threat to U.S. security. This is a vertical recon picture taken on 10 November 1962 by a USAF aircraft.

An invasion force of Army and Marine Corps units had been assembled and moved to Florida and the Canal Zone. Thousands of tons of supplies and equipment had been airlifted by Tactical Air Command's combat airlift squadrons to the bases. They were manned by Air Force Reserve officers and crews, called up by McNamara to operate their 24 Troop Carrier Squadrons.

On October 28, Moscow Radio broadcast a statement that the USSR had ordered the dismantling of "... arms which you described as offensive ..." beginning the following day. The next afternoon, two McDonnell RF-101Cs taxied out for takeoff. Lt. Col. Joseph M. O'Grady and wingman Capt. Jack C. Bowland, from the 29th TRS, took off at 3:00 PM, headed for San Cristobal. Two hours and ten minutes later they landed back at MacDill with pictures showing that the Russians had made good on their promise and were removing the equipment and dismantling the sites.

The missiles were trucked to the harbors and loaded on cargo ships. At-sea inspections were made from the air, as reconnaissance aircraft tracked the departing vessels and photographed their opened hatches and uncovered deck cargos. But back on the airfields, the bombers remained, and Kennedy decided to twist the screws a little harder.

So did Castro. It was clear that Khrushchev had not consulted him before agreeing to remove the missiles. The Il-28 aircraft were Cuban, Castro said, and he was not going to give them up. But on November 20, Khrushchev agreed with Kennedy and the planes were recrated and shipped as deck cargo from Cuba. By December 4, San Julian airfield had been cleared of Il-28s; they were the last remnants of Soviet offensive weaponry in Cuba. The confrontation was over.

In retrospect, it was a very close thing. The Russians, it must be said, had as much right on their side as the United States had. American Jupiter intermediate-range ballistic missiles were emplaced in Turkey, a country sharing a border with Russia, and to Russian eyes they were just as threatening as Russian missiles in Cuba were to U. S. eyes.

Intelligence analysts had first speculated that Khrushchev was attempting to work out a trade of the Cuban-based missiles for the Turkey-based ones. But Kennedy and the administration denied any such compromise with the chairman. Yet within three months after the Russian withdrawal of their missiles, the U. S. brought back its Thor IRBMs from England, and announced that the Jupiter missiles would be leaving Italy. The Turkish government announced a few days later that Jupiters would depart from that country also.

The Cuban crisis emphasized the high value of current and continuing reconnaissance and surveillance. That was the most outstanding performance of the whole Cuban maneuver. McNamara admitted later that there was neither enough airlift capacity nor tactical fighter strength to have supported the planned invasion properly.

By November 28, the regulars had gone back to the routine of USAF life, and the Reserve units were released that day. Some time later, Congress asked McNamara for a cost estimate for the Cuban affair. The Secretary, in his inimitable fashion, put together a lengthy table, allocating so many dollars to each of the services for operations, research and development, procurement, maintenance and salaries. The total came to $183,259,048.

New Weapons, New Strategies

"...safety will be the sturdy child of terror, and survival the twin brother of annihilation."

Sir Winston Churchill, speaking before the House of Commons in 1955, was describing the new global strategies based on the possession of thermonuclear weapons. The keystone of the new strategies was mutual deterrence.

That concept arises from the belief that thermonuclear war is unthinkable because of the mutual destruction that would ensue. It works if both sides are strong enough to survive a first strike by the enemy; launching the counterstrike would so devastate the originator that there would be no real victor.

In fact, mutual deterrence has worked as a national policy. There has been no wartime use of nuclear weapons since August, 1945, even though there has been an ample number of wars since then. The inter-

vening years have seen nation after nation join the nuclear club, and have seen the United States and Russia develop and stockpile enough nuclear weapons to annihilate each other several times over, and to leave the world an irradiated and dying sphere.

The concept of deterrence evolved from the awesome power of atomic explosions and the sober realization by some strategic planners that a nuclear exchange amounts to mutual suicide. It was described in "Strategy for the West", a book written by Marshal of the Air Force Sir John Slessor in the early 1950s, and was introduced to the American public by John Foster Dulles, Secretary of State under President Dwight D. Eisenhower.

Such a national policy drives a specific composition of the air arm: a strategic, long-range bombing force that is equipped to deliver nuclear weapons on enemy

The U.S. Air Force deployed the world's first intercontinental-range cruise missile in 1959. Northrop's N-69 Snark test vehicles, one of which is seen here being launched from Cape Canaveral in 1955, led to the SM-62A Snark which entered service with SAC's 556th Strategic Missile Squadron at Presque Isle. Snark carried a thermonuclear warhead up to 6,325 miles.

The Lockheed T-33A was a popular Air Force trainer and hack for more than 20 years. Here in its twilight years (1969) a pair of T-birds head across the Chugash mountains of Alaska. Unit, 317th FIS, then equipped with F-102A Delta Daggers.

Below right. In 1944 Douglas at Long Beach designed the XC-74, with a planned DC-7 civil version. The latter was cancelled, but the C-74 reached the Air Force in time for the Berlin Airlift. By this time Douglas had designed a new fuselage of even greater capacity to produce the C-124 Globemaster II, in its day the world's biggest production transport landplane. Though missions often took 12 to 18 hours non-stop the C-124 could carry loads too large for other aircraft, including the new ICBMs, loaded through clamshell nose doors. These examples with the 62nd Troop Carrier wing (Heavy) were parked on the ramp at Larson AFB in October 1959.

Test and evaluation of the F-84F Thunderstreak included firing 24 HVAR (high-velocity aircraft rockets) of 5-inch calibre against a ground target at Edwards AFB. After long delays with the engine Republic delivered 2,711 of this more powerful version of F-84.

targets deep inside the borders. To traditionalists, the word "force" was read as a reference to conventional heavy bombers. But to a small and forward-looking segment of the Air Force, the word could just as easily refer to a force of ballistic missiles, the new class of bombardment weapons the Germans had introduced to the battlefield in the last year of the war.

Consequently, after World War 2, the development of a strategic bombing force in the United States—and in other technologically minded nations as well—moved along parallel roads, one leading to improved bombers and the other leading to new missiles.

The policy of deterrence also led to the threat of massive retaliation, another Dulles catchphrase. This grew from the power of nuclear weapons; it was a latter-day "Big Stick" diplomacy. The problem with massive retaliation is that it is a ridiculous application of overkill if the situation demands something much

less. It locks a nation into a policy to which there is no lesser alternative.

Gradually, the concept of massive retaliation softened to acceptance of a limited nuclear war, where only tactical nuclear weapons would be used. That softened even further to limited conventional war, where old-fashioned high explosives would be the weapons of choice.

Changes in policy will force changes in the composition of the force designed to carry out policy. That is why there has been a gradual shift from the preponderance of long-range strategic weapons development right after World War 2 to the current emphasis on battlefield tactical weapons.

The tactics themselves have changed. At the end of World War 2, the accepted way of striking at a distant enemy was with long-range strategic bombers operating at high altitudes. But the development of anti-

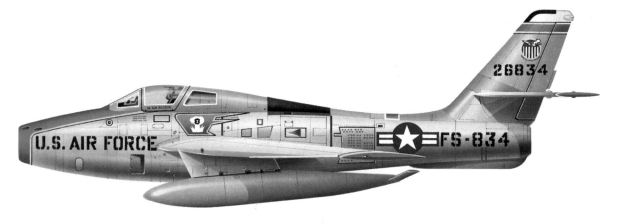

The Republic F-84F was a swept-wing fighter-bomber development of the straight winged F-84E. Its development had been suggested by Republic, but only made possible by the pace of events in Korea during 1952. Deliveries to the USAF began in 1954.

aircraft missiles by the Germans during the war cast a long shadow across the ability to operate that way much longer. Surface-to-air missiles, from the start, were capable of multiples of any bomber's performance. They were easily supersonic, highly maneuverable, and could chase a bomber as well as intercept its predicted flight path. Altitude, speed and maneuverability no longer aided the bomber. Further, radar development moved forward so rapidly that it soon was capable of detecting and tracking aircraft at great distances, using new techniques that extended its electronic vision far beyond the myopia of early equipment.

The bombers then were faced with a dual problem: They could be detected at long range, and they could be shot down at high altitude by missiles. The only alternate was to avoid detection by dropping down close to the ground and approaching the target at very low altitude. That presented problems in navigation, and in the structural design of the airplanes. Flying low and fast is as rugged a set of conditions as can be imposed on an airframe.

So now national policy, strategic concepts and the tactics of weapons delivery have completely changed in a long and evolutionary policy that began at the end of World War 2.

Aircraft Development

That war set the pattern. Captured German data on jet engines, sweepback, airborne radars and rapid-firing aircraft cannon, and the new guided missiles forced industry to review its contemporary design trends. Within a few years, all fighters under development were jet-propelled, most had swept wings, and were armed with cannon, fired by indications on a radar-ranging gunsight. Air-to-air missiles were just emerging, and were still cumbersome.

The classic fighter of the postwar years was the North American F-86 Sabre, eventual ruler of the skies over Korea. Its design concept has lasted for three decades; it used state-of-the-art aerodynamics, propulsion, structures, and systems. It was highly successful at its primary task of air superiority, and it also was a remarkably good fighter-bomber. That dual capability also was a trend-setting factor.

Just as World War 2 set the design pattern for the first postwar generation of fighters, so did the Korean war determine the tactical requirements for a second generation. Remembered as the "Century Series" because their numerical designations began with 100, these were the production USAF fighters and fighter-bombers of the post-Korean period:

• **North American F-100 Super Sabre.** The world's first fighter capable of sustained supersonic speed originated as an unsolicited proposal by NAA in January 1951 for an air-superiority fighter based on the Sabre. Its original concept was basically that of an F-86 with a 45-degree swept wing, and the name Sabre 45. The USAF wanted the fighter to be operational in 1955, but certainly no later than 1957. North American

made good; the first F-100A models achieved initial operational capability (IOC) in September 1955.

• **McDonnell F-101 Voodoo.** This long-range penetration fighter originated as a June, 1946, design for an escort to SAC bombers, the XF-88; it was cancelled because of budget restrictions. It was reinstated after it became obvious that the B-29s could not go north in Korea without an escort. As the improved and redesigned F-101A, it became operational May 2, 1957.

• **Convair F-102 Delta Dagger.** This design was a response to a January 13, 1949, request for proposals

Early B-47s often made dramatic takeoffs using RATO (rocket-assisted takeoff). But the mightly fleet of later B-47E bombers (1,590) that by February 1958 equipped 29 SAC wings did not use RATO despite being cleared to take off at much higher weight of 206,000 lb with 1,870-gallon drop tanks. An immense challenge to air and ground crews, this bomber was the most advanced of its era, and the backbone of SAC through the perilous 1950s.

for a "1954 Interceptor" designed to knock down potential Russian jet bombers. It was the first aircraft to come under the weapons system concept, a USAF management structure to improve the quality and the timetable of aircraft development. Deficient in its early incarnation, the F-102 was redesigned to incorporate the "area rule", an aerodynamic advance that reduced transonic drag. It became operational in April, 1956, about two years late.

• **Lockheed F-104 Starfighter.** Another fallout of the Korean war, the F-104 originated in an unsolicited proposal by Lockheed in November 1952 for an air superiority fighter. USAF issued operational requirements in December 1952 for a lightweight day superiority fighter to replace the F-100 in 1956; the F-104

resulted. It became operational in January 1958, about a year late, and it never did replace the F-100.

• **Republic F-105 Thunderchief.** The company had studied a series of designs to incorporate what was learned in Korea about fighter-bombers and what had since been seen as deficiencies in the F-84F model. Proposed under the general designation of AP-63 in April 1952, the F-105 went through a long seige of development problems to emerge as an operational fighter-bomber in August 1958.

• **Convair F-106 Delta Dart.** This design also was a response to the requirement for the 1954 interceptor, and was conceived as a logical extension of the interim F-102. It finally achieved IOC in October 1959, just five years late. But perhaps it made up for the delay; it

Testing times

The late 1940s and early 1950s were heady times for the test pilots of the U.S. Air Force. The jet engine was still in its infancy, and few planners or designers were yet able to predict with accuracy the effect of combining such a powerplant with the new aerodynamics deriving largely from German research in World War 2. The skies of the U.S. at times seemed filled with an alarming array of futuristic-looking aircraft.

1. Convair's XF-92A was the world's first jet delta-wing aircraft. It surprised many eminent aerodynamicists by flying normally, and it was a stepping stone to the F-102.

2. Far more dramatic was Northrop's YB-49, an amazing eight-jet conversion of the piston-engined XB-35 all-wing bomber.

3. By putting four of the new General Electric TG-180 axial jets into a traditional type airframe Convair got the XB-46 bomber into the air in April 1947.

4. Martin's amazing XB-51 flew in October 1949; it had a small wing and three jet engines, but the Air Force preferred the more traditional British Canberra which Martin made as the B-57.

5. Just a year after the XF-92A Lockheed flew the first XF-90, a fine-looking twin-engined escort fighter which was dived faster than sound.

6. Possibly the noisiest aircraft ever built, the XF-84H was a Thunderstreak rebuilt with a rear jet and front turboprop driving a supersonic propeller. It flew in June 1955.

7. Perhaps the best fighter the Air Force ever cancelled, North American's F-107A was the next generation after the F-100 and flew almost twice as fast.

8. The most powerful aircraft ever to fly — outside the Soviet Union, at least — the North American XB-70 Valkyrie was a fantastic canard delta bomber intended in the late 1950s to replace the B-52. It reached 2,000 mph soon after first flight.

1

3

4

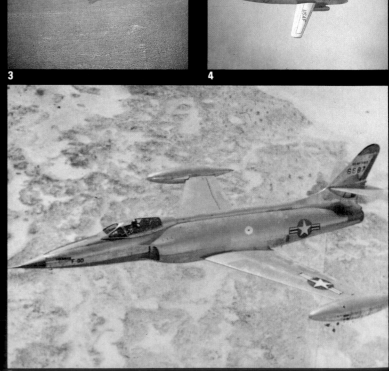

2

5

remains as America's only interceptor today, more than 30 years after its design objectives were laid down.

Jet bomber development, like that of the fighters, began before the war had ended. The USAF initiated a 1944 design competition that produced a batch of bombers that first flew during 1947. North American's XB-45, Convair's XB-46 and Martin's XB-48 were different approaches to the same requirements. They all were interesting designs, all capable of good performance, and all basically conservative designs with a few technical innovations. There was only one thing wrong with each of them: their competition was the radical Boeing XB-47. It whipped them all, handily, and became the mainstay of Strategic Air Command.

Hundreds of the elegant sweptwing bomber were built, and they were deployed all over the world at a network of foreign bases established as the USAF took on increasing global responsibilities.

The B-47, designed for high-speed, high-altitude bomb runs, was forced by circumstances into an entirely different flight regime for survival in the face of enemy radars and missiles. They changed abruptly to low-level delivery tactics, running in with their banked wingtips seeming to scrape the surface of the earth. They developed the "pop-up" delivery: A low-level dash, an abrupt pull-up to a peak altitude, bomb release, and a dash for the ground again. They also used toss-bombing; they flew to a pre-planned point and pulled up into the first part of a loop. On the way

6

7

8

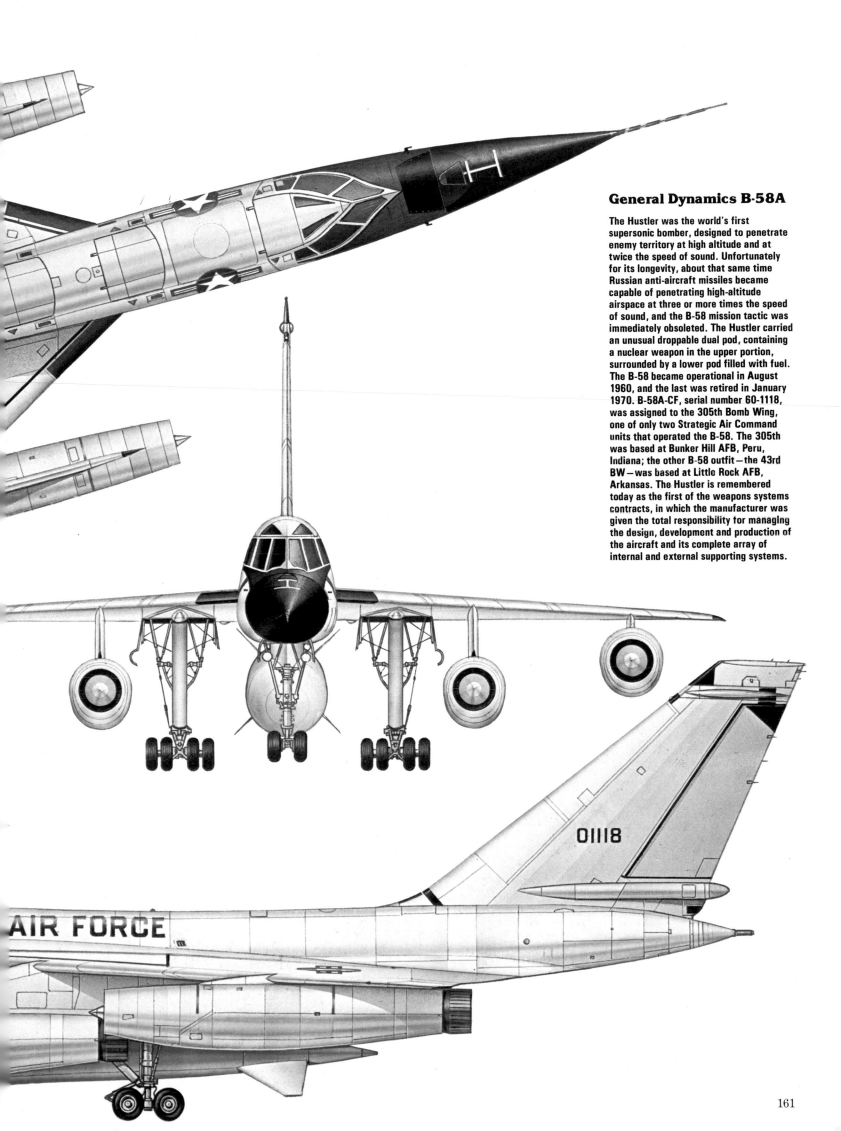

General Dynamics B-58A

The Hustler was the world's first supersonic bomber, designed to penetrate enemy territory at high altitude and at twice the speed of sound. Unfortunately for its longevity, about that same time Russian anti-aircraft missiles became capable of penetrating high-altitude airspace at three or more times the speed of sound, and the B-58 mission tactic was immediately obsoleted. The Hustler carried an unusual droppable dual pod, containing a nuclear weapon in the upper portion, surrounded by a lower pod filled with fuel. The B-58 became operational in August 1960, and the last was retired in January 1970. B-58A-CF, serial number 60-1118, was assigned to the 305th Bomb Wing, one of only two Strategic Air Command units that operated the B-58. The 305th was based at Bunker Hill AFB, Peru, Indiana; the other B-58 outfit—the 43rd BW—was based at Little Rock AFB, Arkansas. The Hustler is remembered today as the first of the weapons systems contracts, in which the manufacturer was given the total responsibility for managing the design, development and production of the aircraft and its complete array of internal and external supporting systems.

AIR FORCE

01118

up, at about the 45-degree tangent to the curve, the nuclear weapon was released to continue on course like a high fly ball being slugged out of the park. The B-47 completed about half of the loop, rolled out and headed for the ground in a dash to get away from the nuclear blast.

In a category by itself was the Boeing B-52, first flown in April 1952. It is a ponderous and wondrous heavy bomber, capable of carrying the largest and heaviest bombs over intercontinental distances. It has ample room for the hundreds of pounds of electronic countermeasures to smooth its way to the target. It, too, has to hug the nap of the earth for survival in the 1970s, producing one of the more thrilling rides available to an Air Force crew.

Long-Range Missile Development

The controlling design requirement in the early development of strategic missiles was the size and weight of the ordinary plutonium bomb. It was huge, weighing on the order of 10,000 pounds. It had to be carried for at least 5,000 miles to make any sense as a weapon.

The first attempts to adapt German A-4 technology to a 5,000-mile range missile quickly failed because of the fundamental principles of rocketry. The range of any ballistic missile is proportional to its speed at engine cutoff. That speed is a function of the mass ratio of the missile, its launching weight divided by the weight of the payload. There was at that time no feasible way to carry a 10,000-pound nuclear warhead a distance of 5,000 miles using a ballistic missile. The resulting structure would have been the size of the Empire State building. Consequently, early ballistic missiles studies remained as studies.

On the other hand, pilotless aircraft could carry the nuclear payloads over great distances, and the USAF funded three strategic missiles in that category:

• **Northrop SM-62 Snark,** a rocket-launched, turbojet-

The new aircraft enter service

The jamboree of experimental aircraft types developed in the late 1940s and early 1950s may at times have seemed like a ludicrous joke perpetrated by the aircraft manufacturers and the U.S. Air Force at the expense of the long-suffering U.S. taxpayer. But though many of the aircraft could never have hoped to reach operational status, research accomplished with these aircraft combined with combat experience with types such as the F-86 Sabre in the Korean War to make possible a new generation of aircraft, many of which are still in service in the 1980s.

1. In 1951 Martin obtained a licence to build the British Canberra, as the much improved B-57.

2. First of the Century-series of supersonic fighters, the North American F-100A Super Sabre reached the USAF in September 1954.

3. After frantic redesign the Convair F-102A Delta Dagger interceptor entered ADC service in early June 1955.

4. The F-106 Delta Dart started life as a re-shaped, re-engined F-102.

5. After remarkably painless development the McDonnell F-101 Voodoo reached squadrons in May 1957; this is a 101B.

6. The unique Lockheed F-104 Starfighter saw only limited combat duty with the Air Force, starting in January 1958.

7. The Air Force never expected to buy the Navy McDonnell F4H at all, but—as the F-110—the Phantom reached TAC in November 1963.

8. When the B-52A Stratofortress entered USAF service in late June 1955 neither Boeing nor SAC expected it to last 40 years.

9. Equally, when Lockheed-Georgia delivered the C-130A Hercules to the Air Force in June 1956 they little thought they would be making it 25 years later.

10. One of the F-105B test models shows the distinctive Thud plan-form that became operational on 27 May 1958.

North American F-100C-20-NA (54-1939)
of the 127th TFS, Kansas ANG, 1969.

powered subsonic cruise missile. Snark was proposed in January, 1946.

• **North American SM-64 Navaho,** a supersonic cruise missile with a massive payload. It was powered by ramjet engines, and boosted by a large rocket-engine system. It was funded in July 1946.

• **Convair MX-774 project,** a research and development program approach to the design of two long-range missiles, one a cruise type. That was later

cancelled, leaving a ballistic missile still under study. That, too, was cancelled in the 1947 budget cuts.

But Convair got permission to use some unexpended project funds to complete three test missiles and launch them. The tests were less than successful, but they did yield some knowledge that paid off later by enabling Convair to get a contract in January 1951 for the MX-1593 project. It was another research and development program for a missile with a 5,500

Republic F-105D Thunderchief of the 192nd Tactical Fighter Group, Virginia ANG, based at Byrd Field, Sandston, Va.

Apart from the German "V-1" the Martin TM-61 Matador was the first tactical cruise missile to go into widespread service (with TAC, from 1955). From it was developed the TM-76 Mace, with longer range, bigger warhead and two types of much improved self-contained guidance. This Mace was launched from a hardened shelter at Cape Canaveral on 29 March 1960.

nautical mile range, a still remote achievement.

Almost two full years later, the Atomic Energy Commission detonated its "Mike" thermonuclear device which indicated that the warhead weight barrier might yield to further experimentation. More laboratory studies in the summer of 1953 added credence. Then the "Shrimp" shot of March 1954 revolutionized warhead design. The hydrogen bomb could be made smaller and portable in the nose of a moderately sized missile launched into a ballistic trajectory.

Part of the nuclear weapons program was the development of low-yield warheads, small atomic bombs with less destructive power than was visited upon Japan. The need was for greater firepower than conventional explosives could offer. The AEC developed a family of them, which became available for tactical weapons. It gave nuclear capability to the fighter-bombers of Tactical Air Command; the Republic F-84Fs were modified to handle the new weapons, while pilots and armament crews were trained in the special delivery and handling required in the technology of nuclear warfare.

The new and light warheads also led to modifications in TAC's first missile family. USAF had contracted with the Martin Co. to develop the TM-61 Matador, a rocket-boosted, turbojet-powered pilotless bomber with high subsonic speed at 40,000-ft. altitude and a range of about 600 miles. First flown January 20, 1949, Matador was built around a warhead with conventional high explosives; its nuclear capability came along later, after the availability of the small bombs. It became operational with NATO ground forces in 1954; in all, four guided missile squadrons were activated and equipped with the TM-61C. Some squadrons later converted to the improved TM-76B Mace, also developed and built by Martin. It was a short-lived program, though; the same arguments against manned aircraft penetration of Russian defenses held for the pilotless aircraft, and they were withdrawn from service.

Atlas Approaches Operational Use

By then the MX-1593 project was well along. Its other technical problems were being solved. A blunt nose shape to resist the extreme aerodynamic heating of re-entry had been conceived and tested at the National Advisory Committee for Aeronautics by scientist H.

Julian Allen. The powerplant was an extrapolation of the North American Rocketdyne engines that had been developed to boost the Navaho into flight.

In June, 1954, Atlas—now the name of the MX-1593 project vehicle—was given the highest priority in the list of Air Force programs. There were many then who held the belief that the United States was doomed if it did not develop an immediate response to Russian missile technology. By October, the USSR had detonated 14 nuclear devices of one type or another, including a hydrogen bomb. There was much evidence that they were working on large booster rockets. Their academicians were commenting that the state of the art now permitted creation of an artificial satellite, or sending a "... stratoplane to the Moon".

The basic drive behind the speedy passage of the Atlas from test vehicle to operational weapon was concurrency. Everything had to be developed on the same time line, with a stated goal of achieving IOC at the end of that line.

Atlas flight testing was an evolutionary process. It began with the simplest test vehicle that could be made to fly in a controlled trajectory, as a means of checking out the basic performance of the systems. Atlas-A firings began in June 1957 and progressed through the Atlas-F series, with a number of experimental launchings in each alphabetical sub-series. Last of the test missiles was fired at the end of 1962. By then, Atlas had been declared operational with Strategic Air Command for upwards of three years, although for the first few months of that time it was optimistic to refer to the Atlas as ready.

By the end of 1957, the USAF had a Ballistic Missile Division established to run its several programs. It was managing the development of Atlas; the Titan I, a two-stage back-up system for Atlas; the intermediate-range Thor, a spectacular success story; and the Minuteman I solid-propellant ICBM. Navaho had been cancelled that year in a budget cut; Snark was still alive, backed by those who still believed that somehow a subsonic airplane-type missile could survive the trip through the rings of anti-aircraft missiles around Moscow. It was finally declared operational in February 1961 and withdrawn from service in June, probably the shortest operational life of any USAF aircraft, piloted or pilotless.

The build-up of SAC missile strength began officially when a "blue-suit" crew from the 576th Strategic Missile Squadron launched an Atlas-D test round September 9, 1959. It was successful; but subsequent USAF firings produced such poor results that a special program called *Golden Ram* was initiated to simplify the launch procedures and improve the performance of SAC crews. A much better firing record resulted, and produced an operational ICBM force within SAC.

With that force came the concept of the strategic triad to keep peace by maintaining a deterrence. The triad is, of course, the intercontinental ballistic missiles and long-range bombers operated by USAF's Strategic Air Command, and the submarine-launched ballistic missiles operated by the U. S. Navy. The theory of the triad is not only deterrence, but assured deterrence by the survival of at least one of the three striking forces. No potential enemy, it is believed, could destroy utterly all three components of the triad. And the surviving force would be strong enough to lay waste the enemy's territories with such devastation that recovery would be impossible.

Through all of this emphasis on the Big Nuclear Stick, there have been some strategists who have worried about the possible consequences of not wanting to use, or not being able to use, nuclear weapons in a massive blow. Suppose the Russians moved an armored ground force across the East German boundaries and into Berlin, continuing to roll into the western portion of the city. What then? It is clearly an act of overt aggression. Should Moscow, Stalingrad and Rostov be leveled in retaliation? Or should the armored column be obliterated? And if the latter, how and with what? It was a question that was to occupy the thinkers from then on.

They were too soon faced with that kind of a problem. Limited wars were being brewed around the world, and the USAF was about to be involved once again.

With the Atlas ICBM (intercontinental ballistic missile) the USAF moved into a totally new era characterized by notions of pushbutton warfare, instant (well, 30-minute) retaliation and conflict in the space beyond the atmosphere. Under intense pressure its development was forced ahead, installations for its deployment were built—in successive different versions, ending with underground silos—and different models of missile were rushed into production at a newly built plant near San Diego. This launch, on 8 December 1959, was the first of the improved D-series with General Electric Mk 3 ablative re-entry vehicle.

F-106A Delta Dart of the 159th FIS, Florida ANG. Today its tail number has an 00 prefix.

Background to a Limited War

"It took us eight years of bitter fighting to defeat you French . . . The Americans are much stronger than the French, though they know us less well. It may perhaps take ten years to do it, but our heroic compatriots in the South will defeat them in the end."

That was Ho Chi Minh, Vietnamese revolutionary, Communist, and venerated "Uncle" to his people, explaining to writer Bernard Fall how he evaluated the coming conflict. He was speaking in late 1962. It did not take ten years.

In the end, the United States was defeated; it did not, nor could it, win the war in Viet-Nam. America, helped by no major power as an ally, engaged in what much of the rest of the world saw as a war of imperialism, and emerged from it spent.

Viet-Nam was a quicksand for America; the more she struggled, the more deeply engulfed she became. Now, it is nearly a decade since the last B-52 dropped its earth-shattering load of iron bombs through the jungle tree canopy, since the last Phantom flew MiGCAP, and the last Wild Weasel went downtown trolling for SAMs. Some of the scars have healed; some of the lessons have been learned, and others have been forgotten already. Too many of the latter, if past wars are any criterion.

America started in that war by forgetting—or choosing to ignore—all the lessons the French learned so very painfully along the Street without Joy, or in the Hell of Dien Bien Phu.

Forever, War in Indochina

The beautiful land of Viet-Nam has been a battlefield for centuries. Ethnic and cultural wars, wars of enslavement and aggrandizement, colonial and imperial wars have washed over the river deltas and through the rice paddies.

World War 2 brought the Japanese against the French colonists, and the French went down to harsh and cruel defeat, outnumbered, outweighed, and finally outfought. French, Cambodian, and Vietnamese soldiers died together before the Japanese onslaught.

In the northern reaches of the country, guerrilla bands were active, drawing political and military support from Mao's units in the Chinese provinces of Kwangsi and Yunnan just across the border. Two of the most active of the Vietnamese guerrillas were young and ardent Communists: Ho Chi Minh, and Vo Nguyen Giap. By late in World War 2, their forces were strong enough to be a factor in the chaos after the surrender of Japan. Ho's forces moved into Hanoi on August 19, 1945, and were there, a de facto government, when the Chinese Nationalist troops arrived to disarm the Japanese and to receive the official surrender.

The American policy in Indochina was much a product of a personal prejudice. President Franklin D. Roosevelt saw the French as the worst of the colonial powers; they had milked the country dry, he believed, and it was time to turn them out and let the people rule their own destiny. He was joined by China, under Chiang, and by Stalin, for his own reasons, and they outmaneuvered and outvoted the French and the British in postwar conferences that settled the fate of millions of innocent and unknowing people.

Internally, Communist leaders were busy with a program of deliberate subversion and a drive to establish themselves as the absolute and recognized government in Indochina. Terror was one of their effective weapons, and they had no scruples whatsoever about using it. In late September, 1945, they incited a mob riot in Saigon that culminated in the murder of 450 French and Eurasian women and children.

As in Korea, the U.S. Air Force drifted into war in SE Asia totally unequipped for this style of conflict. Almost all its defense dollars had been spent on advanced aircraft most unsuited to finding "Charlie" hiding behind a tree. The best answers were older designs, such as the 1944 Navy-designed A-1 Skyraider.

A French air force Douglas B-26 flying an interdiction mission against the Viet Minh forces in Indo-China. The U.S. deployed infinitely greater fire power during their stay in South East Asia—but the end result was the same; frustration and defeat.

Two days later, the Japanese officially surrendered in a ceremony at which the French were conspicuous by their absence. A single French general had been offered a seat somewhere in the rear rows, behind junior Viet Minh officers. No French flag was flown at the ceremony. The French, very obviously hurt and humiliated, did not attend.

In March, 1946, France recognized the Republic of Viet-Nam as a free state, part of the French Union and the Indochina Federation. It was a positive move, and went far toward cementing good relations between France and Ho Chi Minh and the revolutionary council. But it was completely undone by a unilateral decision made May 30, 1946, by the French High Commissioner Admiral Thierry d'Argenlieu. Urged on, and backed by French conservatives who wanted to maintain the status quo, he recognized a southern enclave, the Republic of Cochinchina, as a free state, with the same rights and privileges that had been granted to the Republic under Ho. Cochinchina was clearly a French-sponsored client state, and that single act, unauthorized and unknown, surely triggered a new outburst of war.

Not that the fighting had ever stopped; French occupation troops were still engaged in mopping-up operations, and the Viet Minh were tired of being mistaken for Japanese. Tensions increased, and came to a head November 20, 1946, at Haiphong. Viet-Minh militia opened fire on a French ship in the harbor, and the sound of gunfire alarmed another band of Viet-Minh. They killed a few unarmed French soldiers in the market. The reprisal came two days later, when the French moved troops into the Chinese quarter to rout out the Viet-Minh. The action stampeded a mob out of the city toward the French air base at Cat-Bi. A French heavy cruiser lying offshore saw the running mob, assumed that the base was under attack, and opened fire. In the panic that followed, about 6,000 Vietnamese were either killed outright by gunfire or were trampled to death.

The time for any peaceful solution had passed, and on both sides the military pressures for further action increased. On the night of December 19, the Communists blew up the Hanoi powerplant, blacking out the city. Armed bands of Viet-Minh moved against French civilians in Hanoi and against all French garrisons in the country in a well-planned and well-executed attack.

From then on, it was open warfare. The French tried to hold the entire countryside at first, and then slowly were pushed first out of the border areas and then out of the river deltas. When Mao Tse-tung announced the birth of the new China in September, 1949, it was the beginning of the end for the French. With the Chinese provinces bordering Viet-Nam under Communist control, the Viet-Minh had their own sanctuary, just as the North Koreans had theirs across the Yalu River. The French pulled back to the deltas, then lost parts of them to the Viet-Minh in early 1950. The Vietnamese kept on the offensive, hitting the French forts in the northern part of the country. Lang-Son was abandoned October 17, and by the end of that month, the Vietnamese held absolute control of most of the northern part of North Viet-Nam. It was the worst defeat the French armies had suffered in a colony since the British met them on the Plains of Abraham near Quebec.

The campaign that ended at Lang-Son was, incidentally, paralleled by the Chinese intervention in Korea. Both began late in October, 1950, and both depended on a sanctuary across a border that was not violated by the Americans in Korea or the French in Indochina.

Giap's words, spoken before a group of political commissars about that time, appraised the contemporary situation neatly and were also, read now, chillingly prophetic:

> . . . the enemy will be caught in a dilemma. He has to drag out the war in order to win it, and does not possess, on the other hand, the psychological and political means to fight a long, drawn-out war . . .

Giap tried at first to achieve a decisive series of victories over the French by engaging them in major set-piece battles, a strategy that was doomed to failure. Between January and June, 1951, his forces were beaten thrice in the Red River delta area. He pulled his armies back into the highlands, and there analyzed what had happened. After a few months, Giap went on the offensive again; but in the meantime he had learned not to tackle a modern army in open battle. In September he began assaults on the French positions in the highlands, picking on one outpost at a time and neutralizing them systematically.

By mid-1953, the Korean armistice had taken the pressure off the Chinese, and their instructors were free to leave North Korea and move south to help Giap. With them came huge shipments of captured American weapons.

Change in American Policy

Opinion in the United States by now had swung to favor the French, primarily because they were fighting Communism. In the highly emotional anti-Communist atmosphere of the United States in the 1950s, the enemy of their enemy was their friend. In a small way, the U. S. was trying to help; technicians were sent to assist in the maintenance and repair of the U. S. aircraft that had been supplied to France. Secretary of State Dulles had hoisted the spectre of massive retaliation; but it turned out to be only words. Less than a month later, in at least a partial contradiction of his Secretary, Eisenhower said that he could foresee " . . . no greater tragedy than for the United States to become involved in an all-out war in Indochina." It was a signal to the French that no real help would be forthcoming from that quarter.

For the French, the war really ended in the siege at Dien Bien Phu that began in March, 1954. They had been drawn into a trap, an undefendable position that required air supply of several hundred tons a day. Giap's forces had gathered in the hills around the doomed garrison, and moved in their artillery. From the heights, they could see and adjust the position of practically every shell that landed near the airstrip or

Last-minute supplies are handed up to the crew of a French-operated Douglas B-26 bomber involved in the costly air campaign to support the beleaguered base at Dien Bien Phu in 1954.

the French positions. The terrain forced aircraft into a single approach and departure pattern; pilots on supply runs referred to the flight pattern in the valley as "The Slot". In such a situation, the Viet-Minh anti-aircraft had a fairly easy time of it, and it is a wonder that any planes got past the flak barrage to drop zones.

Now that it was too late, the United States began to consider some sort of active intervention on the side of the French. Covert support was given through the cover of Civil Air Transport, one of the Central Intelligence Agency's creations. It was the remnant of Chennault's China Air Transport, driven out of the mainland by the inexorable advance of the Communists, and now operating out of Hong Kong. CAT began to fly the supply routes, using Fairchild C-119 Flying Boxcar cargo transports transferred from USAF stocks.

At the Joint Chiefs of Staff level, the discussion was divided between two, and perhaps more, proposals. The Navy and Air Force favored a surgical strike by bombers, the B-29 heavies now retired from the Korean conflict. Certainly the question of the weapons to be used must have come up, and certainly nuclear weapons must have been considered. The strike would hit a single strategic Viet-Minh target, preferably at night, and with the U. S. insignia on the aircraft replaced by French markings.

One of the potential targets was the Viet positions around Dien Bien Phu. Brig. Gen. Joseph D. Caldara, then commanding FEAF Bomber Command, had flown a reconnaissance mission over the battlefield in April, and had concluded that a B-29 strike was feasible and could be effective.

Gen. Matthew B. Ridgeway, Army Chief of Staff and former ground commander in Korea, believed that

only troops would make a significant difference for the French position. But he warned that if U. S. ground forces were sent in, the price paid would be higher than the Allied losses in the Korean conflict.

Eisenhower, typically, compromised. He agreed to call for an air strike, if the United States could get support from some of its allies. None stepped forward. Then a debate followed in Congress, with one of the more demagogic statements coming from Senator Lyndon B. Johnson. He came out firmly " . . . against sending American GIs into the mud and muck of Indochina on a blood-letting spree to perpetuate colonialism and white man's exploitation in Asia." (Nine years later, as President, he was to sound very different on the same subject.)

In the end, there was no support either at home or abroad for the planned air strike, and it was cancelled, along with any other planned form of tangible assistance to the French. The air attack was code-named Operation *Vulture*, and the name must have been chosen by someone with a fine sense of black humor. The vulture, you know, watches and waits until a predator has killed and eaten, then flies down to gorge himself on the remnants of the kill, at no risk to himself and with very little effort expended.

Dien Bien Phu ended in a last desperate and glorious attack reminiscent of an earlier day. On the evening of May 7, 1954, with their ammunition exhausted and their ranks decimated, the 3rd Battalion of the 13th Foreign Legion Half-Brigade fixed bayonets. Then, at the bugle call, they charged out of their positions, 600 soldiers against 40,000, going to their certain deaths.

That battle ended the effective French military adventure in Indochina. There were later engagements, but Dien Bien Phu was the last straw for the

One of the controversial aspects of the war in Viet-Nam was the use of USAF transports specially equipped to defoliate trees and other vegetation and thus expose the Viet Cong. These Fairchild C-123 Providers were photographed at Tan Son Nhut in 1965 prior to the most destructive mission of all, the woods-burning strike at Boil Loi.

Operation Ranch Hand Fairchild C-123 Providers equipped for spraying defoliants were among the first USAF aircraft to arrive in South Viet-Nam in 1962.

Among the first U.S. airplanes deployed to South Viet-Nam was the McDonnell F-101 Voodoo, in its RF-101C tactical reconnaissance form. The type's high performance allowed it to evade most enemy defenses, while the six cameras carried (four in the nose and two in a fuselage bay) made possible extensive coverage of ground areas.

government and the people of France. Popular opinion was demanding a withdrawal.

Indochina was lost, and the prophets of doom in the United States had heard their worst dreams echoed by Eisenhower. The loss of Indochina, he said April 7, will cause all of Southeast Asia to fall like a row of dominoes.

The war ended formally in truce talks in Geneva, Switzerland, that began July 21, 1954. The United States neither participated, nor signed the agreements, although a delegation was on hand and did make statements from time to time. Indochina was divided at the 17th parallel. North of that line was the Democratic Republic of Viet-Nam, under Ho Chi Minh and the Communists; south of it was the Republic of Viet-Nam, under Ngo Dinh Diem.

The USAF Presence

The first open USAF military support for the French dated back to the summer of 1950, soon after the outbreak of the Korean war. A Military Assistance Advisor Group (MAAG) had been sent to Saigon early in July, and USAF technicians and some combat crews were also ordered to French Indochina. A detachment of maintenance and supply people was moved from the Philippines to Nha Trang airfield to work on the aging Douglas C-47 transports that the French had gathered to replace their captured German Junkers Ju 52 fleet of antiques. They worked on the C-47s from January to August, 1953, and then returned. In February, 1954, yet another detachment of technicians, numbering several hundred, went to Indochina.

Part of the Geneva truce agreements called for a free election in Viet-Nam during 1956. It was a foregone conclusion that Ho would win by a landslide in both the north and the south, and Diem didn't want to risk that. So he and his government ignored the call for elections, and they were not held. The Communists let that one pass, and began a campaign of terrorism in South Viet-Nam, hoping to force their way into control of the country. By mid-1959, the covert campaign had become overt; the Central Committee of the North Viet-Nam Workers' Party openly called for reunification of the country through armed struggle. The second war began in the south when a Viet-Cong (as the southern Communist unit were named by Diem's people) guerrilla force ambushed a local army unit looking for guerrillas.

In October, the U. S. about doubled the size of its

MAAG team, and the increase included Army Special Forces personnel sent to train the Vietnamese Rangers.

The first airplanes, 25 tired ex-Navy Douglas AD-6 Skyraiders, arrived in September, 1960, followed by four Sikorsky H-34 helicopters in December and seven more between January and April. Many of them were soon out of action because of a lack of maintenance, or parts, or both.

The guerrilla war received an endorsement from Moscow in a speech by Chairman Nikita Khrushchev. The USSR, said Khrushchev, would support wars of national liberation " . . . wholeheartedly . . . ", and he cited the examples of Viet-Nam and Algeria as two such wars.

President John F. Kennedy took office two weeks later, and one of the first acts of his administration was to react to the Kremlin pronouncement by instituting studies and funding programs of counter-insurgency. Then in March, Kennedy announced that Soviet planes were operating in Laos, breaking the signed agreements that accepted the neutrality of that country. He neglected to mention that the U. S. had been violating that neutrality for several years by then.

Two months later, Kennedy sent Vice President Lyndon B. Johnson to Saigon to talk with Diem. One of the results of those discussions was the dispatching of a mobile control and reporting post from the 507th Tactical Control Group, Shaw AFB, SC, to Tan Son Nhut air base outside Saigon. It was operational October 5, and the active, overt participation of the USAF in the war in Viet-Nam dates from that day.

Within a week, a second detachment was authorized to go to South Viet-Nam. The USAF had established the Special Air Warfare Center at Eglin AFB, Florida, in the first flush of enthusiasm for counter-insurgency. It was training a group of Air Commandos under the general project name of Jungle Jim. A group was put together from the Jungle Jim roster, and sent to Bien Hoa. Detachment 2A, 4400th Combat Crew Training Squadron (CCTS), moving under the code name of Farm Gate, took 151 USAF officers and men to Viet Nam. With them went eight North American T-28 trainers converted for counter-insurgency use, four Douglas SC-47 transports, and four Douglas RB-26 light reconnaissance bombers, all carrying the insignia of the Republic of Viet-Nam.

The Farm Gate deployment was authorized by Kennedy October 11, 1961. At about the same time, and under cover of USAF participation in an air show, four McDonnell RF-101C reconnaissance planes were detached to Viet-Nam to fly missions over that country and Laos. Four more were sent to Thailand in November, and later replaced the Viet-Nam detachment. Before the end of the year, they had flown about 200 sorties.

In November, Kennedy authorized the deployment of three companies of Army H-21 helicopters, plus an Air Force squadron of 16 Fairchild C-123 tactical transports. The Vietnamese Air Force was loaned 30 North American T-28 aircraft, fitted for counter-insurgency missions. The most controversial decision, viewed with the perspective of time, was his authorization to move a Ranch Hand flight of six C-123 aircraft from the Philippines to Viet-Nam. Their mission was defoliation of the thick jungle that hid the Viet-Cong.

Late in 1961 came the first of the many rules of operation, telling the Air Force how it was to fight or cooperate with the Vietnamese. That first one prohibited any combat by the Farm Gate detachment unless a Vietnamese crewman was aboard, or unless the South Vietnamese Air Force could not handle the mission.

Those first few months set the pattern: escalation of forces, operational restrictions, control from Washington. It was a frustrating way to go to war, and it had hardly begun.

Retaliation and Rolling Thunder

Indochina is devoid of decisive military objectives and the allocation of more than token U. S. armed forces in Indochina would be a serious diversion of limited U. S. capabilities. The principal sources of Viet Minh military supply lie outside Indochina.

Those two sentences, part of a 1954 study by the Joint Chiefs of Staff, accurately summarized the war in Viet Nam between the French and the Viet Minh. As it was true in 1954, so was it true later.

In fact, the truth of those two sentences is so basic, and the implications of ignoring that truth so serious that one wonders, at this time, how and why the United States' involvement in the war ever came about.

It's glib to say that President John F. Kennedy's Camelot and Premier Nikita Khrushchev's Communism couldn't co-exist, but there is truth in that statement. Under Kennedy, the first escalation of effort occurred, and the basic policies of his administration were inherited and expanded upon by the succession of later Presidents. But predecessor administrations were not blameless. Truman's open support of the French position determined the course of subsequent American policy, and Eisenhower's support of the Diem administration while trying to hurt Ho Chi Minh's government

During the first years of the involvement in Viet Nam USAF aircraft were in general unpainted. Here an F-100D rolls towards its target in the Mekong Delta area, killing speed with airbrake. Absence of other dropped stores shows it is to make a strafing run.

One of the tactical jets that really came into its own in Viet-Nam was the Martin B-57 Canberra. This flew many kinds of close-support, reconnaissance, intruder and FAC missions, and extraordinary results were obtained with a handful of special multi-sensor B-57G aircraft that could have been the regular model had the systems been developed earlier on the evidence of Korean experience. Here a tandem-seat B-57B is readied for a night mission in South Viet-Nam in 1965.

were initial steps on the long road that Kennedy followed and sign-posted for his successors.

For the professional soldiers, sailors and airmen called upon to manage the war, it was to be a continuing frustration. There was no defined objective for the U. S. involvement. There were rules of engagement that severely restricted operations. There were directives, orders, teletypes and visitors from Washington, all taking precedence over the usual prerogatives of a field commander to run the war from the scene of the action.

With no goal, and with no way of measuring the progress toward a goal, it is hardly any wonder that the war degenerated into a conflict whose purpose seemed to be the production of favorable, cost-effective statistics: so many dead Viet Cong in the South, so many bridges destroyed in the North, so many trucks left burning on the Ho Chi Minh trail, so many pounds of rice and rounds of ammunition captured in bivouac areas overrun by so many U. S. troops.

There was another basic truth about the war in Viet-Nam that was never broadly recognized or understood, and it needs to be stated here: ideology can not be destroyed by killing its adherents.

A Decade to Change Minds

Ten years after the JCS had written that Indochina was " . . . devoid of military objectives . . . " they prepared a memorandum to Secretary of Defense Robert S. McNamara. In the opinion of the JCS, the United States should escalate its efforts in Indochina, the memo said. The first step would be the gathering of intelligence by flights over Cambodia and Laos. That would be followed by arming, equipping, advising and supporting the Republic of Viet-Nam (RVN) so that the RVN Air Force (RVNAF) could bomb North Viet-Nam and mine its sea approaches. Finally, the U. S. should bomb specific targets in North Viet-Nam, using U. S. aircraft with Vietnamese markings and with Vietnamese open assumption of responsibility for the action.

That memo was dated January 22, 1964. Less than two months later, McNamara sent a memo to President Lyndon B. Johnson that went further. He called for retaliation that would include open reconnaissance over North Viet-Nam and air attacks against military, possibly industrial, targets in the North. To do that task, McNamara suggested that the RVNAF be augmented by the USAF Farm Gate unit, and that the

Still with its big centreline tank, but with its 16 underwing pylons empty, an Air Force A-1E Skyraider rolls down through light cloud.

Farm Gate squadron be reinforced by three squadrons of Martin B-57s.

Clandestine military operations had begun in the North during February, under Operations Plan 34A, and by April the Joint Chiefs were developing a target list that ultimately included 94 potential bombing objectives in North Viet Nam. The 1st Air Commando Wing had sent its Detachment 6 to Udorn, Thailand, to assist in Laotian air operations, to check out Lao pilots in the North American T-28, and to maintain the planes. Their four T-28s and 41 airmen were ready for operations with the Laos in April.

In May, Gen. Khanh, one of the many South Vietnamese leaders who followed in the turbulent wake of the unsuccessful Diem regime, asked that the United States attack the North. The pressure to escalate began; Khanh's request was only one of several factors.

Then South Vietnamese naval commandos raided a pair of islands lying in the Gulf of Tonkin. In response to the invasion of their territory, the North sent a small force of highspeed patrol torpedo boats into the Gulf, and they intercepted the USS *Maddox*, an American destroyer. They barrelled in, attacked, and fled. Two nights later, they repeated the performance against the USS *C. Turner Joy*. That was the triggering action.

Within twelve hours, a retaliatory strike had been launched, sending USAF and Navy planes against port installations. The Rubicon had been crossed, and the United States was committed to war in Southeast Asia. Ambassador Maxwell Taylor, in Saigon, suggested that the U. S. bomb North Viet-Nam, and the JCS agreed it was a good idea. They proposed that the Americans adopt a provocative strategy; in other words, force the North to do something that would create the reason for retaliation.

The Congress, with minimum debate, passed the Gulf of Tonkin resolution August 7, giving President Johnson almost *carte blanche* to take the country into the war. Two Martin B-57 squadrons moved from Clark Air Base in the Philippines to Bien Hoa AB, and North American F-100 fighters and Convair F-102 interceptors were sent to Da Nang. Other aircraft deployed to Thailand, taking up battle stations. They did not have long to wait. In October, the Johnson administration decided that it would be appropriate to strike against the Ho Chi Minh trail that was being used to infiltrate men and supplies into the south.

The Viet Cong struck back; they attacked the Bien Hoa base, destroying several aircraft with well-placed mortar fire. Ambassador Taylor again urged bombing of the North, and an interagency working group came up with a trio of options for Johnson to consider. First, they suggested, he could order reprisal air strikes and increase the covert operations. Second, he might order bombing of the North until the U. S. got its way. Third, he might begin a graduated air war to be followed by the possible deployment of ground troops.

In December, 1964, Johnson made his choice. He wanted to work the first option for 30 days, to be followed by the third if after a month things had not begun to go the way he wanted them to go.

At the same time, in northern Laos, the Royal Laotian Air Force began flying its T-28s against ground targets in support of the Laotian Army and Neutralist groups who were fighting the Pathet Lao. Laos, according to the Geneva Accords of July 23, 1962, was a country ruled by a tripartite government: Rightists, Neutralists, and Pathet Lao (leftists). It never worked, and quickly degenerated into a Pathet Lao attempt to seize total control. They were backed by the North Vietnamese. In the spring of 1964, the Pathet Lao and their NVN supporters went on the offensive and captured control of the Plain of Jars. The Neutralists called for air strikes against the Communists to save the country, and in response the

United States began the *Barrel Roll* air campaign to support Laotian ground forces.

Background to Rolling Thunder

The Viet Cong attacked a U. S. military compound at Pleiku in February, 1965, and drew down the first reprisal air strike. About 50 USAF and Navy planes hit Donghoi, a major NVN base about 50 miles north of the demilitarized zone (DMZ) on the coast. The Viet Cong then hit a U. S. barracks, and the second reprisal strike went out. These *Flaming Dart* attacks were just a prelude; that same month, Johnson ordered the beginning of *Rolling Thunder*, a sustained air campaign against the North. It began in March.

Its objective was to break the will of the North Vietnamese, a tactic that had been tried before in Korea and in World War 2, and that had failed then. It was to start on a small scale and expand slowly and deliberately, first hitting targets in the South that were associated with the infiltration of men and supplies to the guerilla forces. It would creep northward, hitting a wider variety of targets and striking harder. As a plan, it has been called an "excellent one. But as a concept, it has been called a "colossal misjudgement".

The theories of bombing assume that the country to be attacked is an industrial power, producing at home most of the materiel required by its armed forces. Further, they also assume that those armed forces are to be engaged in large and intensive battles, requiring the movement of large numbers of men and mountains of supplies, and featuring concentrations of troops, armor and munitions.

None of this was true for North Viet-Nam. It was an agricultural country, with inadequate roads, a minor railroad network, and very little industry. The gross national product of the entire North in 1965 was estimated at $1.6 billion, and of that, about $192 million was attributed to industrial output. It had few major industrial complexes; only eight were deemed worth including on the first target list. They made very little in military materiel. Instead, North Viet-Nam's military machine was supplied by China and Russia. Practically every single weapon, every round of ammunition, every airplane, tank and truck came from the two

major Communist powers. True, it had to be moved from outside to key distribution points within North Viet-Nam, and at first glance their transportation system looked like a prime target whose destruction would be worthwhile. But if the rails were knocked out, the roads would remain, and the trails could be used by porters carrying loads on their backs or trundling them along on bicycles.

The primary supply network was the famed Ho Chi Minh trail, first used as a portage route during World War 2, and again during the postwar fighting with the French. In the dry season, the trucks rumbled along its rolling contours; in the rains, the roads were still passable by bicycle and foot. Most of the trail lay within Laos, under a jungle canopy of triple-layered foliage. It was extremely difficult to attack for that single reason.

The weather was a complicating factor. The southwest monsoon caused heavy rains and thunderstorms in South Viet-Nam from May until October, but created the best weather for the strikes against the North. When the northeast monsoon hit from September to May, it made for foul weather over the targets during that period. Typically, only five or six days might be clear enough for visual attacks.

Rolling Thunder was planned as an interdiction campaign, and it was waged simultaneously with other air strikes and campaigns as part of a four-front aerial war. Parallel campaigns included the interdiction strikes against the Ho Chi Minh trail in the Laotian panhandle, the attacks on roads and trails in South Viet-Nam, and the attacks against the Communist lines of communication in northern Laos.

There was a fundamental difference between the opinions of the Joint Chiefs and of some of the intelligence branches of government. The Chiefs were convinced that *Rolling Thunder* and other bombing attacks would achieve their purpose; the intelligence people argued that they would be of little or no value. The JCS countered with the argument, unanswerable then and now, that if the bombing were of little value, it was because of self-imposed restraints.

Those restraints, often compared to fighting the war with one hand tied, were political. Primary among them was the desire to avoid doing anything that would draw in either the Chinese or the Russians, and

Devoid of underwing offensive stores, a North American F-100D fighter banks left to begin a strafing run against suspected enemy positions.

First flown as far back as 1953, the supersonic F-100 Super Sabre proved itself an admirable tactical aircraft in Viet-Nam, flying both ground attack and top cover missions. Particular F-100 units also flew "fast-mover FAC" (forward air control) missions, and altogether the "Hun" flew more than 300,000 sorties in this theatre, a total greater than that flown by almost 16,000 P-51s in World War 2. Here aircraft of the D sub-type from the 120th TFS leave on a mission from Phan Rang on 22 June 1968.

widen the war to a world conflict, possibly with nuclear weapons. In many cases, these rules of engagement were turned against the U. S. and RVN forces. One example: The prohibition on bombing the dikes that dammed the rice paddies of the North. This known, the North Vietnamese installed anti-aircraft batteries and SAM sites alongside or even on the dikes, knowing full well that they would be safe from any deliberate attack.

Target selection was almost invariably done in Washington, and relayed through the Commander-in-Chief, Pacific (CINCPAC), in Honolulu, and the Military Assistance Command, Viet-Nam (MACV), in Saigon. If the strike aircraft were to be working in Laos, or were based in Thailand, there were additional complications as local ambassadors assumed a primary authority.

Such a chain of command has some merit in a long-range, strategic war. But in the fluid tactical environment of Viet-Nam, it led to some ridiculous situations. A target now may not be there in a matter of minutes. It has to be struck now, without waiting for its name or description to appear on a list teletyped from halfway around the world.

Targets and Weapons

The *Rolling Thunder* campaign had a classical target list: radar sites, bridges, rail lines, roads. There were

some notable omissions to complicate things. Neither North Vietnamese MiG airfields nor surface-to-air (SAM) sites were targeted at first. With regard to the SAM sites, there was a popular belief on the civilian side of the Pentagon for some months that the North Vietnamese would not fire the missiles against U. S. planes if the planes did not attack the missile sites. With regard to the MiG airfields, there was probably a belief that either Russian's, or Chinese, or both, might be at those fields as advisers, and it would not have been a good thing to have killed a number of them.

There was a buffer zone at the Chinese border, a 25-mile depth that was sacrosanct. The cities of Hanoi and Haiphong also had restricted zones surrounding them, within which no attack could be mounted.

The targets were well-defended by heavy anti-aircraft. The North had about 1,000 guns in place, located at about 400 sites. Most of it was medium-caliber, 37-mm. and 57-mm., with some larger 85-mm. and 100-mm. weapons. Additionally, one of the most effective weapons of the war was a multiple-barrelled Russian-designed ZSU-23-4, a 23-mm. automatic rapid-firing weapon that hosed the approaches to targets.

A reconnaissance flight by a Lockheed U-2 spotted the first SA-2 (NATO name: Guideline) SAM site early in April, 1965, and by the end of the year more than 50 had been plotted. The North Vietnamese Air Force (NVAF) was equipped with a handful of Russian-designed Ilyushin Il-28 (NATO name: Beagle) light

The capacious air inlets in the wing roots of the Republic F-105 Thunderchief give a clear indication of the type's thirst for fuel, about to be satisfied once the nozzle at the tip of the tanker's flying boom has slotted into the receptacle in the nose of the "Thud".

This "Hun", an F-100D-61-NA, was assigned to the 308th TFS, 31st TFW, based in 1970 at Tuy Hoa AB.

bombers, and a half-hundred miscellaneous MiGs, both the -15 and the -17 models.

The primary USAF strike aircraft was the Republic F-105 Thunderchief, almost universally called the "Thud". It was the only USAF fighter-bomber that could go north and strike at supersonic speed. And, in the words echoed by many pilots, "Speed is life!" The secondary strike aircraft was the North American F-100 Super Sabre, recalled from duty with the Air National Guard to serve in Southeast Asia. Some combat missions were flown by the Lockheed F-104 Starfighter, and the ubiquitous Martin B-57 flew many bombing strikes against targets in the South.

Their supporting forces were Strategic Air Command Boeing KC-135A tankers on racetrack orbits over northern Laos and the Gulf of Tonkin. Low- and high-flying reconnaissance aircraft and drones made up the primary intelligence gathering force, and rescue units were always on standby.

The first of the *Rolling Thunder* strikes was on March 2, 1965, when 25 F-105s and 20 B-57s struck a North Vietnamese Army (NVA) ammunition dump at Xam Bong, just a few minutes flight north of the DMZ. As subsequent strikes moved north, the tactics of defense and offense improved. One of the first increments was the deployment of College Eye, a Lockheed EC-121D aircraft that orbited above the Gulf of Tonkin and controlled traffic, assigned strike aircraft to forward air controllers, warned of MiG attacks forming in the Hanoi area, and relayed immediate intelligence and communications.

In late July, a single McDonnell F-4C became the first victim of a NVA missile. Four days later, a flight of F-105s roared in against a SAM site and knocked it out of action. But strikes against missiles were dangerous and also complicated. One rule of engagement was that a missile whose radar was in the search mode was immune to attack; as soon as the mode was switched to track, the missile site became fair game. The imposition of that demanding a check on the already overloaded pilot probably accounted for a number of losses to the SAMs. The missiles were most effective only after passing some minimum altitude; below a few thousand feet they were still accelerating and still well below their capabilities. The obvious counter was to fly low; but that made the strike force an easy target for the 23-mm. automatic anti-aircraft fire, responsible for most of the losses over the North in the early months of *Rolling Thunder*.

The USAF countered the missile threat with Iron Hand flights, a hunter-killer team of fighters called Wild Weasels. At first, they flew aging F-100F two-seaters that had been modified with additional electronic equipment. They preceded the strike force by about five minutes, going into the target area deliberately to draw missile fire. The plan was that the Wild Weasels would detect and evade a missile launched at them, while firing one of their own AGM-45A Shrike missiles to ride the enemy radar beam backward to its source.

As a weapon, the SAM was not too effective. The NVA fired about 180 of them during 1965, and shot down only 11 American aircraft. But they were very effective in forcing the strike aircraft into an altitude envelope where they were more vulnerable to other types of anti-aircraft weapons.

Further counter-measure support came from Douglas EB-66 aircraft, loaded with chaff and jamming equipment, that were assigned to orbit off the main axis of attack to jam the NVA communications and

When the U.S. Air Force was formed in 1947 piston-engined combat aircraft were generally judged obsolete as a class, yet 20 years later the Air Force was at war with piston-engined aircraft originally designed for the Navy! The A-1 Skyraider combined such payload, endurance and versatility that it played a major role with every branch of the armed services in Viet-Nam. Here an Air Force A-1E single-seater, popularly called the "Sandy" or "Spad", blasts a ground target with a phosphorous bomb in February 1966.

Today tens of thousands of flight personnel from all U.S. armed forces remember with gratitude the role of the ever-present USAF KC-135 tankers. There are even records of disabled fighters being towed long distance via the tanker's boom. Here three very battle-ready F-105Ds are topped up en route for a target in 1966.

Whatever anyone may today think of the U.S. "involvement", the troops at the sharp end were truly great professionals. In November 1966 1st Lt Lee A. Donner (furthest), 1st Lt Victor C. Seavers, Capt John Purves, Maj James R. Brown and 1st Lt Samuel P. Carter Jr listened to Lt-Col Robert B. Tanguy's briefing before going out to their F-4Cs at Da Nang.

ground-controlled intercept radars.

In addition to weather, the defenses and the restraints, there were demanding problems with air traffic control. The few Viet-Nam targets were in a small geographic area, and could only be approached by a few routes. The combination of weather and the number of aircraft to be handled forced the attack patterns into predictable paths, and the NVA was able to move its defenses accordingly. One attempt to bring some order out of the threat of chaos was the division of North Viet-Nam into six Route Packages. They began at the DMZ, with RP 1 extending northward, and ended with RP VI, further subdivided into VI-A and VI-B, both reaching to the buffer zone at the Chinese border. RP V and VI-A, in the northwest, were assigned to the USAF; RP VI-A contained Hanoi. The Navy drew RP VI-B, on the coast and containing the port city of Haiphong.

Rolling Thunder began with about 1,500 tactical sorties during April, 1965, flown by USAF and Navy aircraft. That figure rose to almost 4,000 by September, and then fell off in October as the monsoon swept in. The strikes had been heavy, but relatively ineffective.

The First Bombing Halt

The year ended with one of the many "signals" sent to Ho's government by the Johnson administration. Johnson ordered a bombing halt from the evening of December 24, 1965, to the end of January, 1966, since that time period included both Christmas and Tet, the Buddhist festival. There was no discernible response from the North, and bombing began again in February.

The JCS had been urging the bombing of NVN petroleum supplies since November, 1965. McNamara recommended it in a memorandum in March, 1966, and Johnson decided that it was a feasible idea. Under orders to take great care with their strikes, U. S. tactical air forces went North on June 29 to bomb the oil storage facilities at Hanoi and Haiphong. The capital's tank farm was completely destroyed, and the Haiphong dock installations were listed as 80 percent destroyed. The Seventh Air Force headquarters issued a statement calling the raid the most significant and most important strike of the war. It was, unfortunately, a hollow boast. Even though almost three-quarters of NVN petroleum products storage capacity lay in ruins by the end of July, it did not slow the pace of the war. The North Vietnamese continued to import oil and gasoline, but in barrels instead of in bulk. They

established a myriad of small storage dumps that could be easily concealed and easily moved.

The tactical success and strategic failure of the strikes against the oil system started some rethinking of the role of air power and its employment in the war. One specific assignment was given to the Jason Division of the Institute of Defense Analysis; in September the group reported its consensus:

As of July, 1966, the U. S. bombing of North Vietnam had had no measurable direct effect on Hanoi's ability to mount and support military operations in the South at the current level . . .

Since the initiation of the Rolling Thunder program the damage to facilities and equipment in North Vietnam has been more than offset by the increased flow of military and economic aid . . . The indirect effects of the bombing on the will of the North Vietnamese to continue fighting and on their leaders' appraisal of the prospective gains and costs of maintaining the present policy have not shown themselves in any tangible way. Furthermore, we have not discovered any basis for concluding that the indirect punitive effects of bombing will prove decisive in these respects.

The Jason Division report went to Defense Secretary McNamara who, in turn, wrote a memo to President Johnson.

The increased damage to targets is not producing noticeable results. No serious shortage of POL (Petroleum, Oil, Lubricants) . . . is evident . . . No serious transport problem . . . is evident; most transportation routes appear to be open, and there has recently been a major logistical build-up in the area of the DMZ. The raids have disrupted the civil populace and caused isolated food shortages, but have not significantly weakened popular morale . . . In spite of an interdiction campaign costing at least $250 million per month at current levels, no significant impact on the war in South Vietnam is evident. The monetary value of damage to North Vietnam since the start of bombing in February 1965 is estimated at about $140 million through October, 1966.

There had been two expansions of the *Rolling Thunder* campaign, once in July and again in November, in the latter case moving to targets in the outskirts of Hanoi itself. The tactical air strikes flown by USAF and USN planes totalled 106,500; they were augmented by 208 B-52 sorties. Together they dropped 165,000 tons of bombs. It cost the Americans 45 aircraft.

The defenses had grown stronger. There were more than 150 SAM sites by the end of 1965, a tripling in the course of about 12 months. The NVAF had gone on the offensive with new MiG-21s, armed with infra-red seeker missiles (NATO name: Atoll), and were operating out of five bases within the Hanoi sanctuary area. The Air Force diverted some of its McDonnell F-4Cs, used earlier as strike aircraft, to deal with the aerial threat posed by the MiG-21s. By year's end the MiG inventory had been reduced by 23, 17 of them brought down by USAF planes, at a cost of five losses.

The 1965 and 1966 air campaigns were studied in some depth by the Central Intelligence Agency (CIA). Total estimated casualties in 1965, said the agency, were 13,000 killed; in 1966, the number was 23,000 to 24,000. About 80 percent of these were believed to be civilians. That totalled about 29,000 civilian casualties in the first two years of the bombing offensive.

Rolling Thunder had flown about 55,000 sorties in 1965, and double that in 1966. It had cost $460 million in 1965, and $1.2 billion in 1966 to send those sorties North.

And the study concluded that the bombing in 1966 " . . . accomplished little more than in 1965."

To Fly and to Fight

"The mission of the Air Force is to fly and to fight—and don't you forget it!"

That sentiment, on posters that hang in every fighter squadron briefing or ready room, is a cornerstone of the fighter pilots' creed. It was disappointing to go to war in Southeast Asia and to find that only half the mission was available. The early months of the conflict were characterized by a nearly complete lack of classical air combat. The big fighter sweeps of World War 2 and the Korean war seemed to be things of the distant past, as ancient now as shooting down observation balloons on the Western Front.

The combat forces were fighter-bombers, a mix most often of F-4s and F-105s, all carrying bombs. There were not enough fighters available in the theater to use any of them as dedicated escorts to beat off MiG attacks.

The North Vietnamese Air Force (NVAF) was small and poorly equipped. But they could not be ignored; their MiGs were a constant threat to strike forces headed north, and they could be deadly opponents in a swirling dogfight where their high maneuverability gave them the turning advantage.

Their interception tactics were simple. The NVAF radar system gave ample warning time; the MiGs scrambled and orbited, either high or low, waiting for the strike force to show. Then they would make a high-speed pass at the formation, hoping that the threat of attack would force the fighters to jettison their bombs to prepare for combat.

The primary reason for the lack of fighters was an unusual one. Southeast Asia was a small theater of war, and the distances from strike force bases to Hanoi were relatively short. From Udorn to Hanoi was 325 miles; from Takhli, 550 miles. These distances were well within the limits of the official performance data for the combat radius of both the F-4 and the F-105. But under wartime conditions, with external weapons multiplying the drag and afterburner operations multiplying the fuel flow, those performance figures were

The sentry standing guard over a pair of North American F-100 Super Sabre tactical fighters at a base in South Viet-Nam gives a clear indication of the internal security problem faced in combatting so elusive an opponent as the Viet Cong.

One of the best — and, from the target attitude, most unusual — air combat pictures ever taken, this combat camera picture shows a North Vietnamese MiG-17 trying to escape from an F-4C about 35 miles west of Hanoi.

Unquestionably the most important USAF combat aircraft in Viet-Nam was one which, like the very different A-1, had originally been designed for the Navy. The Phantom II served in air combat, ground attack and dedicated reconnaissance roles in the Southeast Asia theater, flying day and night in all weather.

reduced drastically. The strike force had to have aerial refueling to hit targets as close as 350 miles away.

But not enough tankers could be made available to handle the requirements of shuttle bombing by large forces. SAC, as single manager for tankers, felt the strain. Twice a day, 27 of its big Boeing KC-135A tankers off-loaded fuel to fighters and other elements of the strike forces. More tankers were dispatched to support the B-52 missions in the theater. But both of those tasks were only contingency missions for SAC; the primary role of the tanker fleet was in support of the worldwide deployment of SAC bombers and their continuing training missions that extended thousands of miles and demanded several refuelings on route. The bulk of the SAC tankers were orbiting in trackless skies waiting for a B-52 or an FB-111 to nuzzle up for a drink.

Consequently, the availability of tanker support was a limiting factor on the size of the tactical fighter deployments and missions. It was depressing to fighter pilots, who wanted little more than to fly sweeps to force the enemy to come up and tangle. Instead, they had to load bombs on their planes and become flying artillery. It demanded a different mental set, and it was not what fighter pilots had joined the USAF to do.

Seventh Air Force, annoyed by the frequent attacks by NVAF MiGs, decided to try a Korean-war style sweep, a mass formation of USAF fighters that would head north to try to get the NVAF, by then strengthened by some new MiG-21s, into the air where it could be hurt badly, if not destroyed. Col. Robert F. Olds, an ace in World War 2 and in his second shooting war with the USAF, was given responsibility for planning the sweep — Operation *Bolo* — in detail. Olds, who commanded the 8th Tactical Fighter Wing, designed the

sweep so that it would appear to the NVAF like any other routine strike: A standard formation of F-105s and F-4s, with escorts and Iron Hand flights. But he planned to make the entire force F-4s, and only simulate the strike formation. They would get ready to fight at about the point where the F-105s would begin their steady bomb run and the MiGs would begin their interceptions. Olds' scheme called for two groups of F-4s, one coming in high from Laos, to fight the high-altitude MiG-21 patrols, and the other low from the Tonkin Gulf, to take on the MiG-17s that orbited nearer the ground. The force from Laos also would be able to intercept any MiGs trying to make a run for the Chinese border sanctuary.

Twenty flights — 80 aircraft — headed out from their bases on January 2, 1967, but weather walled out the strike from the Gulf of Tonkin. Only the Laos-based planes got through, and met MiGs popping up through the overcast. In a fast and furious fight, seven MiGs were shot down at no loss to the F-4s. Olds himself got two of the enemy.

It had been the largest air engagement of the war until then, and it was to remain that. Four days later, the NVAF lost two more MiG-21s in a lesser air combat; the shock must have been traumatic, because they seemed to drop out of action altogether for an while to reconsider their tactics.

Seventh AF also reconsidered the situation, and decided that the threat justifed the use of dedicated escorts. From then on, some F-4s were assigned to fighter escort, and they were used to cover attack forces headed north. It was basically the same job that the Mustangs had done in 1944 and that Sabres had done in 1951. Typically, there would be a bombing force of 16 F-105s; their escort would be two flights of four

F-4s each, ahead of and behind the main formation, continuously weaving to cover the strike.

Their early tactics were to stay with the formations and deflect the MiG attacks. Later, they were free to chase and fight the NVAF opposition, a task much more to the liking of the aggressive fighter pilots.

Stop-and-Go Offensive

From February 8 to 12 that year, there was another bombing halt, to attempt negotiations between the two sides. When the try failed, Johnson once again gave orders for an expanded offensive. Hanoi and Haiphong were on the target lists.

The USAF celebrated Washington's Birthday by hitting five city powerplants in the capital and the Thai Nguyen steel plant complex northwest of Hanoi. A third force mined rivers and estuaries in the North. A month later, they hit two thermal powerplants that supplied power to the city of Haiphong. On April 8, Kep airfield — one of the MiG bases formerly within the Hanoi sanctuary — was pounded, and a power transformer near the center of the city was hit. Other targets that day included an ammunition dump and POL supplies in Haiphong, and a cement plant. There was a fifth major strike directed against the thermal powerplant that lay one mile to the north of the center of Hanoi.

These targets were essentially those earlier suggested by the Joint Chiefs. Specifically, they had recommended most of those objectives in a memorandum to the Secretary of Defense in mid-October, 1966. Now they had been hit and badly damaged. But what were the results beyond destruction?

The CIA analyzed those raids and the earlier ones, and in May circulated three separate papers dealing with several aspects of the war to date. In the first, the agency concluded that 27 months of bombing had produced little effect on the North's strategy, its plans for the future, or its approach to negotiations. The second paper stated that the people of North Viet-Nam continued to be stoic, with still-untapped endurance. Clearly their will was not broken. The third credited the air offensive with severely hurting Hanoi's military-industrial base, but pointed out that it still had not lowered the ability of the North to continue the war.

One of those studies recounted the cost of the air operations. The U. S. was losing pilots six times as fast over Hanoi and Haiphong as it did over all the rest of the North; the loss rate was one pilot for every 40 sorties. In terms of percentages, that was two and one-half percent, a relatively low and militarily acceptable rate in a long war of attrition like World War 2. But the U. S. pilot force was not that large, and could not take that rate of loss for long.

Johnson and the Joint Chiefs persevered. In July he again expanded the air offensive, removing more targets from the restricted list. Soon after that, the tactical forces were authorized to strike the Paul Doumer bridge, a key element in the rail and road transportation system that moved supplies to Hanoi.

The Durable Bridge of Paul Doumer

For more than two years, tactical aircraft had been pounding the railroads of North Viet-Nam, as their companions in arms had done earlier in Korea and Europe. And the results were pretty much the same as always. The enemy knew how to make rapid repairs, and how to bypass bombed-out segments.

The much-loved Lead Sled, or Thud, did more than just drop bombs; the F-105F of Maj Arthur L. Kuster and Capt Larry D. Wiggins bagged the second MiG (in this case a MiG-17) to be downed in Viet-Nam, on 3 June 1967. Unit, 469th TFS, Korat AB, Thailand.

The F-4E version of the Phantom was developed to provide an internal gun, on the centreline, but all of this version were later rebuilt (or originally constructed with) large leading-edge slats on the wings to increase manoeuvrability and eliminate stall/spin crashes on heavily loaded attack missions.

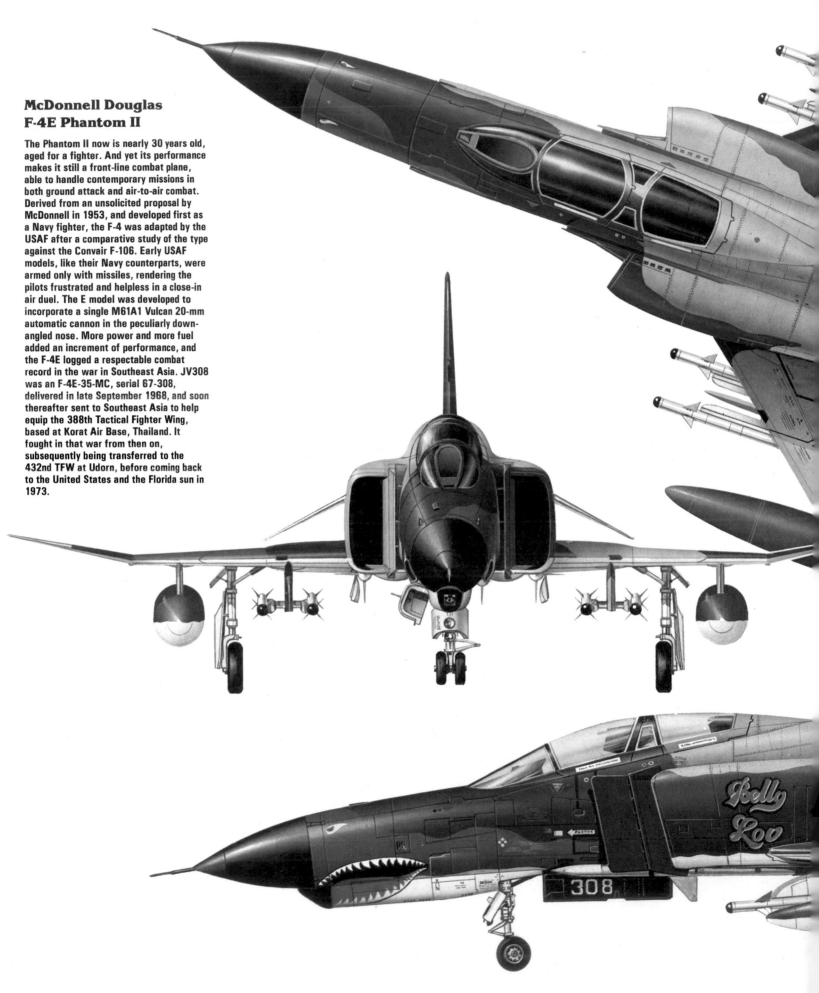

McDonnell Douglas F-4E Phantom II

The Phantom II now is nearly 30 years old, aged for a fighter. And yet its performance makes it still a front-line combat plane, able to handle contemporary missions in both ground attack and air-to-air combat. Derived from an unsolicited proposal by McDonnell in 1953, and developed first as a Navy fighter, the F-4 was adapted by the USAF after a comparative study of the type against the Convair F-106. Early USAF models, like their Navy counterparts, were armed only with missiles, rendering the pilots frustrated and helpless in a close-in air duel. The E model was developed to incorporate a single M61A1 Vulcan 20-mm automatic cannon in the peculiarly down-angled nose. More power and more fuel added an increment of performance, and the F-4E logged a respectable combat record in the war in Southeast Asia. JV308 was an F-4E-35-MC, serial 67-308, delivered in late September 1968, and soon thereafter sent to Southeast Asia to help equip the 388th Tactical Fighter Wing, based at Korat Air Base, Thailand. It fought in that war from then on, subsequently being transferred to the 432nd TFW at Udorn, before coming back to the United States and the Florida sun in 1973.

High over South Viet-Nam an RF-4C multi-sensor reconnaissance Phantom noses in under a KC-135 to take on fuel. The unit may have been the 11th Tac Recon Sqn.

A Sikorsky CH-3E helicopter hovers just above the ground while rescuing an American pilot. Such "choppers", together with the closely related HH-3E, played a significant part in the war by picking up downed airplanes and aircrew.

Most of the supplies that arrived in Hanoi from China came by rail on one of two lines entering from the northwest and the northeast. Materiel was handled at Hanoi and forwarded south to the battlefields. Supplies that came by sea to the port of Haiphong also moved over a 40-mile long railroad to Hanoi. There was still another rail line that carried steel from the Thai Nguyen plant into the city, and a fifth segment that led south out of Hanoi.

The rail system had been built by the French at the turn of the century, and was the brainchild of the Governor General of French Indochina, Paul Doumer. His name was given to the main bridge in the system; it crossed the Red River at Hanoi, and carried trains from four of the five segments of the rail network. Cut that single critical bridge, and Hanoi was cut off from China and the sea. As a bonus, Route National 1, the main highway north out of Hanoi, also was cut, because it crossed the Red River on the Doumer bridge.

It was a monstrous structure for that part of the world, a little longer than a mile, not counting its approach viaducts. Its 38-foot width carried a one-meter gauge rail line in the center with a 10-foot wide highway each side. It was held aloft by 18 hulking piers of reinforced concrete which bore the 19 separate spans of the bridge structure.

North of the bridge lay the floodplain area of the Red River, with villages and rice paddies. Hanoi was south and west of the bridge; to the east was Gia Lam airfield and an industrial complex. Because of the proximity to Hanoi, the bridge remained in the restricted zone until mid-1967.

The attack force was built from the F-4s of Col. Olds' 8th TFW, based at Ubon, Thailand, and F-105s from the 355th TFW at Takhli and the 388th TFW at Korat,

both also in Thailand. Refueling would be the task of the KC-135As of Detachment 1, 4258th Strategic Wing, based at U-Tapao, Thailand. After the strike, the 11th and 432nd Tactical Reconnaissance Squadrons would send paired RF-4Cs to photograph the bomb damage.

One flight of F-105s would be the Iron Hand team, with two F-105 Wild Weasel aircraft and two wingmen armed with iron bombs. Another four-plane flight would fly flak suppression. The main body would be the bombing force of F-105s, carrying two 3,000-lb. bombs each instead of their usual load of 750-pounders, plus some F-4s carrying bombs. One flight of F-4s had been detailed to fly MiGCAP (MiG Combat Air Patrol) to defend against expected interceptors. EB-66Cs went along to jam radars and support the attack with their speciality of electronic warfare.

The defenses of the bridge lay in depth along the approaches to, and the exits from, Hanoi: SAM sites, multiple batteries of automatic 23-mm. flak, plus 37-mm., 57-mm., and 85-mm. anti-aircraft artillery, radar-directed, massed and accurate. A few minutes' flight distant from Hanoi was the entire NVAF MiG inventory. As a final touch, there were radar-directed 85-mm. batteries at each end of the bridge.

Into this potential death trap roared the bombing force, led by Col. Robert M. White, a former X-15 research pilot. Behind him was his command, the 355th; further back in the formation was Olds' 8th TFW and the 388th TFW, led by Lt. Col. Harry W. Schurr. They approached Hanoi from the northwest, crossing the Red River about 95 miles out of town. They had been cruising at 500 knots; now they powered up to Mach 0.9 at their run-in altitude of 10,000 feet. At the northwest end of "Thud Ridge", a major rock outcropping northwest of Hanoi, they

Tactical Fighter Activity

With only negligible air opposition to face, the U.S. Air Force in Viet-Nam was able to use all its fighter strength in the tactical role. Under the control of FACs in slow aircraft, heavy fighters such as the F-100, F-105 and F-4 were able to deliver massive ordnance loads right down the throats of hostile forces in close combat with allied forces. The fitting of extra systems also permitted the use of advanced missiles and "smart" weapons against radar systems and harder targets such as bridges.

1. The Air Force F-4s scored their first victories over MiG fighters when two F-4Cs of the 45th TFS shot down two MiG-17s.

2. This was one of the first RF-4Cs to reach the action; ground crew scramble clear in May 1966.

3. The B-57B served in Viet-Nam almost from the beginning; here Lt-Col Lidie and Maj Planchon (8th TBS) depart Phan Rang.

4. Any Thud jock would immediately recognise these F-105D noses at Takhli RTAFB, February 1966.

5. Urgent rearming of an F-4D of the 37th TFW before a sortie from Phu Cat AB in March 1970.

6. Almost the entire USAF force of seven wings of F-105Ds rotated through Viet-Nam; these are from the 355th TFW.

7. The F-4C was in SE Asia soon after it joined the Air Force, and this one was rocketing a target on March 28, 1966.

8. F-4D Phantoms armed with smart bombs take their turn at the KC-135 during a mission over the North in November 1971.

9. Two F-104C Starfighters over Viet-Nam in December 1965; later these aircraft were camouflaged.

1

2

3

4

5

6

7

8

9

Sikorsky HH-53C

This 20-year old design originated as the Navy's **CH-53A Sea Stallion** helicopter, developed for the Marine Corps and its tactics of assault by vertical envelopment. The copters saw service with the USMC in Viet-Nam, and impressed everybody who saw them working. The Air Force ordered some modified versions in two batches—the latter now designated **HH-53C**—in the late 1960s, primarily for the dangerous and demanding mission of air rescue of downed pilots and other flight crew members. These versions of the chopper could be refueled in flight, had provision for auxiliary fuel tanks, increased power, and a ten-ton winch capacity. A handful of HH-53C helicopters have since been modified for use by the USAF Special Operations Wings for clandestine operations, such as the insertion and retrieval of agents in enemy countries. Outfitted with special night-flying and night-observation systems, these specific aircraft have been a valuable addition to the special operations units of the USAF. CH-53 helicopters achieved an embarrasing notoriety in the aborted rescue attempt in Iran, early in 1980.

An F-100D prepares to depart on a combat mission showing the muzzles of its M-39 cannons. In total the F-100 fired well over a million rounds against ground targets in SE Asia.

The appealing yellow glow of a bursting napalm tank conceals the devastating effect of this weapon against personnel and unprotected ground targets.

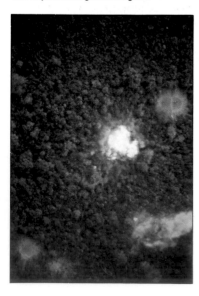

changed course and headed for the bridge. MiGs from Phuc Yen airfield just north of the city tried for a head-on intercept and blew it, vanishing behind the task force. When White sighted the bridge, he turned the force south and began the climb to the bombing altitude of 13,000 feet. It was a struggle for the heavily loaded "Thuds" to get up to that height, but they did. And then they peeled off in pairs, diving at the target in a 45-degree path that kept them in the run for seven long seconds while flak and missiles headed their way. They released their bombs between 7,000 and 8,000 feet, made the pullup and a hard turn downriver heading east. On their way, they reached and passed Mach 1; as they blasted over the "Hanoi Hilton", the U. S. prisoners there knew who was overhead by the characteristic sound of the "Thud" in full afterburner and over the Mach. Later they would tell what a morale boost it was to hear that particular cacophony.

The strike left behind a badly damaged bridge and some shaken and dead defenders. The lead strike had dropped one span, and the two following units had dropped two spans, both on the north side of the bridge. One of the 85-mm. flak batteries at the bridge was reduced to smoking ruin, but the other survived. Two missile sites were pounded into dust, and several more were suppressed successfully during the attack. The Doumer bridge had taken the brunt of hits and near-misses from 94 tons of bombs. And it was restored and carrying traffic again by October 3.

The August 11 strike was only the first of many. A second was mounted October 25, and unloaded 63 tons of bombs from 21 F-105s, against knocking out the bridge. It was back in service by November 20. On the 14th and 18th of December 50 F-105s again visited the bridge, and dropped another 90 tons of the big 3,000-lb.

bombs. By this time the North Vietnamese had gotten the message, and began building a bypass rail pontoon bridge about five miles further downriver; it opened to traffic in mid-April, 1968.

Paul Doumer's big bridge had been attacked by 177 bombers that had dropped 380 tons of bombs. By the time of the last strike of the 1967 air campaign, the defenses were known to include more than 300 anti-aircraft batteries of varying calibers, 84 missile sites with four to six launchers each, and 24 MiG-17 and MiG-21 interceptors. Countless rounds of anti-aircraft artillery had been fired at the attackers, and 109 missiles were launched, according to strike force reports. Two planes were lost to flak—neither during the first strike in August—and 15 were damaged.

But the bridge was to endure, almost until the end of hostilities, and it was to absorb more punishment in future strikes.

The Ghost of Dien Bien Phu

The village of Khe Sanh, in Quang Tri province, lay about 16 miles south of the DMZ and 10 miles from the Laotian border. The Army's Green Berets had built a combat base on a little plateau north of the village, using it as a jumping-off place for long-range reconnaissance patrols that moved around the Ho Chi Minh trail.

Otherwise it had no tactical value; it controlled no major road route. In fact, the combat base was completely dependent on air resupply. A Marine battalion moved in late in 1966, and a few months later the Green Berets left Khe Sanh for another location not far off.

A patrol of Marines ran into a small unit of North

Vietnamese in April, and came back with the conclusion that an attack on the base was among the enemy plans. Two more battalions of Marines were sent to reinforce the base later that month. Still later, the 26th Marine Division arrived to replace the 3rd, and settled into the base to stay.

By late 1967, enemy activity against the outpost had forced the U. S. command to a basic decision either to evacuate Khe Sanh, or to defend it against a possibly very heavy enemy onslaught. The spectre of the French defeat at Dien Bien Phu hung over the reality of Khe Sanh. President Johnson was one of the many troubled by the similarities between the two situations. There were important differences, though, and in the end they made the victory. First, the Marines had logistics support that the French could only have dreamed of, in terms of sizes and numbers of cargo aircraft available. Second, American firepower, both on the ground and in the air, was massive and, in the case of the latter, unlimited.

The decision was made; Khe Sanh would be defended, for political reasons. A minor outpost of no real tactical value was to become the symbol of American determination to win the war.

The weather, on average, was bad. There are two types of monsoons in Southeast Asia, at different seasons. North and South Viet-Nam are hit by complementary ones; when it is monsoon season up north, it is clear down south, and vice versa. Khe Sanh, in the middle, got both. The visibility was bad in the early morning, and the late afternoon.

In addition to the weather hazards, any supply effort would have to run a gauntlet of fire from enemy anti-aircraft batteries on the ridges that lay parallel to the western approach to the small airstrip. The enemy had moved in on the high ground, and seemed to hold every advantage but one: air power.

It was widely believed that the North Vietnamese forces were commanded by Gen. Vo Nguyen Giap, long-time friend of Ho Chi Minh, and defense minister in his government. Whether or not Giap was in the field was never known certainly; most observers believed that he ran the campaign, and was hoping to repeat his victory over the French at Dien Bien Phu.

The North Vietnamese had two full combat divisions in place around Khe Sanh; one of them had fought at Dien Bien Phu. There were reinforcements not far away. Total NVA strength was estimated at 20,000 troops, 72 heavy artillery pieces from 75-mm. to 122-mm. caliber, more than 200 mortars in three calibers, and an unknown number of rocket launchers. They had built and improved the roads between their positions and the Laos border where portions of the Ho Chi Minh supply trail emerged from the jungle canopy. Guns were dug in, and the battleground was set for a major attack on the Marines.

Khe Sanh had a garrison of about 3,600 Marine troops of the 26th Division, plus the 1st Battalion, 13th Marines, a heavy artillery unit. The tactical plan was simple: hold the outpost. Their main supporting force was to be air power, a Niagara of falling bombs and rockets. And Gen. William C. Westmoreland gave that name—Operation *Niagara*—to the massive air strikes planned to back the Marines.

USAF used Strategic Air Command and tactical air as its strike force; the Navy had a carrier task force, TF77, in the Gulf of Tonkin, with its planes and those of the First Marine Air Wing available. About 400 strike sorties each day were easily possible.

The battle began the morning of January 21, 1968. Giap's artillery fired a rolling barrage against the base. An early salvo hit the main ammunition dump, destroying all but two percent of the munitions available. Worse, the shells hit and cratered the airstrip, cutting it so short that none of the heavier transports would be able to land.

Under enemy fire, a Naval construction detachment repaired the runway so that it could handle Fairchild C-123 Provider light tactical transports. Six of them flew in that afternoon and evening with 24 tons of munitions. The next day, 20 more C-123 sorties raised the total to 130 tons, relieving the immediate problem of an ammunition shortage.

Then the battle settled into the characteristic pattern: artillery barrages by the enemy, answering air strikes, plus artillery from the Marine base, and Army artillery from a distant base called the Rock Pile. Marine reinforcements came in, including a South Vietnamese battalion, raising the Khe Sanh combat strength to about 6,000 men. Their supply needs were massive, and between a dozen and 15 cargo transports came into the base area each day to unload. Most of them were Lockheed C-130 tactical transports; they could haul up to 15 tons, more than three times the capacity of the C-123s.

It was a tough supply run. Khe Sanh was not a very good radar target, and it got worse as the Marines dug in more and as the surface structures were hammered by enemy artillery. Visibility was bad. Air traffic was heavy; the incoming flights were controlled by a Marine GCA operator during their final approach to

A constant threat to the sophisticated equipment operated by the U.S. Air Force in Viet-Nam was posed by Viet Cong rocket or mortar attacks. For this reason it was the practice to disperse airplanes, or alternatively to locate them in revetments for protection combined with ease of maintenance. Seen here are seven North American F-100 Super Sabre tactical fighters in such a revetment.

the runway. Two FACs accompanied each transport on its run in, and an escort of fighters orbited around them, ready to suppress any anti-aircraft fire. It there was no cloud or fog cover for the transport, the fighters laid a three-mile long smokescreen to cover the landing.

Once on the ground, the transports became "rocket bait" or "mortar magnets", two of the friendlier nicknames the Marine troops give the big planes. Enemy artillery pounded the airstrip and the unloading areas. Losses were light; surface damage to the runway ruined a lot of tires, and some shapnel holed the planes, but very few were total losses.

By mid-February, the risk was so great that a command decision was made not to let the valuable

Lockheed C-130s land at Khe Sanh any longer. Their greater landing distance meant a much longer taxi run, and a longer time to be a target for enemy artillery and mortar fire. Even the three-minute turnaround time achieved by some crews was too long. So the C-130s made delivery by parachute, or came in low for ground extractions by drag chute or arresting hook.

Heavy Air Traffic above Khe Sanh

The cargo carriers were a minority in the air traffic around Khe Sanh. During any typical day, there would be 350 tactical fighters hitting enemy positions, augmented by the carpet bombing of about 60 B-52s in from Guam. Thirty or so FACs would be working the

Tactical Airlift over S.E. Asia

The ground war in Viet-Nam was essentially a mobile war, in which the conventionally trained and outfitted U.S. and South Vietnamese forces strove to pin down and destroy highly elusive Viet Cong and, later, North Vietnamese forces. In such circumstances a high degree of mobility was vital, and such mobility could only be conferred in Viet-Nam by airplanes, both fixed-wing and rotary-wing.

Perhaps the most graphic example of the type of airlift perfected in Viet-Nam was the siege of the USMC firebase at Khe Sanh. In similar circumstances the Viet Minh had effectively prevented the French garrison at Dien Bien Phu from receiving aerial re-supply, but at Khe Sanh the Americans were able to fly in large quantities of all needed equipment (and some luxuries).

1. After the forklift has loaded the heavy items even the mail for Khe Sanh (foreground) will be delivered by C-130.

2. An Army rigger attaches the static line to the C-130 hook-up cable before para-dropping another load to Khe Sanh.

3. Pallet-mounted supplies sink towards the beleaguered outpost of Khe Sanh from a C-130 in March 1968.

4. Pallet-mounted supplies from a C-130 impact off the DZ at Khe Sanh after overshooting the target in March 1968.

5. C-130s with the 173rd Airborne Battalion aboard marshalled for takeoff at Bien Hoa for Operation Junction City.

6. Marine replacements arriving at Khe Sanh by CH-53A.

7. A USAF sergeant snapped this photograph of a Khe Sanh fuel dump burning after a VC mortar attack.

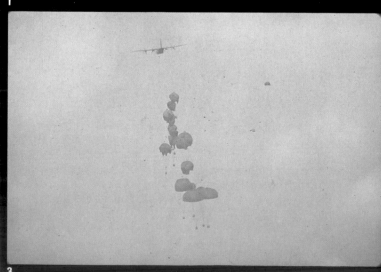

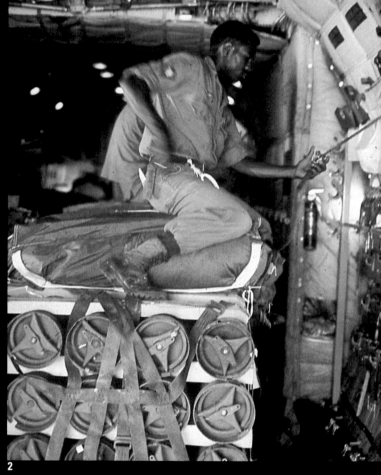

strikes, marking targets and calling in specific aircraft. Ten or a dozen RF-4Cs would race low across the battlefield, cameras rolling. And all of these low-flying planes were working in among the invisible tracks of dozens of shells from enemy, Marine and Army artillery, each one capable of totally destroying an aircraft if it hit. At night, the AC-47 gunships came in, using their batteries of miniguns to shatter the enemy. They also served as night FAC aircraft and battlefield illuminators.

Because of the weather, more than half of the strikes were directed by radar. The Marines had their own TPQ-10 working 20 hours a day and bringing ground support strikes as close as 150 feet from their forward positions. The USAF used one of its Combat Skyspot MSQ-77 radars to direct the B-52 strikes.

All incoming tactical aircraft reported to the airborne battle command and control center, a C-130 in orbit above the area, and were then assigned to a specific FAC to work against his target array. The FAC brought in each individual strike; often aircraft were stacked in holding patterns up to 35,000 feet, waiting to be cleared down to drop their ordnance and get back home.

The B-52s worked their own way. They bombed by the Bugle Note procedure, a system that used a grid map of the area with lines subdividing it into plots one by two kilometers in size. That box was the size of the bomb pattern from a cell of three B-52s. Every 90 minutes, on the average, three of the big bombers

5

6

7

The monster B-52 was generally known as the Buff (Big Ugly Fat Fella). This Buff is a smoky B-52D, leaving the switchback runway at Guam with full water-injection power to carry a load of bombs on a nine-hour round trip to Vietnam in 1967.

arrived at a specific point in the air, were picked up by the MSQ-77, given a route to the target box, and told when to drop their bombs. Late in the battle, the formations changed their timing and size to six every three hours. The effect was the same. Bombs generally were dropped to impact more than 3,000 feet from friendly forces; but in an emergency, the B-52s demonstrated that 1,000 feet was feasible, and made frequent attacks that close to Marine positions during the battle. Tactical strikes worked within a few hundred feet, generally.

The days passed and Giap's troops were held in a grinder that slowly but surely wore them down. Ground sensors, part of the Igloo White system (see Chapter 20), fingered their resupply convoys and targeted them for strikes by tactical aircraft. Marine artillery hammered their positions. B-52s pulverized square miles of their forest cover. And always they took heavy casualties. When the battle slowed to a halt

in mid-March, the North Vietnamese had lost heavily. The Americans never knew just how heavily, but intelligence estimated the decimation of two divisions, with about 10,000 total casualties.

The Marines lost 199 men killed and about 1,600 wounded, with half of them requiring air evacuation. they took nine prisoners, and rounded up 41 suspected Viet Cong guerrillas.

The reconnaissance photographs tell the story. The hills around Khe Sanh, the high ground and the valley were transformed into a lunar landscape. Bomb craters made a contiguous carpet of cutouts. The Boeing B-52s from Strategic Air Command's 3rd Air Division had flown 2,548 sorties and dropped 59,542 tons of bombs. Seventh Air Force had dispatched 9,691 sorties; its planes had dropped 14,223 tons of bombs. The First Marine Air Wing, supporting its ground units, sent off 7,078 sorties to drop 17,015 tons. The Navy sorties totalled another 5,337, with bomb loads of 7,941 tons.

To put this in another perspective, during World War 2 the USAAF dropped a total of 537,000 tons of bombs against targets in the Far East. Most of that tonnage was delivered to the main islands of Japan and dumped on cities and industries.

The bombs dropped at Khe Sanh weighed a total of 98,721 tons. That was about 18 percent—nearly one-fifth—of all the bombs dropped by the USAAF through the 45 months of World War 2 on targets in Asia.

The supplies delivered weighed 12,430 tons, and it required 1,124 sorties by daring tactical transport crews to land them or to drop them in the face of heavy, accurate and deadly enemy anti-aircraft fire.

The final verdict on the battle, as a battle, came from Gen. Westmoreland, in a speech he made to SAC's 3rd Air Div. on Guam. Khe Sanh, said Westmoreland, was " . . . a battle won by you . . . the thing that broke their backs was basically the fire of the B-52s."

The siege of Khe Sanh was lifted by mid-March when Giap's troops began fading back into the jungle. There was no surrender. A relief force of Marines came up Highway 9 on April 1, a day after President Johnson had called a halt to the bombing of the North and had removed himself from the Presidential race.

Later, the base was dismantled and finally, on June 23, 1968, it was abandoned.

Inflight refuelling was an important, if unusual, feature of the capable HH-53 multi-role rescue helicopter. The tanker was almost always the HC-130P model of the popular "Herky bird".

Technology on the Trail

The enemy was a rugged, six-wheel drive open-bed truck, simple, cheap, expendable, and very difficult to find at night. It was designed in Russia and built in a factory named after Lenin. The ZIL-157 could carry two and one-half to five tons of anything, and move it at speeds of up to 40 miles per hour over the roads of Southeast Asia.

It was a key element in the movement of war materiel from distribution points in North Viet-Nam to the army and to the Viet Cong irregulars in the South.

Trucks moving by day are relatively easy targets, exposed on open roads, often trailing a dust plume that can be spotted miles away. But a truck moving at night along a jungle trail covered with a triple layer of foliage is another matter entirely. To try to find and then to kill that truck was a problem that occupied the best brains and the finest tacticians of the war.

The solution evolved into a complex and highly sophisticated system that combined the latest technologies in electronic warfare, aircraft development, and weapons design. It represented at least $1 billion in capital costs, plus the operational costs of the system and of the aircraft that made it effective.

The system was called Igloo White, among other names, and it was a classical example of advanced technology to solve a primordial battlefield problem.

Twilight on the Trail

Igloo White had its roots in the frustrations of trying to stop the infiltration of men and supplies into the South. The distribution system began inside China, and included the rail lines from the northeast and northwest to Hanoi. From there, supplies moved by truck and rail, depending on the season and the state of the roads or railroads after interdiction strikes. As materiel approached the DMZ, it crossed the border into Laos at one of two passes: Mu Gia, about 75 miles north of the DMZ, or the Keo Neua pass at Nape, about 150 miles north.

The effectiveness of the B-52 as a dispenser of vast tonnages of "iron bombs", rained down on targets that were seldom seen and probably often absent, has been a matter for prolonged debate. Certainly it was not what the aircraft was designed to do, and the fact that the B-52 was the weapon most hated by the Viet Cong does not mean its missions were worth their great cost. Here 51 general-purpose bombs of 750-pound size (actual weight about 825 pounds) go down on a suspected VC target.

One of the many unusual kinds of combat aircraft deployed in Viet-Nam was the heavily armed gunship created by rebuilding a cargo transport with advanced night-vision sensors and various weapons. The most important gunship in Viet-Nam was the AC-119 Shadow. In this case the operating unit was the 71st Special Ops Squadron, Nha Trang AB, and the photograph was taken on December 27, 1966.

Facing page. Greatest of the Air Force helicopters in Viet-Nam was the HH-53B, derived from the Marines CH-53 Sea Stallion and popularly called the Super Jolly Green. Here an HH-53 hovers over a downed crewman on 16 June 1970.

Among the new weapons deployed in Southeast Asia, the "smart" (laser-guided) bomb was outstanding. Here over Viet-Nam in September 1972 a formation of F-4D Phantoms of the 8th TFW head for a point target. The nearest aircraft has two smart missiles of the "Paveway" family; this LGB (laser-guided bomb) has a pivoted guidance unit on the nose which continuously homes on the target. The emitting laser was carried in a pod by the second aircraft. Both carry Sparrow missiles for air-to-air defence, but rules on positive eyeball identification made it difficult ever to use such weapons.

Here it entered the Ho Chi Minh trail, in use since World War 2 as a supply route for insurgents. Heavy foliage along the trail provided natural concealment, but there were places where truck convoys were exposed to attack. Consequently, much of the traffic moved at night.

Operation *Steel Tiger* was a limited air campaign to stop or slow enemy movements along the Laotian portion of the Ho Chi Minh trail. The first strike was flown about one month after the Rolling Thunder air campaign began against the North, and it was directed against a segment of the trail in the southern panhandle of Laos.

The first attack was at night, setting the style for many to come. A C-130 flareship and two B-57s sortied on an armed reconnaissance mission on April 3, 1965, hoping to find some targets worth hitting. The makeup of this team was typical for the mission; for daylight strikes, F-100s and F-105s generally flew the sorties.

Some of the latter were on strip alert in Thailand, waiting to be dispatched against targets of opportunity discovered by one of the attack teams.

The seasonal monsoon came along soon after the opening of *Steel Tiger*, slowing the pace of the offensive and the supply movements. In spite of that, more than 1,000 strike sorties were being flown monthly by mid-year, using both USAF and USN aircraft. But as soon as the monsoon season was replaced by the dry months, infiltration increased, stronger than ever, and it was apparent that a limited air campaign of *Steel Tiger*'s scope wasn't enough. The answer was *Tiger Hound*.

It was a systematic air campaign of major size that brought in Army, Navy and Marine Corps aircraft to augment the USAF. The targets were trucks, their park and bivouac areas, bridges, buildings, and anti-aircraft artillery along the Trail. The planes also were assigned to cut roads and to hit choke points wherever they appeared.

Every available type of air weapon was thrown into the campaign. Fairchild UC-123 Ranch Hand aircraft sprayed the Trail with defoliants to denude the trees and deny the natural camouflage. Targets were spotted by McDonnell RF-101C and RF-4C reconnaissance aircraft, using their infra-red sensors and side-looking radars (SLAR). The strike force included forward air controllers (FACs) flying Cessna O-1 and Douglas A-1E aircraft, aided by Royal Laotian AF pilots in their North American T-28s. They got their assignments from an airborne command and control aircraft, at first a Douglas C-47 and later a Lockheed C-130. The Martin B-57, North American F-100, Republic F-105 and Douglas AC-47 gunships hit the targets. At night, the C-130 flareships orbited the areas, often supported by the Army's Grumman OV-1 Mohawk, equipped with infra-red sensors and SLAR.

During the first month of *Tiger Hound* the USAF flew 51 night sorties out of a total of 384; the other services made a total of 425 combat sorties. On December 11, 1965, the first B-52 strike hit the Mu Gia pass, their first attack of many against the trail network. In the dry winter months, the pace quickened. The B-52s were called in more frequently when concentrations of materiel promised worthwhile targets.

In a good month, the fighter-bombers would account for 200 or more trucks. But there seemed to be an endless stream of ZIL-157s, and the jet fighters could only make a few passes before leaving the target area still full of trucks rolling along. The answer was to get a slower aircraft with more loiter time.

For its solution, the USAF reached back two wars and came up with the Douglas A-26 Invader, brought up-to-date in a modification program. In June 1966, just after the start of the monsoon season, the "new" weapon arrived to arm the 609th Air Commando Squadron at "Naked Fanny", the popular name for the Nakhon Phanom Royal Thai Air Force Base. Eight A-26Ks had been resurrected to go to war once again. In Korea, they had performed admirably as night interdictors; in Viet Nam they were to fly the same mission, striking at targets on the trail during the dark hours. Using the radio call sign "Nimrod"—the "... mighty hunter before the Lord"—the A-26Ks combined the capabilities of hunter and killer in a single effective package. They replaced the AC-47 gunships in that phase of the *Tiger Hound* campaign, but structural problems soon grounded the fleet and ended their usefulness on the trail at night.

Taking stock at the end of 1967, the USAF counted 1,718 B-52 sorties in the *Steel Tiger* and *Tiger Hound* campaigns. Against trucks, the most effective killers had been the gunships. The B-57s did somewhat less well. By night, two NC-130Ks with special sensors and a freight hold loaded with bomblet canisters did surprisingly well on their own; they also worked with the A-26s, serving as nighttime FACs. Some strike aircraft pilots even tried using the Army's "Starlight Scope", a night vision-enhancer that had been developed for the M16 rifle.

But all of this effort was stopping the infiltration, and back in the Pentagon, the cost-conscious McNamara was taking another analytical look at the problem.

The Jason Division of the Institute of Defense Analysis, having damned the interdiction effort in a report they issued in mid-1966 (see Chapter 18), suggested as an alternate an electronic anti-infiltration system. It would use electronic sensors to detect the presence and movements of troops and trucks that were crossing the DMZ and the Laotian border. Then, tactical air strikes could be called in to hit specific targets.

The responsibility to develop the system was given to the Defense Communications Planning Group (DCPG) in September 1966, along with the highest authority to get things done. DCPG had top industrial priority and unusual freedom to cut red tape or circumvent routine channels. The USAF named its part of that system Igloo White.

Technology on Test

The building blocks were air-dropped sensors, reacting either acoustically or seismically to the sounds and movements of troops and trucks. Each sensor would transmit its data via an orbiting relay aircraft to a ground station, where computers would analyze the data and present it in displays on CRT (cathode-ray tube) screens. The computers would be able to show the area of activity in terms of coordinates on the trail, and the strike force could be tailored for the mission, which was to cut the enemy lines of communications, and to keep them cut for extended periods of time. That would make it costly and difficult for the enemy to move materiel and men.

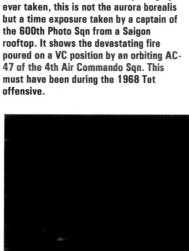

One of the most dramatic war photographs ever taken, this is not the aurora borealis but a time exposure taken by a captain of the 600th Photo Sqn from a Saigon rooftop. It shows the devastating fire poured on a VC position by an orbiting AC-47 of the 4th Air Commando Sqn. This must have been during the 1968 Tet offensive.

The development of ordnance for Igloo White was guided by several intended uses. Bombs would be used to cut the roads. Anti-truck or anti-tank mines would be needed to destroy the moving vehicles on the Trail. Anti-personnel mines would certainly deter, if not prevent, mine clearing operations. Still another type of bomb would be needed to hit trucks that were concentrated by a chokepoint, or parked in a camouflaged area during the day.

Each air-dropped sensor was a self-contained sensing and transmitting system. The acoustic types were modifications of the Navy's basic sonobuoy. Called Spikebuoy and Acoubuoy, both types detected and transmitted acoustic signals only. Spikebuoy, as the name implies, had a long nose spike that emplaced the unit in the ground. Acoubuoy was dropped by parachute and was designed to hang in the trees. The mainstay of the program was the air-delivered seismic intrusion detector (ADSID). It detected a very low level of seismic disturbance and translated it into the presence of a tank, truck, or body of troops. That unit led finally to the development of Acousid, a combined acoustic and seismic detector.

Air delivery of the sensors had to be done with accuracy in order for the system to work at all. The only available aircraft with precision navigational gear were Navy Lockheed OP-2Es, and special squadron VO-67 was formed to do the job under operational control of Seventh AF. Some sensors also were dropped by A-1Es and CH-3 helicopters, both able to make relatively slow runs and accurate drops on the trail. But the drops still had to be referred to map coordinates, and to be coordinated with local FACs.

In June, 1968, a single squadron of F-4Ds with special modifications, including Loran navigational equipment, took over the sensor drops. The Phantoms carried the sensors in various mixes, but generally 16 in each SUU-42/A pod dispenser hung on the outboard wing stations. Typical delivery speed was 300 to 350 knots.

As it turned out, the Loran system was not that accurate. But for nighttime and all-weather placing of the sensors there was no alternate.

On the ground 100 miles away in Laos, Task Force Alpha, a special USAF unit established for Igloo White, had built its Infiltration Surveillance Center (ISC). It was a complex, computerized ground station that received, processed, displayed and transmitted the data and its analysis. Between the sensors on the Trail and the ISC was an orbiting relay aircraft, a dedicated Lockheed EC-121R; it was necessary because the sensor transmissions propagated along lines-of-sight and the ISC was, obviously, out of sight of the Trail. The EC-121R also had the equipment necessary to assess the sensor information, as a backup to the ISC. There was a further backup, the Deployable Automatic Relay Terminal (DART), which had no computers, but enough displays of sensor output to enable an experienced operator to make a real-time evaluation of the situation and to act on that assessment.

Because of the possibility that the EC-121R could become a sitting duck in the event the NVAF really decided to go get it, there was a backup aircraft program, designated Pave Eagle. That program developed a stock Beech Debonair into a piloted or droned relay aircraft with a more powerful engine and increased wingspan. It was also dedicated to relay Igloo White communications, it was more economical to operate than the big four-engined Lockheed, and it could operate as a drone in a high-risk area.

Special Weapons for the Trail

Several other special systems were developed, deployed and evaluated in combat on the Trail. One of these was the Martin B-57G, planned as a self-contained night attack aircraft for solo missions, detecting and destroying targets in total darkness. The standard Martin B-57 airframe was modified by the addition of several sensors, including a forward-looking radar with a moving-target indicator sensitive enough to track slow-moving trucks ten miles off; a low-level-light television (LLLTV) system; a forward-looking infra-red (FLIR) detector; and a laser range-finder. In its belly the B-57G carried a 20-mm. gun turret.

About a dozen of these planes were built; one was lost during factory tests, and a second was shot down in Laos in December 1970, soon after the squadron had become operational. The combat evaluation showed that the planes killed only 2.3 trucks on each sortie, a figure only about one-quarter as good as the gunship kill rate.

Another surprising weapon developed for night war on the Trail was a pair of modified Fairchild C-123 transports. Designated NC-123K, these two planes were equipped with a group of special sensors, including night-vision types, and their bellies were modified to carry dispensers for anti-personnel mines. The usual short nose of the standard aircraft was lengthened by a radome, probably housing a forward-looking radar for nighttime trail navigation. Both planes were equipped with auxiliary wing tanks on short pylons and two auxiliary jet engines on longer pylons just outboard of the two piston engines that were the main powerplant. Standard night camouflage finish was used.

Most of the ordnance used with the Igloo White system was wide-area, rather than precision, type. There were too many variables in the system to result in a small CEP. Typical dive-bombing CEP values were around 400 feet, which is a large miss distance for a small target like a truck. Consequently, wide-area munitions and fragmentation bombs were the bulk of the ordnance dropped on the Trail. Among the specific weapons were these:

• **BLU-31 land mine**, a 750-lb. blunt-nosed weapon designed to penetrate the ground for only a short distance. Its fuze was capable of detecting movement of heavy targets such as tanks.

• **BLU-52 riot control gas bomb**, a standard napalm bomb case filled instead with 270 pounds of either CS-1 or CS-2 riot-control agent. The weapon produces nausea, choking and copious weeping; CS-1 effects last three to five days in an area; CS-2, up to 45 days.

• **CBU-24 fragmentation anti-truck munition**, a com-

The basic operating technique of the gunship was to orbit round a ground target at night, firing at it from all points of the compass. The ultimate gunship was the AC-130 version of the C-130 Hercules. Here one fires its 20-mm. "Gatling guns" at dusk. The aircraft was assigned to the 919th Special Operations Group, AFRes.

bination of the BLU-26/B bomblet and the SUU-30/B clamshell dispenser. It was one of the most effective, and therefore most widely use, munitions against trucks. Its fragments perforated fuel tanks, tires, radiators and drivers equally well.

• **CBU-28 anti-personnel mine,** called Dragontooth. These were carried in canisters and dropped from a dispenser.

• **CBU-33 anti-vehicular land mine** which was designed to destroy tanks. It weighed about 20 pounds. Only about 600 were built; they saw minimum use in the theater because of the limited use of armor by the NVA.

• **CBU-34 wide-area anti-personnel mine** (WAAPM), using a dispenser and canisters containing the bomblets.

• **CBU-42 WAAPM munition** developed by the DCPG specifically for the conditions of the Trail. It had a

longer life than the -34 before it destroyed itself in a time-fused explosion.

• **CBU-49 fragmentation anti-truck munition,** the same basic weapon as the CBU-24 except that the -49 had a random-delay time fuse.

• **EOGB (Electro-Optical Guided Bomb),** a standard 2,000-pound general purpose bomb equipped with an electro-optical guidance head. It was a self-contained weapon, not needing other aircraft to illuminate the target as in the case of the laser-guided bomb. However, it did need daylight with good visual conditions, and a degree of contrast between the target and its background, something not always attainable.

• **Gravel anti-personnel mine,** basically an area-denial munition. It was strewn from an SUU-41 dispenser.

• **LGB (Laser-Guided Bomb),** a 2,000-lb. GP bomb with an attached laser guidance head and oversized

Interdiction in S.E. Asia

Of necessity, the primary roles of the U.S. Air Force have always been the defence of the United States and the deterrence of aggression by a demonstrated capability of strategic retaliation—if necessary, with nuclear weapons. But almost all the fighting the Air Force has actually had to do has been of a totally different nature, centred on local attacks on surface targets associated with distant land warfare. Interdiction is the attack on surface targets well behind the battle zone, and demands clever sensors to find the targets and precision missiles to hit them. At the start of the Korean war the USAF had nothing suitable, and it still had nothing in the early days of the Viet-Nam conflict. Much had to be done, and quickly.

1. An unusually visible section of the Mu Gia Pass showing 26 enemy trucks travelling south.

2. An OP-2E delivering Igloo White sensors.

3. Navy P-2 Neptunes rebuilt as OP-2Es were essential components of Igloo White.

4. Signals from Igloo White sensors were collected by EC-121R Warning Stars.

5. Two A-1H single seaters escorting an HH-53 "Super Jolly Green" on a rescue mission.

6. Napalm being used on suspected but unseen targets.

7. A helicopter landing site created by 15,000-lb bombs pushed out of C-130s.

8. The Cessna A-37B Dragonfly, a useful attack twin jet derived from the Air Force's standard primary trainer.

9. An AC-119K Shadow gunship developed from the Flying Boxcar.

10. Night mission for an AC-26K Invader — a rebuilt B-26 of World War 2 design.

11. A multi-seat A-1E Skyraider delivering ordnance.

TRUCKS - MU GIA PASS AREA
9 FEBRUARY 1967

fins to counter the destabilizing effect of the head. CEP was about 30 feet with this precision weapon.

- **M-36 incendiary cluster** of 182 M-126 incendiary bombs developed for World War 2. The cluster, weighing about 800 pounds, was carried externally on the A-1 and the A-26, internally on the B-57. It was very effective against trucks.
- **Mk-36 destructor,** a retarded GP bomb with a special fuse that sensed the seismic disturbance caused by a moving target.
- **Pave Pat I fuel-air explosive munition,** built into a commercial propane tank. Only 52 were built, and they were dropped from A-1Es during the autumn of 1968 in a combat evaluation that showed them to be rather unsuccessful.
- **Pave Pat II fuel-air explosive bomb** weighing 2,500 pounds, and designed for highspeed aircraft. Three could be carried on a Phantom.

Commando Hunt Campaign

After all bombing north of the DMZ had been halted on order of the Johnson Administration effective November 1, 1968, the North stepped up its infiltration of the South and soon the Trail was carrying more traffic than ever. Since there was no proscription against hitting that region, a new air campaign, *Commando Hunt*, began with the old objective: stopping the flow of supplies down the Trail. As a secondary objective, the campaign would further test the Igloo White system.

Strikes for the latter purpose were designated *Commando Bolt*, and they differed in their pattern from the others. In the ISC an assessment officer monitored the activation of the sensors, looking for some recognizable pattern that was characteristic of the movement of troops, trucks or tanks. He would then call up from the

computer a sketch of the particular section of the Trail where the sensors were being activated, and superimpose a display of the target movement on that sketch. When the target had been located and identified, a call was made to the Tactical Air Control Center (TACC), the strike dispatching unit. They would call on the necessary number of Loran-equipped F-4Ds and transmit the coordinates of the target. The pilots entered those coordinates into the aircraft computer. The target data transmitted to the F-4D included the estimated time of arrival (ETA) at the desired mean point of impact (DMPI). The computer continued to monitor the sensor broadcasts and to calculate the position of the moving target, extrapolating continuously to estimate the DMPI and the ETA over it.

The pilots followed the course indication from the Loran equipment, and the ordnance was dropped automatically when the computer had the bomb ballistics, the aircraft flight path and motion, and the truck movement coordinated to come together at the impact point. And, just in case the precision was not as advertised—and it wasn't, initially—the F-4Ds were loaded with either fragmentation bombs or other wide-area munitions.

Laser-guided bombs were used on *Commando Bolt* strikes beginning in 1968. An AC-130 gunship located and designated the target with a laser, while two F-4s dropped their bombs into the capture area of the designator. It was a tricky procedure and called for some very exacting coordination between the AC-130 and the F-4s.

Later, a handful of F-4s was equipped with laser designators, so that they could illuminate the target themselves after the gunship had located it. As the last step in the development of that weapon system, some FAC OV-10s were fitted with the Pave Nail system, enabling them to designate the targets with a laser, finally freeing the AC-130s for their primary job of truck-killing.

NVA anti-aircraft was heavy and often accurate at night. When it opened up, either an AC-130 or an OV-10 would locate it with infra-red detection and call in an F-4 with a laser-directed bomb. Generally one was enough.

Gunships also were called in for these kills, although they were not considered as part of the *Commando Bolt* strikes because they did not have the necessary on-board equipment. But what they did have on board turned out to be a much more effective killer than almost anything the *Commando Bolt* strikes were able to bring to bear.

Development of the Gunships

Perhaps the most significant, and unquestionably the most effective, weapon to come out of the nighttime war on the Trail was the gunship. It reached its wartime zenith in the AC-130E, a multi-sensor, multi-gunned potent package. These gunships had disadvantages as well; they could only be used against targets that were lightly defended against air attack. The big, slow-moving planes flying on a fixed and predictable orbit were easy targets for enemy fire. But at night, on the Trail, against rifles, machine guns and an occasional anti-aircraft battery shooting in the blind, they were powerful truck-killers and traffic-stoppers.

The concept is based on precise pilotage around a circular orbit whose radius of turn and angle of bank are predetermined. On-board computers take the flight path into account, and calculate impact points for the various weapons, knowing their ballistic characteristics. The armament consists of a mix of automatic weapons from 7.62-mm. to 105-mm., and they are fired from the left side of the aircraft by the pilot, who uses a special gunsight. He needs a backup crew of gun

Lockheed AC-130A

The gunships, converted cargo aircraft that were loaded with batteries of automatic cannon, became the most effective truck-killers on the Ho Chi Minh trail during the dry seasons in Southeast Asia. The pilots flew them in precise left-hand circular orbits, sighting their targets through an electro-optical system that displayed firing information gathered and reduced from the various on-board sensors. The pilots triggered the guns; the rest of the crew loaded them, or operated the sensor systems. This Lockheed AC-130A gunship was converted from a standard and elderly Lockheed C-130A-LM, serial number 55-0046. The "O" prefix to the serial number indicates an aircraft more than 10 years old. Early model gunships carried 4 x 7.62-mm miniguns and 4 x 20-mm Vulcan M61 automatic cannon. Their sensors included night observation devices and forward-looking infra-red (FLIR) systems. Updated models contained paired 7.62-mm, 20-mm and 40-mm cannon, FLIR, low-level light television, a laser target designator, a radar tracking sensor, and "Black Crow", a special system for detecting operating ignition systems of trucks.

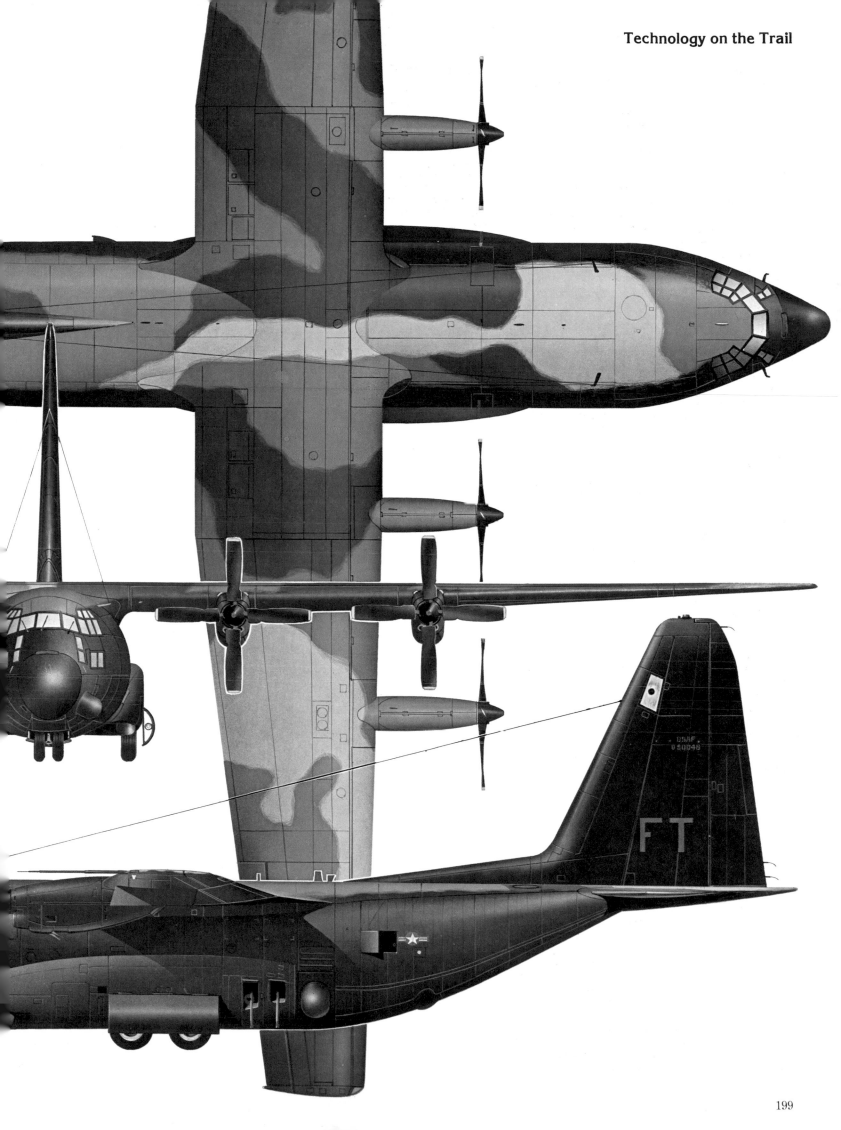

A splendid picture of an A-1H setting out with full ordnance on a rescue support mission on 1 April 1970. The photographer's name is the same as that of the greatest pilot in the history of U.S. airpower: Lt James Doolittle.

loaders, fire control officers, navigators, a flight engineer, and co-pilot to make the whole system work.

First of the line was the venerable Douglas AC-47 in yet another role. Formally called Dragonship or Gunship One, the AC-47s were informally called "Puff, the Magic Dragon" or, most often, "Spooky", their radio call sign. They became operational in Southeast Asia in 1964, and were turned over to the VNAF five years later when updated gunships became available.

The next, Gunship Two, was the Lockheed AC-130A, an early model with four 7.62-mm. miniguns and four 20-mm. M61 Vulcan automatic cannon. It had night observation devices (NOD) and forward-looking infra-red (FLIR) detectors, and was designed to work against trucks. The first of them began operations against the Trail targets during the 1969-1970 dry season.

Third in the series was the Fairchild AC-119 "Shadow", made in two different models. The AC-119G was intended primarily for close support of friendly forces in South Viet Nam. It was armed with four 7.62-mm. miniguns and had NOD. The AC-119K was intended for interdiction missions, primarily against vehicles along the Trail. It was modified by the addition of a pair of jet pods containing J85 engines. Its armament was four miniguns plus a pair of 20-mm. M61 cannon. Its sensors included FLIR. Twenty-six of each model were modified for the Gunship Three program.

The AC-130 program produced two different end products for combat in Southeast Asia:

• **The updated AC-130A,** refitted during summer overhauls in the United States, was built around an armament package of paired 7.62-mm., 20-mm. and 40-mm. automatic cannon, the LLLTV and FLIR sensors, a laser target designator, a radar tracking sensor, and Black Crow, a new sensor that detected operating truck ignition systems.

• **The AC-130E Spectre,** which featured greater survivability and to that end had additional armor protection for the crew stations. It had an increased loiter time at the target, and a heavier punch. Its gun battery included paired miniguns and Vulcans, a single 40-mm. automatic cannon, and a single 105-mm. howitzer in a trainable mount.

On a typical mission, the radar was used as the first detection system, because it had a longer useful range than any other sensor. The LLLTV or FLIR or both picked up the details of the target. Black Crow was very effective when the trucks were running; a truck recently shut down still radiated in the infra-red range and could be detected by the FLIR.

Surprise was important in using the gunships, primarily because of their vulnerability to ground fire. If they could get off a first strike, there was not likely to be enough of the enemy target left to fire back. Visualize a football field; on a single pass overhead, one AC-130E could put a bullet into every square foot of that field. It was an absolutely devastating weapon in its milieu.

During the 1969-1970 dry season, which ran from November through April, the toll on the Trail was 5,950 trucks destroyed, according to post-combat reports and reconnaissance. One year later, the cost to the North had more than doubled; 14,000 trucks were ruined during the 1970-1971 dry season. Toward the end of the latter time period, the gunships were in full cry, with advanced sensors, heavy artillery, and finely honed tactics. By then, they were accounting for between 75 and 80 percent of the kills of trucks on the Trail.

Linebacker ends the War

The frustration and futility of the war in Southeast Asia were summarized most succinctly in a pair of 1968 official communications. The first was a wrap-up cable from Adm. U. S. Grant Sharp, CINCPAC, to the Joint Chiefs of Staff, sent January 1, 1968. It included, among other comments, the following:

From January through 15 December 1967, 122,960 attack sorties were flown in Rolling Thunder route packages I through V and in Laos ... Air attacks throughout North Vietnam and Laos destroyed or damaged 5,261 motor vehicles, 2,475 railroad rolling stock ... the enemy has been able to replace or rehabilitate many of the items damaged or destroyed, and transport inventories are roughly at the same level they were at the beginning of the year ... Economic losses to North Vietnam amounted to more than $130 million dollars in 1967 ...

Simple arithmetic shows that the average dollar damage per sortie was $1,057. For comparison, the laser head for a guided bomb cost $4,000; an EOGB guidance head cost $16,000. A typical strike sortie— one flight north by one airplane—cost $8,400 in direct operational costs, not including the weapons or the value of the pilot's life or time.

The conclusion was all too plain. It was costing many dollars to inflict a single dollar's worth of damage on the enemy. And that was noted in a paper written by Dr. Alain C. Enthoven, who headed the Office of Systems Analysis in the Pentagon.

Until late in the SE Asia involvement all B-52 missions against North Viet-Nam were flown from distant Guam, which made each trip an exhausting and expensive flight averaging nine hours. The tonnage of bombs delivered from the runway at Andersen AFB exceeded that delivered against Japan in World War 2. This picture of the B-52G flight line at Andersen was taken in August 1972. It is still occupied by B-52s and tankers on training missions.

War in Southeast Asia

By many standards the MiG-17, most numerous of the NVAF warplanes met by U.S. forces, was obsolescent in the late 1960s. In addition, many of the pilots were clearly inexperienced, and were seldom aggressive. But the combat manoeuvrability of the early MiG was better than that of almost all the more modern U.S. types, and a further handicap was the self-imposed list of restrictions on air-to-air engagements by U.S. aircraft. Here two MiG-17Fs are seen in a revetment by a USAF recon camera.

The pattern of an SA-2 "Guideline" SAM (surface-to-air missile) site was absolutely distinctive, as were the associated tracking and guidance radars. This SA-2 site, with the usual six launcher emplacements, was photographed 25 miles northwest of Hanoi on 25 November 1966 by a RF-101C.

Our strategy of attrition has not worked. Adding 206,000 more U. S. men to a force of 525,000, gaining only 27 additional maneuver battalions and 270 tactical fighters at an added cost to the U. S. of $10 billion per year raises the question of who is making it costly for whom . . .

We know that despite a massive influx of 500,000 U. S. troops, 1.2 million tons of bombs a year, 400,000 attack sorties per year, 200,000 enemy KIA (Killed in action) in three years, 20,000 U. S. KIA, etc., our control of the countryside and the defense of the urban areas is now essentially at pre-August 1965 levels. We have achieved stalemate at a high commitment. A new strategy must be sought.

Perhaps part of that pessimism was a reaction to the Tet offensive, which still provides some of the most bitter criticism of media coverage heard from military officers. Tet, while certainly no great victory, was in no military sense a defeat, according to them, and yet the reporting made it appear that the offensive was a major beating for the South Vietnamese and their Allies.

But for whatever reason, the beginning of 1968 was the time when the adherents of escalation and de-escalation first began open confrontation over policies in Southeast Asia. It marked President Johnson's decisions to stop the bombing north of the 20th parallel and to withdraw from the 1968 Presidential election campaign. Then later in the year all bombing north of the DMZ was halted, again on Johnson's orders. The man who had urged Navy pilots to ". . . bring back that coonskin and nail it to the wall!" had changed both his tone and his tune.

The inauguration of Richard M. Nixon as President brought about a stated change in policy. It was important that South Viet-Nam take over the responsibility for its own defense, said Nixon, and he promised to bring U. S. troops home as the Vietnamese began to take over the military burden.

Within two months, Nixon had sent B-52 strikes against Cambodia in an open violation of the borders of a neutral country, had directed that it be kept secret, and had set out on a long road of deception that led inexorably to his own downfall. The complicity of the USAF in hiding the location of the strikes did not reflect the ideals of that, or any military, service.

Further, since false reports were filed on the B-52 raids, some officers were quite concerned that their own deeds were actionable, even though they acted under orders. Article 107 of the Military Code of Justice states that any serviceman " . . . who, with intent to deceive, signs any false record, return,

regulation, order or other official document, knowing the same to be false . . . shall be punished as a court martial may direct." Yet the post-strike reports of the Cambodian raids officially showed that the targets were in South Viet-Nam.

At about the same time, since it was obvious that the military might of South Viet-Nam was something less than advertised, the USAF continued to maintain some pressure on the North in attacks that were euphemistically called "protective reaction" strikes. That action followed the apparent breakdown of an understanding reached between North Vietnamese and American negotiators in Paris, which had led to the bombing halt of November 1968. The understanding permitted reconnaissance missions over the North, according to the Americans. But there is always somebody who doesn't get the word, and the North Vietnamese occasionally fired on one of the reconnaissance runs. By February 1970 they had done it once too often, and Nixon authorized the "protective reaction" strikes to hit back at those doing the shooting. Later, they were changed to "reinforced protective reaction" strikes, and were directed broadly against the whole NVN defense system.

The magnitude of the latter strikes can be seen in one of them, a minor air campaign that lasted from May 1, 1970, through May 4. Almost 500 sorties were flown by USAF and USN planes against SAM and anti-aircraft artillery sites north of the DMZ, specifically at two passes on the Ho Chi Minh trail.

The brilliantly conceived and executed raid on the Son Tay prison compound took place November 21, and even though its primary purpose failed, it stands as a classic among rescue operations. On the same day, a heavy retaliation strike was flown to avenge the loss of

a single RF-4C. About 200 USAF and USN aircraft struck targets along the trail, doing heavy damage without suffering any loss.

Operation *Louisville Slugger*, named after a widely used American baseball bat, hit SAM sites in the Ban Karai pass during February 1971. The USAF and USN joined forces for Operation *Fracture Cross Alpha* against SAM sites on March 20 and 21.

The first blind-bombing attack using Loran was on September 21 against POL storage areas that were south of Dong Hoi, a few minutes north of the DMZ. The 196 aircraft destroyed about 350,000 gallons of fuel.

By late in the year, the NVAF had strengthened its inventory of MiG-21s and was coming up to fight more often and more aggressively. Working in an advantageous environment, controlled by ground radars and operating from bases that were still withheld as potential USAF targets, the MiGs managed to inflict real damage on both Air Force and Navy flights. The air combat odds that had favored the Americans by almost two and one-half now dropped closer to even.

Back came the EC-121D College Eye aircraft to take up their positions to warn of MiG intercepts in the making. And the USAF, trying once more to be allowed to attack the NVAF bases, finally got authorization.

They struck November 7 and 8, pounding the runways and installations of Dong Hoi, Quan Lang, and Vinh. With those bases essentially impotent, heavy strikes were mounted against targets south of the 20th parallel that had been in the defense area of those three fields. During the four-day period between December 26 and 30, the Americans dispatched more than 1,000 attack sorties.

"Do you have smart bombs?" someone asked an F-111 pilot; he replied "No, but we have smart airplanes". On its first deployment to Takhli RTAFB in 1968 the clever swing-winger suffered from maddening internal troubles, but in September 1972 a larger force did more than any other in the history of airpower to prove that blind first-pass attacks—coming down among the mountain valleys at 500 knots in thick cloud—can be devastating. Here an aircraft of the 474th TFW lands with pylons empty at Udorn RTAFB during the 1972 deployment.

The Underrated Aardvark

The F-4 Phantom was the workhorse of the war in Southeast Asia, and got most of the attention. But one unsung operational hero was the "Aardvark", as the General Dynamics F-111 models were generally known, and perhaps here is an appropriate place to pay tribute to the much-maligned aircraft.

In the spring of 1967, a test evaluation called Combat Bullseye I proved that the F-111 bombing systems were excellent, and that the early deployment of the plane to Southeast Asia would be desirable. The F-111A, although quite suitable for such tests and evaluation, was far from a combat-ready fighting machine. A modification program called Harvest Reaper began in June to make the plane suitable for war, to fix the existing problems, and to add more avionics, specifically ECM gear. That done, a test detachment of F-111As began the Combat Trident program which included 500 bombing sorties and logged 2,000 flying hours by March 6, 1968. Nine days later the Aardvark was headed for the wars.

The Combat Lancer deployment sent six F-111As as Detachment 1, 428th TFS, 474th TFW, from Nellis AFB to Thailand. They left March 15, arrived March 17, and by the end of the month had flown 55 missions against targets in North Viet-Nam. Two of the planes and their crews had been lost. Two replacements arrived, but when a third F-111A was lost April 22, the planes were removed from combat and saw little action until they were returned to the United States in November, ending the Combat Lancer deployment and combat evaluation.

After a detailed investigation of the probable causes of the accidents, the F-111s were run through a modification program to fix the mechanical problems that had been blamed for the losses. They redeployed to Southeast Asia on September 27, 1972, to become part of the *Linebacker* operation.

Within 33 hours after they left Nellis AFB, they were in combat 55 miles northwest of Hanoi, an impressive performance on any deployment effort. The F-111As continued to fight the air war with the 429th and 430th TFS, 474th TFW, based at Takhli, Thailand. They were the major factor in night inter- diction strikes; they attacked targets in Laos in the middle of the monsoon season, and struck the North in weather that grounded other aircraft. Four of them could carry the bomb load of 20 Phantoms, so that a two-plane element could be a strike force. And they went in alone; no Iron Hand or chaff flights preceded them, no EC-121s vectored them, and no tankers refueled them.

They had problems with the terrain-following and attack radar sets, and with the internal navigation and weapons release systems. Brakes, wheels and landing gear struts were in critical supply. The engine inlets caused powerplant problems occasionally.

The primary use made of the Aardvark was to fly an all-weather mission into a high-threat area. They attacked at low level, using their terrain-following radars, and dropped accurately. They also flew some support sorties for the B-52 raids, going in just ahead of the main force to suppress the defenses and kill the SAM sites.

Between October, 1972, and March, 1973, they flew almost 4,000 combat sorties with one of the lowest loss rates—0.15 percent—ever to show in air combat statistics. Six aircraft were lost during the period, a relatively high absolute loss in terms of the total F-111A force. But the sortie loss rate was extremely low and proved, statistically, what the F-111 pilots had been saying right along it: was—and is—one Hell of a fine airplane.

General Dynamics F-111A

The key to the performance of this remarkable aircraft is its variable-sweep wing. It was the world's first operational aircraft with this feature, which gives the F-111 the ability to takeoff, climb and cruise efficiently, and to make terrain-hugging dashes at high subsonic speed in an efficient, and relatively comfortable, manner. Born of political decisions, fostered in the environment of a stubborn and wrong-headed civilian bureaucracy, the F-111 somehow weathered its massive initial problems and criticisms to become a versatile, capable fighter-bomber, and the best all-weather interdiction aircraft available. The unnamed 67-064 is an F-111A-CF from the 474th Tactical Fighter Wing, Nellis AFB, Nevada. That wing's 428th Tactical Fighter Squadron detached six of its aircraft for a combat trial in the spring of 1968. Under the code name of Combat Lancer, the planes deployed to Takhli Royal Thai Air Base, and went into action almost immediately. After initial misfortune, and a four-year layoff, a second detachment in Southeast Asia finally proved the great worth of this controversial warplane.

Linebacker Operations Begin

During the night of March 29/30, heavy and mechanized North Vietnamese units drove into South Viet Nam, moving south across the DMZ and east from Laos simultaneously in a powerful offensive. The RVNA fell back in disarray, and the defenses were left almost entirely to the air strength of the RVNAF and the Americans. It became a fierce fight, drawing on all available aircraft in the theater plus some deployed from other USAF command areas.

On May 8, Nixon called a halt to the peace negotiations then underway in Paris, and authorized the Air Force to proceed with Operation *Linebacker*. Strikes were permitted again above the 20th parallel, and against a mix of new and old targets. Haiphong harbor and other northern ports were to be mined, and a naval blockade was established. The war had entered on a new phase, and there were developments in its technology that were to make things somewhat easier for the tactical strike forces headed north.

One of these was the maturing of the laser-directed and electro-optical guided bombs. These precision guided munitions (PGM) were extremely effective, and the kill probability of these "smart" bombs became almost unity, instead of the low fractional values that had characterized the earlier iron "dumb" bombs.

Improvements in electronic warfare aided immeasurably. Better Wild Weasel equipment in newer aircraft was available, and the countermeasures pods for fighters and fighter-bombers were more versatile and effective. The EB-66 jammers had been refitted with the latest gear, and some big EC-135s lent their powerful jamming capabilities to shield the strikes north. Chaff corridors were laid down by fast-moving F-4s using new types of dispensers.

The durable Doumer Bridge was targeted again. The first mission against that structure since 1967 was flown on May 10, 1972, by a force made up of 16 F-4s from the 8th TFW, loaded with 2,000-lb. general purpose bombs. Twelve of the planes had laser-guided bombs and the other four had electro-optically guided weapons. Eight more F-4s from the 8th TFW were loaded with chaff, and were to lay down a corridor for the strike force to follow. The 388th TFW sent 15 F-105G Wild Weasel aircraft and four EB-66s for jamming and other electronic warfare. More Phantoms flew MiGCAP.

At 8:00 AM the chaff layers roared off the runway, followed 20 minutes later by the strike force. They flew into defending MiGs, heavy flak and missile fire at the bridge. Pilots reported an estimated 160 missiles fired from the SAM sites along the route, and 41 intercepting MiGs. In spite of that fierce defense, the bombers released from 14,000 feet, dropping 22 LGBs and seven EOGBs. The results were first-class; they got 12 direct hits on the bridge and four probables; 13 other bomb strikes were unobserved due to the heavy defenses and smoke in the target area. But the bridge was out of action, with one span completely destroyed and several badly damaged. No USAF planes were lost.

In a follow-up raid the next day, four Phantoms were dispatched with a covering force to hit the bridge again. One was carrying two M-118 3,000-lb. bombs with laser guidance. The chaff corridor was laid too early and the support aircraft left the scene early, but the strike force continued. The defenders fired missiles, but no MiGs came up to intercept. The F-4s rolled in, dropped, and left. They had launched two M-118 bombs and six standard Mk-84 2,000-lb. iron bombs. They had

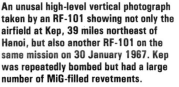

An unusal high-level vertical photograph taken by an RF-101 showing not only the airfield at Kep, 39 miles northeast of Hanoi, but also another RF-101 on the same mission on 30 January 1967. Kep was repeatedly bombed but had a large number of MiG-filled revetments.

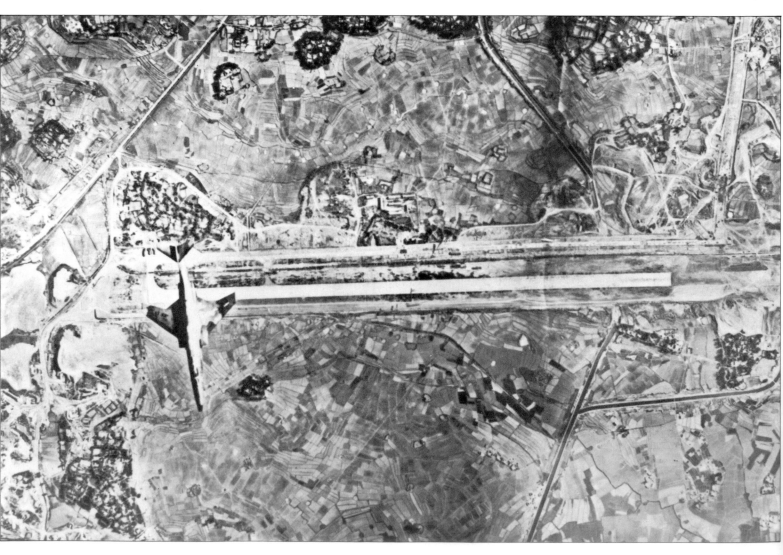

Chief attack types given to the VNAF (air force of South Viet-Nam) were the A-1 and A-37. Here one of the latter is seen on a training sortie near Da Nang in September 1971.

dropped three spans of the bridge into the Red river.

And that, finally, was the end of Paul Doumer's durable bridge.

By the end of June, 1972, the punishment began to tell; the NVA drive had been stopped and control of the ground began to change hands. The RVNA went on the offensive, and Nixon once again proposed a ceasefire and negotiations for a peace agreement. Talks began again in Paris in July.

By October, enough progress had been made to persuade Nixon to call a bombing halt effective October 23. As yet another signal in the long string of signals reaching back into early U. S. involvement in the war, it received the same treatment as the rest. It was ignored, and what was meant to be evidence of good faith on the part of the U. S. was a useless gesture.

The halt was used for continued planning on both sides, and the U. S. evolved an all-out air offensive that would be held in readiness should the North try to back out of the negotiations, or if they resumed their drive to gain control of the South. Some intelligence indicated that the latter was a possibility, and Nixon again authorized air strikes north of the 20th parallel. The air campaign was an extension of *Linebacker*, but different in some respects. Like a Hollywood sequel, it was named *Linebacker II*.

It was the height of the monsoon season, and the weather was true to form: ceilings between 1,000 and 3,000 feet, with a five-mile visibility below the clouds. So the offensive was built around an all-weather force of B-52s, F-111s, F-4s, A-7s, and carrier aircraft, with EB-66s and other elements of the supporting forces. The NVAF MiGs, having limited all-weather performance, were not expected to present much of a threat, and neither were the smaller caliber anti-aircraft weapons which were aimed visually. Missiles were tagged as the primary menace, with radar-directed large-caliber anti-aircraft artillery coming a close second.

The majority of the targets were transportation and supply systems; the remaining 40 percent of the objectives included MiG airfields, SAM sites, communication installations, command and control systems, and urban powerplants.

Specific assignment of targets depended on the capability of the aircraft. The B-52s were tasked to bomb the airfields, storage areas, and the railroad marshalling yards near Hanoi. The F-4s, armed with PGMs, were to strike the Hanoi powerplant, Radio Hanoi, and the rail classification yards. The F-111s

drew the SAM sites, some airfields, and the marshalling yards. Vought A-7Ds were to hit the Yen Bai airfield, and to be led there by Loran-equipped F-4s.

The Buffs Bomb Hanoi and Haiphong

Linebacker II began for the big B-52s at Andersen AFB, Guam, at 2:51 PM local time, December 18, 1972. The first eight-jet bomber began its takeoff run down the two-mile runway, black smoke plumes streaming from its nacelles. It gained speed, lifted free and headed for Hanoi. Behind it, bomber after bomber moved to the runway, ran up to full power and began its cumbersome acceleration to gain flying speed.

The "Buff" force was a mixed group of B-52D and G models; the former had been modified in the "Big Belly" program to carry 108 x 500-lb. bombs. The G models generally were armed with 27 x 750-lb. bombs.

The crews were given three specific rules of engagement, pertinent only to the B-52s. First, they were to try to avoid the defenses wherever possible; they were known to be formidable. Second, if they had to penetrate defended areas, and it was a foregone conclusion that their targets would surely be defended,

During exercise Dewey Danyon II on 1 February 1971 these C-130s were lined up with engines running waiting to be unloaded at Dong Ha, South Viet-Nam, on airlift support for the Laotian offensive.

Groundcrew of the South Vietnamese air force start the laborious process of uncrating and then assembling a Northrop F-5 light fighter. The later stages of the Viet-Nam war were marked by a phased U.S. withdrawal, supposedly accompanied by a marked "Vietnamization" of operations. This naturally involved the allocation to the South Vietnamese forces of much matériel that would otherwise have gone to the U.S. forces.

Facing page. The KC-135 boom operator's view of a B-52D, with full bomb load, as it takes on fuel. The long round trip from Andersen AFB, Guam, needed heavy inflight-refuelling transfers, but these diminished when B-52s moved to Kadena, Okinawa, and vanished (almost) when missions originated from U-Tapao in Thailand. The B-52G with its much greater internal fuel capacity required few inflight refuellings.

In February and March 1973 a total of 591 Americans were released from captivity in North Viet-Nam after what in many cases had been long periods as POWs. This was one of countless pictures taken during the long-awaited homecoming.

they were to try to confuse, spoof, and degrade those defenses with the on-board electronic countermeasures equipment that the big bombers carried in quantity; in that task, they would be aided by other USAF airplanes with ECM equipment, and by a number of Navy Grumman EA-6B Intruders that had enormous and versatile ECM capabilities. Third, if the defenses weren't fooled, they were to strike them and destroy them.

As the planes from Andersen headed for Viet-Nam, other B-52s based at U-Tapao Royal Thai AFB were being readied for the mission. They took off after a planned interval to join the Andersen force on the trip northward. Tankers dotted the approach routes to the targets, laying well off to refuel the B-52s, and moving in closer to handle the myriad of tactical aircraft that would be headed for Hanoi.

The two forces joined and formed three waves of bombers, Andersen's force in the first and third, sandwiching the U-Tapao B-52s. They came in over Hanoi and dropped their bombs on targets.

Salvos of SAMs blasted up to meet them. One returning pilot was asked how many missiles he had spotted; "Hundreds", he said. Another pilot vividly described the way the missiles looked. "Hold your hand at arm's length, fingers bunched and pointed toward your eyes", he said "Now imagine that your fingertips are little points of light, and each one of those lights is a rocket motor on a missile. Now move your hand toward your face, fast, and spread your fingers. Those damned SAMs look like that going by."

Another pilot said that he could have read by the light of the rocket engine as the missile sped past. His co-pilot, he reported, counted 22 missiles on his side alone, and he himself saw 18.

The bombers went out every day until the Christmas one-day standdown. Eleven B-52s had been lost by then, six on a single black day, December 20. When *Linebacker II* began again the day after Christmas, the 24-hour lull had been used to good effect, and a large and strong force took off.

The NVA missile inventory had been estimated at a total of about 1,000, and about 100 were being fired each day at the attacking fleets. At that rate, the defenders could be expected to run out of missiles in about ten days, assuming that interdiction was keeping them from getting any more to the SAM sites. Apparently it did, because for the last two days the B-52s cruised over the targets and were not once struck by enemy fire.

Damage assessment to the targets was done by reference to low-level reconnaissance photography done by Strategic Air Command's drones. They operated below the cloud cover and, being small and speedy, were very difficult to detect and bring down. Their photos were processed in Southeast Asia and rushed to the Joint Chiefs in Washington by a special daily KC-135 courier flight. Within 24 hours after the pictures had been printed from the negatives, they were being used for target damage assessment and planning the next strikes.

Civilian casualties were very low, in spite of the potential for mass killings. By North Vietnamese estimates, between 1,300 and 1,600 civilians were killed, a remarkably low figure and one that, given the source, is more likely to be larger than smaller than the actual number.

The attack force, including SAC's B-52s, destroyed or damaged more than 1,600 military structures, and 373 pieces of railroad rolling stock. About three million gallons of POL stores had been torched or blown into vapor. More than 500 line cuts slowed rail traffic from a torrent to a trickle, and ten airfields were hit.

The B-52s flew 729 sorties, the tactical aircraft about 1,000. Fifteeen B-52s were lost, and eleven tactical aircraft. The North Vietnamese lost eight planes, two of them to B-52 tail gunners.

The results of *Linebacker II* never have officially been linked to the almost immediate resumption of the peace negotiations, but it is impossible to accept that the air campaign did not have that final effect. Whether or not the administration wanted to admit it, the pounding that the North took during those eleven days had to be a factor in their decision to go back to negotiations in Paris.

Linebacker II was the last mighty strike of a terrible war. The U. S. announced a halt to all offensive actions against the Hanoi government on January 15, 1973, and on January 23, a cease-fire was signed to become effective on January 28. One of its most important provisions was for the return of American prisoners of war.

More than 6.3 million tons of bombs fell on Viet-Nam, Laos and Cambodia during the war years from 1964 to early 1973. A little more than one-third of that amount helped defeat the Third Reich and the Japanese Empire during World War 2.

And yet, for all the outward appearance of massive strikes and continued bomber offensives, the air was never run the way the airmen wanted it to be handled. One senior air officer said later, "The way the strikes were flown, they were of no importance. They accomplished virtually nothing. It was not worth the effort."

He felt that a *Linebacker II* operation earlier in the war might have stopped the fighting right then. But was the USAF ready for such an intensive operation any earlier? Would the SAMs, the deadly and concentrated anti-aircraft, and the MiGs have made the cost too high in 1966 or 1967? Could a strategic bombing campaign ever have succeeded against the North, or would it simply have driven the Communists underground, to bide their time and emerge months, years, even decades later to achieve their stated goals?

It was seen as a war of attrition, but the U. S. achieved only a stalemate. By any measurable terms, the United States came out of that war in far worse shape than when it had entered it, and that is one of the definitions of a defeat. The costs of that conflict, in lives, careers, broken homes, inflation and taxes, have yet to be even estimated. The effect of the war is seen daily, in almost every home in America, and felt daily by everyone.

It has been a cruel lesson in fighting the wrong war in the wrong place at the wrong time, to borrow a phrase from an old soldier. May the sound of those drums never be heard again.

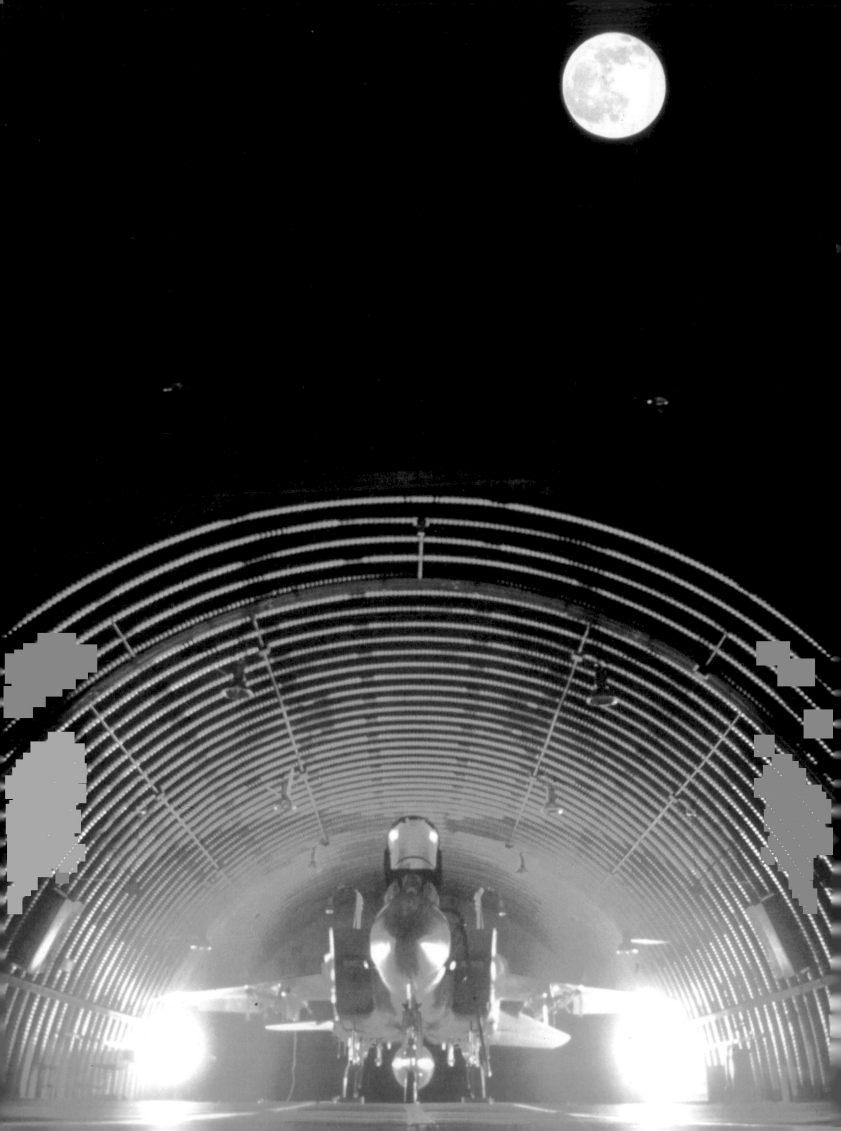

The USAF enters the Eighties

The United States Air Force, at the beginning of a decade of potential peril, faces a difficult and demanding future. The bulk of its aircraft and missiles are between ten and 20 years old. Their quality, once the pride of the USAF, has been matched and frequently exceeded by their Soviet counterparts. Their numbers, once the greatest air force in the world, have long since been surpassed by a USSR build-up of weapons, munitions and personnel on a scale never before seen, and seldom even contemplated, by Americans.

The basic problem confronting the USAF is to maintain its ability to deter nuclear war and to win a tactical war, when badly outnumbered and when matched in the qualitative aspects of weaponry. And that task, as anyone will appreciate, is not an easy one.

For that reason, the USAF is arguing for a number of new programs to increase its effectiveness as a fighting force. There is no likely way that its numbers ever can match the Russian forces. But the current

concept is that technology and the improvements in weapons that result from its application will serve as "force multipliers" that will enable the USAF to outfight, outlast, and beat its Soviet opposition.

When World War II ended, the USAAF had more than 2.2 million personnel in its ranks, and operated more than 50,000 aircraft. At the peak of its activities in the war in Southeast Asia, its aircraft numbered 15,327, and they were operated, maintained and supported by a total of 904,759 officers and airmen.

At the start of 1981, the USAF will field a total of about 9,263 aircraft, both in the active units and the combined forces of the Air Force Reserve and the Air National Guard. Total active-duty personnel will be about 564,000, with an additional 242,000 available in the Guard and the Reserves. These people and assets will occupy 100 active operational bases, 70 Air National Guard bases, and 48 AF Stations in the United States, plus 40 major bases overseas. Additionally, the Air

Cunning work with timing and a telephoto lens captures the Moon above a hardened aircraft shelter housing an F-15A Eagle on round-the-clock alert at Bitburg AB, West Germany. Shelters protect aircraft against many types of aerial attack.

The Soviet Union's MiG design beureau has been responsible for the two biggest shocks ever inflicted on the U.S. military machine by a foreign military aircraft. The first was the MiG-15 in 1951. The second was the MiG-25, known to Western allies as "Foxbat", first seen in the mid-1960s. Even today this all-weather interceptor version is the world's fastest combat aircraft, and it still holds world records for speed, climb and altitude.

Force has 34 major research and development facilities under its aegis.

The decade of the 1980s will be another time of transition for the Air Force, just as the 1970s were. The USAF came out of the war in Southeast Asia with the certain knowledge that it was not well-equipped to handle the kind of war that conflict had become. In former times, the classical task of the Air Force was to seize and hold air superiority over the battlefield, wrestling it from enemy aircraft. With that air umbrella opened, other aircraft then were relatively free to hammer ground targets in support of advancing troops, to fly interdiction missions, and generally raise havoc among enemy ranks, supply lines and distribution centers.

But the face of modern warfare has modified that basic concept. It still holds true, but from now on the adversary is not the enemy's air fleets. It is his ground-based anti-aircraft defense, a formidable assemblage of a variety of guided missiles and deadly automatic artillery that have, in effect, denied a wide altitude range to any air opposition.

Viet-Nam provided the first look at that collection of anti-aircraft weapons. The North Vietnamese fielded a number of Russian-developed anti-aircraft missiles and artillery weapons, and they did so in numbers that began to cause grave concern to U. S. military planners. The pictures they painted were bleak enough. But then the Yom Kippur War erupted in the Middle East and an over-confident Israeli Air Force was almost beaten in the first three days of that fight, hammered into the ground by batteries of well-sited and well-fought anti-aircraft weapons. It was a rude awakening for the *Heyl Ha'Avir*, and its lessons were not lost on the United States.

Some military thought tended to regard the new emphasis on anti-aircraft as comparable in its long-range effects to the introduction of the machine gun during World War 1. That relatively unsophisticated weapon changed the face of war, and condemned the armies on both sides to long years of slow movements along a line of trenches that hardly varied in its position from one month to the next. It was a profound influence on the concepts of fighting in those days, and it totally obsoleted the cavalry charge, the infantry assault across open ground, and a number of the other traditional aspects of pre-nuclear wars.

The Russian deployment of multiple kinds of anti-aircraft weapons has had a similar chilling effect on air warfare. Assigned to Russian armies as integral anti-aircraft defense, these new missiles and cannon have taken the airspace from about 1,000 feet to 15,000 feet away from any attacker, and made that region a death trap.

Consequently, the USAF began to develop new tactics and new countermeasures to take back the advantage in battle. At first, it attempted to counter that problem in Viet-Nam by flying higher, and above available cloud cover. As was expected, it was more difficult to acquire targets and to deliver the ordnance accurately on them. The alternate was to attack from a very low altitude, under the effective threat. This meant coming down to below 1,000 feet, and often to considerably lower altitudes, on the order of a few hundred feet. This seemingly ideal element for the attacker offered the possibility of terrain masking as one way of concealing the approach to the target, coupled with the possibility that the attacker might be lost in the ground clutter of enemy radars until almost too late to do anything about him. Further, by staying low and fast, an attacker was exposed for an absolute minimum of time to enemy defenses. But flying low is very difficult and very wearing on a pilot who has multiple things to do when he is about to attack a target. His work load is compounded by efforts to find the target while avoiding terrain, smokestacks and radio towers, to say nothing of anti-aircraft artillery and even large numbers of troops with rifles.

Defense suppression, which has long been a tactic associated with air power, became even more important. A whole new concept of electronic warfare grew out of the need to degrade or destroy defenses so that attacking aircraft could have an easier run into the target.

These considerations produced superb tactical air force units during the 1970s, equipped with a number of new and specialized weapons fitted to the specific problems of the potential threats that were envisioned during those years. During the 1970s, the USAF set in motion the wheels that developed and delivered such advanced air weapons as the McDonnell-Douglas F-15 Eagle, the General Dynamics F-16 Fighting Falcon, and the Fairchild Republic A-10 Thunderbolt II. Great advances in the technology of command and control, coupled with detection and early warning capabilities, were built into a single airborne package, the Boeing E-3 Sentry. Highly modified Republic F-105G Wild Weasel aircraft, a single-ship hunter-killer team to seek and destroy enemy missile sites, were replaced by an advanced, more-capable McDonnell-Douglas F-4G. New missiles for ground attack and air-to-air missiles for dogfighting moved from experimental prototypes to production deliveries. Electronic countermeasures were built into the aircraft, or added in pods that could be preprogrammed with a variety of threat profiles. And a tactical jammer, the Grumman-General Dynamics EF-111A, became available to mask an attacker in a bright blob on an enemy radar screen.

And then, with the USAF finally well-equipped to fight the war in Southeast Asia again, the Russians forced another switch in design and development. This time, it grew from the synergistic combination of satellite reconnaissance and multiple, independently targetable re-entry vehicle (MIRV) warheads aboard intercontinental ballistic missiles.

Both the United States and Russia had been operating spy satellites, each monitoring what the other was doing. And during the 1970s, what the Russians were doing sent cold chills down the backs of the U. S. military. They were improving the accuracy of their missiles, and they had increased the number of those missiles that carried MIRV warheads. Knowing the exact location of every USAF missile silo from satellite information, the Russians could target those silos—and therefore a major portion of the American retaliatory force—for an ICBM attack.

Taken during the fly-off evaluation to select the Air Force's future ALCM (air-launched cruise missile) this picture shows a B-52G with a full load of 20 AGM-109 Tomahawks, eight internal and 12 on the wing pylons. In the event the rival AGM-86B was the missile chosen.

Suddenly, the pressure was off the development of tactical air power, and was on the development of new weapons for strategic forces. Thus, the decade of the 1980s will be the decade for the growth and improvement of strategic forces. Tactical air will get what it has been programmed to receive, but it will not be the lucky recipient of lots of new airplanes and missiles to do its job. The funds for those purposes will be spent for a new strategic missile system and for upgrading the abilities of the aging fleet of long-range strategic bombers.

The Decade for SAC

For the near-term future, Strategic Air Command (SAC) will be the dominant force within the USAF. Its mission is to be a part of the deterrent forces, those missile and aircraft strengths that would presumably cause any potential aggressor to think more than twice before attacking the United States. The deterrent force is expected to deter nuclear war; obviously its presence did nothing to deter the limited tactical war in Southeast Asia. SAC operates two types of forces: long-range strategic bombers, and intercontinental ballistic missiles. Those paired elements make up two-thirds of the so-called "triad" of deterrent forces, the other third being the submarine-based, sea-launched ballistic missiles of the U. S. Navy.

SAC flies about 350 Boeing B-52D/G/H Stratofortress bombers plus 65 General Dynamics F-111A supersonic low-level bombers. Supporting these is a fleet of more than 600 Boeing KC-135A tankers, the strategic reconnaissance aircraft like the Lockheed SR-71 and U-2, and some highly specialized reconnaissance aircraft that are modified KC-135s.

The ICBM force includes 1,000 Boeing Minuteman missiles and 54 Martin Marietta Titan II giants whose useful life is being questioned as these words are written because of an explosion in one of the silos.

These are the long-range deliverers of nuclear warheads or bombs, and their mission is deterrence or, failing that, the devastation of an enemy's military — and probably civilian — might. But SAC also has contingency missions. Viet-Nam was one, as was the Korean War or SAC's part in the Cuban confrontation over Khrushchev's missile sites on that island. SAC today is an available force to support NATO or the Western Pacific region with conventional bombing, and to assist the Navy with minelaying.

Most recently, the USAF Aerospace Defense Command was disestablished, and the space surveillance and missile warning operations of that organization were assigned to SAC.

The Command's current organization includes the Eighth and Fifteenth Air Forces, the 1st Strategic Aerospace Division, and the 3rd and 7th Air Divisions.

Tactical Air Command is, curiously enough, not primarily a fighting command. Its major mission is to organize, equip and train its assigned forces, and to maintain combat-ready units that can be moved anywhere in the world on short notice. It's important to realize that a deployed TAC unit, sent to some remote base as part of a war plan, leaves operational control of TAC and becomes part of, say, USAFE.

TAC operates 2,285 aircraft under the Ninth and

Twelfth Air Forces, and also serves as the air component of Atlantic Command and Readiness Command. Further, under ADTAC, it operates the interceptors and radars that go with air defense missions it took over from the Aerospace Defense Command.

TAC was the beneficiary of much of the procurement money spent during the 1970s, and its look as a fighting force has changed remarkably. It entered the decade with the bulk of its aircraft fleet composed of the aging, but still potent, McDonnell-Douglas F-4 Phantom II, plus a variety of special-purpose aircraft. Now it fields the two hottest fighters in the skies, the F-15 and the F-16, and sends its tank-busting A-10s out at low level to "root around".

In 1956 the Air Force selected Camp Cooke, near Lompoc, California, as its chief West Coast site for development and training firings of the planned ICBMs (intercontinental ballistic missiles). Renamed Vandenberg AFB it has for more than 20 years been the only location for 'blue suit' firings of long-range missiles. The main task is training launches of the Minuteman, as seen here.

Developed from the T-37 trainer, the Cessna A-37B Dragonfly serves with a number of Air National Guard squadrons. This example was assigned to the 104th Tac Fighter Sqn, Maryland ANG.

Climbing vertically round a loop, the Northrop T-38A Talon has been a standard USAF trainer for 20 years.

The Boeing E-4 is the AABNCP (advanced airborne national command post), which in time of crisis would have the U.S. President and the Commander of SAC on board able to take decisions at the highest level even after the possible destruction of Washington or other decision-taking machinery. The standard aircraft is the E-4B, with General Electric F103 engines.

Three commands take operational control of TAC units during specific deployments overseas. First of these is the Alaskan Air Command (AAC), tasked to provide an early warning of an air attack against the United States and Canada. AAC also is responsible for supporting U. S. ground troops in the area, and for defending the airspace. It has two squadrons of McDonnell-Douglas F-4E fighters for its mission. They often intercept Russian long-range reconnaissance or electronic intelligence aircraft, and have been photographed flying a close formation with their red-starred bogies.

The second major operational command is Pacific Air Forces (PACAF), the air component of the unified Pacific Command. Its Fifth Air Force, based in Japan and Korea, and Thirteenth Air Force, headquartered in the Philippines, are the leading edge of U. S. air power in the Pacific basin. That vast area, the responsibility of Pacific Command, covers more than half the earth, and extends from the West coast of the United States to the East coast of Africa, and from the Artic to the Antarctic. That surface is more than 100 million square miles; the air space that PACAF patrols is more than one billion cubic miles.

The United States Air Forces in Europe — USAFE — make up the third command that would take operational control of TAC units. The units within USAFE are the American commitment to NATO, and include aircraft in three numbered air forces: The Third, headquartered at RAF Mildenhall; the Sixteenth, at Torrejon Air Base, Spain; and the Seventeenth, at Sembach Air Base, Germany.

USAFE strength in place is about 650 aircraft. Badly outnumbered, in war its forces would have to be rapidly augmented by reinforcements.

Military Airlift Command is, as the name states, the prime mover behind the USAF. It operates more than 1,000 cargo and passenger transports, hauling everything from military personnel on a change of station to heavy artillery and armored vehicles for the Army. In wartime, its fleet would be increased by the nearly 500 transports of the Civil Reserve Air Fleet (CRAF), made available by the commercial airlines of the United States. In peacetime, almost half of MAC's aircrews come from the Air Force Reserve.

Additionally, the Command operates the Aerospace Rescue and Recovery Service and the Air Weather Service. It is well known for its special mission capability, and the ubiquitous Air Force One, with the President aboard, is MAC-operated.

The Air Force Reserve (AFRES) not only supplies aircrews to MAC; its highly skilled airmen train with the regular Air Force as if the two organizations were one. AFRES units fly a major share of SAC's tanker missions, operating the gray KC-135s from bases around the country. They augment TAC with two tactical fighter wings, and take great delight in often besting their active-duty counterparts in the tactical skills employed by fighter pilots. Three numbered air forces comprise AFRES: the Fourth, at McClellan AFB, California; the Tenth, at Bergstrom AFB, Texas; and the Fourteenth, at Dobbins AFB, Georgia. They field more than 450 aircraft.

Another great source of Air Force strength is the Air National Guard. It's a unique organization, under the command of the governors of the individual states, but also subject to call-up by the President, Congress, or the provisions of certain Public Laws. The Guard operates more than 1,500 aircraft of many types, and represents almost one-fifth of the total force of the

USAF. For example, the Guard flies 60 percent of the USAF's interceptors, 57 percent of its reconnaissance aircraft, 42 percent of tactical air support, and 30 percent of the tactical airlift.

Training and Support Forces

Before a pilot ever gets to these organizations, he starts his career in Air Training Command. By almost any measure, ATC is of mammoth proportions. More than a teacher of flying, the Command is responsible for the professional military and specialized education within the Air Force, and for the recruiting program that supplies the USAF with personnel. The Command flies almost 1,500 aircraft, predominantly Cessna T-37s and Northrop T-38s, runs the Air University, trains foreign students in English and the subtleties of flight, and shows aircrews how to survive in deserts and after water landings. In a unique aspect of its job, ATC even has its own readiness force, trained aircrews that could become available to operational units in the event of a crisis.

Four major technically oriented Commands are the supporting strength behind the routine operations and the future developments of the Air Force.

AF Communications Command operates in more than 400 locations around the world, providing the Air Force with its communications network, all of its air traffic control, and all of the standardized and auto-mated data processing. In these days of computerized everything, this is an enormous responsibility, and a critical one for the operations of the Air Force.

Air Force Logistics Command manages support, depot maintenance, major modifications and repairs for USAF aircraft and weapons. Working closely with industry, AFLC moves several thousand planes through its depots and industry plants during any typical year, plus additional thousands of engines, missiles, and specialized equipment. Each of its five Logistics Centers has specific assignments in aircraft, powerplants and weapons for depot maintenance, for example, and will perform all the work on the systems in those categories.

Air Force Systems Command is faced with what might be the most difficult mission in the Air Force: Developing advanced technology for future aircraft and missiles. It is a crystal-ball command, because it must look ahead into a dimly illuminated future and try to discern the shapes in the shadows. Further, AFSC manages the procurement of new weapons for the Air Force, so that most of its annual budget actually is spent with industry for hardware. With what is left it operates centers of technology that investigate, re-search and develop new weapon systems.

Finally, the Electronic Security Command is the specialist in electronic warfare. Its major task is to protect USAF's command, control and communications systems and to find ways to disrupt the enemy's similar systems. The findings go directly to combat commanders who can utilize that knowledge tactically to their own advantage. A routine part of the Command's work load is the monitoring of Air Force communications, checking for possible breaches of security on the obvious premise that, if Command specialists can find them, so could an enemy.

These organizations, together with a whole list of associated supporting elements and services, make up the United States Air Force as it enters the decade of the 1980s. Its future direction was spelled out in some detail in early 1980 by the then-Secretary of the Air

Like the HH-3E above, the Lockheed HC-130P is a specialized model of a familiar type developed for the USAF Aerospace Rescue and Recovery Service. One of its functions is the safe retrieval of capsules and vehicles from space missions.

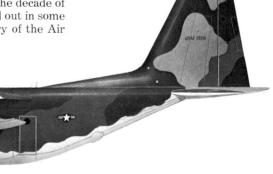

U.S. AIR FORCE

Experience in MAC service showed that the available cube volume in the cargo hold of the C-141 StarLifter was too small for the available payload. Nothing could be done to increase the cross-section, but the fuselage could be lengthened, and this aircraft was the prototype of the stretched C-141B version, which is also distinguished by its universal inflight refuelling installation in the roof behind the flight deck. Adding 23ft 4in to the fuselage of each of 271 aircraft is equivalent to adding an extra 90 aircraft to MAC.

Since the late 1970s the Air Force has been trying out numerous camouflage paint schemes, including some for aircraft of MAC. Here a C-141 shows its new "wrap-around" three-color livery, in a line of aircraft still in the original white tops.

Force, Hans M. Mark. He defined three priorities for the years to come:

- The enhancement of strategic forces, both bomber and missile, to guarantee equivalence with the Russians.

- The enhancement of strategic and tactical airlift for better response to contingencies anywhere in the world.

- The development of doctrine and an organization that will increase Air Force space activities.

But since that list had been described, the world situation had changed. By mid-1980, American eyes were focussed on the Persian Gulf, and on the crisis that was rapidly brewing in that region. And so, for that reason, Secretary Mark revised his priorities. Strategic force enhancement still headed the list; but a newcomer was now in second place: The Rapid Deployment Joint Task Force. The creation of that force, said Mark, " . . . must now have a higher priority than some of the other items . . . "

The Rapid Deployment Joint Task Force had been established on March 1, 1980, at MacDill AFB, Florida, as a separate and subordinate element of the United States Readiness Command. The idea was to create a reservoir of units, based in the United States, that could be moved rapidly to some remote location to defend American interests in the area.

The RDJTF would draw on units of all the services, and combine them in a tailored package to meet whatever threat was at hand. It required no new forces, but would draw from existing units anywhere in the United States. There were special rules applied to the USAF units that could be tabbed for the Task Force: they could come from outside the United States, but they must not be taken from units designated for assignment to NATO or Korea in the event of a crisis there. In other words, the attempt was

to preserve the major strengths of the USAF abroad to fight a major war, and to make available smaller forces for a minor war.

The mission of the RDJTF was defined as the planning, training, exercising, deployment and employment of designated forces responding to non-NATO contingencies. Once on the scene, RDJTF would be the operational command, rather than any other existing command structure, taking its direction from USREDCOM.

Confederate General Nathan Bedford Forrest is reported to have said something to the effect that success in battle was accomplished by getting there first with the most. The RDJTF has been criticized as being a case of getting their last with the least, because it is, obviously, totally dependent on airlift and sealift for its movements.

A fighter wing currently can deploy a squadron to an overseas base within a day after getting the word to go. To get to the Persian Gulf, considerably further than a simple crossing of the Atlantic or Pacific, a fighter wing might take three days. It could fight on arrival, if it knew the territory or had friendly air to serve as a guide for a few sorties. To move an airborne brigade to the Persian Gulf might take from four to five days, using airlift. Its amount of available firepower is not very impressive. An airborne division would take from 12 to 15 days to emplace by air, and an infantry division, moved by sea because of the size and weight of its equipment, could be expected to arrive in 30 to 35 days after it left the United States. Bear in mind that these are travel times only, and do not include the time spent at either end of the trip in getting ready and loading, and in unloading and getting ready to fight.

The air elements of the RDJTF would, naturally, be on the scene first, and could be expected to stage a show of force, a holding action, or a small air offensive with the equipment and supplies it had. But in a very short time, the earliest arrivals would have run out of supplies and weapons and ordnance, and would be helpless on the ground without a ready supply of pre-positioned stocks. The provision of such stocks is to be one feature of the RDJTF, as is the development of a fleet of special ships and aircraft dedicated to the swift movement of the Force.

But even as the announcements of the creation of the RDJTF were being made, some military men were questioning the concept, pointing out that it is perhaps worse to strand a too-small force in a crisis situation than not to respond at all. It is, they argue, just another extension of the principle that the United States should police the world.

The concept is not all that new. There once was a Strike Command, a combined force of ground troops and supporting air, and it existed for a number of years in the organizational structure of the U. S. military. It vanished quietly about the time of the Viet-Nam war, only to resurface in reminders of its existence when the first rumors of the RDJTF began to appear.

Proponents of the system believe that it is an idea whose time has come, to coin a cliche. True or not, a substantial portion of Air Force strength is earmarked for possible future deployment with the Task Force, and that is a matter of some concern to the leaders of the USAF.

Is that to be one pattern of their future involvement with crises? They only can wait and see.

Changing Threats and New Weapons

The Fulda river rises in the Rhoen mountains of eastern Hesse, in the Federal Republic of Germany. It meanders down the slopes of the hills and through a town that takes its name from the river itself. The medieval town, with its roots deep in ninth-century Catholicism, lies about 55 miles northwest of the metropolis centered on Frankfurt-am-Main. Around that latter city is a complex of military bases that house and support German, American and other NATO units.

The border with the German Democratic Republic is hardly more than ten miles from Fulda, forming a local bulge that is part of the irregular trace the border makes between the two Germanies. It runs generally east for about 100 miles, and then swings southeast to divide Czechoslovakia from the West German state of Bavaria.

On the East German side, opposite Fulda and running almost to the Czech border, is the Thueringer-wald, a dense and mountainous forest. There are road networks, stamped out by the treads of armored vehicles, through those thick woods.

And now it is a cold and wintry morning. The first faint light of the approaching dawn has just begun to brighten the low cloud cover. The sun, if it appears, will only be a silver disc seen dimly against the backdrop of pale gray. The wind blows from the West, driving a light flurry of snow before it.

Under the trees that line the roads and in the nearby forest groves lie the great green shapes of armored vehicles, their sides marked with scrawled writing. Cyrillic letters identify their drivers' goals: "To the Channel!"; "Defend the Motherland!"

At the head of one long line of tanks, a lone engine begins its starting cycle, its gas turbine whining into life. Within seconds, another and another begin the low groan that rises to a shriek as compressors spin. Fuel spurts into combustion chambers; sparks ignite the furnace; turbine blades begin to whirl under the impace of highspeed, high-temperature streams of

The Fairchild Republic A-10A Thunderbolt II has the most powerful gun (measured in terms of muzzle horsepower) ever fitted to any aircraft. Here ground crew bring up the hydraulically driven handling system which feeds the 1,174 milk-bottle-size rounds of ammunition.

pale yellow gases. Power moves through gears and shafts to the treads, and the long column begins to move out, forming into squadrons as it clatters along. Out of the forest it streams and into the open land behind the border, noses headed straight for the throughway to the English Channel: The Fulda Gap.

This has been the classic, studied scenario for a conflict between the NATO countries and the Warsaw Pact nations for years now. It assumes an armored thrust by the Pact countries, out of the East in a Blitzkrieg, streaming onto the plains of northern Germany, dashing for the Channel. Some military writers have implied that such a charge could reach its goal in about two weeks. But others, NATO planners included, believe that the Red drive would be blunted, held and driven back in disarray.

A major part of the defenses ranged against such an attack are the United States Air Forces in Europe, squadrons that are assigned to the European theater and either based there, or deployed there rapidly from their home bases in the United States. Staff and command studies over recent years have concentrated on the Fulda Gap scenario in planning USAF responses to a crisis in Europe.

But a second troubled area also has attracted much attention during the decade of the 1970s, and has been studied in detail, although not to the point of near-obsession that has characterized the concentration on the Fulda Gap. There remains unfinished business in Korea, according to the basic assumptions behind this second concept of potential conflict. Once the North Koreans feel strong and confident enough, the view is that they will again move south, as they did in June 1950. That drive also will be an armored Blitz, supported by strong tactical air power. It will be met by Republic

of Korea air units augmented by USAF squadrons now based there, and reinforced within hours by other USAF units deployed from Japan and the United States.

The exercises that have studied these two common scenarios of a future war have influenced the deployment of forces to those threatened regions. They have influenced the training exercises that are a constant feature of today's military climate. They have further influenced the types of aircraft and weapons that the USAF has developed and allocated to those two areas.

But recent events have begun to alter the perceptions of the planners about how war might come to the United States and, more specifically, where it might begin. The arena of new and critical focus is the Middle East, and particularly the countries that surround the Persian Gulf.

Its waters lap the shores of states that produce much of the world's oil supplies: Iran, Iraq, Kuwait, Saudi Arabia. To the east of the Persian Gulf lies the Gulf of Oman; the two bodies of water are connected by the narrow and curving waterway called the Straits of Hormuz. Through this slim passage move huge tankers, laden with crude oil from the Gulf states. And that whole region historically has been an area characterized by turmoil.

Through all of the past struggles in the region, with one recent exception, oil has continued to flow to the world markets. The United States, preoccupied with its extensive commitments to Europe and the Far East, has tended to leave the affairs of that sector of the world in the hands of those countries it regarded as friendly: Iran, Saudi Arabia, Jordan, Egypt and Israel. The overthrow of Iran's Shah brought the political and religious realities home with sudden emphasis. With

Devastation wrought by political instability. Only a year previously the U.S. and Iran were close allies and held numerous joint maneuvers. Within months of the Shah's overthrow mobs had taken the U.S. Embassy and held 52 citizens hostage. President Carter authorised a bold rescue bid that ended in appalling failure. A unit of C-130s and HH-53 helicopters attempted to reach Tehran. Of the eight helicopters that set out from the carrier "Nimitz", two developed faults, one was forced to turn back and a fourth collided with one of the C-130s. The mission was aborted leaving eight service men dead in the attempt.

Though a long-range aircraft, the C-141 StarLifter frequently would have been helped by an inflight refuelling capability. One of the improvements in the stretched C-141B version is a refuelling receptacle in the roof of the forward fuselage. This was one of the trial hook-ups behind a KC-135A over Edwards AFB.

the Shah gone, the outlook for continued American influence in his country became very bleak. And when revolutionaries took control of the American Embassy in Teheran and held its staff hostage, it was painfully obvious that U. S. influence in Iran had dwindled to zero, and that in the Gulf states it was precariously low. And then, in the early autumn of 1980, open warfare broke out.

There is disputed area on the border between Iran and Iraq, dating back to the days when the powerful Shah tried to establish control over the flow of oil in the Persian Gulf. Iraq seized the opportunity to attack Iran while the latter country was still struggling with the internal problems caused by the revolution, with an active rebellion in the northwest, and with fanatic demands for a holy war against any who chose not to follow the precepts of its religious leaders. The stated Iraqi goal was to take and hold the disputed land, primarily in a small area at the northern end of the Persian Gulf where the Shatt-al-Arab waterway debouches.

The Iraqi-Iranian war triggered an examination of current U. S. military strength and how it might best be applied if the situation went from bad to worse. It pointed up the immediate problems of wars in remote locations, with no U. S. bases in the region to serve as staging areas.

The available U. S. force for such a situation is the Rapid Deployment Joint Task Force (RDJTF), an organization containing mobile elements of all the services under a single command. The force concept visualizes an initial deployment of airborne troops and air support in a package airlifted to the scene of action. Simultaneously, ships would begin to move the mountains of supplies, equipment and backup personnel needed to maintain whatever position the advance elements were able to secure.

Such a plan looks excellent on paper and in the theoretical staff exercises. But it still seems geared to the conditions of World War II, or perhaps the Korean conflict of the 1950s. Such a plan assumes time to react, to deploy, to supply and resupply. And time may be the most precious commodity in any future conflict. A war between the major powers threatens to be short and sharp, with heavy initial losses and a rapid drawdown of forces. It is entirely possible that a future conflict could last only a week to ten days before combat losses had decimated the available forces. Supply ships still would be at sea, making their few knots against the concerted opposition of long-range enemy bombers and prowling submarine packs.

As one exasperated U. S. general said, "The thing (the Iraqi-Iranian conflict) has really driven home that there are no good answers to the question of how the Hell we would get there and what we would do when we landed."

Crises Beget New Weapons Systems

What has been described here are some of the driving forces that determine the kinds of weapons that are developed for the military forces of the United States, and specifically for the Air Force. The first is the basic threat: what country will the United States have to fight, and what is its strength? The second is the basic scenario: will it be a space war above continents and oceans, or a limited tactical war on some sandy peninsula?

For many years past, the answers to those two points have been simply stated. The U. S. expected that it would have to defend itself against a Russian attack, and it would be an intercontinental war, with ballistic missiles delivering nuclear and thermonuclear warheads. Those statements were reflected in the development of a large U. S. retaliatory force, a mix of manned bombers, land-based intercontinental ballistic

Soaring costs and various problems afflicted the development of the Lockheed C-5A Galaxy, the world's most capable logistic freighter and on some counts the world's biggest aircraft. Procurement was cut to only 81, of which 76 are now in the active inventory. Even now there are problems, and Lockheed-Georgia is making complete new wings for the entire fleet to remove airframe limitations and give a service life of 30,000 hours.

There are possibly more sub-types of KC-135 and C-135 Stratotanker and Stratolifter series than of any other aircraft. This is a basic KC-135A tanker. Originally these aircraft were unpainted and lacked several of today's electronic items.

missiles, and submarine-based ballistic missiles. The Air Force's Strategic Air Command controlled the manned bombers and the land-based missiles; the Navy commanded the remainder of the strike force.

It was a concept that had begun during the Cold War of the 1950s, after the Russians began bragging about their possession of nuclear weapons. It was refined by the technology of the 1960s and 1970s. But obviously it was an all-or-nothing arsenal of weapons, clearly unusable except in retaliation to the extreme—perhaps the final—case of a nuclear attack on the United States.

The war in Southeast Asia de-emphasized that singular view. Because it was a politically limited war, it called for the employment of small units of strength, measured in squadrons of tactical aircraft, battalions of troops, and single Navy carriers. It would have been unthinkable to have used nuclear weapons in such circumstances, although there are indications that it was thought about, and even suggested, on more than one occasion.

The Air Force learned from that war that it was not very well prepared to fight and win a limited conflict; it had neither the weapons nor the tactics to gain a clear-cut victory. It learned that a classical tactical threat was changing. The enemy defenses, batteries upon batteries of anti-aircraft missiles and automatic cannon, denied continuing control of the air to the USAF.

Some theorists postulated that the nature of air war had been changed, just as the nature of land war had been changed by the introduction of the machine gun on the Western Front during World War 1. The anti-aircraft defenses, they said, were the new machine gun. They certainly posed a comparable threat, and it was demonstrated not only in Viet-Nam, but also in the Arab-Israeli war of 1973. The IAF, reeling from its initial losses, might have been soundly defeated if it had not been for the support of the United States, which drew from its own limited resources in Europe and home to supply fighters, missiles, and electronic countermeasures equipment to the hard-pressed Israelis.

Following that conflict, an Arab oil embargo of Western nations and a series of successive price rises for barrels of crude oil began to have a geometric inflationary effect on the cost of weapons. Not only did it cost more to fly aircraft, but it also cost more to purchase them and the sophisticated weaponry that they carried aloft.

The conventional concepts of the ways to build air power were changing, driven by a changing threat and rising costs. And at about the same time, the Russians began a long-term, sustained effort to produce military weapons in huge quantities, delivering every year the equivalent of a major element of a U. S. force in tanks or aircraft. Added to this were the clandestine shipments of small arms and man-transportable rocket launchers to insurrectionists and terrorists.

The emerging picture was one of formidable strength. Russian military might, augmented by the armed forces of the Warsaw Pact countries, could pose a very real threat to NATO and its defenses. There was some expression of doubt that the Russian threat was very real, or that the intentions behind the threat were actually directed westward. Some argued that the Russians were really building to be able to handle China, while maintaining enough strength in the West to deter any help that might have been contemplated for the Chinese in such circumstances. Still, hundreds of modern tanks continued to arrive in border regions, where they could clearly be observed from reconnaissance aircraft. And, as one general said, "What the Hell else can the Russians do with those thousands of tanks? They're only good for one thing!"

Equating the two sides in any potential conflict is a game for fools, yet it has to be done. It is done, to a first approximation, by a simple listing of orders of battle, and by the numbers of weapons and troops available. But such a paper balancing act never takes into account—nor can it—the varying degrees of loyalty, of training, of determination, of support in the field, at the depots and at home, and of the myriad of factors that finally determine the effectiveness of a military force in action.

So, because of these very uncertainties, military planners work on "worst cases", assumptions that include being outnumbered by a very strong and capable enemy, and having to fight alone, without the support of any allies.

On that basis, the U. S. saw a need for "force multipliers", weapons whose effectiveness is so great that they would compensate for the existing numerical inferiority of the U. S. to Russia or the Warsaw Pact nations.

Force multiplers are, by definition, improved weapons that are very capable. Capability equates to complexity, and complexity equates to cost. Consequently, force multipliers also turn out to be cost multipliers. That brings into the equation another factor that influences the kinds and quantities of weapons that will be supplied by a country for its use by its military forces. That new factor is a constantly rising cost, and it has become increasingly important in the recent development of force multipliers.

The costs of individual aircraft and their associated systems skyrocketed in the decade of the 1970s, due both to inflation and to the force-multiplying technologies that increased the capabilities of weapons. Single fighters like the McDonnell-Douglas F-15 series, then well along in production, cost upward of $15

The termination of the B-1 as a bomber for the Air Force inventory in 1977 was a controversial decision, which could later be found to have been a very serious error. Here the first B-1 is seen on its second test flight on 23 January 1975.

million each. Further, that number was conservative because of many indirect costs that did not get factored into the final accounting to the bedeviled taxpayer.

Cost affected other aspects of the Air Force in addition to controlling the numbers of aircraft and weapons it could buy. Fighter pilots in training were severely hampered by the high cost of flight hours, of ammunition, and of the sophisticated weaponry they would carry aloft to aerial battle. Tactical Air Command pilots flew only one exercise per year in which each pilot fired a live missile against a target drone maneuvering over an instrumented range. With the luck of the draw, some of those pilots got malfunctioning missiles that bored a hole in a different quadrant of the sky from the one they were aimed at, or they got a drone out of control that caused an abort of the entire mission.

Clearly it no longer is possible, if it ever was, for the United States Air Force to buy all the aircraft and missiles it deems necessary to fulfill its mission requirements. There are too many uncertainties, and uncontrollable factors, in addition to the basic ones of threat, scenario, and cost. Weapons procurement has become a major political issue, and the availability of funds for development and production varies with the ebb and flow of partisan politics and the nearness of elections.

New Strategic Arms

There have been at least three follow-on programs planned to develop and produce a long-range strategic bomber to replace the B-52. All of them have been cancelled, for a variety of reasons, and the aging Stratofortresses continue to be modified and updated. During the four years from 1976 to 1980, B-52s were modified or scheduled for modification to incorporate these improvements:

• The ability to carry and deliver the new GBU-15 glide-bomb family.
• The ability to make a low-level nuclear weapon laydown from an altitude of about 150 feet.
• Wing strengthening and damping of critical vibration frequencies to increase the safe-life limits on the airframe. The program was called Pacer Plank, and applied only to B-52D models.
• The addition of much new electronic counter-measures equipment, including an AN/ALQ-153 tail-mounted radar warning system and an AN/ALQ-117 defensive jamming system. This was the Rivet Ace program.
• An electro-optical viewing system, added to the B-52G and H models. AN/AAQ 6 steerable forward-looking infra-red (FLIR) and AN/AVQ-22 low-level light television sensors display their information on

One of the sub-types of B-52 remaining in active service, the B-52G introduced wet (integral-tank) wings for greatly extended range, and also a shorter vertical tail. This example has the EVS (electro-optical viewing system) blisters beneath the nose.

Giants in their lair on Strategic Air Command major maintenance include all three types of B-52 remaining in the SAC inventory. Those with tall tail are B-52Ds, still with black sides and undersurfaces from the Viet-Nam war. The others are Gs and (nearest camera) Hs, which equip the SAC bomb wings in the front-line force based in the United States.

The Boeing E-4A advanced airborne national command post was originally based on the civil 747, with JT9D engines. Subsequently this aircraft was brought up to E-4B standard with various modifications including a change to General Electric engines.

a cathode-ray rube to the right of the pilot's instrument panel.

• An offensive avionics system, also for the G and H models, improving navigational and weapons-delivery accuracies. It featured a new set of sensors, except for the main forward-looking AN/ASQ-38 radar, plus a central computer to handle the generated data.

• Installations of equipment and systems to carry the Boeing AGM-86B air-launched cruise missile (ALCM) on the B-52G models. Twenty can be carried, 12 under the wings on two racks, and eight inside the bomb-bay on a rotating launcher that is interchangeable with the one developed for the Boeing AGM-69A short-range attack missiles (SRAM).

A key weapon in the future SAC B-52 force will be the ALCM (air launched cruise missile). Also built by Boeing, the AGM-86B ALCM is a miniature aircraft which, after being released from the parent bomber (a B-52G as here, or a B-52H), unfolds wings, horizontal tail and turbojet air-inlet scoop, and flies to its target, if necessary making changes of height or direction. The B-52 can carry eight internally and 12 more on underwing racks.

SRAM and ALCM are complementary weapons. The older SRAM was designed for a short-range mission, on the order of 30 to 100 miles. Armed with a 200-kiloton thermonuclear warhead, the rocket-powered SRAM missiles streak to their targets at Mach 3. In addition to the 20 carried on each Boeing B-52G or H, the missile can also arm the General Dynamics FB-111A, which holds two under each wing and two more in the bomb-bay.

ALCM, on the other hand, is a long-range missile, powered by a turbofan engine and cruising at a speed of Mach 0.7, more comparable to the best velocity of the B-52 carrier aircraft itself. The airframe was derived from a Boeing development of a subsonic decoy; it is carried in a stowed state, with its tiny wings, tail surfaces and inlets retracted. On release, they deploy and the missile resembles a small airplane. Its range is about 1,500 miles, and it can deliver a 200-kiloton warhead.

SAC's land-based strategic missiles also have been updated. The Boeing LGM-30G Minuteman III is being hardened; its silos are being strengthened, its silo suspension systems improved, and a remote retargeting system has been installed, so that new data can be played into the existing, installed target tapes, avoiding the earlier cumbersome routine of inactivating the missile while a target team removed the old tapes and installed new.

Further, up to 200 of these models of the Minuteman can be retargeted from an airborne command post, after an attack that presumably might wipe out the ground-based facilities for so doing. The Air Force will keep 350 of the current force of 550 Minuteman III missiles in service, and replace the other 200 with the MX missile, according to the latest plans.

The MX is the most controversial of the new strategic systems. It is a mobile, long-range ballistic missile, capable of delivering up to 10 warheads, each of 335 kiloton strength, to targets more than 8,000 miles distant. There is some disagreement, even within the Air Force, whether or not such a weapon is needed. There is considerable disagreement on the best method of basing the movable missile. The reason for making it mobile is, of course, to confound Russian targeters who have tabbed the fixed Minuteman silos for first-strike attention. But under the SALT agreements with the Russians, it must be possible to check on the location and quantity of these missiles. So the Air Force developed a strategic shell game, and plans to move the missiles on a random basis, each to any one of 23 shelters within its own particular complex. Two hundred of these complexes are scheduled for installation on public lands generally north and east of Nellis Air Force Base, near Las Vegas, Nevada. The MX will be launchable from ground or airborne control centers.

Any incoming Russian missiles would be detected soon after their launch by one of the several long-range systems designed for that purpose and placed along the northern reaches of the world. The latest addition to these radars is a pair of phased-array, dual-faced early-warning systems, code-named Pave Paws, which can monitor launches over a 3,000-mile range and keep an eye on low-orbit earth satellites. The first two of a planned chain of these radars have been installed at Otis AFB, Massachusetts, and Beale AFB, California.

Complementing these new radars are the older BMEWS and DEW (Ballistic Missile Early Warning System and Distant Early Warning) radars. BMEWS badly needs improvements, specifically in its computers. Developed almost 30 years ago, the now-ancient computers no longer are supported by their manufacturer, making it necessary for the Air Force to cannibalize existing sets to maintain their dwindling numbers.

There is an overall command structure that controls this whole unity of radars, missiles and bombers. The National Command Authority—the President, the Secretary of Defense and their authorized deputies—would assume control in the event of crisis or war. For survivability of the NCA, Strategic Air Command operates a Boeing E-4A, a modified commercial 747 jet transport, which holds the systems to control the weapons of war. From the airborne command post, SAC missiles and bombers can be alerted, launched, and directed to attack. The three E-4As in service in early 1981 used the equipment developed for earlier airborne command posts. The USAF then was trying to get funding for new systems for installation in the trio, and for procuring new aircraft which would be designated E-4B.

This is a glimpse, then, of the new strategic weapons in being, in development, or in the hopes of the Air Force. The chances are quite good that all of them will be carried through, because of the stated policy of that service to concentrate on strategic weapons for the next few years.

Additionally, the Air Force would like to get money to develop the cancelled Rockwell International B-1 bomber, the swing-wing supersonic aircraft developed as a long-range penetrator. Primarily for economic reasons, President Carter followed through on the policies of his predecessors in that office, and finally cancelled the B-1. The remaining prototypes were being used to investigate the potential of the aircraft

as a penetrator, and the USAF thought that perhaps it would be able to fund a development of the airplane was a dedicated cruise-missile carrier. There are, of course, studies for new bombers to replace the B-52, and for more advanced missiles to replace the SRAM and ALCM.

But whether or not any of these advanced ideas ever will come to fruition is unpredictable, and dependent on too many unknowns.

Tools for Tactical Air Power

The cutting edge of America's air power is wielded by tactical air forces, skilled and well-equipped, flying an increasing number of new fighters armed with capable new weapons, and augmented by older warhorses that are still very capable of first-line performance.

One of the USAF units "up at the sharp end" confronting a hostile neighbour is the 51st Composite Wing, based at Osan AB, South Korea. One of the F-4E Phantoms from the 336th TFS is seen making a slow fly-by with the slats extended, during Team Spirit '77, a joint U.S. and Korean tactical exercise.

This F-4E was until recently on the strength of the 32nd TFS at Camp Amsterdam, Soesterburg, Netherlands, as part of USAF Europe. This unit is now equipped with the F-15C.

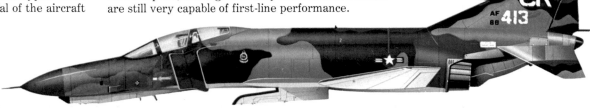

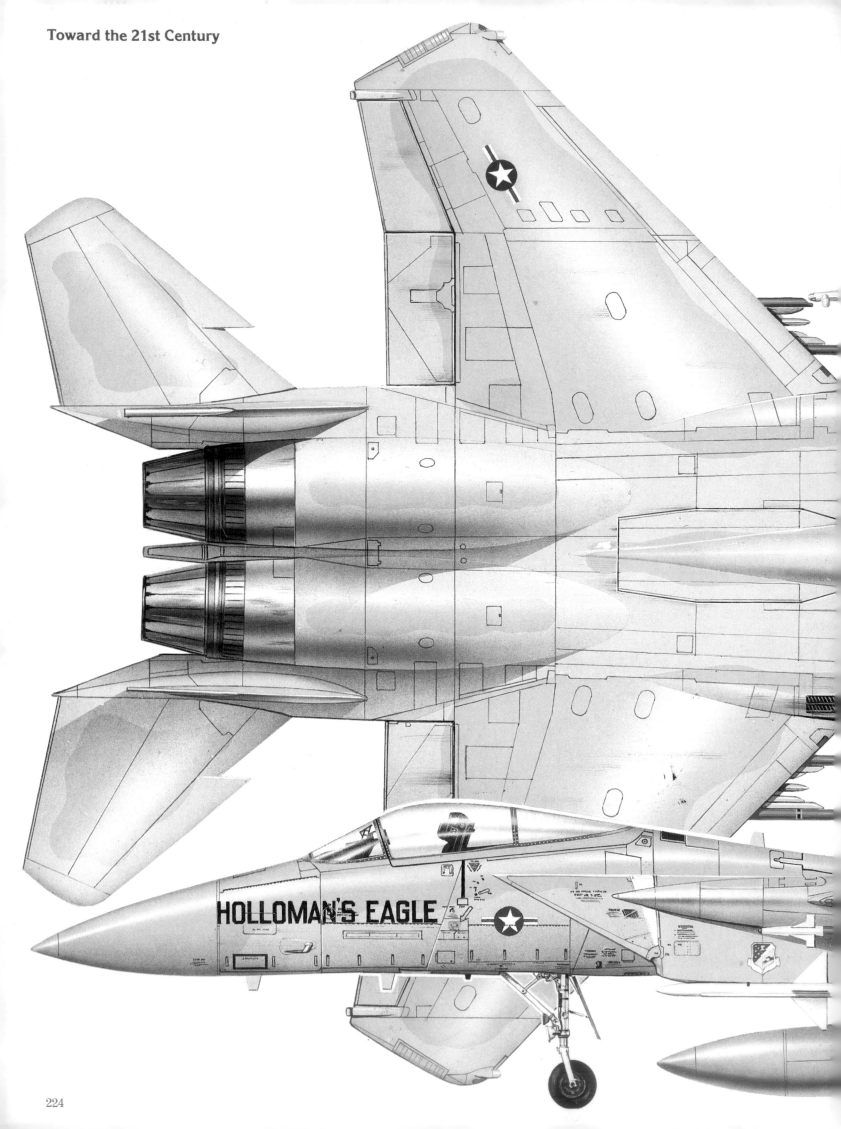

HOLLOMAN'S EAGLE

McDonnell Douglas F-15A Eagle

It is hard to believe that this massive and powerful air-superiority fighter is now almost 13 years old. But it dates back to the post-show shock of the Russian air display at Domodedovo in 1967, where the MiG-25 "Foxbat" and MiG-23 'Flogger' were first revealed. An Air Force competition and contract award for a "Foxbat" counter followed in 1968. The F-15 was optimized to fight and win in the blood sport of air combat. To do that, it was developed around a wing of large area and aerodynamic elegance and simplicity. Added to that was a powerplant whose installed thrust exceeded the airplane's

weight, which meant that the F-15 could accelerate vertically. Combining that with excellent radar, a heads-up display, and a range of weapons from the far-ranging radar Sparrow missiles, through the medium-range infra-red Sidewinders, to the close-in guns, made the Eagle a potent combat threat. "Holloman's Eagle" was flown by the commander of the 49th Tactical Fighter Wing, Holloman AFB, New Mexico. Just by arranged coincidence, she carries a serial number to match the wing designation: 76-00049.

McDonnell Douglas F-15A in the blue camouflage common on entry to service, in this case with the 58th Tac Training Wing at Luke AFB, Arizona.

Today's USAF tactical air forces field about 3,400 aircraft of all types, and perhaps one-third of them are the indispensable and versatile McDonnell-Douglas F-4 Phantom series. They serve as interceptors, air-to-air fighters, ground attackers, and reconnaissance aircraft. Some have special weapons delivery capabilities, which means they can delivery tactical nuclear weapons. Others fly defense suppression missions as Wild Weasel aircraft. This preponderance of the F-4 is slowly shifting as the F-15, F-16 and A-10 are being phased into operational squadrons. Current inventory includes eight different aircraft types, some of which have been modified for several tasks.

The grandfather of them all is the F-4 series, with technology that dates back about thirty years. Mc-Donnell began paper studies of the airplane in 1953, intending it as a high-performance single-seat fighter for the Navy, then a primary customer of long standing. The Navy awarded the company a development contract in 1954, and the first aircraft flew in Navy markings May 27, 1958. Almost four years later, the official go-ahead on an Air Force version was forwarded by the Office of the Secretary of Defense. The first USAF version, then redesignated F-4C from its earlier model number of F-110, flew May 27, 1963.

The Phantom II first became operational with the 12th Tactical Fighter Wing, then based at MacDill AFB, Florida, in October, 1964. Later that year the first F-4Cs were deployed to Southeast Asia, where they soon proved that their lack of an internal cannon installation was a real drawback in air-to-air combat. Missiles are great, said the pilots, but I want to get in close and shoot the bastard down. Hurriedly, SUU-16A gun pods, equipped with a General Electric M61A1 20-mm. cannon, were made available. They took a little getting used to; carrying the guns added some extra

drag and decreased the performance.

But aside from the gun, the rugged and angular Phantom could carry a formidable array of armament. Four AIM-7D or E model Sparrow missiles were slung underneath its fuselage, and four AIM-9B or D model Sidewinders, or four AIM-4D Falcons could be carried on its wing pylons. Four of the AGM-12B or a pair of the larger AGM-12C Bullpup missiles could be carried on the wing stations, or they could be loaded with four AGM-45A Shrike anti-radiation missiles or two Genie rockets. Or ordnancemen could upload special (nuclear) weapons or conventional bombs or TV-guided Navy Walleye missiles.

The F-4C, which was the original model to see combat, was supplemented later by the F-4E model, with an improved bombing and aerial combat capability. That same model was the first equipped with a laser-designator pod, for pinpoint delivery of modified bombs. The F-4E model mounted an internal cannon, and had a slotted stabilator, and leading edge slats. It went to Southeast Asia in late 1968, just about one year after achieving initial operational capability with the Air Force.

The standard tactical reconnaissance aircraft is yet another model of the Phantom, the RF-4C. Basically a C model with photographic and electronic sensors, the RF-4Cs were used tellingly, and at high cost, in the Viet-Nam war. They went there in October 1965, and stayed to the end.

Still another version was the Wild Weasel Phantom, extensively modified aircraft that carried a variety of electronic countermeasures equippment, and whose job was to go fishing for North Vietnamese anti-aircraft missiles. They preceded a strike into the target area, monitoring the missile radars as they came on the air, and avoiding the launched weapons

Three F-15A Eagles from the 36th TFW at Bitburg, West Germany, participating in Arctic Express '78 on detachment to Bodo AB, Norway. This was a multinational combat readiness exercise, at a time when combat readiness of many front-line USAF units—including those equipped with the F-15—was abysmally low.

General Dynamics F-16 Fighting Falcon in the two-tone blue/gray camouflage used on entry to service, since superseded by low-visibility gray with low-contrast national markings.

while firing their own anti-radiation missile to blast the enemy battery. Only a few of the F-4 models were reworked to this configuration during the war years; most of the task was being done outstandingly well by the Republic F-105G Wild Weasel. But beginning in 1979, the F-105Gs have been phasing out of the active USAF inventory, to be replaced by F-4G Wild Weasel aircraft of greatly enhanced capabilities.

The planned F-4 replacement was the McDonnell-Douglas F-15 Eagle, an air-superiority fighter, designed to take control of the upper reaches of the sky and hold them against any comers. It originated as an FX study in 1965 and received official go-ahead in December 1969. The first flight was made July 27, 1972, and the first delivery to Tactical Air Command occurred in November 1974. Current deliveries to TAC are of the F-15C single-seat and F-15D two-seat models.

The Eagle carries four AIM-7F Advanced Sparrows, an all-aspect, all-weather, beyond-visual-range (BVR) missile. Another four AIM-9L infra-red homing Side-winder dogfight missiles can be carried, for the shorter-range, visual engagement. And for the "six o'clock kill" from directly behind the enemy, the Eagle mounts a single M61A1 cannon.

Even though the design was optimized for the air combat role, the F-15 can haul ordnance for the ground-attack mission. It can, for example, carry 18 of the 500-lb. bombs used in those missions, and still outperform an unloaded F-4E. Further, it is the only USAF aircraft that can carry and release its multiple stores in super-sonic flight.

The key to its performance as a fighter is an outstanding light-weight Hughes AN/APG-63 radar, which has long range and can track moving targets from high altitude down to the treetops. Its information is presented on a heads-up display on the windshield.

In the early days of the F-15 development, when fighter costs were beginning to escalate, there was a technology program that began to look as if it ought to be eased into procurement. The program had funded the development of a pair of lightweight, low-cost, simple mission "austere" fighters, the General Dynamics YF-16 and the Northrop YF-17. In the late 1960s, it seemed as if three or four of those kinds of fighters could be bought for the cost of a single Eagle. General Dynamics got the nod in January 1975, one year after the first flight of its YF-16, and the full-scale development began.

The result was one of the most elegant creations of a design team since the Lockheed XP-80. Small and light, the YF-16 looked fast and tough just sitting on the ground. It had advanced technology written all over it. Its automatic leading-edge flaps produced, in effect, a variable-camber wing. Composite materials decreased its weight. Wing and body blended into an aerodynamic whole. Vortex lift was generated by forward strakes where the wing met the fuselage. It was planned to be flown by powered controls, signalled by electrical impulses flowing through wires, instead of by hydraulic fluids running through piping. Its stability requirements were relaxed. It had a belly engine inlet. The cockpit was closely followed by the rest of the airplane, and it featured a reclining seat that enabled the pilot to take a higher body "G" load during high-speed maneuvers. The control stick was a stub, mounted on the right-hand console and fixed. Pilots pressed it in the direction they wanted to go, and the control system did the rest.

TAC deliveries began in January 1979, and the 388th Tactical Fighter Wing, the first recipients, became operational in early 1981.

There was one bitter note about all of this. The low-cost airplane became a higher-cost airplane, and at one point appeared to be not much less expensive than the unit price of a large buy of F-15s.

All-weather interdiction strikes deep in enemy territory are the specialty of the General Dynamics F-111 series. The remembered victim of a long and acrimonious Congressional investigation into its origins as one component of the TFX program, today's F-111 has gained a reputation for being a formidable weapon, like by pilots who fly it and disliked by people who maintain it.

No fighter in the world surpasses the F-16A for its cost/effectiveness which rests on advanced engineering design. This view emphasizes the all-round visibility from the reclining ejection seat, with a small glass square in front of the pilot to give a HUD (heads-up display).

General Dynamics F-16A Fighting Falcon

The F-16A was derived from a 1972 lightweight and — it was hoped — inexpensive fighter prototype development program that featured the application of advanced technology. After winning a flyoff competition with the Northrop YF-17, the F-16A was developed into a battler that now is seen as useful in both air combat and ground-attack missions. Its belly engine intake and stalky landing gear immediately mark it as a different and newer breed of airplane, and a plan view confirms it. That blended wing-body combination is a result of sophisticated aerodynamics that required many hours of computer time and wind-tunnel testing. So is the use of automatically controlled leading- and trailing-edge flaps for maneuvering; the concept of relaxed stability requirements, and the fly-by-wire control system, operated by a side-stick control on the right side of the cockpit. The F-16A-CF shown here, serial number 75-0747, was one of the first batch of eight ordered by the USAF after the flyoff decision had been made in favor of the Fighting Falcon. (Note for historians: The F-16A is undoubtedly the first-ever airplane to be named after a second-rate college football team.)

One of the numerous weapons cleared for operational use from the A-10A Thunderbolt II close-support aircraft is the AGM-65 family of Maverick missiles. Here an AGM-65A, the original TV-guided model, is fired from an A-10A against a simulated point target on a U.S. range.

F-111 technology dates back to the 1950s and drew extensively from wind-tunnel studies done at the National Advisory Committee for Aeronautics (later the National Aeronautics and Space Administration) on variable-sweep wings. Specifically, a General Operational Requirement was issued March 27, 1958, describing the basic characteristics and performance of a tactical fighter for service in 1964. It was expected to be capable of V/STOL performance; but that was soon ruled out in the light of the available means to do that bit of levitation. While the desired performance was studied and restudied, Defense Secretary Robert S. McNamara entered the scene and decided that the program should be modified to develop a tactical fighter — the TFX — common to both the Air Force and the Navy. The Request for Proposals was mailed September 29, 1961, and General Dynamics was selected as contractor November 24, 1962.

The first F-111A development aircraft flew December 21, 1964; the A models became initially operational with TAC in April, 1968. They were followed by F-111E, D and F models, each with its own peculiarities and not exactly interchangeable with its predecessors. The F-111 is, aeronautically speaking, the equivalent of a medium bomber in an earlier Air Force time, but its devastating weapons load makes it the equivalent of many wings of World War II medium bombers. Comparing it to a more-modern medium bomber, like one of the ground-attack versions of the McDonnell-Douglas F-4, dramatizes the F-111 advantage. Four of them carry the bomb load of 20 F-4s, and further, they can deliver it with high accuracy at night, in foul weather, flying on the automatic impulses from a complex navigational and terrain-following radar system.

A major criticism of the Air Force continues to be that it is a fair-weather force, and that combat by night and in all-weather conditions is beyond the capabilities of most of its fleet. Unfortunately, that is largely true, although steps are being taken to redress the uneven balance between day- and night-fighting capabilities. Particularly critical is the European environment; a winter month in central Europe has little daylight and much bad weather. Some calculations have shown that a typical three-day cycle in January in Europe will produce conditions that restrict day-fighter operability to about 40% of the daylight hours, assuming a need for a minimum cloud base of 3,000 feet, and a three nautical-mile visibility. Further, it assumes that a typical tactical mission needs a four-hour "window" in which to prepare, launch and recover aircraft. An all-weather fighter can raise that operability fraction to 90% of the daylight hours and probably the same

Fairchild Republic A-10A of the 354th TFW, which previously flew A-7s, based at Myrtle Beach AFB, SC. This aircraft is shown in one of the two-tone blue/gray schemes, and has the "Pave Penny" laser pod installed under the nose.

percentage during the night. In that situation, the F-111 is the airplane of choice for the mission.

The F-111s were deployed to Southeast Asia during the war years and—after some initial troubles—made an impressive combat record in a comeback from the edge of disaster. That experience is described earlier in this volume.

A number of "Aardvarks", the Air Force's highly unofficial name for the F-111, are being converted to "Electric Foxes", the EF-111A tactical jammer. This version will accompany strike forces into the target area, screening them with powerful noise jamming or specific countermeasures. The system installed in the EF-111A is the AN/ALQ-99E, a modification of the Navy-developed ALQ-99 designed and built by Airborne Instruments Laboratory and installed and operational for at least a decade in the Grumman EA-6B. Additionally, the EF-111A has self-protection electronic countermeasures. It is entering service now, and will be a valuable addition to TAC's strike force composition.

Speaking of "Aardvarks", the Air Force also fields another unusual beast, the "Warthog". The reference is to the Fairchild Republic A-10A Thunderbolt II, an airplane with an uninspired, though historic, name and inspired performance. It's a tank-killer, pure and

simple, built around an enormous 30-mm. automatic GAU-8 cannon, whose one-pound slugs containing depleted uranium can penetrate Soviet armor and shred whatever is inside those steel hulls.

The A-10A was the first USAF airplane to be designed specifically for close air support of troops. Every other previous airplane assigned to that mission was a reluctant draftee from the USAF roster of fighters. The need was formulated in 1966, when military planners began paying serious attention to the problems that might face NATO in the European scenario at some time in the future. Things moved fast; the RFP went out in March 1967, and study contracts were awarded in May. It was a successful study program, because the Air Force learned from it what should have been requested in the original RFP. The second try went out in May 1970 and six designs were submitted in August. Both Fairchild and Northrop got a go-ahead in December for prototypes that would compete in a fly-off.

Fairchild's entry first flew May 10, 1972, just a couple of years after the RFP date. The following January, after a comparative evaluation with the Northrop airplane, Fairchild was selected to begin full-scale development. Production authority was granted in December 1974, and the first production aircraft

The devastating punch of the 30-mm. cannon that forms the principal inbuilt armament of the Fairchild A-10A is well illustrated in this shot of a target being torn apart by its shells.

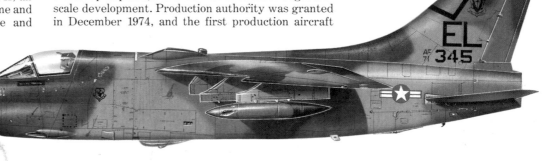

Vought A-7D Corsair II of the 23rd TFW, England AFB, La. This aircraft displays the "wrap-around" three-tone camouflage, without off-white undersurface and with unit emblem in outline only.

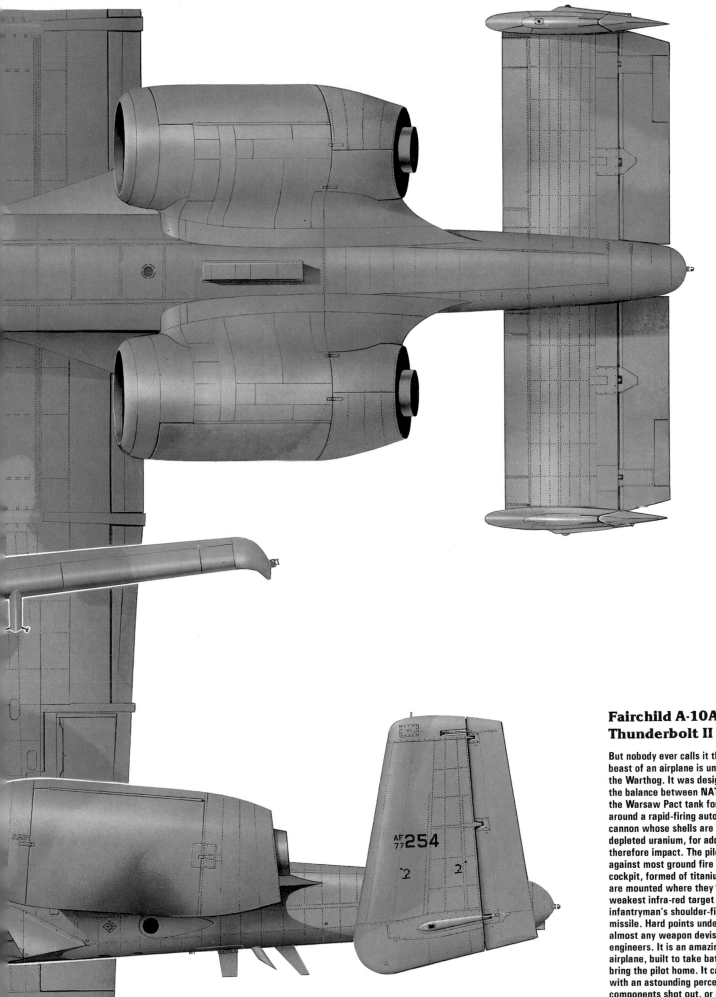

Fairchild A-10A
Thunderbolt II

But nobody ever calls it that; this great
beast of an airplane is universally called
the Warthog. It was designed to redress
the balance between NATO airpower and
the Warsaw Pact tank forces, and it is built
around a rapid-firing automatic 30-mm
cannon whose shells are fabricated from
depleted uranium, for added mass and
therefore impact. The pilot is protected
against most ground fire by an armored
cockpit, formed of titanium. The engines
are mounted where they will present the
weakest infra-red target for an enemy
infantryman's shoulder-fired anti-aircraft
missile. Hard points under the wing hold
almost any weapon devised by armament
engineers. It is an amazingly rugged
airplane, built to take battle damage and to
bring the pilot home. It can maintain flight
with an astounding percentage of
components shot out, or off. The "charcoal
lizard" camouflage scheme is the
latest—and most permanent—of a number
that were tried on the Warhog to add
deception and to complicate detection. "It
ain't pretty," said one of its pilots, "But it's
sure mean!"

233

Certainly the fastest aircraft at present known to be flying anywhere in the world, and holder of the world absolute speed record at 2,193 mph, the Lockheed SR-71A is the unique platform for special recon missions by the 9th SRW at Beale, a SAC element which also uses models of the U-2.

flew October 12, 1975.

A-10As new equip active-duty and Air National Guard units. Their performance in exercises and joint maneuvers with Army troops and helicopters has been exceptional. Pilots were at first reluctant to be assigned to fly the big, brutal-looking beast, which obviously was a slow airplane with a mission in the mud. But they found right away that the "Warthog" was fun to fly. They could legally do all the flying at low altitudes that they liked to do, and had to risk reprimand for earlier. And once they had sampled the maneuverability of the A-10A near the deck and had flown it in a couple of exercises, they became its staunchest supporters. In Red Flag exercises, the simulation of wartime conditions in an arduous and demanding training environment, "Warthog" pilots have been bounced from above by enemy fighters. The first recommended tactic is evasive action; but some of the A-10 pilots soon discovered that they could put up one Hell of a dogfight. They turned into the oncoming fighters, spinning their slower aircraft around on a dime, and sprayed the attacker with a burst of 30-mm. fire—simulated, of course—that would have fragmented him.

The aircraft described here are the major elements

Certainly the most capable "electric fox" (EF) platform of any air force, the EF-111A electronic-warfare aircraft is a total rebuild of F-111A attack aircraft by Grumman. It houses the ALQ-99 tac-jammer system, but without the two extra crew of the Navy EA-6B.

of a strike force as now envisioned by TAC. Major, in the sense that these are the carriers of weapons, the seizers of the skies, the suppressors of missiles and flak defenses, the electronic spoofers. But there is another echelon of aircraft within a tactical air force, and these have to do with command and control, and with communications.

The Air Force operates a number of airborne command and control aircraft, including the Boeing EC-135 series, which basically are tankers modified by the installation of the necessary electronic gear, and Lockheed EC-130s, which are similarly outfitted. Some of these aircraft also are capable of electronic intelligence missions, and can gather data on the enemy electronic order of battle. The nature of their mission precludes any extensive description of what they do and how they do it.

Two totally different, unique aircraft operate far above the battlefield, and some miles away. Soaring highest is the Lockheed TR-1, a derivative of the U-2 strategic reconnaissance aircraft. The TR-1 is equipped with advanced side-looking radar, a mapping device of astonishing capability. The plane loiters at 60,000 feet or so, scanning the distant horizons and making images of the enemy's deep positions. That information can be

relayed directly to the ground by a data link, and displayed in combat and control centers to assist air and ground commanders in their development of tactics.

The other high-altitude loiterer, although it works considerably below the levels of the TR-1, is the Boeing E-3A Sentry, the AWACS aircraft. Its task is a complex one; it monitors the airspace over the battlefield, and—in a manner analogous to the control of air traffic around a busy terminal area—controls the air traffic of a strike force, or a defense. Sentry can oversee an enormous volume of airspace; early tests, for example, publicized the ability of the plane to track every radar beacon-equipped aircraft in the entire Northwest United States. Its rotating disc antenna picks up thousands of bits of information, which are processed by one-board computers that send their output to display consoles manned by senior battle staff members. Sentry is, in effect, the air boss of the battle, and it serves as the airborne command post for any tactical situation.

Force Modernization

No force in being ever can be considered totally equipped. The requirements imposed by enemy threats constantly change; components age, and their designs grow obsolete. Electronics, particularly, have known an explosive increase in capabilities, and need almost constant updating to maintain even a semblance of currency.

There are a number of modification programs in being or in the hopes of planners that are aimed at improving the effectiveness of a tactical air strike force, and particularly one with the numerical inferiority of the USAF/NATO combination. Two existing and ongoing programs as examples are the EF-111A tactical jamming system, and the conversion of F-4Es to F-4G Wild Weasel aircraft. Those two weapon systems, one a combined hunter and killer of enemy defense missiles and flak artillery, and the other a powerful and versatile spoofer, are only as good as their sensors. The Air Force has planned a precision location strike system, universally known by the acronym of PLSS (pronounced "Pliss"), to be integrated with the EF-111A, the F-4G, Army helicopters and artillery in a cohesive system to destroy or degrade the enemy air defense umbrella. PLSS is an all-weather system that would locate and guide the attack to the threat radars, and that could also be directed against non-radiating targets such as bridges and airfield, critical to strike in a tactical air war. One method of suggested deployment of the PLSS system has been to use the TR-1 reconnaissance aircraft as an airborne relay platform.

Another part of such a defense-suppression system is the frequently overlooked expendable drone harassment aircraft. There was a flurry of interest in these types a few years ago, which subsided in the funding cuts of later times. But the program has surfaced again, and the United States and the Federal Republic of Germany have cooperated on a program designated Locust, to develop a low-cost and expendable miniaturized aircraft equipped with sensors for automatic

Toward the 21st Century

Vought A-7D Corsair II

Its nickname is SLUF, and the first three letters stand for short, little and ugly, attributes that reasonably well describe the Corsair II. But the true description of a combat plane is voiced by its performance, and on that score, the A-7D is a remarkable airplane. Designed for the Navy in a May 1963 competition for an attack aircraft, and ordered by the USAF late in 1966, the Corsair II features a lot of "magic", those avionic systems that augment or supplement man's own judgment and abilities to produce a fighting team of pilot and plane. All weapons and targeting data are presented to the pilot on a heads-up display inside his windshield. The bombing accuracy established by the Corsair II in service has been phenomenal, averaging somewhere around ten yards when an experienced pilot is flying. This particular A-7D was flown by the wing commander—note the four tail color stripes, one for each squadron—of the 355th Tactical Fighter Wing, Davis-Monthan AFB, Arizona. In recent months, the USAF inventory of A-7Ds has been reduced through transfer of these aircraft, and their mission, to Air Force Reserve and Air National Guard units.

Toward the 21st Century

acquisition of enemy radars or other electronic emitters. It would then attack them, and—depending on the lethality of the warhead loaded into the available space—could either destroy or severely damage the threat.

To bolster the nighttime capability of tactical air strike units, the USAF would like to proceed on LANTIRN, an apt acronym for Low-Altitude Navigation Targeting Infra-red for Night. That pretty much describes the system; it is intended to be able to acquire, track and destroy ground targets in a night attack, and to do so while minimizing the pilot's workload, on the theory that he has quite enough to do to stay alert and alive while hurtling through the darkness.

A further step after LANTIRN and its associated aircraft and weapons is a program to produce an autonomous tactical all-weather strike (ATAWS) aircraft. This type would fill the attack gap between front-line assaults by such aircraft as the A-10s, and the deep interdiction strikes by the all-weather F-111s. Behind any armored attack is a long "tail" of replacement tanks and other vehicles, moving up to the battle over good all-weather roads, generally under the cover of night, or other conditions of poor visibility. These tanks, for example, move in batches of less than a dozen, and are generally rigged for travel rather than an offensive maneuver. In the event of war, there would be little trouble finding them. They and other vehicles would clutter the network of roads leading toward the battle front.

ATAWS aircraft would be launched on a low-altitude, high-speed penetration of the missile belt, using every sensor available: radar, forward-looking infra-red, and terrain-following equipment. Once the pilot or weapon-system operator (WSO, pronounced "Whizzo") detected a road, the ATAWS aircraft would be flown to follow it, to the inevitable contact with some worthwhile target. The tanks or other vehicles would be fingered by a laser designator, and the WSO would launch a fire-and-forget missile on the first pass. The tactic is then to keep right on going, and find another target, not to try to circle back and nail another one or two in the same area.

The ATAWS study has looked at two candidate aircraft for the job, one being the modified A-10 two-seater currently flying, and the other being a modified F-15, equipped for the ground-attack role.

One other development initiative is earmarked for the F-15, and for the F-16 as well. The AIM-7F/M radar-guided Sparrow missiles that now are part of the offensive armament of both fighters, are due for replacement by an advanced medium-range air-to-air missile (AMRAAM). It would also be an all-aspect, all-weather type, designed for greatly improved performance.

Development and procurement of any of the advanced weapon or detection systems listed here will depend in the future, as in the past, on the funding that is made available. Even if all of these should become operational with the near-future Air Force tactical units, there would remain a continuing need for further improvement and modernization, built around the new technologies of the 1980s.

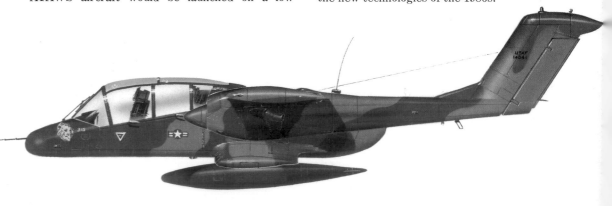

Fastest Guns in the West

The classic engagement in air combat remains; it is the deadly duel between two pilots, flying their fighters to the limits of their performance, hurtling through the upper air on the edge of a stall one moment, and unloading to accelerate in the next. This is the mission that fighter pilots are born for, they believe, and for which they train and train and train during their entire careers.

The evolution of that mission is well known; it began with air combat in World War 1, at first short and simple engagements between individuals, and later the clashes of formations that quickly broke into a sky full of swirling dogfights. World War 2 added another dimension: The discipline of tactics, of formations, of the concepts of team fighting. That war also saw the introduction of innovations in both the form of the airplane and the style of its weapons. Jet propulsion—both by turbojet and by rocket—raised aircraft performance to a new plateau that eased closer to the speed of sound itself. And guided missiles and fixed-fin

rockets foretold the development of deadlier generations of fighter weapons to come.

The jet-with-jet combat in the arena of MiG Alley during the Korean conflict pioneered a new way of fighting, air combat at blinding speeds and gut-straining maneuvers, with the constant need for surveillance of the skies and avoiding the terrible presence of an enemy in the six o'clock position.

Technological gains after that war, particularly in the development of air-to-air missiles, suggested that there was another change coming in air combat. The strongest proponents of missiles believed that any future air combat would be fought with the robot weapons at long ranges, rather than by the close-range tactic of hosing the enemy with cannon shells or machine-gun bullets. Airframes were getting tougher, to withstand the stresses of high-speed flight and maneuvering, and ranges between the paired combatants were increasing, because of the speed of flight and the distance that it took to turn a high-speed

The dorsal speed brake helps slow this F-15A Eagle of the 49th TFW as it arrives at Holloman AFB on 20 December 1977 after the unit had converted at Luke AFB. The fin badge is that of TAC.

TAC uses about 82 T-38 Talons as well as 66 F-5E Tiger II fighters in air-to-air combat training with Red Flag and Aggressor programmes. This T-38A serves with the 6th Fighter Weapons School, and unlike ATC Talons is painted in a combat-style camouflage.

fighter. Both these factors led to the conclusion that it would become increasingly difficult to shoot down an opponent with guns, and that guided missiles would be the only salvation for future fighter pilots.

So be it. The word went out, and in the late 1950s, fighters were designed around a battery of air-to-air missiles. Their noses carried radars, and their wings carried hard points for the attachment of the new breed of weapons. There was no place, either in the airplane itself, or in air combat, for the machine gun or the cannon.

Then along came Viet-Nam, and that war became a series of duels again, with USAF and Navy pilots mixing it with North Vietnamese experts flying their MiG-21s. The expectation was that something like the decimating kill rate achieved in the Korean war by the Sabres would be repeated by American fighter pilots against their Vietnamese opposition. Not so. The kill ratio was much too low for comfort, and far too close to a one-for-one trade.

And one reason was that both the Navy and the Air Force were flying the F-4C Phantom II, a fair airplane in a dogfight, except that it had no guns. Further, the missiles weren't performing too well; it required the launching of several to score a sure victory.

There were investigations and studies and reports, and out of all the paperwork and inputs from fighter pilots came some conclusions. First, air combat training was just not adequate to the combat task. Second, total reliance on missiles was probably not the correct way to go; guns were needed, not only for the occasions when the fighting closed to short ranges, but also to avoid the feeling of helplessness that a pilot had after he had fired his missiles and had no remaining offensive armament.

One of the first suggestions to come out of the studies was that air combat training be extended to

include dogfighting between dissimilar airplanes. Earlier, fighter squadrons had trained with their own kind. If you flew Phantoms, you fought Phantoms. It was convenient to do so, and that kind of combat training could be conducted within the squadron itself. Dissimilar air combat tactics (DACT) training changed all that. The first USAF organization to establish a program of DACT was the Aerospace Defense Command. It was logical; their General Dynamics F-106 interceptors were never going to have to intercept other F-106s. Somebody in the Navy noticed that the F-106 was a pretty good simulation of a MiG-21, and suggested to the Air Force that the F-106s be worked into a joint program to train pilots for Southeast Asia. From this and other developments, both the Air Force and the Navy eased their way into a series of planned programs for DACT training.

As a sidelight, the Navy sent pilots with that kind of training back to the war, and the Navy kill ratio increased several times over.

Today's DACT training is a very prominent part of the program within Tactical Air Command. TAC pilots practice the routine daily, flying against their Marine and Navy counterparts in combats that test the combinations of airplane, pilots and weapons to the utmost.

A most unusual adaptation of technology has proven invaluable in the assessment of the results of air combat training exercises. Modern radars, coupled with computers, have made it possible to track individual fighters through the intricate steps of their aerial ballet. Each participating aircraft carries a radar beacon in a pod with the size and aerodynamic characteristics of a standard Sidewinder missile. The pod is mounted on the left wing of the aircraft, and activated for the flight to the range area and the combat that ensues there. Triangulating radars track up to eight

A partner to the aircraft pictured above is the F-5E Tiger II, here serving in an Aggressor role with the 57th Tac Training Wing at Nellis but also used by the 527th Aggressor Sqn at RAF Alconbury, England.

Northrop F-5E Tiger II of the 64th FITS, 57th Fighter Weapons Wing, Nellis AFB, in "snake" camouflage.

F-5E of the 527th Tac Ftr Training Agressor Sqn at RAF Alconbury in "ghost" camouflage.

F-5E of the 64th FITS, 57th FWW, painted in the so-called "lizard" camouflage scheme.

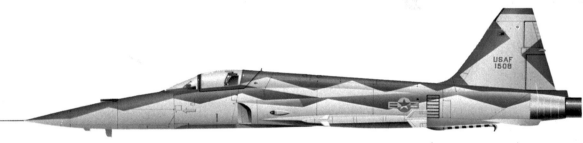

F-5E of the 57th FWW in one of the several experimental schemes with low-visibility insignia.

fighters in the same patch of sky, and present their flight paths as displays on a large monitoring screen in a ground station. From there, the progress of the combat can be watched.

But there is a much larger benefit from the ACMI (Air Combat Maneuvering Instrumentation) range data. After the pilots have come back, they debrief the mission with the aid of replays from the ACMI. The versatile computers can recreate any portion of that battle from the three-dimensional radar data, and replay it in slow motion. Further, to settle arguments about who killed whom, the presentation can be displayed as if it were seen through the windshield of any single fighter, to prove, beyond argument, whether or not that pilot had indeed locked on to his target when he fired the missile and called a hit.

The entire air battle can be replayed to study the tactics of the two opposing sides. It can be seen from one side of the airspace, as if it were being viewed from an attacker heading into combat. Or it can be followed from above, in what the pilots call the "God's-eye" view, showing the maneuvers in light tracery against the screen. It's a marvelous system which shows better than any other currently available post-mission analysis what really happened.

From Red Baron to Red Flag

It is difficult to talk about fighter tactics without referring again and again to Baron von Richthofen. This time it is because his name was given to a study of the air combat in Southeast Asia. The purpose was to analyze what happened, why certain pilots seemed to get the larger percentage of the kills, and what their background was that made them effective. Similar studies had been done in earlier wars; there are references to a survey of records kept during World War 2.

Red Baron and other earlier informal studies pointed to one common factor: if a pilot survived his first ten combats, his changes of continuing survival went up from something like 50% to approximately 90%.

Out of that observation was born the idea for one of the most significant training exercises ever developed: Red Flag.

Red Flag is a combat scenario, using a typical tactical air task force, and sending it off to a battle area which simulates the threats in a very realistic manner. The exercises, for they now are an almost continuing program, are flown on the range complex at Nellis AFB, Nevada. The range area is the size of Switzerland, just to put things in perspective, and you are liable to spot an East German airfield, a Russian armored column, a battery of their surface-to-air missiles, or a GCI radar among the hills and rolling contours of the range.

You're a fighter pilot, assigned to a Red Flag along with your squadron. You deploy to Nellis, and brief for the exercises. The morning of the first test, you're up early for the briefing. Your job is to fly top cover with the F-15 in a mixed strike force of USAF F-4s, Navy F-4s and Marine A-4s, accompanied by Wild Weasels. There will also be some A-10s in the battle area, working with Army helicopters and FACs. Expect a SAC B-52 low-level strike in the middle of the range, and watch out for enemy air.

So far, it sounds like any other exercise; a little more complicated, perhaps, but nothing you can't handle.

An F-15A Eagle of the 57th Fighter Weapons Wing stands by during Red Flag 1981/2. The 57th is the resident wing at Nellis AFB comprising of twelve squadrons.

All the surviving F-102 Delta Dagger interceptors on USAF strength have been rebuilt as Sperry PQM-102 RPVs (remotely piloted vehicles) for use in threat evaluation, as target drones and in many other tasks. Here a PQM-102A takes off; note the empty cockpit.

And so you plan your mission with the other fighter pilots in the squadron, head out to your planes and light the fires. You launch and establish the task-force formation as you head for the target area.

For a while, things are uneventful; the sun comes up, the desert floor is a lot of pretty colors, the airplane slides along nicely, radio discipline holds. Your head turns, looking for something, and you spot two tiny dots headed your way. The radar has them spotted also and suddenly the sky comes alive. One F-15 breaks sharply left and down, and the radios go wild. Your leader calls a break and you pull through it in a gut-wrenching turn, trying to follow the thin-winged shapes that are moving rapidly across your line of sight. Your leader is good, and suddenly you're above and behind a Northrop F-5E, all shining metal and red stars on the wings. Red stars? The aggressors! The fastest guns in the West!

Actually, they are the friendliest enemy the USAF has. They're highly skilled and methodically trained pilots who have immersed themselves in the Warsaw Pact way of flying and fighting. They know the tactics, the formations, and the way those pilots are taught to fight; they painstakingly transfer that knowledge to the "new boys" who have never been in a Red Flag before, or fought with the travelling circus of aggressor squadrons in the environment of Europe or the Far East.

Based at Nellis, RAF Alconbury, and Clark Air Base in the Philippines, the aggressor pilots fly the Northrop F-5E, camouflaged in the colors or bare metal of the Warsaw Pact air forces. The F-5E was chosen for its resemblance to the MiG-21 in terms of its radar signature and its size.

The aggressors, like Red Flag itself, stemmed from the Red Baron study. One of the conslusions of that study was the recognized need to train under the simulated conditions of combat. The reason for Red Flag and the presence of the aggressors grew out of the need to give an inexperienced fighter pilot his first ten "combat" experiences in a situation where he would not be killed if he made a tactical mistake. By learning from the aggressors in the world of air combat, and the framework of a Red Flag, the new pilot gets the equivalent of ten combat experiences.

And at the end of that time, he is far more ready and able to fight than he would have been under any other system of air combat training earlier devised.

Red Baron also pointed up the importance of visual acquisition of the target, the need for reliable and interference-free communications, and the total awareness of enemy tactics, particularly their excellent use of ground-controlled intercept (GCI) radars and experienced controllers.

The aggressors are the bridge between the intelligence community and the pilot in the cockpit. They furnish him the vital information he needs in order to be able to cope with his Pact counterparts, and to be able to outlast them in combat.

The aim in TAC is to get each unit to one Red Flag per year. Some squadrons will go more often, simply because they are equipped with a specific type of aircraft that is needed for the exercises. The Red Flag exercise lasts two weeks, with ten days of combat sorties, each thoroughly debriefed for lessons learned. One of the most unusual experiences available is to sit in one of these debriefings and listen to the pilots exchange notes and arguments about who shot down whom and how. To do that twice, once at the beginning of the exercise and once near the end, is very informative. One sees the first-time Red Flag pilot come back dejected, having been an easy mark for one or more aggressors. Some days later, you see the same pilot stride into the debriefing, claim two kills, and hear an aggressor pilot — who debriefs with the attack force — praise him for his superior performance in combat.

This war over Nevada is as real as simulation can make it. Live ordnance is dropped against some ground targets, but obviously all combat is simulated, as are the ground-based anti-aircraft artillery and missile firings. The complex scoring system tied to a common digitized time line solves the problem of who got killed first: the SAM site or the attacking F-4.

One thing the Red Flag war can't provide is the actual firing of an air-to-air missile in a simulated combat condition. For that, fighter pilots must go with a detachment from their squadrons to the Tactical Air Warfare Center (TAWC) at Eglin AFB, Florida. There under controlled conditions, they fire live missiles against drone targets over the Gulf of Mexico.

Typically, a unit comes in with five aircraft, and six pilots, and perhaps will rotate two more pilots through before the program is complete. It's part of WSEP (Weapon System Evaluation Program) and its goal is two-fold. First, it enables fighter pilots to experience the real thing, the firing of an AIM-7F Sparrow or an AIM-9J Sidewinder against a moving target. Second, it gives the Air Force a statistical check on the overall reliability of the armament systems on board their fighters.

Firing a live missile is a rare experience. Pilots don't know quite what to expect, in terms of the flash, exhaust plume, noise and their own reactions. WSEP is the first place they find out, and it is better to learn the tricks of the trade under those conditions than to have to learn them under fire from a MiG somewhere. There is a second major difference between the live firings and the simulated firings of Red Flag. In the latter exercise, unless the aircraft's avionic systems go out completely, everything works with 100% perfection. The entire chain, from the ground taxi to the actual flight of the missile itself, works right the first time. In real life, things are different. Generally USAF assumes an 85% probability that things will work in the systems. With a live launch, there are five places where the missile can develop a malfunction: on the ground before flight, in the cruise phase, during the attack, at the launch, and during its flight to the target. If the 85% probability is applied to each step of that path, the overall probability that the pilot will get a successful missile flight is only 44%. Knowing that, and knowing the value of the experience to the pilot, TAWC decided to guarantee the pilot one sure shot. He may have to make several flights to get that one off, but he will be allowed to do so. His intended victim may

be the Teledyne Ryan BQM-34 drone, a tiny target; the Sperry-converted General Dynamics F-102 that has been modified to the PQM-102 drone aircraft, a much more MiG-like target; or the Boeing Bomarc, once an anti-aircraft missile and now a simulator of the Russian MiG-25 Foxbat.

The AIM-7 is fitted with a telemetry package instead of a live warhead. Only a direct hit will destroy the drone, and the statistics favor a near miss that will be recorded by instrumentation aboard the drone. That miss distance can be converted to a lethality probability, and the determination of a kill. With the telemetry pack, an AIM-7F costs about $100,000, or about the same amount as a missile with a standard warhead and fuze.

Odd Acronyms for Evaluations

Red Flag and WSEP are part of the routine training of contemporary USAF pilots. Additionally, the Air Force conducts a number of tests and evaluations and, for the sake of economy and experience, generally uses operational units as participants.

In the latter half of 1977, the Air Force and the Navy joined in a pair of evaluations, one of air combat (ACEVAL) and the other of air intercept missiles (AIMVAL). Flown above the range at Nellis, the two test operations pitted Navy Grumman F-14A Tomcats and USAF F-15s as the Blue Force against the F-5E Red Force.

They flew 6,600 sorties, all in air-to-air combat under visual conditions, that is, all targets had to be eyeballed and positively identified before the simulated firings could be made. It was a handicap for an airplane like the F-14, which was designed for long-range engage-

A pair of RF-4Cs from the 363rd Tactical Reconnaissance Wing deployed from their usual base at Shaw AFB, South Carolina, depart Nellis AFB, afterburners blazing. They are taking part in a total mission package designed to improve not only the performance of the RF-4s but coordination with other elements taking part in Red Flag 1981/2.

By the standards of even the immediately preceding generation of combat aircraft (such as the F-4) the F-15 is astronomically costly; but its capabilities are far greater than any air force has ever had before. In 1981 the 600 in service were expected to be brought up to the standard of the definitive F-15C (two-seater, F-15D) with 2,000 lb additional internal fuel, FAST (fuel and sensor, tactical) packs and radar with a programmable signal processor.

ment of targets beyond visual range. There were many other constraints not at all typical of the real world of air combat: there were no specified missions, only a weak threat simulation, no ground fire, no jamming, no flying at low altitude, immortal crews and no kill removal.

In spite of that, the combatants and the services agreed that much was learned. ACEVAL showed that there would be a very intense environment in air combat, and that it was likely that up to 20% of the force would be lost before they even got their first shots off. AIMVAL showed some of the anomalies of the fight under visual spotting conditions, but nevertheless was able to supply useful input to a number of conceptual air-to-air missiles.

One interesting sidelight was the animosity generated by the test programs. The F-5Es were flown by the USAF aggressor squadrons and by instructor pilots from the Navy's Top Gun program. They are considered the best in the service, except by all other fighter pilots, and feelings ran high during the debriefings. More than once it seemed that the air combat was going to be finished off in the debriefing room with fists.

But argumentative pilots always are cautioned to save it for the real fight. That fight is a fluid situation, with a lot of unknowns. Near the end of the 1970s, the Russians added a formidable air weapon to the Warsaw Pact forces: the armed helicopter, the types designated Hip and Hind in NATO terminology. These are heavily armed and armored, and fast and relatively small, and they are assessed as being very tough customers. In fact, there was considerable worry that such versatile aircraft would be a threat to anything in the low-altitude flight envelope.

The Army and the USAF developed a joint exercise —J-CATCH, Joint Countering of Attack Helicopters— to study and develop the tactics that might help defeat Hip and Hind helicopters. It was begun with studies in the air-combat simulator developed by NASA at the Langley Research Center, just across the field from TAC Headquarters at Langley AFB, Virginia. Phase 2 was helicopter-to-helicopter combat at Ft. Rucker, the Army's rotary-wing school. For that event, TAC's 20th Special Operations Squadron was tasked to be the Red Force. They camouflaged their helicopters until they looked as if they had just flown out of East Germany. They added an infra-red seeker aboard the big Sikorsky CH-3s and a Minitac—a Canadian innovation that mounts a single machine gun below the belly—on their

Bell UH-1s, and headed for the wars. The helicopter duels were deadly, and yet out of the exercise came a whole set of special tactics to counter the Russian rotary-winged weapons.

The third phase pitted the armed helicopters against fighters, in what everybody presumed would be a fairly futile effort. F-4s, F-15s, A-10s and Army gunship helicopters flashed into sight, roared across the target area and sped out, apparently unharmed during their run-in and the break after. But the only reason they were unharmed is because the 20th SOS helicopters were not shooting real rounds. The gun camera films showed a slaughter of the fixed-wing types. They were hit during the brief moments they fixed on the target, and again when they were coming off the target. The armed helicopters picked them off, one by one, and it was a very sober bunch of fighter jocks that viewed the gun-camera films each night after the exercises.

There was a Phase IV, after the previous phases had been studied, and a whole series of new tactics had been evolved. It combined the lessons learned and the new tactics, and allowed a departure from the fixed scenarios for what fighter pilots call "free play", improvised air combat under near-real conditions. This time the score was not nearly so one-sided. The armed helicopters now represent just another threat, not the primary one.

The Electronic Environment

EWCAS stands for Electronic Warfare during Close Air Support, and it promises to be one of the largest and longest test evaluations conducted by the Air Force. It began as the result of studies of the combat in Southeast Asia, with the specific directive to analyze the aspects of electronic warfare. That dictated a very complex test program which, after it was developed, proved to be impossible to fund, let alone accomplish. A replanning arranged the program so that much of it could be done during other exercises, using the units deployed for those exercises rather than creating a dedicated test force. EWCAS began on a building-block basis, starting with what seemed the easiest to accomplish: tactical jamming of communications in the close-air support environment. The program will continue to add complexity and players, until it is working with a combined force in an integrated tactical situation along a segment of a battlefront perhaps 10 by 40 kilometers in size. It's a formidable undertaking, and yet a vital one that should produce a much better understanding of the deficiencies of Warsaw Pact equipment and tactics, and provided strong counters for USAF and the Army.

TASVAL is shorthand for Tactical Aircraft Effectiveness and Survivability in Close Air Support of Anti-Armor Operations. It was done during a large-scale joint exercise using Army armored and air cavalry regiments, the Army's Air Defense School, and aircraft from the Tactical Fighter Weapons Center at Nellis.

The exercise assumed the defense-rich environment of a Pact armored attack, aimed at keeping the Army AH-1S Cobra helicopter gunships and the USAF A-10A Warthogs from clobbering the tanks. It took two months of exercises in the field, at Ft. Hunter Liggett, California, and eight months of post-exercise evaluations to come up with the final analysis. New tactics were developed, along with a detailed understanding of the special needs of such an air-ground engagement.

It won't let up. By the time these words appear in print, the chances are that the Air Force will have evolved several new exercises or test operations, aimed at meeting the ever-changing conditions of future battles. Versatility and flexibility are two of the most useful attributes of a fighting force and its commanders, and USAF is taking every step to assure those qualities in the Air Force of the 1980s and 1990s.

The Future: Conditional and Tense

For the foreseeable future, the threat remains the same. On one hand, the fear persists of a nuclear war involving the two major powers, perhaps aided by a third or fourth. From this threat come new mobile strategic missile systems, new reconnaissance and warning satellites, advanced ground-based radars to monitor the skies. On the other hand, the continuing presence of small wars that might expand is the major factor in the evolution of new tactical aircraft and weapon systems.

The hope remains that nuclear war, leading to a human holocaust of global dimensions, will continue to be deterred by the cold logic of mutual suicide. If it isn't, the world ends. Period. The recent comments in the United States and elsewhere that tend to play down the horrors of nuclear war and raise hopes for the possibilities for survival come from people who may be well-intentioned, but whose heads contain not one grain of sense about the subject. It sends a cold shiver down the back to hear politicians glibly discussing nuclear weapons, when many of them can not even pronounce the word "nuclear" correctly.

To repeat, global nuclear war is the end. Period.

Tactical nuclear war, a possibility often mentioned in high-level strategy discussions about warfare in Europe or in the oceans, remains a possibility. Serious studies of a possible World War 3 include the destruction of a single enemy city or industrial complex somewhere as a logical escalation of the tactical battles. That's a terrible road to set out upon, and one that can also lead to a general nuclear exchange. Does anyone seriously believe that the parties to such a conflict would be willing to consent to an equal trade? Minsk for Birmingham, for example?

The possibilities remain: nuclear holocaust, tactical nuclear war, and their ramifications. Any prudent planner must account for those, simply to preserve his own reputation and his position. But a tactical non-nuclear war offers many permutations and combinations of threats and countermeasures, and is the type of war that will most influence the design and development of future fighter types.

We describe only future fighter aircraft here for a number of reasons. First, their evolution is an accurate reflection of the pace of technology. Their performance demands are such that they must utilize the latest

The inexorable trend towards what appear at the time to be impossibly high costs for not only weapon systems but also all the other hardware that has to be bought by an air force can be slowed by good engineering design and long production runs. An outstanding example is the General Dynamics F-16 Fighting Falcon, which though originally sponsored in 1972 as a mere technology demonstrator (to see to what extent an operationally useful fighter could be made cheaper than the F-15), matured into an exceptional and versatile combat aircraft able to fly almost all missions except long overwater patrol and interception in all weather. Over 200 had been delivered to six air forces by early 1981; this example is with the 388th TFW at Hill AFB, Utah.

Takeoff of a Lockheed SR-71A from Beale AFB, California, home base of the 9th Strategic Reconnaissance Wing. This unit is the only operator of this uniquely capable but demanding aircraft, which is air-refuelled with special (JP-7) fuel by another Beale resident, the 100th Air Refuelling Wing with its own tanker version, the KC-135Q.

The threat in a future tactical war will be basically the same as now, but greater. The evolution of defensive weapons will assure us that the Russian mobile surface-to-air (SAM) missiles will have shorter reaction times. The missiles themselves will be faster, and they will cover the lower fringes of the sky better than they do now. Above the battle, Russian AWACS aircraft will control the deployment and employment of their forces, working with fighters that have look-down and shoot-down capabilities. It will be very difficult for a tactical aircraft to penetrate that network of defenses.

Given that situation, there are two possibilities in the event of a war. One is a short, sharp fight, with a sky full of airplanes and missiles for a few days before it's all over. The other is a long war of attrition, with forces committed in packages of strength that may or may not escalate in capability during the drawn-out fighting.

Each imposes its own constraints on the design of future fighters. A short, sharp war calls for weapons with a very high kill rate. The war of attrition calls for ways to kill many targets at low cost. Further, a short was has to be won—or lost—with the weapons on hand, perhaps even on the scene, because there will be little or no chance to augment them with replacements, and absolutely no chance of replacing them with new production.

The potential statistics of the short war are staggering. Operations analysts, who develop elegant mathematics to describe battlefield situations quantitatively, have calculated some comparisons of the air battles typical of World War II and of a future conflict. One such set of numbers assumes a friendly force of 100 aircraft, for convenience. The half-life of that force, that is, the time for it to be reduced to 50 aircraft without being augmented by replacements, would have been 19 months, during World War II. It would have taken them about six months to kill 100 enemy aircraft. If their mission had been air-to-ground strikes against vehicles, they could have killed 1,000 of them in 35 days, and the half-life of the friendly force would have been reduced to eight months.

Translate those forces to today's battle environment. The half-life of the friendly air combat force would be

aerodynamics, the newest structural concepts, the most modern powerplants, the most sophisticated weaponry. Second, reading about the development of strategic weapons—or describing them, for the writer—is about as exciting as browsing through the pages of a telephone directory. The contents are always predictable; it's only the arrangement that differs from year to year. All strategic missiles are cylindrical things with one end pointed and the other blunt, and the pointed end is the one that is aimed at the target. That's about all one needs to know, except that the Russians paint theirs green and we paint ours white. There may be some great psychological meaning hidden there.

And, still in a lighter vein, it's obvious that the Boeing B-52 is going to last forever, and that neither American nor Russian bomber designs are technological breakthroughs. So let's dismiss future manned bomber technology, also.

McDonnell Douglas has funded a developed F-15 called Strike Eagle with synthetic aperture radar and other changes giving it the ability to make blind attacks on point targets from standoff ranges, in any weather. The prototype, seen here, has the F-15C features plus an enhanced capability of carrying up to 24,000 lb of external weapons. Some of this capability is retrofittable on the USAF's F-15s already delivered.

ACCESS THRUST
TERMINATION
DEVICE PIN

LOADED

seven days, instead of 19 months, and they would destroy 100 enemy aircraft in just two and one-half days, instead of six months.

The half-life of the ground-attack force would be nine days, instead of eight months, and they would kill 1,000 enemy vehicles in just a day and a half, instead of 35 days.

Those sharp contrasts in lifetimes and lethalities point up the seriousness of the game today. It demands the best weapons, the most sophisticated electronics, and the finest pilot training and tactical exercising that can be devised.

How can a force survive longer in such an environment? It must be equipped with all-weather weapons of exceptional survivability. It must be able to generate a large number of sorties rapidly, and its pilots must make multiple kills on each sortie. Further, they must do it with weapons that have a low life-cycle cost.

Those terms would make any designer think twice or three times. They seem to be contradictory, but — following careful study — they seem to point in a single direction: stand-off weapons. It may be that the day of the penetrator is fast fading. Tomorrow's tactical aircraft may hurtle toward the battle, pull up into a sudden climb, loose a weapon and break fast for the rear, leaving the smaller pilotless aircraft to cruise on its one-way mission to the target.

Once this philosophical approach is accepted, it means that the weapon becomes the critical portion of the design, and that is a departure from past practice. Most contemporary aircraft — perhaps all of them — were designed as exercises in technology. Their aerodynamics were compromised for the best overall performance, their structures were designed to take the predicted loads, and their powerplants were

whatever was available at the time that would run at maximum thrust without blowing up for a least an hour. When the Air Force, or the Navy, or the Army, pointed out that they wanted to be able to hang bombs and guided missiles and jamming pods and fuel tanks somewhere, the designers looked hurt, and offered to make hard points on the wings and fuselages from which those horrid excrescences could be suspended. It would absolutely ruin performance, they pointed out, but if you want it that way, we guess we'll have to go along.

In this case, it was the chicken that came first; it eggs were considered later. But that approach is obsolete. The demands of modern warfare, let alone future conflict, require absolutely that the primary consideration in an aircraft design be the weapons it is going to carry. It must be built around those weapons, to carry and launch and guide them most efficiently and at least danger to the pilot, who must live to launch again and again and again.

Further, those weapons can no longer be the kind that have to be delivered to the target, like a salvo of iron bombs, or even a short-range glide bomb guided by television, radar, or an active seeker. The weapons must be long-range stand-off missiles, released far from enemy threats, capable of streaking along a few yards above the terrain to their targets.

That is an expensive solution; but the alternates are far more costly, and perhaps not even possible. Given that, there are again two ways to go. The weapons can be integrated into a completely new design, optimized to meet the performance characteristics of the ordnance load. Or they can be carried externally on a modified contemporary aircraft. Obviously, the less costly approach is the second one. A large measure of

Essentially the whole of the West's land-based strategic missile capability rests in a force of 1,000 Boeing LGM-30 Minuteman ICBMs (intercontinental ballistic missiles) deployed in SAC squadrons and flights throughout the US Midwest. This Minuteman II is seen in its silo at one of the 10-missile flights of the 44th Strategic Missile Wing, Ellsworth AFB, South Dakota.

tomorrow's tactical aircraft, therefore, should look very familiar. They will be today's fleet, modified to increase their range, endurance, and payload, and festooned with a variety of externally hung weapons. Their performance in that condition will be abysmal, compared to their former speeds and altitudes, but their survivability will be enhanced many times over.

Designing Tomorrow's Tactical Aircraft

A modified General Dynamics F-16 is the test vehicle for a fascinating program to develop a type of technology that will radically change the way aircraft are flown. There is a joke among pilots, who often caution each other in mock tutorial terms to " . . . make sure you keep the pointy end forward!" The modified F-16 doesn't to that; its pointy end may slew several degrees from forward, and may point up, down or sideways when the airplane is flying straight and level.

The goal is to develop a fighter that is maneuverable in six degrees of freedom, one that is not constrained to bank in a turn, or unable to pull its nose inside a turn to fire at an enemy. The airplane and its flight path are decoupled, to use the technical term. No longer is there a fixed relationship between the two. It is done with additional control surfaces that supply side loads or other maneuvering aids, and that can effectively point the airplane away from its flight path.

Immediate advantages come to mind. In a ground-strafing run, the pilot will be able to hold the nose on his target in a curving dive. He will be able to pickle his bombs off in a climbing turn. If he wants, he can keep his wings level for the entire strafing or bombing run.

Evasive action will be easier, with the possibility of pulling up to 2G side load. The resulting erratic flight path will help to confuse enemy gunners, whose automatic anti-aircraft cannon use simple linear prediction to calculate the lead angle for their firing. Imagine target which appears to move literally by zigs and zags through the sky. ("Too much vodka, Comrade Gunner?")

One advantage of the F-16 tests is that such control systems obviously can be installed on existing aircraft, and don't require a completely new platform to be designed, developed and built. It offers one of the more exciting applications of current technology.

Fighters for service before the year 2000 are going to be designed with what is basically today's knowledge. The time cycle for advanced aircraft development underscores that fact. The F-15, for example, originated in studies in 1966, and became operational a little more than 10 years later. The F-16 began life in 1969, and became operationally ready by the end of 1980.

The biggest challenge to the designer is keeping the size and weight of any future aircraft to a minimum. Size and weight both equate directly with cost, unfortunately. Since the mid-1960s, the starting time for most current fighters, there have been major advances in aircraft structural design and in fabricating techniques. The use of composite materials, cloth impregnated with carbon or metallic fibers, has produced lightweight structures stronger than steel and lighter than aluminum. Unusual forming and joining techniques have eliminated the rows upon rows of rivets. A Grumman study of recent date shows that a fighter equivalent to the F-111A in capability could be designed today for half the F-111's original weight, using composites and new fabrication techniques.

The Air Force has funded studies for a "mission-adaptive" wing, a surface with automatically actuated leading- and trailing-edge devices. Such a wing is less

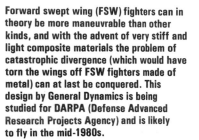

Forward swept wing (FSW) fighters can in theory be more maneuvrable than other kinds, and with the advent of very stiff and light composite materials the problem of catastrophic divergence (which would have torn the wings off FSW fighters made of metal) can at last be conquered. This design by General Dynamics is being studied for DARPA (Defense Advanced Research Projects Agency) and is likely to fly in the mid-1980s.

sensitive to gusts; it can, in its response to the air, distribute the wing loads to reduce the bending moments and therefore reduce the weight of the necessary resisting structure. Or it can produce more lift at a lower angle of attack, which improves the lift-drag ratio and therefore makes for a more-efficient cruise.

There is, in technology, an almost inexorable relationship between advances and the calendar. There is such a thing as the state of the art, the availability of technology at some particular point in time. Ideas that emerge before the technical environment is ready for them are fated to blush unseen. But sweep-forward may be one of those ideas whose time has finally come.

The air doesn't care whether the wing is swept forward or backward. The basic aerodynamic effect — the reduction of drag — occurs with either case. If drag reduction is the only problem, either solution works. But there are other considerations. A wing has been usually swept back, rather than forward, because it produces a lighter structure. Why? It's because of what happens when wings respond to air loads. A sweptback wing, bending upward under air loads, shows a decreasing angle of attack from wing root to wing tip. That dynamic change in angle may produce a tendency to flutter; if it does, that instability can be controlled by making the wing stiffer, or by adding weights. The engines on today's commercial jet transports act as anti-flutter devices.

If the wing is swept forward, though, the angle of attack increases toward the wing tip when the wing bends upward. Under load, the wing tries to twist and may literally be torn off the fuselage unless it is very strong, very stiff, and — consequently — very heavy. For that reason, the World War II German experiments with swept-forward wings found few postwar partakers of their technology.

But with that obvious disadvantage, the swept-forward wing shows a great advantage in its behavior near the stall. With a sweptback wing, the stagnant air nearest the surface literally slides sideways and begins to pile up near the tip. The tip, operating in an airstream of greatly reduced velocity, has little else to do but stall, which it does before the wing root stalls. Asymmetries in construction and the vagaries of flow fields generally produce a local stall at one wingtip before the other, and the airplane may roll viciously entering the stall. But sweep the wings forward, and it is the wing root section that stalls first. And that is a good thing, because asymmetry makes essentially no

difference at the inboard sections of the wing, and entry to the stall is less violent.

So with that excellent stall behavior, there would seem to be good reason to use a swept-forward wing, if one could be built strong enough to stay attached to the fuselage.

Enter composites, and a Lt. Col. Krone, USAF, writing his doctoral dissertation at the University of Maryland. Krone was studying the use of composite materials in aircraft design, and he found that these unusual materials could be used to tailor the dynamic characteristics of a wing. Because the directional characteristics desired can be designed into composite wing structures, they can be built extremely stiff in torsion, with controlled twist as they deflect. Krone suggested that perhaps the swept-forward wing might be successful, if it were made of composites with directed strengths, instead of metals with their homogeneous characteristics.

What eventually resulted was a series of USAF study contracts, awarded to Grumman and Rockwell, to investigate the swept-forward wing and to design some applications to a future fighter type. Both companies did so, conducting wind-tunnel tests and building mock-up structures. At this writing, funding had been made available for the construction of simple prototype.

Building the Quiet Airplane

In this case, "quiet" means one that won't wake up the enemy defenses, an airplane that can sneak in, stealthily, and not alert enemy radars and other sensors until the very last moment.

Stealth design concepts are not really new at all, despite the lurid revelations of the 1980 Presidential campaign in the United States. Designers have known for years that radar "signatures", the characteristics of reflections given off by an airplane, can be minimized by keeping the size and the weight of the airplane to a minimum.

That's a start; next the designer goes to work on the shape of the aircraft, changing its lines to present curved surfaces to the enemy radars rather than slab-sided barn doors that bounce the beam back brightly. But reducing radar reflections is not the only necessary task. The enemy uses infra-red detection methods, and to the average IR detector, a jet engine looks like a Fourth-of-July firework. But it won't, if it can be shielded. One way of doing this was adapted by the

Though NASA (US National Aeronautics and Space Administration) is a civilian agency, much of its research is of interest to the Air Force. For example the AD-1 slew-wing research aircraft, first flown in December 1979, could well assist the development of future long-range military jets. Here the AD-1 wing is set at its extreme angle of 60°.

Dramatically exemplifying the Air Force's budget problems is the Boeing YC-14, possibly the most advanced military transport ever built. Designed as a contender for the AMST (Advanced Medium STOL Transport) to replace the C-130, it has two F103 turbofans installed to give USB (Upper-Surface Blowing) for fantastic takeoff and climb with heavy loads. The Air Force simply lacks money to procure a fleet of these impressive aircraft.

Toward the 21st Century

The McDonnell Douglas F-15 Eagle, climbing through the horizon into the brighter sky above, epitomizes the strength and advanced technology that are carrying this great service forward into the uncertain days in the closing years of the 20th century.

HiMAT (Highly Maneuvrable Aircraft Technology) is a joint research programme run by the Air Force Flight Dynamics Lab at Wright-Patterson AFB and the NASA Dryden Flight Research Center. This is one of two pilotless Rockwell HiMAT aircraft undergoing test in California. Rather smaller than manned combat aircraft, it comprises an advanced jet "core aircraft" to which can be attached different arrangements of wings, canards, tails, engine inlets and jet nozzles. A host of novel ideas are being tried out on these exciting aircraft, to keep the Air Force ahead in the 1990s.

designers of the A-10A. They planned the locations of its twin jet engines and the twin vertical tail surfaces so that the tail masked much of the hot part of the engine. By the time the airplane was in a position to make a significant signal on an IR detector, it was already past the detector and heading toward safety.

It's also possible to eyeball an airplane, to see it at a great distance because it glistens in the sky. That's why dull camouflage paints are used, among other reasons. Their primary function is to make the aircraft difficult to see against the ground or sky. By choosing the right shapes for windshields and canopies, which can't be camouflaged, the designer can reduce the reflections of the aircraft—its "glint"—and make it that much more difficult to see.

Finally, it is known to even inexperienced designers that a radome has to be made out of non-metallic materials so that the radar can "see" through it. Exactly the same phenomenon works in reverse; an all-plastic airplane is much harder to detect by radar than an all-metal one. Radar-absorbent coatings and materials have been developed and used for years. Adding them to the carefully designed "stealth" airplane would reduce its apparent visibility even further.

One of the best current examples of an airplane designed with some stealth techniques is the Lockheed SR-71 high-altitude supersonic reconnaissance aircraft. Its nose contours, curving gently, and its dull finish of special paint reduce its forward radar signature to a minimum. And its blinding cruise speed gives it a large margin of safety, even though its powerful engines generate a large infra-red return.

Will tomorrow's fighters be armed with laser guns and charged-particle beams? Not likely. Today, those futuristic weapons are of weight and volume that require large aircraft, not the crammed and cramped dimensions of a fighter. The current airborne test vehicle for a laser weapon is a modified Boeing KC-135, and a major portion of its cavernous interior is taken up with the equipment necessary to generate the pencil-like beam of coherent light.

Lasers and charged particle beams have great potential as weapons, and the laser has demonstrated impressively its possible performance. In 1973, the Air Force shot down a drone—probably one of the BQM-34 category—with a laser beam. Three years later, the Army had its turn, destroying a number of fixed-wing and rotary-wing drones. The Navy lasered, if that becomes the right word, a TOW missile in flight in

1978, indicating that a high-speed, low-level missile is susceptible to this new kind of weapon, and that the laser beam is versatile and responsive enough to handle the high-speed geometry of that situation. And why not? Nothing moves as fast as the speed of light except light.

The laser works by putting enough light energy into a concentrated beam to burn through its target. Industrial lasers are used for metal cutting, and surgical lasers are used to refasten detached retinas in the human eye. They are precise, controllable, and offer the potential for unusual weaponry.

Charged particle beams, on the other hand, do their damage by directing a stream of sub-atomic particles against their targets. The electrons, ions, or protons transfer their energies to the material of the target, and fragment it, either by cracking it or by melting it.

Current extrapolations of developmental experiments to practical weapons envision three types of use. One would be as a ground-based anti-aircraft or anti-missile beam weapon. The second would be as a naval fleet defense weapon against aircraft and missiles. And the third possible weapon is the one that has been described the most: a satellite killer, carried into space aboard an orbiting hunter or other spacecraft.

Note that these applications work the weapons in their most effective manner. Their performance is degraded by fog, dust and clouds, and so the best use is in a manner that avoids those spoilers.

So: tomorrow's fighter will be smaller, lighter, built of mixed materials, will possibly feature some unusual wing geometries, and will be maneuverable in six degrees of freedom. It will be flown by wire or even by fibre optics that will transmit control inputs to the surfaces. The pilot will sit—or perhaps recline is the more appropriate word—in a cockpit remarkably like the one now in the F-16, regarded as a really outstanding design.

Notice the words, " . . . the pilot . . . " in that description of the future fighter. There will continue to be pilots in the combat aircraft of tomorrow. No matter how smart sensors and computers can be made, they will not likely have more than limited judgment circuitry. They may be able to decide whether or not to fire a missile, or to turn at a way-point. They may be able to analyze the erratic behaviour of the engine and to suggest a way to correct it. They may even be able to ease the pilot down through the worst weather and onto a tire-squeaking landing without his ever seeing the runway. But there will come times when the weather is foul, and the electronics have been hit. The automatic pilot has packed up, and only the emergency control system is left to be man-handled. There is a hole in the left wing that no amount of automatic aileron trim can compensate for, and only a tiring wrist and a forearm of a human being will be able to hold the wings level.

And that most elegant, complex, and versatile computer of all—the human brain—will be working in top gear, rejecting and accepting suggestions, cues, sensed motions, indicator readings, lights, and the feedback of the controls, and integrating them all into a dynamic process that gets the pilot home and down safely.

And so the history of the United States Air Force, written by some future historian, may read much like these pages, except for the wonders of new weapons and new aircraft to carry them. But they are, and will continue to be, beautiful but lifeless chunks of sculptured metal, capable of doing only what they are told to do by their pilots.

And history is, ultimately, the story of people and what they did with what they had. The USAF has done much, and now faces its greatest challenge. What it is able to do in that uncertain future will be done, as always, by its dedicated people.

Index

We are sincerely grateful to the following for their help with additional photographs.

Air Force Museum
Associated Press (page 218)
Boeing-Wichita
James J. Garrity
Ingram T. Hermanson
Elmer Huhta
Mrs. Thomas Isley
Raymond W. Krout
A. F. Migliaccio
Donald L. Miller
Dr. Lyman C. Perkins
Del Shaffer
Gordon S. Williams
Ron E. Witt